PENGUIN BOOKS

NATIVE AMERICAN TESTIMONY

Peter Nabokov is a professor of American Indian Studies and World Arts and Cultures at UCLA. He is the coauthor, with Robert Easton, of *Native American Architecture* and author of *Indian Running, Two Leggings: The Making of a Crow Warrior*, and *Architecture of Acoma Pueblo*.

NATIVE

A CHRONICLE OF
FROM PROPHECY TO

PENGUIN BOOKS

AMERICAN TESTIMONY

INDIAN-WHITE RELATIONS
THE PRESENT, 1492–2000

EDITED BY PETER NABOKOV

WITH A FOREWORD BY VINE DELORIA, JR.

PENGUIN BOOKS
Published by the Penguin Group
Penguin Putnam Inc.,
375 Hudson Street, New York, New York 10014, U.S.A.
Penguin Books Ltd, 27 Wrights Lane, London W8 5TZ, England
Penguin Books Australia Ltd, Ringwood, Victoria, Australia
Penguin Books Canada Ltd, 10 Alcorn Avenue,
Toronto, Ontario, Canada M4V 3B2
Penguin Books (N.Z.) Ltd, 182–190 Wairau Road,
Auckland 10, New Zealand

Penguin Books Ltd, Registered Offices:
Harmondsworth, Middlesex, England

First published in the United States of America by Thomas Y. Crowell 1978
Expanded edition published
by Viking Penguin, a division of Penguin Books USA Inc., 1991
Published in Penguin Books 1992
This revised and updated edition published 1999

3 5 7 9 10 8 6 4 2

Acknowledgments for permission to reprint material from various
publications and collections appear on pages 473

Illustrations credits appear on pages 495–6:

Photographs on pages iv and v:
Red Lake Chippewa visiting Washington, D.C., in 1901.
(Smithsonian Institution; photos by DeLancey Gill)

THE LIBRARY OF CONGRESS HAS CATALOGUED THE HARDCOVER AS FOLLOWS:
Native American Testimony : a chronicle of Indian-white relations from prophecy
to the present, 1492–1992 / edited by Peter Nabokov ; with a foreword by
Vine Deloria, Jr.
p.   cm.
Includes bibliographical references and index.
ISBN 0-670-83704-0 (hc.)
ISBN 0 14 02.8159 2
1. Indians of North America—government relations—Sources.   2. Indians of
North America—History—Sources.   I. Nabokov, Peter.
E93.N3   1991   970.004'97—dc20   90-23579

Printed in the United States of America
Set in Meridien and Copperplate Gothic
Designed by Beth Tondreau Design
Maps by Bernhard H. Wagner

CONTENTS

PART TWO
RESERVATION TO RESURGENCE   185

FOREWORD

The celebration of the quincentennial of Columbus's discovery of the western hemisphere contains the potential for great reconciliation or immense misunderstanding. The tendency for many Americans will be to celebrate the successes of this invasion while sweeping under the rug the excesses that made it possible. Missing in this celebration will be the indigenous peoples of the western hemisphere. We will appear only as faded but familiar stereotypes: the noble savage, the gentle Thanksgiving visitors, and the bloodthirsty barbarians seeking to prevent the civilization of an untamed wilderness. The lessons that *should* have been learned and *could* have been learned will not be apprehended.

Very little understanding of the cultural and philosophical gulf which has always existed between the natives of this hemisphere and the rest of the world will be discerned. Even worse, there will be no appraisal of the dreadful condition of the environment, no recognition that within half a millennium the European immigrants stripped this continent of its original forms of life and created a civilization of waste, supported by an artificial technology which itself is in decline.

The selections in this book can significantly assist in creating the proper debate about these and other issues, particularly if they are understood as a prolonged commentary on the differences between red and white. A century ago, Sitting Bull summed up the difference admirably: "The love of possessions is a disease among them." In various ways these selections demonstrate the Indian response to this disease, their commentaries on the behavior which such a disease engenders, and the impact that such actions had on the native peoples.

Standard textbooks and histories concern themselves with the arrangement of historical artifacts—the dates, policies, movements, and institutions which mark the progress of the human transformation of the North American continent. Anthologies, for the most part, attempt to illustrate a general theme of the conflicting values that characterized the settlement of America. The missing dimension in our knowledge is the informality of human experience, which colors all our decisions and plays an intimate and influential role in the historical experiences of our species.

◀ XVII

Peter Nabokov attempts to move beyond the impasse of historical knowledge by bringing two themes together, thus allowing the traditionally articulated conflict of the races to become an underlying context within which actual people take part in and respond to actual events. This method of understanding history, comparable in many respects to earlier efforts by such people as Bernard De Voto, imprints memorable events and personalities on the reader, outside the sort of sterile academic setting that commands a narrow interpretation of the data. Instead of the usual process of reading to gain comprehension, the reader of this anthology will find him- or herself engaged in historical experiences in which the trivial becomes meaningful and the pompous event finds itself reduced to a human dimension.

The selections in this collection bring together occasions during which we can transcend the limitations of time and space and participate in the meaning of life as others who have come before us have known it. Thus the joy and tragedy of the past enable us to renew the clouded but intense vision of our own lives; as we walk with our ancestors through the incidents of the past, we come to a realization of the underlying meaning of human activities. Some of the selections found here are not unusual in any sense; if we evaluate human expression by its power to suggest a reality beyond our senses, they record in a few instances events of the most minor importance. Yet these same incidents, placed within the proper context, reveal the common condition we share with all previous generations. They remind us that while we may *misunderstand*, we do not *misexperience*.

What can be learned from these selections that would make the next half-millennium a more humane and morally productive era? Is it enough to excoriate the white man once again with the hope that he will finally come to his senses? The lesson which seems so hard to learn is that of dignity and respect. Some of the voices contained herein may appear to be complaining about the loss of land, the loss of a way of life, or the continuing propensity of the white man to change the terms of the debate to favor himself. But deep down these are cries about dignity, complaints about the lack of respect. "It is not necessary," Sitting Bull said, "that eagles should be crows."

The final chapters of the story have yet to be written. Old prophecies relate that the white man will surely come to dominate the continent, but that his time in the sun will be the shortest of all the people who will dwell here. He has not, as yet, come to grips with the land on which he lives. Luther Standing Bear's prediction that the white man cannot live in peace until he comes to understand and love this land still stands as a warning to our wasteful consumer society. The land itself must be seen to have a measure of dignity and respect and when it does not receive these accommodations, human beings who live on the land are accordingly incomplete. If the reader understands that beneath everything else lies this basic demand of respect, he or she will see the outlines of another way of living, the way of life that stood in opposition to the relentless invasion of these lands.

The sole requirement for reading and enjoying this collection is that the reader discard presumptions and preconceptions and immerse the soul in the richness of the human condition. Provocations of emotion are much superior to provocations of the mind alone, and these selections are designed to burst sterile barriers of communication and lead the reader through the twists and turns of human life. The assumption that one party or the other was fated to arrive at its present condition eliminates any possibility of understanding how events occurred and what people felt in the immediate situation and upon later reflection. The skillful balancing of selections here enables one to move along the line of emotions and participate in the grandeur which has made the story of North America among the most exciting episodes of human history. I hope the reader will enjoy this dimension of the book among all the others.

—VINE DELORIA, JR.

NATIVE AMERICAN TRIBES AND CULTURE AREAS, CIRCA 1650

INTRODUCTION

ıılıılıılıılıılıılıılıılıılıılıılıılıılıılıılıılıılıılıılıılıılıılıılıılıılıılıılıılıılıılıılıılıılıılıılıılıılıılıılıılıılıılıılıılıılıılıılıılıılıı

L ike many Native Americans before and after him, Edward Goodbird, a Hidatsa Indian from North Dakota, puzzled over the
behavior of white people.

"When a Hidatsa comes into the cabin," Goodbird observed in the summer of 1914, "he is given a place to sit, or a chair . . . he does not get up and
pace about. . . . If he should do so our people would think he acted fool-
ishly." But whites, Goodbird noticed, "pace back and forth in their rooms.
We Indians think it is because the white man's mind is working while he
has nothing to do; that he himself may be idle, yet his mind keeps working."

The Yaqui Indians of the Arizona Southwest also reflected upon the
thought processes of these different human beings. They called whites *gente
de razones* One tribesman explained, "Yes, you are a people of reasons, you
always have reasons for this, reasons for that."

This anthology chronicles, through Indian eyes and experiences, the Native American encounter with these restless and rationalizing Europeans
and their descendants. Its selections span nearly five hundred years of Indian and white relations—from prophecies about the coming of strangers to
memories of "first contact" to contemporary debates over reburial of Indian
bones and return to tribal sovereignty. They cover famous and little-known
aspects of Indian and white history. They highlight recurrent attitudes and
persistent problems as Native Americans dealt with these busy, nosy newcomers who were not just visiting—who were here to stay.

Actually this is two books. Part One includes the complete text (with one
substitution) of my earlier documentary history of Indian and white relations, the original *Native American Testimony*, which was published in 1978.
Subtitled "First Encounter to Dispossession," that collection closed with the
onset of the Reservation period. Here I have added a longer Part Two,
"Reservation to Resurgence," which opens around 1865 and moves from
the neglected early-twentieth-century Native American experience to the
year 2000 and beyond.

When my research turned up a number of Indian-spoken or -written accounts whose themes echoed or resonated with each other, I figured I was
touching the pulse of the hidden Indian histories of this land. These were
not just new versions of past events. More important, they were expressions

◄ XXI

of underlying feelings and commentaries about those events and the role-relationships Indians shared with whites from 1492 to 1992. Then I chose selections which expressed those perspectives most intimately and dramatically.

Throughout my hunting I preferred stories rather than shrill polemics or impersonal position papers. Ironically, strong narratives were easier to find for the earlier centuries. Over years of recounting, many incidents of Indian and white relations were summarized in well-worn folklore—sometimes even encoded as humorous Trickster tales in which the Coyote or Raven antihero (protector of Indians) overpowers some threatening feature of white culture. Or I would uncover a crisp fragment of oral history with some forgotten Indian's account of a glancing encounter with white society which was often more graphic and persuasive than any chief's oratory. Occasionally edged with anger or subtle irony, but often astonishingly understated and free of corrosive hate, these narratives stood for other Indian testimonies that would never be heard.

As my research entered the twentieth century, however, events were too fresh to lose their pain and confusion; good stories, localized and detailed but conveying deeper truths, were harder to find. Fortunately, the proliferation of Indian autobiographies in this century, and the growth of American Indian journalism in the form of hundreds of on- and off-reservation newspapers, enriched this part of the book.

Part One covers the era of Indians encountering the first explorers, their interactions with early traders, missionaries, settlers, frontier diplomats, and soldiers. Different Indian societies encountered representatives from various European countries on both east and west coasts at different times. This produced many contrasting microhistories of cultural interaction.

As time wore on, however, certain European expectations became familiar to Indians no matter the region. White men expected them to hunt predominately those animals whose furs were desired in faraway markets, thereby altering irrevocably their traditional cycles of hunting, foraging, fishing, or gardening. They wanted Indians to embrace Christianity, to learn to read and write, and to work by the clock. They desired permanent access to their forests, rivers, mountains, and valleys, and as well to unseen resources within the earth itself. They encouraged Indians to be good neighbors, but they also frequently wanted them out of the neighborhood. They insisted that Indians sign documents in which they accepted goods and services in exchange for whatever the white man wanted.

While Part One moves generally from the dawn of European pioneering to the late nineteenth century, its chapters are ordered less by chronology than by general categories of white-Indian interaction such as religion, land, diplomacy, and warfare. In Part Two, however, which opens with the year 1865, the chapters stride through distinctive time periods. Now attention shifts from the battlefield and the treaty table to the Indian reservation and the political forum. Part Two engages what might be termed "modern" Indian history as tribes leave the frontier spotlight to fend for themselves with dwindling resources, many regulations, and words and symbols as their new weapons.

In this expanded version of *Native American Testimony*, we watch Native Americans carry that challenge into the third millennium. These accounts of personal recoveries of native identity and the controversy over Indian gaming and revivals of spiritual traditions also demonstrate how the history of Indian-white relations still brings unexpected surprises.

This anthology bears witness to those instances when Indians were compelled to turn from their private worlds to interact with new cultures from across the sea. Hopefully it helps us glimpse what Native Americans have seen and thought as they have coped with the most cataclysmic event in more than ten thousand years of cultural development—the permanent presence of the white man.

PART

I

FIRST ENCOUNTER
TO DISPOSSESSION

(Preceding page) *In 1906, the sacred Blue Lake was appropriated from New Mexico's Taos Pueblo for Carson National Forest. But the lake was the old village's holiest shrine; for more than fifty years the Indians maintained a peaceful campaign to recover it. Finally, in 1970, the U.S. government restored Blue Lake and the forty-eight thousand acres surrounding the glacial pool to Taos in perpetuity.*

PREMONITIONS AND PROPHECIES

Acoma Pueblo

Before the coming of the white man, bronze-skinned men and women from northern Asia had been exploring and settling the Americas for anywhere from ten to fifty thousand years, according to archeological estimates. They almost certainly began by trekking in small bands from Siberia to Alaska, across a land bridge spanning what is now the Bering Strait. By the fifteenth century their descendants had spread southward to populate both continents.

◀ 3

When Christopher Columbus came ashore in the Bahamas, North America alone was home for an estimated two to ten million people. The Spanish admiral, believing he had found the long-sought western passage to the Asian mainland, made the notorious error of dubbing them "Indians." By then these Native American peoples had developed some three hundred distinct cultures and spoke over two hundred different languages. In North America their numbers were most concentrated along the coastal strip that is now California—about fifty-six people every fifty square miles. The Southwest was a second major population center—nearly fourteen inhabitants per fifty square miles—while east of the Mississippi lived an average of nine natives per fifty square miles.

Like human societies everywhere, these Indian cultures had not been standing still. By 1492 North America had already seen the rise and fall of an array of Native American civilizations. From Canada to Florida, from the Atlantic Coast west to California, archeologists have discovered many thousands of pre-Columbian earth mounds, the result of the work of tens of thousands of Native Americans. Some of the earthworks were foundations of temples built by Ohio and Mississippi River valley peoples who also produced striking art in pottery, copper, and shell. Other mounds were burial sites, constructed by farming groups who flourished over three thousand years ago. Excavations at Cahokia, Illinois, near present-day East St. Louis, have uncovered the remains of a prehistoric city, which once contained, it is estimated, from forty to sixty thousand inhabitants. And throughout the canyons and mesas of southern Colorado and northern New Mexico, pre-Columbian apartment-house remains can still be visited, stone-and-adobe terraced dwellings skillfully built up to four and five stories in height. Erected by the fabled Anasazi, centuries before the arrival of the white man, they were the homes of highly religious and relatively peaceful farming societies.

Some of these cultures had disappeared entirely by the end of the fifteenth century. Others were undergoing profound social transformation. It is intriguing to imagine what civilizations might have developed if the natural evolutionary process had been allowed to continue. Nonetheless, the white explorers and settlers who brought it to a halt found an impressive range of Indian groups. The word "tribe" does not do justice to the extreme variety of their political organizations, methods of food-gathering, cultural and religious patterns, and population size.

In the Northeast the first whites arrived after the five Iroquoian tribes had established a permanent political union. Their Great League, founded in the late fifteenth century by the legendary Hiawatha and Deganawidah, became so formidable that the French and British were forced to negotiate with them as an equal sovereignty. In the Southeast, whites encountered the thousands of loosely knit Muskogean-speaking Indians who came to be known as the Creek Confederacy. In Louisiana they met the last remnants of the aristocratic Natchez, whose hierarchical society was ruled by an absolute monarch known as "The Sun." In Virginia they discovered that the Powhatan Confederacy linked together two hundred villages and thirty different tribes. In California they stumbled upon a seemingly endless succession of independent, isolated groups with widely different languages, and bands so small they are better classified as "tribelets."

These native bands, tribelets, pueblo city-states, nations, and confederacies were as culturally different from each other as the nations of Europe. Most had developed elaborate mythologies with stories for the origin of the rivers, mountains, and valleys in their region. In both the East and the West their territories were covered with "traces," networks of narrow, moccasin-worn paths, trails that had been followed by hunters and warriors for generations. In the Midwest and on the Great Plains their lands were crisscrossed with wider, equally ancient thoroughfares along which entire tribes intercepted migrating buffalo and cut through mountain ranges.

Thus North America was well discovered by the time Columbus and his kind set foot on its shores. And actually Columbus was not the first European to arrive. In fact, some scholars suggest that the first non-Indians came from Asia. There are Buddhist texts that tell of five beggar priests who sailed from China in A.D. 458. Drifting on the Japanese Current, they are believed to have landed either in Mexico or in Guatemala, a realm they called the Kingdom of Fu-Sang. And it has definitely been established that sometime between A.D. 1006 and 1347, Viking seafarers from Scandinavia fought and traded with the natives of Greenland, Labrador, and Nova Scotia.

In practically every corner of North America one can find tribal stories anticipating the white man's coming. On what is today Martha's Vineyard, an Indian seer said a great white whale would foretell the coming of a strange white race who would crowd out the red men. In Mexico there existed the myth of the bearded white god, Quetzalcoatl, who would return to reclaim his kingdom. Indeed, only a few years before 1519, when the first of the Spanish conquistadores, Hernando Cortez, arrived in Mexico, the

Aztec emperor Montezuma saw ghostly people in his polished, volcanic-glass mirror: they seemed to be "coming massed, coming as conquerors, coming in war panoply. Deer bore them on their backs."

It is possible that some tribes received advance word of early Indian-white meetings, then turned these rumors into predictions. When you read the examples that follow, it is important to remember that "first contact," as the initial encounters between Native Americans and whites are termed by anthropologists, occurred at different times in different places. Generally, the more eastern and southern the locale, the earlier was the first contact. Thus the Hopi Indians of Arizona and the Hurons of eastern Canada had both experienced their first meeting with Europeans by about 1540. But the Sioux of the Dakota plains would not have firsthand knowledge of them for another one hundred and fifty years, and the Wintu of northern California for a half century after that.

Indian society was on the eve of what was to be the most catastrophic confrontation in its history. The Wasco Indians of Oregon have a prophecy story in which a wise old man dreams of strangers with hair on their faces coming from the direction of the rising sun. When he awakens, he gives this advice to his fellow tribesmen: "You people must be careful."

1

HE WILL USE ANY MEANS TO GET WHAT HE WANTS

*D*an Katchongva—*his Hopi surname means White Cloud Above Horizon—was a revered spiritual leader from Hotevilla, one of Arizona's twelve Hopi towns. When he repeated this prophecy in 1955, during testimony at a Washington congressional hearing, he was in his eighties. Within the oral tradition of the "peaceful ones," as the Hopi call themselves, are narratives foretelling the future of mankind. They often mention the Bahana, the Hopi's lost white brother, who vowed to return to the Hopi to establish peace and spread wisdom. Some Hopi say they wait for him still.*

IN ANCIENT TIMES it was prophesied by our forefathers that this land would be occupied by the Indian people and then from somewhere a White Man would come. He will come either with a strong faith and righteous religion which the Great Spirit has also given to him, or he will come after he has abandoned that great Life Plan and fallen to a faith of his own personal ideas which he invented before coming here. It was known that the White Man is an intelligent person, an inventor of many words, a man who knows how to influence people because of his sweet way of talking and that he will use many of these things upon us when he comes. We knew that this land beneath us was composed of many things that we might want to use later such as mineral resources. We knew that this is the wealthiest part of this continent, because it is here the Great Spirit lives. We knew that the White Man will search for the things that look good to him, that he will use many good ideas in order to obtain his heart's desire, and we knew that if he had strayed from the Great Spirit he would use *any* means to get what he wants. These things we were warned to watch, and we today know that those prophecies were true because we can see how many new and selfish ideas and plans are being put before us. We know that if we accept these things we will lose our land and give up our very lives.

DAN KATCHONGVA, *Hopi*

2

WHITE RABBIT GOT LOTSA EVERYTHING

In 1939, Lucy Young, a member of the Wintu tribe of northern California, told a local historian her life story. Although she was nearly blind from cataracts and over ninety years old at the time, her storytelling gifts remained sharp. The humorous, poignant events she recalls here probably took place in the 1840s, just before gold was discovered in Humboldt and Mendocino counties. Later in her reminiscences Mrs. Young describes her family's terrible experiences during the gold rush itself. The gold rushers and homesteaders who flooded into California then were responsible for murdering over fifty thousand Native Americans between 1848 and 1870 alone.

Lucy Young

MY GRANDPA, before white people came, had a dream. He was so old he was all doubled up. Knees to chin, and eyes like indigo. Grown son carry him in great basket on his back, every place.

My grandpa say: "White Rabbit"—he mean white people—"gonta devour our grass, our seed, our living. We won't have nothing more, this world. Big elk with straight horn come when white man bring it." I think he meant cattle. " 'Nother animal, bigger than deer, but round feet, got hair on his neck." This one, horse, I guess.

My aunt say: "Oh, Father, you out your head, don't say that way."

He say: "Now, Daughter, I not crazy. You young people gonta see this."

People come long way, listen to him dream. He dream, then say this way, every morning.

They leave li'l children play by him. He watch good. Have big stick, wave round, scare snake away. He had good teeth. All old people had good teeth.

One time they travel, they come to big pile of brush. My grandpa stop, and look at it. He say: "This, good wood. When I die, burn my body to ashes on top of ground. Here gonta be big canoe, run around, carry white people's things. Those White Rabbit got lotsa everything."

"How canoe gonta run round on dry ground all round here?" we askum. "Don't know," he say. "Just run that way." He mean wagon, I guess.

I never grow much. They call me "Li'l Shorty," but I know pretty near everything that time. My grandpa put his head on my head, smoove my hair, and hold his hand there.

"Long time you gonta live, my child," he say. "You live long time in this world."

Well, I live long enough. I guess 'bout ninety-five next summer, if I living till then.

My grandpa never live to see white people, just dreaming every night 'bout them. People come long way, listen [to] him dream.

My grandpa move down by big spring. One day he couldn't get up. He say: "I gonta leave you today. I used to be good hunter, kill bear, elk, deer, feed my children. Can't feed my children no more. Like old root, just ready for growing now. Pretty soon dead. Speak no more."

All seem like dream to me. Long, long ago. Night-time, he die, and in morning, all tied up in deerskin with grass rope. Sit up knees to chin. They tie him up too soon. He roll over, and come back. Scare everybody. He ask for water, and ask for packstrap to basket always carry him in. He ask for li'l basket he always use for cup. He drink lots.

"I starve for water, and want my strap," he say. "That's why I come back."

Then he die. Our people dig big hole, put stick across. Put brush. Put body in. Put more brush. Burn all to ashes. They put basket and strap, too, with him, when he go where people go at last.

LUCY YOUNG, *Wintu*

3

VISITORS FROM HEAVEN

T*he artist Norval Morriseau painted a colorful mural that covered an entire wall of the Indians of Canada pavilion at Montreal's 1967 Exposition. But Morriseau, or Copper Thunderbird as he is known in his native Ojibway language, is a writer as well as a painter. In his book,* Legends of My People, the Great Ojibway, *he narrates his grandfather's story of the conjuring of mysterious fabrics that presaged the white man's coming.*

The "shaking tent" performance he describes here was unique to the ceremonialism of the subarctic peoples. Inside the enclosure's skin or bark covering, the medicine man communicated with spirits who entered and left through a single opening at the top; those gathered outside witnessed the spirits shaking the tent and heard their eerie voices.

The Hudson's Bay Company mentioned in the selection was originally chartered in 1670 by English traders who were anxious to gain control of the traffic in beaver pelts. The company grew to dominate commerce in frontier Canada.

THIS STORY was told to my grandfather many years ago.

One time, about two hundred years ago, in a place called Fort Hope, Ontario, there was a settlement of Ojibway Indians where there was a medicine man who brought visitors from heaven to a huge wigwam shaped like a beaver house. Each spring the medicine man would make this great wigwam and place holes in the top and sides, so that the great wind, if it blew on the top, would also blow out the sides.

After everyone was seated in a big circle about ten feet from the tent, the medicine man inside would speak to the people outside and would say,

The framework of an Ojibway "shaking tent"

"Now we shall have visitors again," and begin to pound his medicine drum. The great skies were clear, and there was no wind.

All of a sudden a wind was heard to blow from the heavens and into the top of the wigwam, and from the holes on the sides came a refreshing breeze. In mid-air a rustle of people was heard, but none were seen. Everyone was now looking and listening, and from inside the wigwam people, men and women, were heard talking. The medicine man inside spoke to the Indians without, saying, "Our visitors are here. Listen."

In those days the Indian people had never seen silk or satin, for everyone wore buckskin clothing. From the side of the opening on the wigwam appeared the finest silk in colors of red and blue and white. These, the Ojibway Indians believe, were the dresses of the visitors. The material came from the sides of the wigwam because the wind was blowing from heaven into the open top, forcing some of the clothing worn by the visitors to appear on the sides. After about an hour the drum was beaten again and the visitors were heard to leave. Everyone looked at the top, but nothing was to be seen and everything became quiet. Then the medicine man appeared at the door of the wigwam and spoke to his people, "My people, you have again seen and heard our visitors from heaven. Next spring we shall invite them again."

The old lady who told this to my grandfather about fifty years ago was very old; she was ninety-nine. She said, "We were all surprised, not at the great magic but at the material we saw at that time. For everyone then wore buckskin clothing and no silk or satin was known to the Indians. Afterwards, when the Hudson's Bay Company came to us, they brought with them the material we had previously seen and touched, that had blown out of the great medicine lodge."

NORVAL MORRISEAU, *Ojibway*

THUNDER'S DREAM COMES TRUE

The Sauk Indian leader Black Hawk gained renown for the short-lived re-sistance he led in 1832 against federal troops; he was fighting to regain his Illinois homeland, which had been taken over by white settlers. Black Hawk was born in 1767 at the mouth of the Rock River. His precocious exploits as a young warrior against the Osage and the Cherokee, his intelligence, spellbinding oratory, and talent for summoning other tribes to his cause, place him among the foremost of Native America's "patriot chiefs." In the book Black Hawk: An Autobiog-raphy, first published in 1833, he recounts his great-grandfather's dream of the coming of the whites. The unnamed French visitor mentioned in the selection could have been Samuel de Champlain, who in 1611 established a trading post at Montreal.

MY GREAT-GRANDFATHER, Nanàmakee, or Thunder (according to the tradition given me by my father, Pyesa), was born in the vicinity of Montreal, where the Great Spirit first placed the Sauk Nation, and inspired him with a belief that, at the end of four years, he should see a *white man*, who would be to him a father. Consequently he blacked his face, and ate but once a day (just as the sun was going down) for three years, and continued dreaming throughout all this time whenever he slept— when the Great Spirit again appeared to him, and told him, that, at the end of one year more, he should meet his father—and directed him to start seven days before its expiration and take with him his two brothers *Namah*, or Sturgeon, and *Paukahummawa*, or Sun Fish, and travel in a direction to the left of sun-rising. After pursuing this course five days, he sent out his two brothers to listen if they could hear a noise, and if so, to fasten some grass to the end of a pole, erect it, pointing in the direction of the sound, and then return to him.

Early next morning they returned, and reported that they had heard sounds which appeared near at hand, and that they had fulfilled his order. They all then started for the place where the pole had been erected; when, on reaching it, Nanàmakee left his party, and went alone to the place from whence the sounds proceeded, and found that the white man had arrived and pitched his tent. When he [Nanàmakee] came in sight, his father came out to meet him. He [the white man] took him by the hand, and welcomed him into his tent. He told him that he [the white man] was the son of the King of France—that he had been dreaming for four years—that the Great Spirit had directed him to come here, where he should meet a nation of people who had never yet seen a white man—that they should be his children, and he should be their father.

BLACK HAWK, *Sauk*

5

EASY LIFE OF THE GRAY-EYED

The old Acoma Pueblo in New Mexico's Valencia County stands atop a steep rocky mesa 357 feet high. Today most of the Acoma people inhabit communities closer to the highway and Albuquerque—sixty miles from Acoma. But in summertime many families return to their adobe houses high on the mesa. Then the narrow, dusty streets bustle almost as in the old days. James Paytiamo spent his childhood there, and his reminiscence of daily life at Acoma, Flaming Arrow's People, was published in 1932. This excerpt differs from the other prophecy stories in that during Paytiamo's childhood, the existence of the white man was an established fact. What the old Acoma caciques, or headmen, seem to foretell here are the destructive influences white culture will have on the traditional Acoma way of life.

I CAN JUST REMEMBER the old men of my village. Old age was simply a delightful time, when the old men sat on the sunny doorsteps, playing in the sun with the children, until they fell asleep. At last they failed to wake up.

These old, old men used to prophesy about the coming of the white man. They would go about tapping with their canes on the adobe floor of the house, and call to us children:

"Listen! Listen! The gray-eyed people are coming nearer and nearer. They are building an iron road. They are coming nearer every day. There will be a time when you will mix with these people. That is when the Gray Eyes are going to get you to drink black, hot water, which you will drink whenever you eat. Then your teeth will become soft. They will get you to smoke at a young age, so that your eyes will run tears on windy days, and your eyesight will be poor. Your joints will crack when you want to move slowly and softly.

"You will sleep on soft beds and will not like to rise early. When you begin to wear heavy clothes and sleep under heavy covers, then you will grow lazy. Then there will be no more singing heard in the valleys as you walk.

"When you begin to eat with iron sticks, your tones will grow louder. You will speak louder and overtalk your parents. You will grow disobedient. Then when you mix with these gray-eyed people, you will learn their ways, you will break up homes, and murder and steal."

Such things have come true, and I compare my generation with the old generation. We are not good as they were; neither are we healthy as they were.

How did these old men know what was coming? That is what I would like to know.

JAMES PAYTIAMO, *Acoma Pueblo*

6

THE SPIDER'S WEB

One of the classics of Native American literature is Black Elk Speaks, *the autobiography of an Oglala Sioux holy man, recorded and edited by John G. Neihardt, a noted Nebraskan poet. By the end of the nineteenth century, Black Elk, a relative of the famous Sioux leader Crazy Horse, had seen his tribe transformed from buffalo-hunting lords of the Great Plains to hungry, impoverished prisoners, pent up on thirteen government reservations. At the age of nine, Black Elk had gone into a trance and experienced a wondrous vision in which the Six Grandfathers—West, East, North, South, Earth, and Sky—granted him unusual spiritual powers. Thereafter he was dedicated "to bringing to life the flowering tree of his people" by revitalizing the seven sacred rites of the Oglala. In this brief selection Black Elk remembers the ominous dream of an earlier Sioux medicine man.*

A LONG TIME AGO my father told me what his father told him, that there was once a Lakota [Sioux] holy man, called Drinks Water, who dreamed what was to be; and this was long before the coming of the Wasichus [white men]. He dreamed that the four-leggeds were going back into the earth and that a strange race had woven a spider's web all around the Lakotas. And he said: "When this happens, you shall live in square gray

Black Elk (left), taken during an extended European dance tour from 1887 to 1889

houses, in a barren land, and beside those square gray houses you shall starve."

They say he went back to Mother Earth soon after he saw this vision, and it was sorrow that killed him. You can look about you now and see that he meant these dirt-roofed houses we are living in, and that all the rest was true. Sometimes dreams are wiser than waking.

BLACK ELK, *Oglala Sioux*

FACE TO FACE

The Cheyennes' first encounter with white men, on the Missouri River, portrayed by the nineteenth-century Cheyenne artist Howling Wolf

I n 1006 a Viking ship, captained by Thorvald, son of Eric the Red, landed somewhere along the coast of Nova Scotia. We will never know what the *Skrellings*—"barbarians" or "weaklings," as the Vikings termed the natives—felt when the two peoples first set eyes on each other. They cannot have remained neutral for long; minutes after landing, Thorvald's sailors killed eight of them.

On Friday, October 12, 1492, when Christopher Columbus and his men hauled their armed landing boat up on the island in the Bahamas to which he gave the name San Salvador, the local Taino Indians were awestruck. "They believe very firmly that I, with these ships and crew, came from the sky," Columbus wrote in his journal, "and in such opinion they received me at every place where I landed, after they lost their terror." We do not know if the Taino were less respectful after Columbus forcibly took ten of them to Spain to display at the court of King Ferdinand and Queen Isabella. Two years later he shipped off five hundred West Indian natives as slaves; nearly all of them died of disease. Thus began the wholesale enslavement of the island Indians by Spain, which virtually annihilated the native peoples of the Caribbean.

The explorers, treasure hunters, traders, missionaries, trappers, soldiers, and colonists who followed in the wake of Columbus represented a number of separate cultures. Each brought to the New World their own national characteristics and particular interests.

Spain viewed the Indians both as potential converts to Catholicism and as slave labor for its silver mines in Mexico and the Southwest and its plantations in the Caribbean. The battle-hardened gold-and-glory-seeking conquistadores left small outposts in their wake—the missions and scattered land-grant colonies. But Spain never settled there on a massive scale. Following the explorations of Hernando de Soto (1539–42) and Francisco Coronado (1540–42), St. Augustine was founded (1565) to secure Spain's claim to the Florida peninsula, and Santa Fe would later (1609) become the capital of the Southwest. The region known as New Spain—extending unbroken down the Pacific Coast from Vancouver Island to the tip of South America and inland as far east as the Mississippi River, with the Florida peninsula as an isolated holding—was held mainly in the futile hope that it would add to the wealth and power of Spain.

France was always associated with tribes and territories which could be visited via inland waterways. Their first New World explorer, Jacques Cartier, saw the St. Lawrence River in 1534 and was warmly welcomed by five local Huron Indians there a year later. Of all the newcomers, the French were probably the most congenial to the Indians. While the Spanish sanctioned white-Indian marriages after the fact, they fundamentally considered the Native Americans to be both pagan and inferior. The French, on the other hand, often became absorbed in Indian life, adopting Indian customs and dress, learning native languages, and intermarrying. As the French voyageurs paddled their canoes up and down the rivers of the New World, their main goal was to dominate the fur trade. French exploration reached its height with Sieur de La Salle's arrival at the Gulf of Mexico in 1682. Within the expanse that was claimed as New France—west of the Appalachian Moun-

tains to the Mississippi River, south from Canada to the Gulf of Mexico—
the French established a few major towns like Quebec (1608) and Montreal
(1642). But they were generally busier forging their trade network than
building a permanent empire.

The English colonists were a different breed altogether. The families who
began populating the South after Jamestown's founding (1607) and the
religious idealists and middle-class townsfolk who founded the more northern settlements, such as Plymouth, Massachusetts (1620), had come to stay,
to transplant their own ideas of civilization in the New World. The Puritans
and Pilgrims even hoped to improve it with stricter religious discipline.
Unlike England's governmental representatives—the soldiers and traders—
these dissident colonists had little use for Indians. The Indians were "savages" (being hunters) and "devil-worshipers" (not being Christians); they
were nuisances who blocked the growth of this new English-speaking colonial world.

Just as the white man discovered many different Indian ways of life, so
the Indian learned that the white man came with many different languages
and national personalities. Besides the Spanish, French, and English, there
were explorers and traders from Portugal, Sweden, Denmark, Holland, and
even Russia. Then, too, Frenchmen in Canada behaved differently from
Frenchmen in Louisiana. English-speaking people presented at least three
regional personalities—in the North, the South, and along the Cumberland
Mountains. When the three major European nations—England, France, and
Spain—began their struggle for domination of the New World, each looked
for Indian allies to fight alongside them. The tribes made compacts, declared
war, or remained neutral, based on their first impressions of these varied
brands of white men.

The last major "first contact" occurred in 1818 when the polar Eskimos,
encountering a British naval expedition, learned they were not the only
humans on earth. By then, virtually every other Indian tribe in North America had already made some sort of accommodation to the white presence.

Some early Indian-white encounters had boded well. Others immediately
erupted into hostility, usually because the Indians had been forewarned
about the aggressive intentions of the foreigners. Such was the case with
the Zuñi Indians of the Rio Grande. In the summer of 1540, they sent their
women and children into hiding just prior to the arrival of the conquistador
they had never seen, Francisco Coronado. He promptly killed twelve of the
Zuñi warriors protecting their leading town of Hawikuh, then sacked it.

Other tribes shared the instinctive reaction of the proud Kiowa of the Plains, who could not tolerate the presence of "ears sticking out" and "growlers"—two Kiowa names for whites—in their hunting grounds.

Stories based on these dramatic face-to-face encounters became a part of tribal folklore. It is interesting how many of the selections that follow underscore the cultural conflicts that have plagued Indian-white relations down to the present day.

1

THEIR WONDROUS WORKS
AND WAYS

I n 1862 the eastern Sioux Indians, the Santee of Minnesota, rose up against white settlers, killing some 800 men, women, and children within a month. American retaliation was swift, and Charles Alexander Eastman, then four years old, was among the Santee refugees who fled to Canada for sanctuary. When his father was turned over to United States authorities, relatives raised the boy near Fort Ellis in southern Manitoba.

Born with the Indian name "the Pitiful Last," but later called "the Winner" (Ohiyesa), Eastman did not see a white person until he was sixteen. He then became one of a stream of Indians who since the eighteenth century had attended Dartmouth College. In 1890 he earned his medical degree from Boston University. Just after the turn of the century his books on Sioux life and philosophy gained great popularity, especially among young readers. In this selection from the autobiographical work, Indian Boyhood (1902), Eastman recalls his own amazement at his uncle's eyewitness report on white culture.

I HAD HEARD marvelous things of this people. In some things we despised them; in others we regarded them as *wakan* (mysterious), a race whose power bordered upon the supernatural. I learned that they had made a "fireboat." I could not understand how they could unite two elements which cannot exist together. I thought the water would put out the fire, and the fire would consume the boat if it had the shadow of a chance. This was to me a preposterous thing! But when I was told that the Big Knives had created a "fire-boat-walks-on-mountains" (a locomotive) it was too much to believe. . . .

I had seen guns and various other things brought to us by the French Canadians, so that I had already some notion of the supernatural gifts of the white man; but I had never before heard such tales as I listened to that morning. It was said that they had bridged the Missouri and Mississippi rivers, and that they made immense houses of stone and brick, piled on top of one another until they were as high as high hills. My brain was puzzled with these things for many a day. Finally I asked my uncle why the Great Mystery gave such power to the *Washichu* (the rich)—sometimes we called them by this name—and not to us Dakotas [Sioux].

"For the same reason," he answered, "that he gave to Duta the skill to make fine bows and arrows, and to Wachesne no skill to make anything."

"And why do the Big Knives increase so much more in numbers than the Dakotas?" I continued.

"It has been said, and I think it must be true, that they have larger families than we do. I went into the house of an *Eashicha* (a German), and I counted no less than nine children. The eldest of them could not have been over fifteen. When my grandfather first visited them, down at the mouth of the Mississippi, they were comparatively few; later my father visited their Great Father at Washington, and they had already spread over the whole country.

"Certainly they are a heartless nation. They have made some of their people servants—yes, slaves! We have never believed in keeping slaves, but it seems that these *Washichu* do! It is our belief that they painted their servants black a long time ago, to tell them from the rest, and now the slaves have children born to them of the same color!

"The greatest object of their lives seems to be to acquire possessions—to be rich. They desire to possess the whole world. For thirty years they were trying to entice us to sell them our land. Finally the outbreak [Minnesota, 1862] gave them all, and we have been driven away from our beautiful country.

"They are a wonderful people. They have divided the day into hours, like the moons of the year. In fact, they measure everything. Not one of them would let so much as a turnip go from his field unless he received full value for it. I understand that their great men make a feast and invite many, but when the feast is over the guests are required to pay for what they have eaten before leaving the house. I myself saw at White Cliff (the name given to St. Paul, Minnesota) a man who kept a brass drum and a bell to call

Charles Alexander Eastman

people to his table; but when he got them in he would make them pay for
the food!

"I am also informed," said my uncle, "but this I hardly believe, that their
Great Chief (President) compels every man to pay him for the land he lives
upon and all his personal goods—even for his own existence—every year!"
(This was his idea of taxation.) "I am sure we could not live under such
a law. . . .

"In war they have leaders and war-chiefs of different grades. The common warriors are driven forward like a herd of antelopes to face the foe. It is on account of this manner of fighting—from compulsion and not from personal bravery—that we count no *coup* on them. A lone warrior can do much harm to a large army of them in a bad country."

It was this talk with my uncle that gave me my first clear idea of the white man.

CHARLES ALEXANDER EASTMAN, *Santee Sioux*

2

BEFORE THEY GOT THICK

T his tale of the Lipan Apache reads like a southwestern version of the story of the Plymouth Colony legend: Native Americans help white pioneers survive by bringing them gifts of pumpkin and corn seeds and showing them how to plant them. Related by Percy Bigmouth in 1935, it describes events that probably took place in the early nineteenth century when his ancestors were living near the Texas-Louisiana border. During the Indian wars in the Southwest (1845–56), when official policy in Texas called for the brutal extermination of all Indians, the Lipan hid in Mexico. Eventually they made their home with their kinsmen, the Mescalero Apache, in New Mexico.

MY GRANDMOTHER used to tell this story; she told it to my mother. It is about the time when they lived near the gulf. She says that they lived at a place called "Beside the Smooth Water." They used to camp there on the sand. Sometimes a big wave would come up and then they would pick up many seashells. Sometimes they used to find water turtles. They used to find fish too and gather them and eat them.

One time they had a big wave. It was very bad. They thought the ocean was going to come right up. It came up a long way. Living things from the water covered the bank, were washed up. Then, when the sun came out and it was hot all these things began to swell and smelled bad.

One day they looked over the big water. Then someone saw a little black dot over on the water. He came back and told that he had seen that strange thing. Others came out. They sat there and looked. It was getting larger. They waited. Pretty soon it came up. It was a boat. The boat came to the shore. The Indians went back to the big camp. All the Indians came over and watched. People were coming out. They looked at those people coming out. They saw that the people had blue eyes and were white. They thought these people might live in the water all the time.

They held a council that night. They were undecided whether they should let them live or kill them.

One leader said, "Well, they have a shape just like ours. The difference is that they have light skin and hair."

Another said, "Let's not kill them. They may be a help to us some day. Let's let them go and see what they'll do."

So the next day they watched them. "What shall we call them?" they asked. . . .

Some still wanted to kill them. Others said no. So they decided to let them alone.

The Lipan went away. After a year they said, "Let's go back and see them."

They did so. Only a few were left. Many had starved to death. Some said, "Let's kill them now; they are only a few." But others said, "No, let us be like brothers to them."

It was spring. The Lipan gave them some pumpkin seed and seed corn and told them how to use it. The people took it and after that they got along all right. They raised a little corn and some pumpkins. They started a new life. Later on the Lipan left for a while. When they returned, the white people were getting along very well. The Lipan gave them venison. They were getting along very well. After that, they began to get thick.

PERCY BIGMOUTH, Lipan Apache

3

SILMOODAWA GIVES A COMPLETE PERFORMANCE

Following the example set by Christopher Columbus, the Spanish conquistador Hernando Cortez continued the ritual of sending Indians to Europe in order to parade them before royalty. At the court of Charles V, Aztecs posed for artists and juggled for gawking lords and ladies. Later, in the eighteenth century,

Indian chiefs went abroad to discuss disputed territorial boundaries and present petitions. And in 1827, a party of Osage Indians undertook a three-year sightseeing tour of France. Such trips were encouraged not only for the entertainment Indians provided, but because officials wished to impress Native Americans with the splendors of Europe and the power of their governments. In 1870 an anonymous Micmac Indian—from Canada's Maritime Provinces—told the Reverend Silas T. Rand the following story about one "Real Live Indian" who turned the tables on his aristocratic audience.

SHORTLY AFTER the country was discovered by the French, an Indian named Silmoodawa was taken to Planchean [France] as a curiosity. Among other curious adventures, he was prevailed upon to exhibit the Indian mode of killing and curing game. A fat ox or deer was brought out of a beautiful park and handed over to the Indian; he was provided with all the necessary implements, and placed within an enclosure of ropes, through which no person was allowed to pass, but around which multitudes were gathered to witness the butchering operations of the savage.

He shot the animal with a bow, bled him, skinned and dressed him, sliced up the meat, and spread it out on flakes to dry; he then cooked a portion and ate it, and in order to exhibit the whole process, and to take a mischievous revenge upon them for making an exhibition of him, he went into a corner of the yard and eased himself before them all.

ANONYMOUS, *Micmac*

|||||||||||||||||||||||||||||||||||||||||||||||||||||||||| 4 ||||||||||||||||||||||||||||||||||||||||||||||||||||||||||

A DIFFERENT KIND OF MAN

T*his melancholy tale of a solitary white man who spent years among the Assiniboine of the northern Great Plains was told by Bad Hawk to James Larpenteur Long (First Boy), a half-Assiniboine historian of his people. A trader's clerk, cattleman, grocery-store owner, tribal official, and a member of the men's secret warrior society, Long interviewed Bad Hawk in the 1930s as part of a government-sponsored oral-history program. The identity of Lone White Man is lost forever.*

MY GRANDUNCLE, Tall Man, was a member of a war party of about twelve, that camped on the south side of the Missouri River, above where the government has built the great Fort Peck Dam.

When the party resumed their journey early the next morning, the two scouts, who had left earlier, came running back. "There is a strange man walking towards the river with a gun on his shoulder," they said. So the party circled about and hid in the path of the man.

When he came closer, one from the party rose and walked towards him, at the same time lifting his hand as a sign for the man to stop. In sign language he was asked as to what tribe he belonged, but instead of an answer the man dropped his gun and raised his hands high above his head.

The rest of the party, when they saw the act, ran over and surrounded the man. Several spoke up, "Don't any of you kill him, he is a different kind of man, let's look him over."

He stood there terrified and continued to look from one to the other.

The man was tall and his hair was down to his shoulders. With the exception of his forehead, eyes, and nose, his face was covered with a heavy beard. His chest, his arms down to the tops of his hands, and his legs were covered with a hairy growth. Nothing like that had ever been seen among the tribe, only animals were that way.

"This must be what is called a white man, that we have heard about," they said among themselves.

His clothing was torn to shreds, and he was thin and seemed to be starved. Apparently all he had had for food were several pieces of a large cactus that he had peeled. These he kept in the shot bag that was attached to the powder horn. They took him along, made camp right away, and prepared some food, which he devoured like a hungry animal.

He stayed with the war party until they returned home. Fortunately for the white man, there were no encounters with the enemy on that trip.

My granduncle took the man home and new clothing was made for him. The man gave the gun, which was without ammunition, to my granduncle. He stayed with our people for many years and my granduncle adopted him as a brother, because they were about the same age and height. He was named Lone White Man.

When he learned our language, he told of being with a party of white men who came up the Missouri River. He was with a group of hunters who supplied game for the party. When the crew started their journey upstream

Possibly commemorating an early encounter with whites, this Chumash rock painting in southern California's Santa Monica Mountains includes four non-Indians on horseback.

each day, the hunters traveled away from the river, then paralleled it until they joined the crew at the night camp with game killed that day.

On one of those jaunts, Lone White Man failed to meet the party. Each day he expected to find them, but after several days he came to the conclusion that he was lost. As he had enough ammunition to last only a day or so, it was not long before he was out [of game] entirely. Berries and roots were all he had to eat after that.

On the morning that he was seen by the war party, he was on his way to the river, thinking he might see a boat. He had kept near the river all the time hoping to find his party.

Even after the whites were numerous, Lone White Man showed no desire to leave our people. One day he met one of the steamboats and did some trading. Among other things, he brought home some bacon and a frying pan. He told my granduncle that he had wanted fried liver and bacon for so long that he was going to satisfy that desire. He prepared a large stack of fried liver and bacon on which he feasted all alone. With so many different kinds of meat to be had at that time, our people never ate liver, which they used only for tanning hides.

Lone White Man lived among our people for many years, but never married. Granduncle never told if the man died out here or finally left the country.

FIRST BOY, *Assiniboine*

5

I HID MYSELF AND WATCHED

To *have peered as a child at strangely dressed, hairy-faced, sunburned, edgy, loud-voiced strangers must have been a common "first-contact" experience for many Indians. In the first of the two selections that follow, Pretty Shield, a Crow woman from Montana, tells of an encounter with white trappers, men who were probably in the employ of a Missouri River fur company, which must have taken place about 1860. In the second, a Navajo from western New Mexico, known to us only as Jaime, remembers the day, a half century later, when bearded strangers surprised him in the midst of a Navajo boy's most common chore—sheepherding.*

WHEN I WAS six snows old . . . these white men, trappers, with many packhorses, came to our village. At first my people did not call the white man *Masta-cheeda* (yellow-eyes) as they do now. Our first name for the white man was *Beta-awk-a-wah-cha* (Sits on the Water) because my people first saw the white man in a canoe on Big river. The canoe was far off. The white man in it looked as though he sat on the water; and so my people named him, and his tribe. . . .

The three white trappers wore beards that did not look nice. And yet one of those men had kindly eyes, I remember. I saw a little girl shake hands with him. There was white in one's beard, I noticed. All the others' were brown. I hid myself and watched the three go into the lodge of our chief, Walks with the Moon. I did not see inside, nor hear what was said in the lodge of Walks with the Moon, and yet I know that the three white men gave the Chief some tobacco, and that they smoked with him, saying that

Pretty Shield

they had traveled a long time looking for the Crows. My mother told me that these white men had asked if they might stay with our people, and that Walks with the Moon had answered "No," giving them a night and a day to rest before going away. When, the next morning, I looked to see the white man with the kindly eyes, he was gone. I never saw him again.

Later, when I was eleven years old, three other men who wore beards, but who were not white men, came to our people. These three caused trouble. I do not remember what it was that they did to make my people angry; but I know that two of them were killed. The other one lived for a long time with our people.

PRETTY SHIELD, *Crow*

O N E   D A Y   I   S A W a man coming along with big white whiskers all over his face. The skin that showed was around his eyes, just a little bit. I had never seen a white man before. I ran away home and told the people I had seen something out there coming toward the sheep. It looked like a man, I said, but had wool all over its face. I thought the whiskers were wool, and I wasn't sure it was a man.

Roberto, my grandfather, was sitting outside the hogan having coffee and Navajo bread. He said, "That must have been a white man you seen." Pretty soon the man came up, walked up to Roberto, reached under his vest, and pulled out below the left arm a bunch of chili peppers. He peeled off three and gave them to Roberto, then he pointed to the bread and then down his throat. The women didn't want to feed him, but Roberto said, "Give him some." The pile of bread soon went way down.

Then the white man stood up, pointed away to the west, and walked off that way. Next day some of the Indian boys trailed him to see which way he was going. They found where he had spent the night, dug a hole and lit a tiny fire and laid down by it all night. Then his tracks went on toward the west.

JAIME, *Navajo*

EXCHANGE
BETWEEN
WORLDS

Cree trappers bringing beaver skins to the Hudson's Bay post at Fort Pitt in Saskatchewan, Canada

A t the time of the Creation, the Cherokee say, the white man was given a stone, and the Indian a piece of silver. Despising the stone, the white man threw it away. Finding the silver equally worthless, the Indian discarded it. Later the white man pocketed the silver as a source of material power; the Indian revered the stone as a source of sacred power. This prophetic story underscores the profound differences in Indian and white value systems. In time the Indian would be forced to use the white man's currency as his medium of exchange, but the white man would never appreciate the Indian's sense of the spiritual potential of an ordinary pebble.

Long before the coming of "the makers of hatchets," as whites were called by the Iroquois, Indians throughout the continent of North America had traded with each other. In the Far West a popular trading spot was the present-day Oregon town of The Dalles. Here a salmon-rich stretch of boiling rapids on the Columbia River divides the world of the Pacific Coast from that of the inland Plateau. To this hub of thriving Indian commerce, controlled by Chinook Indian traders who even exacted tolls along the river, came goods from the Northwest, the Great Plains, the Great Basin, and sometimes from as far away as the Great Lakes. Dealings were conducted in a universal trading language, the "Chinook jargon," which was a potpourri of Salish, Nootka, Chinook, and, later, English words.

In California the Pomo bartered their homemade strings of disk shell beads for abalone and dried kelp from the coastal Yuki, fiber cord and sinew-backed bows from the forest-dwelling Patwin, and furs and iris cord from the inland Yuki. Farther east, Native American trade was just as active. The agricultural Hurons routinely exchanged their corn with the northern Nipissing, a hunting people, for fish and venison. Copper from northern Michigan found its way to tribes in Virginia. Throughout the plains, obsidian, red pipestone, colored slate, flint, and salt were transported over long distances, from village to village.

The first commercial exchange between Indians and whites probably took place in the eleventh century, when natives of Nova Scotia received Viking knives and axes in return for gray fox and sable pelts. In the years ahead, this swap—the exchange of furs for metal—would become the core of Indian and white commerce.

In the fifteenth and sixteenth centuries, as timber, fur-bearing animals, and other natural resources became scarcer in the Old World, Europeans looked across the seas for raw materials. The majority of the renowned early explorers of North America—men like John and Sebastian Cabot (1497), Jacques Cartier (1534), and Henry Hudson (1609)—were actually business agents on the lookout for new markets. Before long, the French, the English, the Dutch—and later the Americans—were competing for exclusive trading privileges with Indian tribes, enticing them with bribes of trinkets, liquor, and guns.

Indians guided Europeans to salt, tobacco, wood, and fish which they then managed to harvest and ship back across the Atlantic. But in collecting furs and hides, native expertise and manpower were essential. Indians possessed skills to lure and trap animals and techniques for skinning and soft-tanning hides. Next they transported these semifinished goods to white trading posts or waterfront docks. As Indians were encouraged to abandon intertribal trade and devote themselves exclusively to cleaning out the hidden stream dens of mink, marten, ermine, otter, sable, and muskrat, it was the beaver which came to enjoy highest value. Europe's hatmakers were building a multimillion-dollar industry. Whether for their furs, in the North, or for tanned deerskins, the main native commodity in the South, Indians received a range of new goods they quickly found indispensable: knives, the popular tomahawk, scissors, awls, needles, woolen cloth, mirrors, hawk bells, German silver to pound into ornaments, sheet metal to file into arrowheads and lance heads, brass kettles, "demon rum" (from the English), brandy (from the French), and above all, muskets, powder, and shot. By the mid-seventeenth century, such items had become an integral part of woodland Indian life.

Preferring to do business via the rivers, the French fur traders stowed their goods in forty-foot-long birchbark cargo canoes. The English packed their stores on muleback and rode overland to bargain with Indians. Eventually, toward the end of the eighteenth century, individual peddler-traders would be largely replaced by companies that operated strings of frontier trading outposts. Indians hauled their prime winter pelts to these posts in the spring, or bartered with company agents who caught up with tribes on the move.

All this trade transformed patterns of Indian life that had existed unchanged for centuries. Suddenly tribes found themselves competing for white business. As trapping sites were stripped of beaver, Indians battled among themselves for more westerly, fur-rich lands. Commercial agreements between the French and Huron Indians, for example, so angered the Iroquois that they joined forces with both the Dutch and the British, getting ample supplies of firearms in return. This alliance not only contributed decisively to British victory in the French and Indian War, it also enabled the Iroquois to ruthlessly dominate the northeastern fur trade.

When the rebellious colonies—the "thirteen fires" as the Iroquois called them—won independence from England, the United States entered this commercial war. Some posts along the Missouri River profited, but northward the Canadian Blackfoot refused to do business with the Americans. They resented the American habit of sending out white trappers—the legendary mountain men who were indebted to Indians for learning to maneuver in the wilderness—to compete against them in their own territory.

By 1840 high silk hats had become the fashion, and the fur trade was drying up. The Rocky Mountain beaver was nearly extinct. For a while a market in buffalo hides filled the vacuum, but soon white hunters with .50-caliber rifles made those animals just as rare. Between 1872 and 1874 over three and a half million buffalo were slaughtered for their hides, the meat left to rot on the plains.

Thanks in large part to the Indian, North America's natural resources greatly enriched European and American lives and pocketbooks. But white goods had a far more profound effect on the Indian world. In the Northeast, for example, traditional intertribal commerce was shattered in large measure by the new intense focus on one commodity—furs. With the animals gone, the prosperity that Indians had enjoyed as a result of trade with whites was followed for many by dependency on white goods, especially on the powder and shot they now needed to protect themselves and to hunt for food. Meanwhile many white traders had proved themselves unscrupulous, manipulating their Native American customers with watered-down liquor spiced with tobacco and red pepper and dealing in shoddy, mass-produced goods.

Farther west, on the Great Plains, Native American life had been transformed by the arrival of the horse. When Antonio de Espejo first rode into Hopi land in 1583, the Indians—who had never before seen a horse—paved the ground with ceremonial kilts for the sacred beasts to walk upon. By the end of the seventeenth century, Wyoming Shoshonis were getting horses from Colorado Utes who had stolen them from Spanish settlements in New Mexico. The eastern Sioux, a canoeing people in the 1760s, were a mounted people thirty years later. The rapid spread of the horse throughout the Plains caused the flowering of an entirely new Indian way of life characterized by the Appaloosa-riding, war-bonneted warrior who would symbolize American Indianism around the world.

For the crop-raising Pueblo Indians along the Rio Grande in the Southwest, metal hoes and shovels made life a little easier but had no deeper effect upon tribal customs. The Navajo way of life, however, was eventually transformed by Spanish sheep and goats. Originally a hunting people, the Navajo became expert shepherds, making their livelihood by trading animals they had bred and blankets from the wool they had woven. Along the Northwest Coast the traditional wood carvings grew brighter as artisans applied European housepaints to their cedar totem poles. On the Plains, silk ribbons, pearl buttons, English red and blue cloths, and Venetian glass beads greatly embellished native costumes. But trade goods sometimes hastened the decline of some ancient crafts, such as pottery and porcupine-quill embroidery.

The western trading posts gave migratory groups a new focal point for their wanderings, as well as expanded contact with neighboring tribes. In the spring Indians who might otherwise be blood enemies would pitch camp side by side, and bargain away their stocks of prime winter pelts. Later it was often at these same stockaded trading posts that defeated Indian leaders met governmental representatives of the United States to discuss terms of surrender and treaties of peace. By then the Indians' principal source of wealth—furs and hides—had been exhausted. All they had left that interested the white man was their land, which could usually be acquired without fair exchange.

The selections that follow offer glimpses of various Native American responses to white goods and frontier commerce.

1

THUNDER, DIZZYING LIQUID, AND CUPS THAT DO NOT GROW

*T*he white man's magical offerings—guns and metal utensils and liquor—all play a part in this Menominee folktale. The time is around the 1660s; the ''sea'' in the story is probably Lake Michigan; the Frenchmen are very likely traders who followed in the wake of the French missionary-explorer Jean Nicolet; the speaker is named Waioskasit.

As their trade with the French blossomed, the Menominee exchanged their mixed-economy, which blended hunting, gardening, and harvesting wild rice, for a seminomadic life focused around fur-trapping. This bound them more tightly to the French, who encouraged them to buy goods on credit against future payment in furs. Yet the partnership, strengthened by extensive intermarriage, also made the Menominee a dominant power in the Great Lakes area.

WHEN THE MENOMINEE lived on the shore of the sea, they one day were looking out across the water and observed some large vessels, which were near to them and wonderful to behold. Suddenly there was a terrific explosion, as of thunder, which startled the people greatly.

When the vessels approached the shore, men with light-colored skin landed. Most of them had hair on their faces, and they carried on their shoulders heavy sticks ornamented with shining metal. As the strangers came toward the Indians, the latter believed the leader to be a great manido [spirit], with his companions.

It is customary, when offering tobacco to a manido, to throw it into the fire, that the fumes may ascend to him and that he may be inclined to grant their request; but as this light-skin manido came in person, the chief took some tobacco and rubbed it on his forehead. The strangers appeared desirous of making friends with the Indians, and all sat on the ground and smoked. Then some of the strangers brought from the vessel some parcels which contained a liquid, of which they drank, finally offering some to the Menominee. The Indians, however, were afraid to drink such a pungent liquor indiscriminately, fearing it would kill them; therefore four useless old men were selected to drink the liquor, and thus to be experimented on, that it might be found whether the liquid would kill them or not.

The men drank the liquid, and although they had previously been very silent and gloomy, they now began to talk and to grow amused. Their speech flowed more and more freely, while the remainder of the Indians said, "See, now it is beginning to take effect!" Presently the four old men arose, and while walking about seemed very dizzy, when the Indians said, "See, now they are surely dying!" Presently the men dropped down and became unconscious; then the Indians said to one another, "Now they are dead; see what we escaped by not drinking the liquid!" There were sullen looks directed toward the strangers, and murmurings of destroying them for the supposed treachery were heard.

Before things came to a dangerous pass, however, the four old men got up, rubbed their eyes, and approached their kindred, saying, "The liquor is good, and we have felt very happy; you must try it, too." Notwithstanding the rest of the tribe were afraid to drink it then, they recalled the strangers, who were about to return to their boats.

The chief of the strangers next gave the Indians some flour, but they did not know what to do with it. The white chief then showed the Indians some biscuits, and told them how they were baked. When that was over, one of the white men presented to an Indian a gun, after firing it to show how far away anything could be killed. The Indian was afraid to shoot it, fearing the gun would knock him over, but the stranger showed the Indian how to hold it and to point it at a mark; then pulling the trigger, it made a terrific noise, but did not harm the Indian at all, as he had expected. Some of the Indians then accepted guns from the white strangers.

Next the white chief brought out some kettles and showed the Indians how to boil water in them. But the kettles were too large and too heavy to carry about, so the Indians asked that they be given small ones—cups as large as a clenched fist, for they believed they would grow to be large ones by and by.

The Indians received some small cups, as they desired, when the strangers took their departure. But the cups never grew to be kettles.

WAIOSKASIT, *Menominee*

2

KEEP YOUR PRESENTS

A Pawnee, Curly Chief, *recollects here a fellow tribesman's rejection of European wares. Actually a federation of four central Plains peoples, the hunting-and-farming Pawnee lived in large earth-lodge villages along the Platte River in Nebraska. In the early decades of the nineteenth century, their lands lay in the path of American pioneers whose wagons were rolling toward the Southwest. This contact with whites brought them social dissolution and disease—in 1849 they lost a fourth of their people to smallpox and cholera. In 1875 the tribe was moved to northern Oklahoma. There is no record of which treaty session Curly Chief is remembering here.*

I HEARD that long ago there was a time when there were no people in this country except Indians. After that, the people began to hear of men that had white skins; they had been seen far to the east. Before I was born, they came out to our country and visited us. The man who came was from the Government. He wanted to make a treaty with us, and to give us presents, blankets and guns, and flint and steel, and knives.

Curly Chief (front row, third from left), *in a portrait by the noted Western photographer William Henry Jackson*

The Head Chief told him that we needed none of these things. He said, "We have our buffalo and our corn. These things the Ruler gave to us, and they are all that we need. See this robe. This keeps me warm in winter. I need no blanket."

The white men had with them some cattle, and the Pawnee Chief said, "Lead out a heifer here on the prairie." They led her out, and the Chief, stepping up to her, shot her through behind the shoulder with his arrow, and she fell down and died. Then the Chief said, "Will not my arrow kill? I do not need your guns." Then he took his stone knife and skinned the heifer, and cut off a piece of fat meat. When he had done this, he said,

"Why should I take your knives? The Ruler has given me something to cut with."

Then taking the fire sticks, he kindled a fire to roast the meat, and while it was cooking, he spoke again and said, "You see, my brother, that the Ruler has given us all that we need; the buffalo for food and clothing; the corn to eat with our dried meat; bows, arrows, knives and hoes; all the implements which we need for killing meat, or for cultivating the ground. Now go back to the country from whence you came. We do not want your presents, and we do not want you to come into our country."

CURLY CHIEF, *Pawnee*

3

GIVE US GOOD GOODS

T rade often led to a dependency on white goods. Indians could not turn away from such conveniences as brass kettles and cloth once they became accustomed to them, or such pleasures as sugar and liquor once they had been tasted. And guns and knives became essential to the Indians' very survival. Many tribes came to be at the mercy of the trader, as reflected in this 1743 plea to a Hudson's Bay dealer named Isham, who copied down the chief's words in his journal.

Y O U T O L D M E last year to bring many Indians. You see I have not lied. Here is a great many young men come with me. Use them kindly! Use them kindly I say! Give them good goods, give them good goods I say!

We lived hard last winter and in want, the [gun] powder being short measure and bad, I say. Tell your servants to fill the measure and not to put their fingers within the brim. Take pity on us, I say!

We come a long way to see you. The French sends for us but we will not go there. We love the English. Give us good black tobacco, moist and hard twisted. Let us see it before opened.

Take pity of us, take pity of us, I say! The guns are bad. Let us trade light guns small in the hand, and well shaped, with locks that will not freeze in the winter. . . .

Let the young men have roll tobacco cheap, kettles thick and high for the shape and size, strong ears [handle loops], and the baile [handle] to lap [fall] just upon the side.

Give us good measure in cloth. Let us see the old measures. Do you mind me!

The young man loves you by coming to see you, take pity, take pity I say! And give them good, they love to dress and be fine. Do you understand me!

ANONYMOUS, *tribe unknown*

4

YOU ROT THE GUTS OF OUR YOUNG MEN

*D*istilled liquor was the bane of Indian existence everywhere, wrecking family life, causing humiliating sprees of self-destruction, and insidiously used by corrupt whites to confuse Indians before trade or land negotiations. Here a mid-seventeenth-century chieftain of the Catawbas—a large tribe inhabiting the Carolinas—scolds North Carolina authorities with a complaint frequently expressed by Indian leaders. Known as King Haglar by English colonists, the chief spoke these words on August 29, 1754. Although he continued to petition for years for an embargo on firewater, by the close of the eighteenth century liquor, along with successive epidemics of smallpox and attacks by the Iroquois, had decimated his people.

BROTHERS, here is one thing you yourselves are to blame very much in; that is you rot your grain in tubs, out of which you take and make strong spirits.

You sell it to our young men and give it [to] them, many times; they get very drunk with it [and] this is the very cause that they oftentimes commit those crimes that is offensive to you and us and all through the effect of that drink. It is also very bad for our people, for it rots their guts and causes our men to get very sick and many of our people has lately died by the effects of that strong drink, and I heartily wish you would do something to prevent your people from daring to sell or give them any of that strong drink, upon any consideration whatever, for that will be a great means of our being free from being accused of those crimes that is committed by our young men and will prevent many of the abuses that is done by them through the effects of that strong drink.

KING HAGLAR, *Catawba*

5

SOME STRANGE ANIMAL

T*he "sky dogs," as the people of the far western plains called horses, inspired a cultural revolution. Suddenly tribes could cut their hunting time by a significant fraction and roam great distances to trade and raid. The costume art of the Plains Indian blossomed; tipis became taller, and their furnishings very elaborate. Ceremonies increased in complexity. Personal wealth was tallied in mounts.*

Whereas in 1730 the southern Blackfoot were relatively defenseless against attacks by mounted northern Shoshoni, three generations later they had become lords of the northern Plains. Around the turn of the nineteenth century, Wolf Calf, a Piegan—the southernmost of the three Blackfoot tribes—told the Plains Indian scholar George Bird Grinnell this story of the tribe's first sight of horses and of a chief whose name appropriately changed from Dog to Many Horses.

THE FIRST HORSES we ever saw came from west of the mountains. A band of the Piegans were camped on Belly River, at a place that we call "Smash the Heads," where we jumped buffalo. They had been driving buffalo over the cliff here, so that they had plenty of meat.

There had come over the mountains to hunt buffalo a Kutenai who had some horses, and he was running buffalo; but for some reason he had no luck. He could kill nothing. He had seen from far off the Piegan camp, but he did not go near it, for the Piegans and the Kutenais were enemies.

This Kutenai could not kill anything, and he and his family had nothing to eat and were starving. At last he made up his mind that he would go into the camp of his enemies and give himself up, for he said, "I might as well be killed at once as die of hunger." So with his wife and children he rode away from his camp up in the mountains, leaving his lodge standing and his horses feeding about it, all except those which his woman and his three children were riding, and started for the camp of the Piegans.

They had just made a big drive, and had run a great lot of buffalo over the cliff. There were many dead in the pískun [corral] and the men were killing those that were left alive, when suddenly the Kutenai, on his horse, followed by his wife and children on theirs, rode over a hill nearby. When they saw him, all the Piegans were astonished and wondered what this could be. None of them had ever seen anything like it, and they were afraid. They thought it was something mysterious. The chief of the Piegans called out to his people: "This is something very strange. I have heard of wonderful things that have happened from the earliest times until now, but I never heard of anything like this. This thing must have come from above (i.e., from the sun), or else it must have come out of the hill (i.e., from the earth). Do not do anything to it; be still and wait. If we try to hurt it, may be it will ride into that hill again, or may be something bad will happen. Let us wait."

As it drew nearer, they could see that it was a man coming, and that he was on some strange animal. The Piegans wanted their chief to go toward him and speak to him. The chief did not wish to do this; he was afraid; but at last he started to go to meet the Kutenai, who was coming. When he got near to him, the Kutenai made signs that he was friendly, and patted his horse on his neck and made signs to the chief. "I give you this animal." The chief made signs that he was friendly, and the Kutenai rode into the camp and were received as friends, and food was given them and they ate, and their hunger was satisfied.

The Kutenai stayed with these Piegans for some time, and the Kutenai man told the chief that he had more horses at his camp up in the mountains, and that beyond the mountains there were plenty of horses. The Piegan said, "I have never heard of a man riding an animal like this." He asked the Kutenai to bring in the rest of his horses; and one night he started out, and the next day came back driving all his horses before him, and they came to the camp, and all the people saw them and looked at them and wondered. . . .

This young man . . . finally became head chief of the Piegans. His name at first was Dog, and afterward Sits-in-the-Middle, and at last Many Horses. He had so many horses he could not keep track of them all. After he had so many horses, he would select ten boys out of each band of the Piegans to care for his horses. Many Horses had more horses than all the rest of the tribe. Many Horses died a good many years ago. These were the first horses the Piegans saw.

When they first got horses, the people did not know what they fed on. They would offer the animals pieces of dried meat, or would take a piece of backfat and rub their noses with it, to try to get them to eat it. Then the horses would turn away and put down their heads, and begin to eat the grass of the prairie. . . .

White people had begun to come into this country, and Many Horses' young men wanted ropes and iron arrowpoints and saddle blankets, and the people were beginning to kill furs and skins to trade. Many Horses began to trade with his own people for these things. He would ask the young men of the tribe to kill skins for him, and they would bring them to him and he would give them a horse or two in exchange. Then he would send his relations in to the Hudson's Bay post to trade, but he would never go himself. The white men wanted to see him, and sent word to him to come in, but he would never do so.

At length, one winter, these white men packed their dog sledges with goods and started to see Many Horses. They took with them guns. The Piegans heard that the whites were coming, and Many Horses sent word to all the people to come together and meet him at a certain place, where the whites were coming. When these came to the camp, they asked where Many Horses' lodge was, and the people pointed out to them the Crow painted lodge. The whites went to this lodge and began to unpack their things— guns, clothing, knives, and goods of all kinds.

Many Horses sent two men to go in different directions through the camp and ask all the principal men, young and old, to come together to his lodge. They all came. Some went in and some sat outside. Then these white men began to distribute the guns, and with each gun they gave a bundle of powder and ball. At this same time, the young men received white blankets and the old men black coats. Then we first got knives, and the white men showed us how to use knives; to split down the legs and rip up the belly— to skin for trade.

WOLF CALF, *Piegan*

6

BUTTOCKS BAGS AND
GREEN COFFEE BREAD

I n this humorous story from the Jicarilla Apache of northern New Mexico, the "white people" referred to are probably not the Spanish, who set up a mission among the Jicarilla in the mid-eighteenth century, but the Americans. In 1854, United States troops quelled the Jicarilla rebels, but in 1878, some warriors took to cattle rustling again. In 1887, the tribe was placed on the northern New Mexico reservation where they live today as successful cattle ranchers.

WHEN THE WHITE PEOPLE first came to this country, they gave the Indians hats, pants, shoes, and coats. Dishes and blankets were also given out, and food, such as flour, sugar, and coffee.

These foolish people received some too. They heard the other people say "buttocks bag" [pants were called *tlatsizis*, "buttocks bag"], and they asked, "What is this bag for? What do you put in it?"

"Why, you throw your buttocks in it," was the answer.

So they decided to do it. They put the pants in a low place and got up on a cliff above them. They hopped in place, getting ready to jump. Then they tried to get in the pants. Their feet missed, and they fell. Then they tied the pants around themselves, but the leg part hung down behind. Some put the pants on backward; some had the legs hanging down in front. That's the way they went around. They put the shirts on. Some wore them in the right way; some put them on backward. The hats they used for carrying water. They didn't know what hats were for. They thought a hat was some kind of dipper. They didn't know what all those things were.

They wouldn't keep gloves. They said, "This must be Bear's hand." The shoes they wouldn't keep either. "These must be the bear's moccasins," they said.

They didn't know what flour was either. They just threw it away. They kept nothing but the sack and emptied out the flour. All the Indians did this, even those who were not foolish. And the baking powder they threw away too.

At first they tried to eat bacon. They made soup of it and ate too much of it. A lot of them died from eating it.

A celebrated trading center for the Navajo, Lorenzo Hubbell's post, in Ganado, Arizona

At first they tried to make the flour into a mush. They tried to use it like cornmeal. But it was too sticky, and they threw it away. The brown sugar they liked though. Some of the children ate it like candy. They tasted the salt. They knew what that was. The white people gave them beans too. The beans they recognized. They knew how to eat them.

They were all given green coffee. This is what all the Apaches did with it, not just the foolish ones. They boiled the green beans for two days. They didn't get any softer. The people couldn't eat it. So they pounded it up and thought they would make a mush of it. It didn't taste good even though they stirred sugar into it. So they tried to make bread of it after grinding it. That didn't taste good either. They gave it up then and threw it away.

ANONYMOUS, *Jicarilla Apache*

7

THE BEWITCHED PALE MAN

A gifted raconteur from the Dogrib tribe, one of the largest native nations in Canada's Northwest Territories, Vital Thomas lived near old Fort Rae. But his story of one man's especially potent ink'on ("a power") probably originates from the days before that post was established in 1852—when Dogrib traders had to venture further west, to the Simpson post along the Mackenzie River.

FORT SIMPSON is an old, old fort. In the fall, the Dogribs used to go to Simpson to trade. One time, one bunch went on ahead of another bunch by four or five days. When they got to Simpson, the Hudson's Bay manager wouldn't give them any credit. He was mad at them. He said, "You guys haven't paid me from last year. I won't give you a thing." Those poor Indians, there was nothing they could do but go back. They were one day out from the fort when they met the other bunch coming along to trade. They said to the other bunch, "There is no use going on, you might as well turn back. The Hudson's Bay man won't give us credit. There is nothing there for you."

There was an old fellow with the second bunch. He was Seretton's father— not that Seretton who is living here now but another one. That old man listened to all the talking, and then he said to his bunch, "Well, we might as well go on in and see what it is like. We can't turn back now." That night when they made camp, those fellows asked the old man if he couldn't change the Hudson's Bay man's mind, because they had come from a long, long way, from Snare Lake or Indin Lake maybe. They offered to pay the old man, so finally he said, "I'll do the best I can to change his mind."

So the old man started to sing, "Hey hey, Pale Man! hey hey." And he started to work his arms down into the earth. Finally he was down into the earth about halfway up his arms. He was still singing, "Hey hey, Pale Man!" when he said, "Here is the man we have been talking about," and he brought the Hudson's Bay man up out of the ground as far as his armpits. Then he began to rub his hands over the Hudson's Bay man's head as if he was pulling or cupping up water. All of a sudden he clapped his hands loudly and said, "Here it is! I got his mind right here in my hands!" And the

Hudson's Bay man sank back through the earth. "He has gone home now without his mind. We got to hurry to get there. We got to do our trading fast and go right back because I can't hold his mind very long."

They started out early and got to Simpson about the middle of the day. When they went in the store, the Hudson's Bay man acted like he was dreaming, kind of like he was asleep. The Dogribs started to ask for things. And that trader gave them everything they asked for, just like he was half drunk. They got everything they could think of on credit. And then the old man said to them, "We might as well go home now. I can't hold it any longer." And as soon as they got back into the bush, the old medicine man sent the Bay man back his mind.

VITAL THOMAS, *Dogrib*

BEARERS OF
THE CROSS

Sisnajini (Blanca Peak or ''White Shell Mountain''), the sacred mountain of the east to the Navajo

To many Native American peoples much of the land they inhabited was sanctified. They conceived of the earth, the heavens, and cardinal directions as supernatural forces. Their religious leaders could point to the cave or hill or lake from whence, according to their mythology, they as a people had first emerged from an ancient underworld. Or they told of a sacred spring or tree where clan ancestors had first descended from the sky. The surrounding trees, plants, seas, rivers, deserts, animals, and other forms of wildlife often figured as personalized forces in their myths and stories.

Their spiritual reference points were prominent environmental landmarks. In Arizona the Navajo universe was bounded by four sacred peaks. A hundred miles to the east, the San Juan Pueblo's world was circumscribed by four different sacred mountains. Everywhere tribes enshrined caves, springs, mesas, and lakes, leaving prayer sticks and food offerings for the unseen spirits living there. They felt toward these natural landmarks as a Taos woman spoke of Blue Lake: "I think of it as an altar."

Many Native American peoples cherished a belief in a sort of Golden Age when humans and animals had lived and talked together. Northwest Coast families proudly proclaimed their descent from the eagle, the raven, and the wolf. Medicine men in nearly every tribe were initiated into their roles as mystical healers and prophets by animal instructors who had appeared to them in visions. Through elaborate ceremonies refined over centuries, young Indian men and women learned how to revere the sacred forces of the living, natural world. The yearning for a dimly remembered time of wholeness, when humans lived in equivalence with all of nature, was found in their highest rituals as well as in the activities of their everyday lives.

"The old people came literally to love the soil," wrote the Sioux author Luther Standing Bear. "They sat on the ground with the feeling of being close to a mothering power. It was good for the skin to touch the earth, and the old people liked to remove their moccasins and walk with their bare feet on the sacred earth. The soil was soothing, strengthening, cleansing and healing."

When white men first witnessed Indians impersonating animal spirits in costume and dance, and worshiping rocks and rainbows, they failed to see this as a form of deep religious expression. To their Christian minds, these were deplorable pagan rites. Worship of more than one deity, and sacrificial offerings directed at the natural world, stamped Indians as a misguided, lesser form of mankind. Here were Christless heathens crying to be rescued from eternal damnation.

For their part most Native Americans were not averse initially to Christianity. Before the white man appeared, tribes had absorbed new waves of religious thought. To them a fresh form of worship did not negate the old. The great value they placed on their own traditional beliefs made them especially curious about the magical deeds of this new medicine man, the Son of God. They were courteous listeners even when they did not understand a word of a missionary's preaching. They were fearful, too. For a people so aggressive and determined as the whites must have powerful spirits. But this openheartedness did not always satisfy the missionaries. Their insistence upon an exclusive devotion to one God, and the criticism meted out when their Indian converts disappointed them, caused centuries of conflict, for not many Indians were about to repudiate their own traditional religions. Even when Christianity forced their children to doubt the old ways, they devised new religious ceremonies blending both Christian and Indian concepts and symbolism to keep their hopes and heritage alive.

The first missionaries came from Spain. Traveling in partnership with the conquistadores, these Roman Catholic padres belonged to the Dominican, Jesuit, Franciscan, and Augustinian orders. In Florida, in the Southwest, and in California they created self-sufficient missions where Indians were to live, worship, and work away from tribal influences. The native converts were trained to tend fruit orchards and grow crops, graze sheep and cattle, read and chant holy scripture, and develop their skill as craftsmen in weaving, leatherwork, blacksmithing, and in the manufacture of olive oil and soap.

Stern with their Indian "children," the padres depended on soldiers garrisoned at each mission to round up neophytes, as newly baptized Indians were known. Each night the Native American men and women were locked into separate dormitories. The Spanish soldiers flogged runaways and those found secretly practicing tribal rites; they quelled the frequent rebellions against strict mission discipline.

But some priests, torn between the prevalent attitude toward Indians and their own consciences, protected their converts. The Native American's earliest white champion was a Spanish missionary, Father Bartolomé de Las Casas. Published in 1544, his proposed *New Laws for the Indies* pleaded for an end to Indian peonage. Later mission priests were often forced to shield their converts when silver-mine bosses or large ranchers tried to conscript them for cheap labor.

By 1635 more than forty thriving Spanish missions had been established in Florida. They lasted for another hundred years until British soldiers from the north, with their Creek and Catawba allies, destroyed them and sold thousands of Indian converts into slavery.

The most durable missions lay in the Southwest. But there Christianity was eventually forced to an accommodation with traditional Indian ritual. By 1633, following an intensive construction campaign of adobe-and-timber churches among the Zuñi, Hopi, and other Pueblos, sixty thousand Indians had been baptized, and ninety chapels were scattered throughout seven missionary districts. Mass was compulsory. Natives who practiced their traditional ceremonies were beaten or executed. Such oppression against this proud and sophisticated people finally led to the famous Pueblo Rebellion of 1680, when all the Spanish missions were destroyed and those priests and colonists who survived were driven south across the Rio Grande into Mexico. When the government of New Spain reconquered the region twelve years later, the churches were rebuilt, and Catholic priests still serve in some of them today. But hereafter both Christ and the kachinas—the masked gods of Pueblo religion—were worshiped in a unique mixture of indigenous and imported ritual.

In California the first Spanish mission was erected on July 16, 1769, near the present-day site of San Diego. Over the next fifty years Native American labor constructed twenty more missions northward along the Pacific Coast to San Francisco. But after 1826, having won its independence from Spain, the Mexican government began ordering the padres to abandon their churches. Although the intention was that the land should be distributed among the Indians who had come to rely on the missions for food and shelter, it wound up in private hands. The Mission Indians were generally evicted, left without livelihood, and ill prepared to return to their former mountain hamlets. Between 1769 and 1830 disease, brutality, and drastic dietary changes, particularly affecting the Mission Indian population, had reduced the coastal Native American population from seventy thousand to twenty-four thousand Indians. By 1840 only six thousand Mission Indians were left, eking out their livelihood as serfs on large ranches.

In New France, Jesuits often accompanied the trader-explorers opening up river routes, men like Père Marquette, who traveled with Louis Jolliet on his 1673 voyage down "the Great Water" (the Mississippi River). The

Jesuits baptized tribesmen in northeastern Canada and the Mississippi Valley. Generally they were humane and tended to adjust to the natives' way of life. In northern New England, for example, a French Jesuit named Sébastian Rale lived alone among the Abnaki Indians for thirty-four years, speaking their language and fighting by their side against the British.

In the British colonies, however, the Protestant clergy was more disposed to ignore or damn the Indians than to proselytize them. There were rare individuals like the Rhode Island minister Roger Williams, who spoke out on behalf of religious freedom and land rights for the Narranganset Indians. But extremist seventeenth-century Protestant leaders—like the Puritan preacher Cotton Mather—considered Indians "agents of Satan."

English-speaking missionaries dispatched Indian converts far and wide to deliver in broken English testimonials of salvation from alcohol and savagery, but they rarely collected sizable native congregations. Not until the late eighteenth century did Protestant proselytizing gain any significant momentum. By then the great aim of numerous Protestant missionary societies was to "civilize" the Indians. Native American boys and girls were indoctrinated into the "gospel of soap" and the ethics of hard work, personal sacrifice, and economic independence. In 1865 the United States government formalized an arrangement whereby Protestant groups would administer the government-owned Indian boarding schools. Their efforts did more to crush Indianness than any other missionary campaign.

Since in traditional Indian life, religious ritual permeated nearly every political, social, and economic activity, the message of most Christian missionaries was that Indians had to reject most aspects of their own culture. The following selections reflect in some measure the range of tribal response to this requirement, from acceptance by the California Luiseño to rebellion by the New Mexican Pueblos to adoption of a blend of old and new religious beliefs as described by the Kiowa-Apache, Jim Whitewolf.

1

BURN THE TEMPLES,
BREAK UP THE BELLS

The Pueblo Rebellion of 1680, incited by eighty years of especially harsh treatment of Native Americans in the Southwest, caught the Spanish off guard. Within a matter of weeks, over four hundred of them were massacred. Priests were slain before their altars; the mission churches and livestock were put to the torch; and twenty-five hundred soldiers were driven south to Mexico.

In an effort to discover how such an attack could possibly have been planned under their noses, Spanish inquisitors interrogated Indian prisoners, among them Pedro Naranjo of the San Felipe Pueblo. This excerpt from Naranjo's replies to his questioners describes how Popé, a San Juan medicine man and the leader of the "Indian sorcerers" mentioned in Naranjo's statement, received spiritual guidance for the rebellion. As its main strategist, he prepared the secret timing by which all nineteen of the Rio Grande Pueblos rose up in arms simultaneously. Until the Spanish "reconquest" in 1692, the Southwest was Indian country once more.

[UNDER OATH, Pedro Naranjo declared that the Indians] have planned to rebel on various occasions through conspiracies of the Indian sorcerers, and that although in some pueblos the messages were accepted, in other parts they would not agree to it, and that it is true that during the government of the said señor general seven or eight Indians were hanged for this same cause, whereupon the unrest subsided. . . .

Finally, in the past years, at the summons of an Indian named Popé who is said to have communication with the devil, it happened that in an estufa [sacred meeting place or *kiva*] of the pueblo of Los Taos there appeared to the said Popé three figures of Indians who never came out of the estufa. They gave the said Popé to understand that they were going underground to the lake of Copala. He saw these figures emit fire from all the extremities of their bodies, and that one of them was called Caudi, another Tilini, and the other Tleume; and these three beings spoke to the said Popé, who was in hiding from the secretary, Francisco Xavier, who wished to punish him as a sorcerer.

A baptismal font carved by a Tsimshian artist from the Northwest Coast

They told him to make a cord of maguey fiber and tie some knots in it which would signify the number of days that they must wait for the rebellion. He said that the cord was passed through all the pueblos of the kingdom so that those which agreed to it [the rebellion] might untie one knot in sign of obedience. . . . As a sign of agreement and notice of having concurred in the treason and perfidy they were to send up smoke signals to that effect in each one of the pueblos singly. The said cord was taken from pueblo to pueblo by the swiftest youths under the penalty of death if they revealed the secret.

Everything being thus arranged, two days before the time set for its execution, because his lordship had learned of it and had imprisoned two Indian accomplices from the pueblo of Tesuque, it was carried out prematurely that night, because it seemed to them that they were now discovered; and they killed religious, Spaniards, women, and children. . . .

Finally the señor governor and those who were with him escaped from the siege, and later this declarant saw that as soon as the Spaniards had left the kingdom an order came from the said Indian, Popé, in which he commanded all the Indians to break the lands and enlarge their cultivated fields, saying that now they were as they had been in ancient times, free from the labor they had performed for the religious and the Spaniards, who could not now be alive. . . .

Asked for what reason they so blindly burned the images, temples, crosses, and other things of divine worship, he [Pedro Naranjo] stated that the said Indian, Popé, came down in person, and with him El Saca and El Chato from the pueblo of Los Taos, and other captains and leaders and many people who were in his train, and he ordered in all the pueblos through which he passed that they instantly break up and burn the images of the holy Christ, the Virgin Mary and the other saints, the crosses, and everything pertaining to Christianity, and that they burn the temples, break up the bells, and separate from the wives whom God had given them in marriage and take those whom they desired.

In order to take away their baptismal names, the water, and the holy oils, they were to plunge into the rivers and wash themselves with amole, which is a root native to the country, washing even their clothing, with the understanding that there would thus be taken from them the character of the holy sacraments. . . . He saw to it that they at once erected and rebuilt their houses of idolatry which they call estufas, and made very ugly masks in imitation of the devil in order to dance the dance of the cacina [kachina]; and he said likewise that the devil had given them to understand that living thus in accordance with the law of their ancestors, they would harvest a great deal of maize, many beans, a great abundance of cotton, calabashes, and very large watermelons and cantaloupes; and that they could erect their houses and enjoy abundant health and leisure. . . .

PEDRO NARANJO, *San Felipe Pueblo*

2
A GOOD INDIAN'S DILEMMA

Even *when an Indian was baptized as the missionaries insisted, racial bigotry kept him from gaining fuller acceptance by whites. The Fox, or Mesquakie, Indians of the southern Great Lakes region provide this ironic anecdote about a convert's can't-win plight.*

ONCE THERE WAS an Indian who became a Christian. He became a very good Christian; he went to church, and he didn't smoke or drink, and he was good to everyone. He was a very good man. Then he died. First he went to the Indian hereafter, but they wouldn't take him because he was a Christian. Then he went to Heaven, but they wouldn't let him in—because he was an Indian. Then he went to Hell, but they wouldn't admit him there either, because he was so good. So he came alive again, and he went to the Buffalo Dance and the other dances and taught his children to do the same thing.

ANONYMOUS, *Fox*

3
WE NEVER QUARREL
ABOUT RELIGION

In *this excerpt from a famous speech delivered in 1828, the Iroquois leader Red Jacket replies to a representative of the Boston Missionary Society named Mr. Cram. The missionary had asked for approval to spread his faith among tribes within the Iroquois sphere of influence in northern New York State. When the meeting was over, Cram refused to shake the Indians' outstretched hands. There could be no fellowship between the religion of God and the works of the devil, he announced. The Iroquois are reported to have smiled.*

FRIEND AND BROTHER! It was the will of the Great Spirit that we should meet together this day. He orders all things, and he has given us a fine day for our council. He has taken his garment from before the sun, and caused it to shine with brightness upon us. Our eyes are opened that we see clearly. Our ears are unstopped that we have been able to hear distinctly the words you have spoken. For all these favors we thank the Great Spirit, and him only. . . .

Brother! Continue to listen. You say that you are sent to instruct us how to worship the Great Spirit agreeably to his mind; and if we do not take hold of the religion which you white people teach, we shall be unhappy hereafter. You say that you are right and we are lost. How do we know this to be true? We understand that your religion is written in a book. If it was intended for us as well as for you, why has not the Great Spirit given it to us; and not only to us, but why did he not give to our forefathers the knowledge of that book, with the means of understanding it rightly? We only know what you tell us about it. How shall we know when to believe, being so often deceived by the white people?

Brother! You say there is but one way to worship and serve the Great Spirit. If there is but one religion, why do you white people differ so much about it? Why do not all agree, as you can all read the book?

Brother! We do not understand these things. We are told that your religion was given to your forefathers, and has been handed down from father to son. We also have a religion which was given to our forefathers, and has been handed down to us their children. We worship that way. It teacheth us to be thankful for all the favors we receive, to love each other, and to be united. We never quarrel about religion. . . .

RED JACKET, *Iroquois*

‖‖‖‖‖‖‖‖‖‖‖‖‖‖‖‖‖‖‖‖‖‖‖‖‖‖‖‖‖‖‖ **4** ‖‖‖‖‖‖‖‖‖‖‖‖‖‖‖‖‖‖‖‖‖‖‖‖‖‖‖‖‖‖

JANITIN IS NAMED *JESÚS*

Sometime between 1820 and 1830, a Kamia Indian named Janitin was brought under guard to the San Miguel Mission in California, south of San Diego. As an old man in the year 1878, he told an interviewer what he had experienced at the mission and displayed the scars he had received at the hands of

the Dominican fathers. Not all Spanish priests behaved so harshly. Some Francis-
cans in the Southwest were actually welcomed by the Indians, because, in the
natives' own words, "These go about poorly dressed and barefooted like us; they
eat what we eat, they settle down among us, and their intercourse is gentle." But
the success of the California padres was judged by the number of Indian names on
their baptismal rolls and the amount of farm and craft goods produced at the
missions. That called for fresh crews of Indian laborers.

I AND TWO of my relatives went down from the Sierra of Neji to the
beach of el Rosarito, to catch clams for eating and to carry to the sierra as
we were accustomed to do all the years; we did no harm to anyone on the
road, and on the beach we thought of nothing more than catching and
drying clams in order to carry them to our village.

While we were doing this, we saw two men on horseback coming rapidly
towards us; my relatives were immediately afraid and they fled with all
speed, hiding themselves in a very dense willow grove which then existed
in the canyon of the Rancho del Rosarito.

As soon as I saw myself alone, I also became afraid of those men and ran
to the forest in order to join my companions, but already it was too late,
because in a moment they overtook me and lassoed and dragged me for a
long distance, wounding me much with the branches over which they
dragged me, pulling me lassoed as I was with their horses running; after
this they roped me with my arms behind and carried me off to the Mission
of San Miguel, making me travel almost at a run in order to keep up with
their horses, and when I stopped a little to catch my wind, they lashed me
with the lariats that they carried, making me understand by signs that I
should hurry; after much traveling in this manner, they diminished the pace
and lashed me in order that I would always travel at the pace of the horses.

When we arrived at the mission, they locked me in a room for a week;
the father [a Dominican priest] made me go to his habitation and he talked
to me by means of an interpreter, telling me that he would make me a
Christian, and he told me many things that I did not understand, and Cun-
nur, the interpreter, told me that I should do as the father told me, because
now I was not going to be set free, and it would go very bad with me if I
did not consent in it. They gave me *atole de mayz* [corn gruel] to eat which
I did not like because I was not accustomed to that food; but there was
nothing else to eat.

One day they threw water on my head and gave me salt to eat, and with this the interpreter told me that now I was Christian and that I was called *Jesús:* I knew nothing of this, and I tolerated it all because in the end I was a poor Indian and did not have recourse but to conform myself and tolerate the things they did with me.

The following day after my baptism, they took me to work with the other Indians, and they put me to cleaning a *milpa* [cornfield] of maize; since I did not know how to manage the hoe that they gave me, after hoeing a little, I cut my foot and could not continue working with it, but I was put to pulling out the weeds by hand, and in this manner I did not finish the task that they gave me. In the afternoon they lashed me for not finishing the job, and the following day the same thing happened as on the previous day. Every day they lashed me unjustly because I did not finish what I did not know how to do, and thus I existed for many days until I found a way to escape; but I was tracked and they caught me like a fox; there they seized me by lasso as on the first occasion, and they carried me off to the mission torturing me on the road. After we arrived, the father passed along the corridor of the house, and he ordered that they fasten me to the stake and castigate me; they lashed me until I lost consciousness, and I did not regain consciousness for many hours afterwards. For several days I could not raise myself from the floor where they had laid me, and I still have on my shoulders the marks of the lashes which they gave me then.

JANITIN, *Kamia*

5

THE FREEDOM TO WORK

When he was about thirteen years old, a Luiseño Indian named Pablo Tac related this fond reminiscence of life at the Mission of San Luis Rey de Francia, at one time the largest of the Spanish missions in California. In 1822, twenty-four years after the mission was founded, Tac became the 3,896th Indian child to be baptized there. His depiction of its daily activities nicely fits the Spanish missionary's dream of how mission life should flow. Tac was such an exemplary pupil that the mission's founder took him to Rome and enrolled him in Urban

College. There he died of disease just before he turned twenty. The industrious work of the Indian "neophytes" at San Luis Rey de Francia was short-lived; after 1834 the mission was abandoned.

THE GOD WHO was adored at that time was the sun and the fire. Thus we lived among the woods until merciful God freed us of these miseries through Father Antonio Peyri, a Catalan, who arrived in our country in the afternoon with seven Spanish soldiers.

When the missionary arrived in our country with a small troop, our captain and also the others were astonished, seeing them from afar, but they did not run away or seize arms to kill them, but having sat down, they watched them. But when they drew near, then the captain got up (for he was seated with the others) and met them. They halted, and the missionary then began to speak, the captain saying perhaps in his language, *"Hichsom iva haluon, pulluchajam cham quinai."* "What is it that you seek here? Get out of our country!" But they did not understand him, and they answered him in Spanish, and the captain began with signs, and the Fernandino

Luiseño women at San Luis Rey Mission, once the richest of California's missions

[missionary], understanding him, gave him gifts and in this manner made him his friend. . . .

The Fernandino Father remains in our country with the little troop that he brought. A camp was made, and here he lived for many days. In the morning he said Mass, and then he planned how he would baptize them, where he would put his house, the church, and as there were five thousand souls (who were all the Indians there were), how he would sustain them, and seeing how it could be done. Having the captain for his friend, he was afraid of nothing. . . .

He [Father Peyri] ordered the Indians to carry stone from the sea (which is not far) for the foundations, to make bricks, roof tiles, to cut beams, reeds, and what was necessary. They did it with the masters who were helping them, and within a few years they finished working. They made a church with three altars for all the neophytes (the great altar is nearly all gilded), two chapels, two sacristies, two choirs, a flower garden for the church, a high tower with five bells, two small and three large, the cemetery with a crucifix in the middle for all those who die here. . . .

The Fernandino Father, as he was alone and very accustomed to the usages of the Spanish soldiers, seeing that it would be very difficult for him alone to give orders to that people, and, moreover, people that had left the woods just a few years before, therefore appointed alcaldes [official leaders] from the people themselves that knew how to speak more Spanish than the others and were better than the others in their customs. There were seven of these alcaldes, with rods as a symbol that they could judge the others. . . . In the afternoon, the alcaldes gather at the house of the missionary. They bring news of that day, and if the missionary tells them something that all the people of the country ought to know, they return to the villages shouting, "Tomorrow morning . . ."

Returning to the villages, each one of the alcaldes wherever he goes cries out what the missionary has told them, in his language, and all the country hears it. "Tomorrow the sowing begins and so the laborers go to the chicken yard and assemble there." And again he goes saying these same words until he reaches his own village to eat something and then to sleep. In the morning you will see the laborers appear in the chicken yard and assemble there according to what they heard last night.

With the laborers goes a Spanish majordomo and others, neophyte alcaldes to see how the work is done, to hurry them if they are lazy, so that they will soon finish what was ordered, and to punish the guilty or lazy one who leaves his plow and quits the field keeping on with his laziness. They work all day, but not always. At noon they leave work, and then they bring them *posole*. (*Posole* is what the Spaniards of California call maize in hot water.) They eat it with gusto, and they remain sated until afternoon when they return to their villages. The shoemakers work making chairs, leather knapsacks, reins and shoes for the cowboys, neophytes, majordomos and Spanish soldiers, and when they have finished, they bring and deliver them to the missionary to give to the cowboys. The blacksmiths make bridle kits, keys, bosses for bridles, nails for the church, and all work for all. . . .

In the Mission of San Luis Rey de Francia the Fernandino Father is like a king. He has his pages, alcaldes, majordomos, musicians, soldiers, gardens, ranchos, livestock, horses by the thousand, cows, bulls by the thousand, oxen, mules, asses, 12,000 lambs, 200 goats, etc. There are five gardens that are for all, very large. The Fernandino Father drinks little, and as almost all the gardens produce wine, he who knows the customs of the neophytes well does not wish to give any wine to any of them, but sells it to the English or Anglo-Americans, not for money, but for clothing for the neophytes, linen for the church, hats, muskets, plates, coffee, tea, sugar and other things. The products of the Mission are butter, tallow, hides, chamois leather, bear skins, wine, white wine, brandy, oil, maize, wheat, beans and also bull horns which the English take by the thousand to Boston.

PABLO TAC, *Luiseño*

6

A SHAMAN OBEYS

I n 1916 Pedro Encinales, one of California's last Salinan Indians, told an anthropologist about this clash between a San Antonio Mission priest and a Native American medicine man. When the Catholic missions in California were finally boarded up in the mid-1830s, Encinales's family, like countless others, clung to the outskirts of the crumbling adobe buildings and the orchards and fields where they once had labored so faithfully. Their plight became a popular philanthropic cause around the turn of the nineteenth century.

LONG AGO there was an old shaman who had a reputation as a rainmaker who could make rain whenever he wished.

One year there was a long drought and the Padre of the Mission said, "We will test his powers." He gave orders that the old man should be caught and brought before him. Then he said to him, "If you do not make it rain so that it will fill these barrels I will have you tied and whipped."

"It is good," replied the shaman, "I will try." Then he sang. Soon the sky became overcast with clouds and it thundered. Then came the rain furiously; it did not delay long. The barrels which the Padre had placed were filled quickly. Then he told the man to stop the rain. And it stopped. "We do not wish any more," he said. "No, there is enough already!"

PEDRO ENCINALES, *Salinan*

7

ALWAYS GIVE BLESSINGS
AND BE THANKFUL

J im Whitewolf, *a Kiowa Apache of southwestern Oklahoma, was born around 1878. In his autobiography he implicitly compares Christian values as he acquired them from missionaries with the Kiowa Apache code of conduct handed down by his grandfather. Unlike the tribes with whom they were most closely associated—the Cheyenne, Arapaho, and Kiowa, who were practically their brothers—the Kiowa Apache had a reputation for friendliness toward whites.*

WHEN I WAS still pretty small, I remember that east of the Agency near Anadarko, there were some Catholic sisters sitting under an arbor in the camp. Someone was calling out to us to come over there because they had something to tell us. My mother and father took me over there. A fellow was there, named Bill Brownbear, who was interpreting for the Catholic sisters. There was another man with those sisters. This man who was with the sisters prayed, and then there was singing. He took out a black book; it was a Bible. He started reading from it. I didn't understand it at that time. The only thing he was doing that I knew was good was the praying because we had always had praying in the Indian way. Every now and then I could

Jesuits had a reputation for seeking out Indians where they lived. Here, a Father Crimont, S.J., visits the Crow Indians in 1890.

understand a little bit, like when he talked about "our Father," but the rest of the time I didn't know what he was talking about.

When the service was over, they said that they would give some of us rosaries. They said that next time they came back they would give out more of them. The men got larger rosaries than the children got. I didn't get any, but my father did. Every two weeks we went to the camp for rations. We went back there again one time—I think it was on Sunday. They had church and went through the same thing as the first time. Then one of the sisters went through the crowd and gave out rosaries. That time I got one. They told me to wear mine all the time. I felt proud of it. I never took it off. I wore it when I slept and even when I went in swimming. People would go back to that service every Sunday, but they went just to get a rosary with beads on the chain. A lot of them didn't even believe in it, but they wanted those beads. I guess those Catholics went around to the Kiowas, too.

The next thing I knew was that the missionary, Mr. Methvin, was building a church right north of the old Agency. I saw them working on that building. After it was finished, they went around and told people that, when they heard the bell, they should come over there. The people around camp were talking about how this man was going to show them how they could come back after they died. They thought that he was some kind of a medicine man. What he meant was that, if you led a good life, your soul would have eternal life. But the Indians thought that he could bring the dead back to life. Everybody started sending their children to that church. My mother told me that, if I should die, I wouldn't be gone forever but would come back to life. This all happened before I ever went to school.

Another boy and I went to church one time. The preacher was talking and there was a Kiowa fellow alongside him interpreting. Then they divided us up into groups and gave us each a little paper. After that I went to church all the time. Soon some of the older people started to come to church. Later on I began to understand that they meant that when you die you don't return to earth but go up to heaven.

Years after that, I heard that they were going to build another church down by Cache Creek. Then some white people came there. Mr. Curtis came there. Some of us helped haul rocks to build this church. On Sundays Mr. Curtis would come out to where we were camping and talk to us. This was before the church was finished. Bill Brownbear was interpreting for them. Some of the Indians started to believe in it. I guess it was because most of them always had believed in praying.

One time Mr. Curtis said that he was going to read us the Ten Commandments. All I got out of it was the one that says, "Thou shalt not steal." I remembered that one. He said that if you stole you wouldn't go to heaven. Henry Brownbear got up and said, "I used to steal horses, but I don't do it any more." Another old man got up and repeated the commandment, "Thou shalt not lie." He said, "I don't lie. I always tell the truth." Henry Brownbear would get up after every commandment that was read and repeat it. His Indian name was "Old Man Nervous." That was because he had a tremor of the hands. He repeated every single commandment. He was the only one who kept jumping up like that. When Mr. Curtis got to the commandment that said you should not go with another man's wife, Henry Brownbear just whistled and said, "That's too much. I want that woman sitting over there. I guess I'll just have to go to hell. . . ."

When I was little I stayed with my grandfather. He was a tall, slim man. My grandfather's cousins used to come. They were all old men. My grandfather would bring them over, just one of them at a time, and they would sleep with me and tell me stories. My grandfather told me that the Indians didn't fight among themselves any more. He told me to be friendly to people and never to steal or lie about anything. He said that in the old days the Apaches used to ride from up near the Kansas line down to Mexico, looking for good hunting grounds. Whenever they met up with the Sioux, there would be a fight. He told me always to get up early in the morning. He said that when I grew up to be a man, always to get up early and feed and water my horses. He said to take care of the horses and keep them fat, because they would take care of me and help me to find something to eat. He told me that now I didn't need to have a fast horse to do fighting, but that he wanted me to take care of my horses so I could use them to farm with, like the white people were doing, so I would have something. He said not to forget to plant corn to feed my horses with, and to eat. He said there were many ways to use corn and that there were going to be many more, and that was why I should never forget to raise it. He said that someday I would have a home of my own and I should always have lots of wood to cook food with. At that time they prayed for wood, because it helped to prepare food for them and it kept them warm. He told me always to give blessings for food and to be thankful for my home.

JIM WHITEWOLF, *Kiowa Apache*

LIVING BESIDE
EACH OTHER

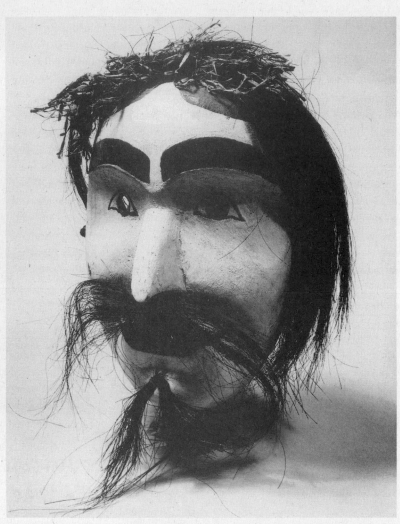

*A mask, representing a bearded white man, carved by a Kwakiutl from the
Northwest Coast*

Were red men and white "two distinct races with separate origins and separate destinies," as the Duwamish chief Seattle is said to have told the governor of Washington Territory in 1854? Was there no chance for neighborly coexistence between the two peoples?

At first most Atlantic Coast Indians were hospitable to the newcomers, who in return dubbed native chiefs as kings and their wives and sons and daughters as queens, princes, and princesses. With a mixture of kindliness and curiosity, these tribes helped the newcomers stay alive in the wilds. All across the country Indians would become known for harboring non-Indian passersby; they did not inquire if their guests were outlaws or misfits. Nor were they particularly upset when their women bore half-white children; they did not insist on taking white women. "Squaw men"—slang for whites who lived with Indian women—found acceptance among Indians when white society shunned them. If "half-breed" offspring were ostracized from white communities, they always found Indian homes. Growing up bilingual and bicultural, they were well suited to fill the critical frontier roles of interpreter and trader. In the regions marked by Spanish occupation, a *mestizo* class soon arose, mingling the blood of *Indios* and *gente de razón,* or European Spaniards. In Canada intermarriage between French and Indian became so prevalent that it there produced an entirely distinct, mixed-blood group, the Red River métis.

But one cannot dream up two more contrary ways of life and systems of belief than those represented by Native American and European societies. The enormous differences in religious values and practices, in the conduct of family and social life, in concepts of property ownership and land use, in traditional attitudes toward work and leisure, made intimacy between Indians and Europeans all too rare. Much of the time they viewed each other as total barbarians. In a talk with Benjamin Franklin, a Delaware tribesman observed, "If a white man in traveling through our country enters one of our cabins, we all treat him as I treat you. We dry him if he is wet, we warm him if he is cold. . . . But if I go into a white man's house in Albany and ask for victuals and drink, they say, 'Get out.' . . . You see they have not learned those little good things we need no meeting to be instructed in because our mothers taught them to us when we were children."

Should an Indian venture inside a white man's home, he often found the etiquette constraining, as an elderly holy man humorously complained to the nineteenth-century missionary Cephus Washburn. "When you come to my cabin I always say to you, 'Go and eat.' . . . But when I come to see you, I never see any food in any of your dwellings; and it is only at certain definite hours that I can find any food; then the bell rattles, ding, ding, ding! and all must go then and eat, or all will soon be out of sight." (Native Americans today still joke about the white man who needs a clock to tell him when he is hungry.)

A major stumbling block between Indians and whites was their opposite attitudes toward the land. In the New World, whites cleared the forests and cultivated the ground, slaughtered wild game in massive quantities, mined the earth's gold and silver as if they would never end, and began peopling villages and towns blocked out after those in their homelands. Yet the Indians generally viewed themselves as the earth's occupiers and custodians, not as its surveyors and engineers. Defining land as a commercial product like sugar or gunpowder, the whites measured it, bought it or stole it, fenced it, tilled or built upon it, with an abandon that horrified Indians. At the same time the colonists, whose society was founded on private ownership and consolidation of personal riches, looked disapprovingly at Indian customs of sharing land in common.

Such differences in cultural outlook did not lead to problems as long as the colonial presence was limited. Friendship between the two peoples could flower when sensitive whites found themselves in Indian company, and early pioneer families often enjoyed squatting and hunting privileges in Indian territory. In those instances the two peoples had space and time to feel each other out. Moments of peace were also possible when tribal and colonial self-interests overlapped, as with matters of trade.

But the white population increased too rapidly for equilibrium to last. Indians were usually trying to eke out a living on the very lands the burgeoning white population coveted. As eastern forests were thinned of game, stories of white settlements pushing Indians ever westward became commonplace. Tribesmen clinging to ancestral territory suffered racial prejudice and religious intolerance. Whatever fragile understandings had existed were torn asunder in the rush of westward expansion. The main justification for usurping tribal lands, the concept of "right of discovery," had been invented as early as the sixteenth century in Spain. Later explorers customarily claimed vast territories in the name of the monarch or commercial interest who had paid for their ventures. In 1823, the United States Supreme Court upheld the notion that "discovery gave exclusive title to those who made it." And where "right of discovery" did not suffice, right of conquest through armed takeover generally would.

Tribes that survived on the outskirts of white communities witnessed their villages torn between pro- and anti-white factions, between "breeches" (pants-wearing Indians who adopted white habits) and "blanket" (traditional) Indians. Despite these wrenching tensions and incessant pressure to choose sides among the embroiled European powers, for the two hundred years of the colonial period most tribes did not consider themselves a conquered people. They held to the vision of retaining their own independent identity. Over the centuries, a theme repeated again and again in tribal speeches is the plea that whites recognize the Indians' right to be distinctly themselves. As a Pawnee leader named Petalesharo tried to impress upon President James Monroe in 1822, "He [the Great Spirit] made my skin red and yours white; he placed us on this earth and intended that we should live differently from each other. He made the whites to cultivate the earth, and feed on domestic animals; but he made us, red skins, to rove through the uncultivated woods and plains, to feed on wild animals, to dress in their skins. . . ."

But entreaties to Live and Let Live, no matter how eloquently expressed, usually fell on deaf ears. The white colonists could not keep from looking down upon the Indian, an attitude that did not escape the natives. "Why come the English hither," a Narraganset Indian questioned Roger Williams, "and measuring others by themselves?"

As early as the mid-seventeenth century the British hoped to establish domestic tranquility between colonies by setting aside living space for friendly, usually Christianized Indians. But these prototype reservations still did not solve the question of how to handle the "wild" Indians. Finally, in 1763, the British drew up a proclamation calling for a boundary line between their "civilization" and "Indian Territory"—which was defined as "any lands beyond the heads or sources of any of the rivers which fall into the Atlantic Ocean from the West or Northwest." Yet even the immensity of the great American West was soon insufficient for this separate-but-equal scheme. The Creek chief Speckled Snake summed up the experience of most tribes: "I have listened to a great many talks from our Great Father. But they always began and ended in this—Get a little farther; you are too near me."

In the nineteenth century, most white Americans came to believe that it was God's will for them to rule from sea to shining sea. By and large, neighborly coexistence between Indians and whites was already a dead dream. To the beleaguered western Indians this notion of Manifest Destiny meant the final series of campaigns to wrest from them their tribal birthright, their traditional land base. The only destiny they could now pursue was as fugitive or conquered nations.

1

REMOVE THE CAUSE
OF OUR UNEASINESS

During the winter of 1607, the new colonists at Jamestown, Virginia, lost half their number through starvation and disease. Without the help of their Native American neighbors in the Powhatan Confederacy, made up of some thirty tribes, the English would have altogether perished: In this 1609 plea for a continuation of friendly relations, copied down by Captain John Smith, the sixty-year-old leader of the confederacy Wahunsonacock—or King Powhatan as he was called by the English—warns of the very abuses that finally drove his people to rise against the Jamestown community. In the spring of 1622, the Indians killed nearly 350 settlers in a matter of hours.

I AM NOW grown old, and must soon die; and the succession must descend, in order, to my brothers, Opitchapan, Opekankanough, and Catataugh, and then to my two sisters, and their two daughters. I wish their experience was equal to mine; and that your love to us might not be less than ours to you.

Why should you take by force that from us which you can have by love? Why should you destroy us, who have provided you with food? What can you get by war? We can hide our provisions, and fly into the woods; and then you must consequently famish by wronging your friends. What is the cause of your jealousy? You see us unarmed, and willing to supply your wants, if you will come in a friendly manner, and not with swords and guns, as to invade an enemy.

I am not so simple, as not to know it is better to eat good meat, lie well,

To seal their friendship with Quaker colonists of Pennsylvania, the Delaware Indians presented them in 1682 with this wampum shell-bead belt, depicting an Indian and a white man (with hat) *holding hands.*

and sleep quietly with my women and children; to laugh and be merry with the English; and, being their friend, to have copper, hatchets, and whatever else I want, than to fly from all, to lie cold in the woods, feed upon acorns, roots, and such trash, and to be so hunted, that I cannot rest, eat, or sleep. In such circumstances, my men must watch, and if a twig should but break, all would cry out, "Here comes Captain Smith"; and so, in this miserable manner, to end my miserable life; and, Captain Smith, this might be soon your fate too, through your rashness and unadvisedness.

I, therefore, exhort you to peaceable councils; and, above all, I insist that the guns and swords, the cause of all our jealousy and uneasiness, be removed and sent away.

WAHUNSONACOCK, *Powhatan Confederacy*

2
MARY JEMISON BECOMES AN IROQUOIS

A curiosity of the history of Native American and white relations are the *"captivity narratives," firsthand accounts by whites who had been abducted by Indians. For three centuries this early American literary genre was relished by the general public, and the often lurid tales of torture and hardship generally reinforced the popular image of the Indian as a bloodthirsty savage. A few of these narratives, however, such as the story of the abduction in 1758 of*

*Mary Jemison, age fifteen, by a Shawnee raiding party and her subsequent adoption
by the Iroquois, tell of the captive's integration into Indian culture. For Indians,
race was usually no barrier to this sort of reverse assimilation, as Mrs. Jemison
describes in this excerpt from her autobiography, published in 1824. She died at
the age of ninety, an Iroquois grandmother on the Buffalo Creek Reservation in
northern New York.*

HAVING MADE FAST to the shore, the squaws left me in the
canoe while they went to their wigwam or house in the town, and returned
with a suit of Indian clothing, all new, and very clean and nice. My clothes,
though whole and good when I was taken, were now torn in pieces, so that
I was almost naked. They first undressed me and threw my rags into the
river; then washed me clean and dressed me in the new suit they had just
brought, in complete Indian style; and then led me home and seated me in
the center of their wigwam.

I had been in that situation but a few minutes, before all the squaws in
the town came in to see me. I was soon surrounded by them, and they
immediately set up a most dismal howling, crying bitterly, and wringing
their hands in all the agonies of grief for a deceased relative.

Their tears flowed freely, and they exhibited all the signs of real mourning.
At the commencement of this scene, one of their number began, in a voice
somewhat between speaking and singing, to recite some words to the following purport, and continued the recitation till the ceremony was ended;
the company at the same time varying the appearance of their countenances,
gestures and tone of voice, so as to correspond with the sentiments expressed
by their leader:

"Oh, our brother! Alas! He is dead—he has gone; he will never return!
Friendless he died on the field of the slain, where his bones are yet lying
unburied! Oh, who will not mourn his sad fate? No tears dropped around
him; oh, no! No tears of his sisters were there! He fell in his prime, when
his arm was most needed to keep us from danger! Alas! he has gone! and
left us in sorrow, his loss to bewail: Oh, where is his spirit? . . . His spirit
has seen our distress, and sent us a helper whom with pleasure we greet.
Dickewamis has come: then let us receive her with joy! She is handsome
and pleasant! Oh! she is our sister, and gladly we welcome her here. In the
place of our brother she stands in our tribe. With care we will guard her
from trouble; and may she be happy till her spirit shall leave us."

In the course of that ceremony, from mourning they became serene—joy sparkled in their countenances, and they seemed to rejoice over me as over a long-lost child. I was made welcome amongst them as a sister to the two squaws before mentioned, and was called Dickewamis; which being inter-preted, signifies a pretty girl, a handsome girl, or a pleasant, good thing. That is the name by which I have ever since been called by the Indians.

I afterwards learned that the ceremony I at that time passed through, was that of adoption. The two squaws had lost a brother in Washington's war, sometime in the year before, and in consequence of his death went up to Fort Pitt, on the day on which I arrived there, in order to receive a prisoner or an enemy's scalp, to supply their loss. . . .

It was my happy lot to be accepted for adoption; and at the time of the ceremony I was received by the two squaws, to supply the place of their brother in the family; and I was ever considered and treated by them as a real sister, the same as though I had been born of their mother.

During my adoption, I sat motionless, nearly terrified to death at the appearance and actions of the company, expecting every moment to feel

Young Santiago McKinn, a white captive in a Chiricahua Apache camp

their vengeance, and suffer death on the spot. I was, however, happily disappointed, when at the close of the ceremony the company retired, and my sisters went about employing every means for my consolation and comfort.

Being now settled and provided with a home, I was employed in nursing the children, and doing light work about the house. Occasionally I was sent out with the Indian hunters, when they went but a short distance, to help them carry their game. My situation was easy; I had no particular hardships to endure. But still, the recollection of my parents, my brothers and sisters, my home, and my own captivity, destroyed my happiness, and made me constantly solitary, lonesome and gloomy.

My sisters would not allow me to speak English in their hearing; but remembering the charge that my dear mother gave me at the time I left her, whenever I chanced to be alone I made a business of repeating my prayer, catechism, or something I had learned in order that I might not forget my own language. By practising in that way I retained it till I came to Genesee flats, where I soon became acquainted with English people with whom I have been almost daily in the habit of conversing.

My sisters were diligent in teaching me their language; and to their great satisfaction I soon learned so that I could understand it readily, and speak it fluently. I was very fortunate in falling into their hands; for they were kind good natured women; peaceable and mild in their dispositions; temperate and decent in their habits, and very tender and gentle toward me. I have great reason to respect them, though they have been dead a great number of years.

The town where they lived was pleasantly situated on the Ohio, at the mouth of the Shenanjee: the land produced good corn; the woods furnished plenty of game, and the waters abounded with fish. Another river emptied itself into the Ohio, directly opposite the mouth of the Shenanjee. We spent the summer at that place, where we planted, hoed, and harvested a large crop of corn, of an excellent quality. . . .

The corn being harvested, the Indians took it on horses and in canoes, and proceeded down the Ohio, occasionally stopping to hunt a few days, till we arrived at the mouth of Sciota river; where they established their winter quarters, and continued hunting till the ensuing spring, in the adjacent wilderness. While at that place I went with the other children to assist the hunters to bring in their game. The forests on the Sciota were well stocked with elk, deer, and other large animals; and the marshes contained large numbers of beaver, muskrat, etc., which made excellent hunting for the Indians; who depended, for their meat, upon their success in taking elk and deer; and for ammunition and clothing, upon the beaver, muskrat, and other furs that they could take in addition to their peltry.

The season for hunting being passed, we all returned in the spring to the mouth of the river Shenanjee, to the houses and fields we had left in the fall before. There we again planted our corn, squashes, and beans, on the fields that we occupied the preceding summer.

About planting time, our Indians all went up to Fort Pitt, to make peace with the British, and took me with them. We landed on the opposite side of the river from the fort, and encamped for the night. Early the next morning the Indians took me over to the fort to see the white people that were there. It was then that my heart bounded to be liberated from the Indians and to be restored to my friends and my country. The white people were surprised to see me with the Indians, enduring the hardships of a savage life, at so early an age, and with so delicate a constitution as I appeared to possess. They asked me my name; where and when I was taken—and appeared very much interested on my behalf. They were continuing their inquiries, when my sisters became alarmed, believing that I should be taken from them, hurried me into their canoe and recrossed the river—took their bread out of the fire and fled with me, without stopping, till they arrived at the river Shenanjee. So great was their fear of losing me, or of my being given up in the treaty, that they never once stopped rowing till they got home.

Shortly after we left the shore opposite the fort, as I was informed by one of my Indian brothers, the white people came over to take me back; but after considerable inquiry, and having made diligent search to find where I was hid, they returned with heavy hearts. Although I had then been with the Indians something over a year, and had become considerably habituated to their mode of living, and attached to my sisters, the sight of white people who could speak English inspired me with an unspeakable anxiety to go home with them, and share in the blessings of civilization. My sudden departure and escape from them, seemed like a second captivity, and for a long time I brooded the thoughts of my miserable situation with almost as much sorrow and dejection as I had done those of my first sufferings. Time, the destroyer of every affection, wore away my unpleasant feelings, and I became as contented as before. . . .

Not long after the Delawares came to live with us [during the first summer], my sisters told me that I must go and live with one of them, whose name was Sheninjee. Not daring to cross them, or disobey their commands, with a great degree of reluctance I went; and Sheninjee and I were married according to Indian custom.

Sheninjee was a noble man; large in stature; elegant in his appearance; generous in his conduct; courageous in war; a friend to peace, and a great lover of justice. He supported a degree of dignity far above his rank, and merited and received the confidence and friendship of all the tribes with whom he was acquainted. Yet, Sheninjee was an Indian. The idea of spending my days with him, at first seemed perfectly irreconcilable to my feelings: but his good nature, generosity, tenderness, and friendship towards me, soon gained my affection; and, strange as it may seem, I loved him! To me he was ever kind in sickness, and always treated me with gentleness; in fact, he was an agreeable husband, and a comfortable companion. We lived happily together till the time of our final separation, which happened two or three years after our marriage, as I shall presently relate. . . .

MARY JEMISON, *Iroquois*

3

OUR VERY GOOD FRIEND KIRK

President Thomas Jefferson *was shrewd to assign a Quaker to the Shawnee tribe when he implemented his plan for "civilizing" Indians. Jefferson wanted the Indians to don European-style clothing, attend school, and most important, abandon hunting in favor of farming. The Quaker creed of nonviolence and interracial harmony had made the Pennsylvania Colony, founded in 1681 by William Penn, an oasis of neighborliness between white and Indian. In this selection, written in 1809, the Shawnee petition Jefferson to retain a Quaker named Kirk, possibly a government agent, of whom they were particularly fond. Their tribe had occupied their western Ohio villages for only fourteen years when they sent this note. In another twenty years, they would be forced to sell that homesite and move west yet again.*

IT HAS BEEN three years since we met together at the seat of Government you then told us that we ought to take care of our women and children and provide well for them[.] we took your advice, at that time you told us you would send a man to help us and that man a Quaker went by us coming from you. You thought him a good man in appointing him.

Since that man has come to live with us, our women and children have found the benefit of it. they have had plenty to eat and he has helped us to make fences round our cornfields. Since he has been with us we have done well by his assistance to work with the young men that we find the benefit of it now, and you told us if we would cultivate the Land with him that we would become independent. we find this to be true. last summer we had plenty of corn and every kind of vegetables. our young men are always very glad to have our friend working with them. our friend is now about building a mill for us. We hope to find the benefit of it when it is done. our young men is glad to see it and we hope you will go through the work as it is begun and we will be independent in a short time[.] our friend likes all our people and when they meet they are always glad to see each other. he always gives them good advice.

Since our friend Kirk has lived with us, we have always found him a good man. we are very fond of him. the white people in the State of Ohio are also fond of him. we do not want to part with him as he is a good man. we wish him to return and live with us. the white people all wish him to return. The Wyandotts are also very fond of him and have requested us to say that they wish him to return and take charge of our business again. We hope our Father [the President] will not listen to the bad stories that have gone about against our friend for they are all false. we therefore hope our Father will send him back to us.

Our hearts felt sorry when we found our friend was dismissed. all our people are fond of him and we are sorry to part with him. we hope our Father will not take him away from us but send him back again soon. we hope he will send an answer to this soon in order to make our minds easy, as our hearts will feel sorry until we hear of his coming back. this is all we have to say[.] it is the sentiments of our hearts.

Signed,	THE OLD SNAKE his mark	X
"	THE WOLF his mark	X
"	CAPT. BUTLER his mark	X
"	THE BLACK HOOF his mark	X
"	YOUNG SNAKE his mark	X
"	THE BEAVER his mark	X
"	a Deleware Chief WAHAPPI	X

THE OLD SNAKE ET AL., *Shawnee*

4

THE FRENCHMAN DREAMS
HIMSELF HOME

This Winnebago tale, concerned with intermarriage and half-white offspring, emphasizes the high value Native Americans place upon their children. The narrative, describing the reintegration into the tribe of a part-Winnebago, part-French boy, clearly shows that cultural allegiances were more important than racial purity. As happens with much oral tradition, more than one story has been interwoven here. The account of how these People of Real Speech, as the Winnebago called themselves, first met the French in the mid-seventeenth century has been grafted on to the story of the later arrival in Wisconsin of a Frenchman known to us only as Decora. The resulting legend of the founding of the Decora family lineage among the Winnebago was told to the anthropologist Paul Radin around 1910.

O N C E   S O M E T H I N G   A P P E A R E D in the middle of the lake [Green Bay in Lake Michigan]. They were the French; they were the first to come to the Winnebago. The ship came nearer and the Winnebago went to the edge of the lake with offerings of tobacco and white deerskins. There they stood. When the French were about to come ashore, they fired their guns off in the air as a salute to the Indians. The Indians said, "They are thunderbirds." They had never heard the report of a gun before that time and that is why they thought they were thunderbirds.

Then the French landed their boats and came ashore and extended their hands to the Winnebago, and the Indians put tobacco in their hands. The French, of course, wanted to shake hands with the Indians. They did not know what tobacco was, and therefore did not know what to do with it. Some of the Winnebago poured tobacco on their heads, asking them for victory in war. The French tried to speak to them, but they could not, of course, make themselves understood. After a while they discovered that they were without tools, so they taught the Indians how to use an ax and chop a tree down. The Indians, however, were afraid of it, because they thought that the ax was holy. Then the French taught the Indians how to use guns, but they held aloof for a long time through fear, thinking that all these things were holy.

Suddenly a Frenchman saw an old man smoking and poured water on him. They knew nothing about smoking or tobacco. After a while they got more accustomed to one another. The Indians learned how to shoot the guns and began trading objects for axes. They would give furs and things of that nature for the guns, knives, and axes of the whites. They still considered them holy, however. Finally they learned how to handle guns quite well and they liked them very much. They would even build fires at night so that they might try their guns, for they could not wait for the day, they were so impatient. When they were out of ammunition, they would go to the traders and tell their people that they would soon return. By this time they had learned to make themselves understood by various signs.

The second time they went to visit the French, they took with them all the various articles that they possessed. There the French taught them how to sew, how to use an ax, and how to use a knife. Then the leader of the whites took a liking to a Winnebago girl, the daughter of the chief, and he asked her parents for permission to marry her. They told him that her two brothers had the right to give her away in marriage. So he asked them and they consented. Then he married her. He lived there and worked for the Indians and stayed with them for many years and he taught them the use of many tools. He went home every once in a while and his wife went with him, but he always came back again. After a while a son was born to him and then another. When the boys were somewhat grown up, he decided to take his oldest son with him to his country and bring him up in such a way that he would not be in danger, as was the case here in the woods. The Indians consented to it and they agreed that the mother was to bring up the youngest child.

So he took his oldest boy home with him, and when he got home, he went to live with his parents, as he had not been married in his own country. He was a leader of men. The boy was with him all the time and everyone took a great liking to him. People would come to see him and bring him presents. They gave him many toys. However, in spite of all, he got homesick and he would cry every night until he fell asleep. He cried all the time and would not eat. After a while the people thought it best to bring him back to his home, as they were afraid that he would get sick and die. Before long they brought him back. The father said: "My sons are men and they can remain here and grow up among you. You are to bring them up in your own way and they are to live just as you do."

The Indians made them fast. One morning the oldest one got up very early and did not go out fasting. His older uncle, seeing him try to eat some corn, took it away from him and, taking a piece of charcoal, mashed it, rubbed it over his face, and threw him out of doors. He went out into the wilderness and hid himself in a secret place. Afterwards the people searched for him everywhere, but they could not find him. Then the people told the uncle that he had done wrong in throwing the boy out. The latter was sorry, but there was nothing to be done anymore. In reality the uncle was afraid of the boy's father. They looked everywhere but could not find him.

After a full month the boy came home and brought with him a circle of wood [i.e., a drum]. He told the people that this is what he had received in a dream, and that it was not to be used in war; that it was something with which to obtain life. He said that if a feast was made to it, this feast would be one to Earthmaker, as Earthmaker had blessed him and told him to put his life in the service of the Winnebago.

From this man they received many benefits. He was called to take the foremost part in everything. They called him the Frenchman, his younger brother being called *Tcaposgaga,* Whitethroat. And as they said, so it has always been. A person with French blood has always been the chief. Only they could accomplish anything among the whites. At the present time there is no clan as numerous as the descendants of that family and the object that he said was sacred (the drum) is indeed sacred. It is powerful to the present day. His descendants are the most intelligent of all the people and they are becoming more intelligent all the time. What they did was the best that could be done. The ways of the white man are best. That is the way they were brought up.

This is the end of the history of the Decoras.

ANONYMOUS, *Winnebago*

5

INCIDENT AT BOYER CREEK

This account of a run-in between Omaha Indian hunters and Mormon farmers in western Iowa dramatizes basic conflicts in Indian and white philosophies of life. Particularly it reveals how the issue of the land simmered just beneath

the surface in nearly all Indian and white dealings. Differences in food-gathering
habits and in concepts of ownership of property lie behind this story of a skirmish
that never became a war. It was told in the 1880s by an unidentified Omaha to
the anthropologist J. O. Dorsey; the incident took place in 1853.

WE KILLED DEER when we went on the autumnal hunt. We
hunted all sorts of small leaping animals. When we approached any place
to pitch the tents, we were in excellent spirits. Day after day we carried into
camp different animals, such as deer, raccoons, badgers, skunks, and wild
turkeys. We had ten lodges in our party. As we went, we camped for the
night. And we camped again at night, being in excellent spirits.

At length we reached a place where some white farmers dwelt. They gave
us food, which was very good. At length they assembled us. "Come, ye
Indians, we must talk together. Let us talk to each other at night."

"Yes," said we.

As they came for us when a part of the night had passed, we said, "Let
us go." They came with us to a very large house. Behold, all of the whites
had arrived. That place was beyond the Little Sioux River, at Boyer Creek,
where the first white men were, across the country from this place. They
talked with us.

"Oho! my friends, though I, for my part, talk with you, you will do just
what I say," said one.

"We will consider it. If it be good, we will do so," said the Omahas.

"I am unwilling for you to wander over this land," said the white man.

White Buffalo in the Distance said, "As you keep all your stock at home,
you have no occasion to wander in search of them; and you dwell nowhere
else but at this place. But we have wild animals, which are beyond our
dwelling place, though they are on our land."

"Though you say so, the land is mine," said the white man.

"The land is not yours. The President did not buy it. You have jumped
on it. You know that the President has not bought it, and I know it full
well," said White Buffalo in the Distance.

"If the President bought it, are you so intelligent that you would know
about it?" said the white man, speaking in a sneering manner to the Omaha.

White Buffalo in the Distance hit the white man several times on the
chest. "Why do you consider me a fool? You are now dwelling a little
beyond the bounds of the land belonging to the President. It is through me

that you shall make yourself a person [i.e., you shall improve your condition at my expense]. I wish to eat my animals that grow of their own accord, so I walk seeking them," said White Buffalo in the Distance.

"Nevertheless, I am unwilling. If you go further, instead of obeying my words, we shall fight," said the white man.

"I will go beyond. You may fight me. As the land is mine, I shall go," said White Buffalo in the Distance.

"Yes, if you go tomorrow, I will go to you to see you. I shall collect the young white people all around, and go with them to see you," said the white man.

Having removed the camp in the morning, we scattered to hunt for game. I went with three men. About forty white men arrived, and stood there to intercept us. They waved their hands at us, saying, "Do not come any further." As we still went on, they came with a rush, and tried to snatch our guns from us. When we refused to let them go, they shot at us: "Ku! ku! ku!"

As we went back, we were driven towards the rest of our party. The leader of the white men said, "Do not go. If you go, I will shoot at you." We stood on an island; and the white men surrounded us.

"You have already shot at us," said the Omahas.

The white men doubted their word, saying, "It is not so about us."

"You have already shot at us, so we will go at all hazards. I am following my trail in my own land. I am going to hunt. Why do you behave so? Make way for us. We will go to you," said White Buffalo in the Distance.

"If you speak saucily to me, I will shoot at you," said the white man.

"Ho! if you wish to do that, do it," said the Omahas. As they departed, the whites made way for them.

We went along a bluff, and then downhill, when we reached a creek. It was a good place for us to stay, so we remained there.

At length about two hundred white men came in sight. We were just thirty. We were in the hollow by the edge of the stream. Wanacejiñga . . . arrived in sight. He looked at them. When he made a sudden signal, he was wounded in the arm. "They have wounded me! There is cause for anger! They have wounded me severely," said he.

"Oho! come, let us attack them at any rate," said the Omahas. We all stood, and gave the scalp yell. Having formed a line, we went to attack them. We scared off the white men. All of them were mounted; but only one Omaha, Agahamaci, was on a horse. He rode round and round, and gave us directions what to do. "Miss in firing at the white men. Shoot elsewhere every time," said he.

At length the Omahas intercepted the retreat of the whites. "Come, stop pursuing. Let us cease. It is good not to injure even one of the white people, who are our own flesh and blood," said Agahamaci. We returned to the women. Then we departed. We reached a place where we pitched the tents. There were a great many deer; they were exceedingly abundant.

ANONYMOUS, *Omaha*

6

OUR STOCK OF FOOD AND CLOTHES

*W*hites who lived alongside Indians found it difficult to accept the idea that native hunters enjoyed any sense of property. They seemed to roam at will. How could they "own" land or resources as the white man did? As a Chippewa man explained to anthropologist Frank G. Speck, however, his people had definite customs regarding territorial rights, which were trespassed at high cost.

Among Indian groups in California, the Northwest Coast, along the Atlantic seaboard, and elsewhere as well, Indians commonly recognized inherited tenure for berry patches, fishing banks, trapping or hunting grounds—sometimes marking them with visible signs such as boulders or blazed trees. The Chippewa speaker is Aleck Paul, from the Temagami band located at Bear Island, Ontario.

IN THE EARLY TIMES the Indians owned this land where they lived bounded by the lakes, and rivers, and hills, or determined by a certain number of days' journey in this direction or that. These tracts formed the hunting grounds owned and used by the different families. Wherever they went the Indians took care of the game animals, especially the beaver, just as the Government takes care of the land today.

So these families of hunters would never think of damaging the abundance or the source of supply of the game, because this had come to them from their father and grandfather and those behind them. . . .

The Indian families used to hunt in a certain section for beaver. They would only kill the small beaver and leave the old ones to keep on breeding. Then when they got too old they too would be killed, just as a farmer kills his pigs, preserving the stock for his supply of young. The beaver is the Indian's pork, the moose his beef, the partridge his chicken. And there was the caribou or red deer, that was his sheep. All these formed the stock on his family hunting ground, which would be parceled out among the sons when the owner died.

He says to his sons, "You take this part. Take care of this tract. See that it always produces enough." That was what my grandfather told us. His land was divided among two sons, my father and Pisha'bo (Tea Water), my uncle. We were to own this land so no other Indians could hunt on it. Other Indians could travel through it and go there, but could not go there to kill the beaver. Each family had its own district where they belonged and owned the game. That was each one's stock, for food and clothes.

If another Indian hunted on our territory we, the owners, could shoot him. This division of the land started in the beginning of time, and always remained unchanged. I remember about twenty years ago some Nipissing Indians came north to hunt on my father's land. He told them not to hunt beaver. "This is our land," he told them; "you can fish but must not touch the fur, as that is all we have to live on." Sometimes an owner would give permission for strangers to hunt for a certain time or on a certain tract. This was often done for friends or when neighbors had had a poor season. Later the favor might be returned.

When the white people came they commenced killing all the game. They left nothing on purpose to breed and keep up the supply, because the white man don't care about the animals. They are after the money. After the white man kills all the game in one place he can take the train and go three hundred miles or more to another and do the same there.

You can write this down for me. If an Indian went to the old country, England, and sold hunting licenses to the old country people for them to hunt on their own land, the white people would not stand for that. The Government sells our big game, our moose, for $50.00 license and we don't get any of it. The Government sells our fish and our islands or gets the money, but we don't get any share.

What we Indians want is for the Government to stop the white people killing our game, as they do it only for sport and not for support. We Indians do not need to be watched about protecting the game; we must protect the game or starve. We can take care of the game just as well as the game warden and better, because we are going to live here all the time. . . .

ALECK PAUL, Chippewa

7

IF I COULD SEE THIS THING

Native Americans lacked all resistance to what in the long run proved to be the most deadly aspect of living in company with whites—their diseases. The dread smallpox began killing Indians as early as 1514, when it first appeared in Panama. Successive epidemics of it continued throughout the nineteenth century. Disease was the overwhelming cause for the estimated 90 percent drop in Indian population between 1492 and 1900. No tribe was left unscathed, as smallpox, cholera, "the great red skin" (measles), tuberculosis, scarlet fever, and influenza took a greater toll than warfare, slavery, or starvation.

Here George Bent, a part-white, part-Cheyenne trader, describes the terrible cholera scourge of 1849. Originating in the ports of New York and New Orleans, the disease was carried to the Great Plains by gold rushers, where it struck Bent's relatives.

I N ' 4 9 , the emigrants brought the cholera up the Platte Valley, and from the emigrant trains it spread to the Indian camps. "Cramps" the Indians called it, and they died of it by the hundreds. On the Platte whole camps could be seen deserted with the tepees full of dead bodies, men, women and children.

The Sioux and Cheyennes, who were nearest to the road [wagon train], were the hardest hit, and from the Sioux the epidemic spread northward clear to the Blackfeet, while from the Cheyennes and Arapahos it struck down into the Kiowa and Comanche country and created havoc among their camps.

Our tribe suffered very heavy loss; half of the tribe died, some old people say. A war party of about one hundred Cheyennes had been down the

In 1856 one of many smallpox epidemics struck the North Dakota Mandan. Running Face was five years old at the time, and carried scars from the disease until his death.

Platte, hunting for the Pawnees, and on their way home they stopped in an emigrant camp and saw white men dying of cholera in the wagons. When the Cheyennes saw these sick white men, they rushed out of the camp and started for home on the run, scattering as they went; but the terrible disease had them already in its grip, and many of the party died before reaching home, one of my Indian uncles and his wife dying among the first.

The men in the war party belonged to different camps, and when they joined these camps, they brought the cholera with them and it was soon raging in all the villages. The people were soon in a panic. The big camps broke up into little bands and family groups, and each little party fled from the rest.

[My] grandmother (White Thunder's widow) and [my] stepmother, Yellow Woman, took the children that summer out among the Chéyennes, and they went to the Canadian, I think, where the Kiowas and Comanches were to make medicine. During the medicine dance an Osage visitor fell down in the crowd with cholera cramps. The Indians broke camp at once and fled in every direction, the Cheyennes north toward the Arkansas. They fled all night and halted on the Cimarron.

Here a brave man whose name I have forgotten—a famous warrior—mounted his war horse with his arms and rode through the camp shouting, "If I could see this thing [the cholera], if I knew where it was, I would go there and kill it!" He was taken with the cramps as he rode, slumped over on his horse, rode slowly back to his lodge, and fell to the ground. The people then broke camp in wild fright and fled north through the big sand hills all that night.

GEORGE BENT, *Southern Cheyenne*

THE LONG
RESISTANCE

A battle between southern Plains Indian warriors and United States troops, as depicted on a Kiowa tipi cover

T he Native American homelands were not seized without a fight, many fights in fact. The four centuries of bitter warfare between red man and white took place in overlapping phases from the East Coast to the West between 1500 and 1900. The overriding cause was Native American resistance to white encroachment on tribal lands. The inevitable outcome—on the field of battle, at least—was Indian defeat.

The European powers were accustomed to waging grand military campaigns to resolve their territorial disputes. They had developed a professional-soldier caste and elaborate strategies for pitting trained armies against one another.

The Indian tribes, on the other hand, never kept standing armies. Their warriors were never exclusively professional soldiers in the European sense. Generally their raids were undertaken for reasons of personal revenge and not to build an empire or to exterminate their foes. With the coming of the horse to the Great Plains, intertribal feuding grew into almost a formalized blood sport.

The ordinary Indian man, although perfectly ready to defend his life or community, was at the same time family man, provider, craftsman, and participant in his people's demanding social and religious schedule. Even in the face of overwhelming threat to his existence, he strove to maintain the accustomed way of life. Thus, in 1814, the Creek warrior William Weatherford described the ideal conditions for defending his nation against the Georgia state militia: "I would have raised corn on one bank of the river and fought them on the other."

Combat between whites and Indians in North America falls into three major periods. The first saw the tribes resisting the rapacity of the Spanish, a sequence of hostilities that began shortly after the arrival of Columbus and lessened only after Spain reconquered the Pueblo Indians in New Mexico in 1692—although Spanish and Indian animosity would persist until Spain was finally forced to abandon her colonies in the 1820s. Overlapping this warfare in the Southwest was the incredibly complex period of incessant hostilities east of the Mississippi among the English, the French, and a multitude of Native American peoples, beginning with the Virginia uprising in 1622 and ending with the close of the War of 1812. Finally came the Indian efforts to hold off domination by the United States, starting with a series of wars in the 1790s and ending symbolically a century later with the tragic massacre at Wounded Knee in South Dakota.

The Spanish threw veteran soldiers of fortune and skilled cavalry against relatively peaceful, settled Indian communities in Florida, California, and the Southwest. These hardened campaigners shocked the Indians as they unhesitatingly enslaved or ruthlessly destroyed any native societies that stood between them and the gold and silver they sought.

During the Colonial era the British, French, and Spanish used the new continent as a battleground for their Old World rivalries. Wise Indian leaders sensed the danger of being swept into this power struggle. "Why do not you and the French fight in the old country and the sea?" the Delaware chief Shingas asked the British in 1758. "Why do you come to fight on our land? This makes everybody believe you want to take the land from us by force and settle it." (The British later considered Shingas such a threat that in 1775 their General Braddock offered a 200-pound bounty for Shingas's scalp, along with five pounds for the scalp of an ordinary warrior.)

Like many Indian headmen, Pontiac, an Ottawa chieftain from what is now the state of Michigan, became caught up in England and France's contest over New World supremacy. His dislike for the British stemmed from their trade policies—they had stopped dealing in rum and gunpowder with the Indians—and their mistreatment of the Allegheny mountain tribes. Although the French had lost the French and Indian War and been decisively defeated in Canada, Pontiac still hoped to revive their prominence.

Together with a Delaware Indian seer known as "the Enlightened," Pontiac formed the greatest alliance of fighting tribes since King Philip's confederacy of Indians had fought the New England colonists in 1675. The war he started in 1763 spread like wildfire across the Ohio Valley, but when his followers learned that France and England had secretly concluded a peace treaty, Pontiac's conspiracy collapsed. Although the Pontiac uprising caused the British government to issue a proclamation forbidding settlement in the Ottawa tribal lands, that restriction meant little to the American settlers who shortly flooded into the territory.

Most tribes found it impossible to maintain their neutrality; they were swayed by bribes, or they were bound by trade alliances, or they chose to exploit the strife to get revenge on old enemies. In the Southeast many Indian communities now found themselves caught between the British and the colonists. When the Mississippi Chickasaws were belatedly asked in 1782 to join the side of the American colonists in the Revolutionary War, they replied, "Our making a Peace with you doth Not Intitle Us to Fall out With Our Fathers the Inglish for we Love them as They were the First People that Ever Supported Us to Defend Our Selves Against Our former Enimys the French & Spaniards & All their Indians."

Other tribes, including the Shawnee, Mohawk, Seneca, and bands of the Delaware and Cherokee, sided with the Redcoats (the British) against the upstart Long Knives (the Americans). As a Delaware chief explained the alliance, "The father [England] has called on his Indian children, to assist him in punishing his children, the Americans. . . . At first I looked upon it as a family quarrel, in which I was not interested. However at length it appeared to me, that the father was in the right; and his children deserved to be punished a little. That this must be the case I concluded from the many cruel acts his offspring had committed from time to time on his Indian children. . . ."

During and after the Revolution, the United States took revenge against England's Indian allies. In August 1779, American troops launched a "scorched earth" campaign, burning to the ground forty Iroquois towns. Thereafter, among the Onondaga, Seneca, and Mohawk, George Washington was known as "the Town Destroyer." The tribes knew they were no longer warring to preserve political independence as had seemed to be the case in the 1760s. Now they were defending themselves against annihilation.

In 1789 the United States War Department was created, in part to handle all Indian matters. When a separate Bureau of Indian Affairs was established in 1824, it remained under War Department control. For the next quarter century, until the Bureau of Indian Affairs was transferred to the Department of the Interior, the "Indian problem" was considered a military matter.

The United States wars with the Indians concentrated on three major fronts: (1) 1790–1832, the northeast wars, where American forces subjugated the remaining nations who had befriended the British; (2) 1849–1887, the southwestern campaigns across Arizona, New Mexico, and northern Mexico to vanquish the Navajo and Apache; (3) 1849–1892, the western Indian wars, a series of desperate clashes from Texas north to the Canadian border and westward to the Pacific Ocean.

In the seventeenth and eighteenth centuries, bows and arrows could hold their own against the smooth-bore muzzle-loaders used by the Europeans, though tribesmen eagerly sought to trade for these flintlocks whenever possible. But in the latter half of the nineteenth century, repeating rifles, constant troop replacements, and the contributions of Indian scouts tipped the balance in favor of the American soldiers. Often short of powder and shot for whatever firearms they had acquired by trade or theft, the Indians had but one real advantage: familiarity with the terrain. Whether darting through the Eastern Woodlands, wheeling on horseback across the Great Plains, or disappearing into the expanses of desert in the Southwest, hit-and-run Native American guerrillas usually tried to avoid the costly, decisive battles so common to white warfare. In disbelief, Black Hawk, the Sauk chief, witnessed the British fighting during the War of 1812: "Instead of stealing upon each other, and taking every advantage to kill the enemy and save their own people . . . they march out, in open daylight, and fight, regardless of the number of warriors they may lose! After the battle is over, they retire to feast, and drink wine, as if nothing happened; after which, they make a statement in writing, of what they have done—each party claiming the victory!"

During the Revolution only a handful of Indians had served as American scouts, but in the western struggles with the Indians the United States Army took full advantage of old tribal animosities, recruiting scouts from among the Osage, Kansas, Crow, Arikara, Pawnee, and Apache. These "red blue-coats," often formed into special Indian scouting units, were invaluable in guiding cavalry columns, spotting the movements of hostile Indians, and later policing the new reservations.

In the long history of Indian-white warfare, the majority of Native American "uprisings" occurred when Indian territory was being encroached upon or some local incident ignited a frontier already tense with injustice toward the Indians. This was the case in 1675 when the execution of three Wampanoag tribesmen in Plymouth Colony touched off the long-smoldering anger of the New England tribes. Led by King Philip, himself a Wampanoag, the tribes waged a six-month campaign against white settlers, a war that represented the first major Indian effort to mount a multitribal offensive.

During later conflicts, actions by Indians were often exaggerated by settlers and sensationalized by frontier newsmen to justify a cry for troops that would smash the Indians once and for all. Within the Native American world,

For centuries whites hired Indians to fight Indians. Here, a Warm Springs Indian Scout, Loa-Kum-Artnuk, aims his Spencer rifle against Modoc hostiles during the famous 1872 war along the Oregon-California border.

resentments against white injustices were frequently given focus by an accompanying native religious revival. Indian leaders often had a prophet-seer at their side, who prophesied a restoration of Indian traditional life once the whites were driven into the sea, or once the Indians learned to reject white ways and vices.

On the military scoreboard the Indians enjoyed a few short-lived successes, including Opechancanough's 1622 rout of the Jamestown settlers; the 1680 crushing of Spanish rule in the Southwest by the united Pueblo tribes; Little Turtle's thrashing of General Arthur St. Clair's American troops in the Ohio Valley in 1791; Little Crow's surprise attacks on Minnesota pioneers in 1862; the victory of Red Cloud in 1868, when the use of the Bozeman Trail, which ran through Indian-held territory guaranteed by treaty, had to be abandoned; and the annihilation of General George A. Custer's command in 1876. But the Native American was never able to follow up on such successes; his strategy was always short-range. Even his most charismatic leaders could not keep a multitribal military force together for long. And neither stealthy ambushes nor full-scale assaults could stem the unending stream of white reinforcements. In the end the Indian was simply outnumbered as well as outarmed. Warfare against the whites was at best only a holding action. Native fighting prowess was judged finally by how long a tribe could prolong its retreat or delay its surrender.

The accounts that follow represent but a handful of the countless campaigns, massacres, and skirmishes that took place and add up to the longest war in American history.

1

WE MUST BE UNITED

*A*fter the colonies were free from England's domination a remarkable Shaw-nee leader began rallying many of the same Indians who had fought beside Pontiac. His name was Cougar Crouching for His Prey, or Tecumseh, and he had earned his warrior's reputation fighting in the defeats of General Harmer at Fort Wayne (1790) and General St. Clair on the Wabash River (1791). Now the enemy were the Americans who had settled along the Monongahela, Allegheny, and Ohio rivers. Like Pontiac, too, Tecumseh's movement was furthered by a holy man, his *brother, who was called "The Prophet." Tecumseh envisioned a vast coalition of tribes who would fight to recover the Ohio Valley lands lost through a succession of dubious treaties negotiated by the wily American governor of Indiana Territory, William Henry Harrison.*

In 1810–11, Tecumseh traveled from the Great Lakes to the Gulf of Mexico, trying to elicit support for his cause. In the selection that follows, he is speaking to the Osage. Before returning from this trip, however, American troops found Tecumseh's stronghold, known as Prophet's Town, on the Tippecanoe River and burned it to the ground. The great leader's gathering storm never broke. Tecumseh died in Canada on October 5, 1813, fighting on the British side against his old adversary William Henry Harrison in the Battle of the Thames.

B R O T H E R S—We all belong to one family; we are all children of the Great Spirit; we walk in the same path; slake our thirst at the same spring; and now affairs of the greatest concern lead us to smoke the pipe around the same council fire!

Brothers—We are friends; we must assist each other to bear our burdens. The blood of many of our fathers and brothers has run like water on the ground, to satisfy the avarice of the white men. We, ourselves, are threatened with a great evil; nothing will pacify them but the destruction of all the red men.

Brothers—When the white men first set foot on our grounds, they were hungry; they had no place on which to spread their blankets, or to kindle their fires. They were feeble; they could do nothing for themselves. Our fathers commiserated their distress, and shared freely with them whatever the Great Spirit had given his red children. They gave them food when hungry, medicine when sick, spread skins for them to sleep on, and gave them grounds, that they might hunt and raise corn.

Brothers—The white people are like poisonous serpents: when chilled, they are feeble, and harmless, but invigorate them with warmth, and they sting their benefactors to death.

The white people came among us feeble; and now we have made them strong, they wish to kill us, or drive us back, as they would wolves and panthers.

Brothers—The white men are not friends to the Indians: at first, they only asked for land sufficient for a wigwam; now, nothing will satisfy them but the whole of our hunting grounds, from the rising to the setting sun.

Brothers—The white men want more than our hunting grounds; they wish to kill our warriors; they would even kill our old men, women, and little ones.

Brothers—Many winters ago, there was no land; the sun did not rise and set: all was darkness. The Great Spirit made all things. He gave the white people a home beyond the great waters. He supplied these grounds with game, and gave them to his red children; and he gave them strength and courage to defend them.

Brothers—My people wish for peace; the red men all wish for peace; but where the white people are, there is no peace for them, except it be on the bosom of our mother.

Brothers—The white men despise and cheat the Indians; they abuse and insult them; they do not think the red men sufficiently good to live.

The red men have borne many and great injuries; they ought to suffer them no longer. My people will not; they are determined on vengeance; they have taken up the tomahawk; they will make it fat with blood; they will drink the blood of the white people.

Brothers—My people are brave and numerous; but the white people are too strong for them alone. I wish you to take up the tomahawk with them. If we all unite, we will cause the rivers to stain the great waters with their blood.

Brothers—If you do not unite with us, they will first destroy us, and then you will fall an easy prey to them. They have destroyed many nations of red men because they were not united, because they were not friends to each other.

Brothers—The white people send runners amongst us; they wish to make us enemies, that they may sweep over and desolate our hunting grounds, like devastating winds, or rushing waters.

Brothers—Our Great Father over the great waters [the king of England] is angry with the white people, our enemies. He will send his brave warriors against them; he will send us rifles, and whatever else we want—he is our friend, and we are his children.

Brothers—Who are the white people that we should fear them? They cannot run fast, and are good marks to shoot at: they are only men; our fathers have killed many of them; we are not squaws, and we will stain the earth red with their blood.

Brothers—The Great Spirit is angry with our enemies; he speaks in thunder, and the earth swallows up villages, and drinks up the Mississippi. The great waters will cover their lowlands; their corn cannot grow; and the Great Spirit will sweep those who escape to the hills from the earth with his terrible breath.

Brothers—We must be united; we must smoke the same pipe; we must fight each other's battles; and more than all, we must love the Great Spirit; he is for us; he will destroy our enemies, and make his red children happy.

TECUMSEH, *Shawnee*

2

BLACK HAWK STANDS ALONE

The next celebrated defender of Native American independence was the Sauk chief named Big Black Bird Hawk, who had joined Tecumseh and fought with the British in 1812. This version of the series of skirmishes that became known as the Black Hawk War was related by tribal elders around 1910 to the part-Fox anthropologist William Jones. It does not identify the treaty that set Black Hawk against the Americans. In 1804 Governor William Henry Harrison had prevailed upon three Sauk and Fox chiefs to sell, without tribal approval, all their north-western Illinois lands; Harrison is said to have gotten the Indians drunk first.

After Black Hawk and his people were finally expelled from their Rock Island wigwams in 1831, the chief crossed the Mississippi and returned to his Illinois homeland the following spring with a thousand followers. Immediately hounded by the Illinois militia, Black Hawk successfully fought them off, but he had a harder time with federal troops and Indian mercenaries under the command of General Henry Atkinson. The Battle of Bad Axe along the Mississippi River, where more than two hundred of his people were killed—men, women, and children—effectively ended Black Hawk's four months of rebellion.

THE SAUKS AND FOXES were living together at the time, in the Rock River country. White people had been coming in for some time, and helping themselves to the land. Wherever they selected places to live, there they settled down and began to make homes for themselves. The people beheld these doings, and were not at all pleased. When they made protests, the reply they got was that the land was no longer theirs, that it was now the white man's.

About this time came officers of the government, and the chiefs and head men met them in council. The white men presented a paper. It said that an agreement had been made between officers of the government and head men of the Sauks and Foxes; that according to the agreement, the people had given up the possession of all the Rock River country, in return for which the government had paid money, sugar, coffee, pork, tobacco, salt, and whiskey; and at the bottom of the paper was signed the names of the men of both sides who made the agreement. The principal man on the side of the government was the head official at Shallow Water (St. Louis); and the principal man on the side of the Sauks and Foxes was Kwaskwami. The agreement had been made in the wintertime.

The whole business came with great surprise upon the chiefs and councillors. The paper made clear one thing: it verified the ugly rumors that had gone from mouth to mouth about Kwaskwami. It was known to all that he had gone to spend the winter near Shallow Water. His object was to be near a trading post where he could dispose of his pelts as fast as he got them. But it was rumored that he spent much time at the post, and that he hunted little; that he hobnobbed with the big official there, and that he had much money to spend; that he drank a great deal, and was often so drunk that he was absent from his camp for a long period at a time; and that all the while, even up to the time of his departure, he had plenty of food to eat.

Now, all this was very strange, and the people wondered how it had come to pass. Then, as now, they knew they kept tab on the wealth of one another, and it was easy to guess the limit of one's possessions. Moreover, it was particularly easy to guess how much a man like Kwaskwami had. . . . Kwaskwami and the men whose names were on the paper denied ever having touched the pen. They must have lied, or else they were drunk at the time and did not know they had touched the pen.

The chiefs and councillors tried to explain to the officers the position of Kwaskwami—that the man was not a chief; that he had no power to make a treaty with another nation; that his act was not known before or at the time he did it; that he was not made a delegate to make a treaty on behalf of his people; and that what he did, he did as an individual. They tried to explain to the officers that it was necessary, when a question came up about the cession of land, to let the whole nation know about it; and that when a cession was made, it was necessary first to get the consent of every chief and councillor.

It was of no use to talk about these things. The officers said that the agreement had been made, and that both parties would have to stand by it; that they had come, not to talk about the treaty, but to tell the people to move as soon as possible across to the west bank of the Mississippi.

Naturally the people were loath to leave their old homes; but some had made up their minds to make the best of a bad bargain, and go to the new country. Those most of this mind were the Foxes. Pawicig was chief of the Foxes then, and he led his people over across the river. With the Foxes went a band of Sauks.

Among the Sauks was a man who had been prominent in council; his name was Keokuk.

Most of the Sauks were not for going, especially men of the younger class. There was at this time among the Sauks a great warrior; he was of the Thunder Clan, and his name Big Black Bird Hawk. The young men rallied about him, and talked to him about holding the old home, even if it meant war with the white man. He was not willing at first, because the number of his Sauk warriors was not big enough for a long, hard fight; and they had few guns and little ammunition, though they all had bows and arrows. He had fought with the English and with the Shawnee Tecumseh, and knew what it was to fight against the government.

In the midst of these events, he was visited by emissaries from other nations—from the Potawatomies, Kickapoos, Winnebagoes, Omahas, and the Sioux—all of them offering help to drive back the white man. A prophet among the Potawatomies told of a vision he had of the manitou [sacred spirit] by which power came to him to foretell events. He said that the Big Black Bird Hawk was the man to lead the nations and win back the old homes of the people; that when the fight began, speedily would rise the dead to life again, and the warriors would be without number; that back would come the buffalo and the game-folk that had disappeared; and that in a little while the white man would be driven to the eastern ocean and across to the farther shore from whence he came.

In the end the Big Black Bird Hawk was prevailed upon to go to war. No sooner had he begun, when he discovered that he would have to do the fighting with only the warriors of his own nation and a few others that came from the Kickapoos and Foxes. The chief of the Potawatomies who had urged him so strongly to fight gave the alarm to the white people, and took sides with them as soon as the fighting began. Instead of the Sioux and Omahas coming to his help, they fought against him; and when the Winnebagoes saw how things were going, they joined also with the whites. Indeed, there was little fighting between the Sauks and the white men; most of the fighting was between the Sauks and the other nations. It was the Winnebagoes who made the Big Black Bird Hawk captive. They turned him over to the white men, who carried him away to the east and kept him there a prisoner. After a time he was permitted to return to his people, whom he found living on the west bank of the Mississippi. A short while after he died. Some white men stole his skeleton, and placed it in a great building, where it was on view. The great building caught fire; and it was burned up with the bones of the warrior of the Thunder Clan.

WILLIAM JONES, *Fox*

3

BLOOD SCATTERED LIKE WATER

T*he Bloody Island Massacre of 1850 took place during the darkest period of California Indian history. Anti-Indian sentiment was at a fever pitch. Over the next two decades thousands of Native Americans—contemptuously termed Diggers—were killed by the military, by citizen-organized "Indian hunts," and by disease. Between 1850 and 1863 an estimated ten thousand California Indians—children preferred—were sold or indentured for cheap labor in the United States and Mexico.*

Among such outrages was the murder of over a hundred Pomo Indian men, women, and children on an island in Lake County's Clear Lake—"a perfect slaughter pen" in the words of the United States army officer whose troops did the deed.

Here Chief William Benson, born twelve years after the event, gives his people's version of what happened. It opens with the murder of Stone and Kelsey, two former trappers, who had abused a band of starving, semi-enslaved Pomos. At-

tempting to rustle cattle to stay alive, the Indians accidentally lose their overseers'
horse. Realizing they will be punished, they decide to kill Stone and Kelsey, their
bosses. Although they flee, it is with a foreboding sense of the terrible retaliation
that awaits them.

THE FACTS OF Stone and Kelsey Massacre, in Lake County, California, as it was stated to me by the five Indians who went to Stone and
Kelsey's house [with the] purpose to kill the two white men. After debating
all night.

Shuk and Xasis. These two men were the instigators of the massacre. . . .
Shuk and Xasis was foremans for the herds [of Stone and Kelsey]. And only
those herds got anything to eat. Each one of these herders got four cups of
wheat for a day's work. This cup would hold about one and a half pints of
water. The wheat was boiled before it was given to the herders. And the
herders shire [shared it] with their families. The herders who had large
families were also starving. About twenty old people died during the winter
from starvation. From severe whipping, four died. A nephew of an Indian
lady who was living with Stone was shoot to death by Stone. . . . [the
Indians suffered] whipping and tieing their hands together with rope. The
rope [was] then thrown over a limb of a tree and then drawn up until the
Indian's toes barly touch[ed] the ground and let them hang there for hours.
This was common punishment. When a father or mother of young girl was
asked to bring the girl to his house by Stone or Kelsey, if this order was not
obeyed, he or her would be whipped or hung by the hands. Such punishment
occurred two or three times a week. And many of the old men and women
died from fear and starvation. . . .

The starvation of the Indians was the cause of the massacre of Stone and
Kelsey. The Indians who were starving hired a man by the name of Shuk
and another man by the name of Xasis. To kill a beef for them. . . .

Shuk got a chance and threw the rope on the large ox. Xasis came as
quick as he could, [but] the band then began to stampede. The ox also
started with the band. The ground was wet and slippery, and [it was] raining.
And before Xasis could get his rope on, Shuk's horse fell to the ground. The
horse and the ox got away. Xasis tried to lasso the horse but could not get
near it to throw the rope. . . . The two went back to the camp and reported
to the people who hired them. Told them the bad luck they had. . . .

All the men who [had] hired Shuk and Xasis had gathered in Xasis' house. Here they debated all night. Shuk and Xasis wanted to kill Stone and Kelsey. They said Stone and Kelsey would kill them as soon as they would find out that the horses was taken without them known; one man got up and suggested that the tribe give Stone and Kelsey forty sticks of beads which means 16,000 beads, or 100 dollars. No one agreed. Another man suggested that he or Shuk, tell Stone or Kelsey that the horse was stolen. No one agreed. And another man suggested that the other horse should be turned out, and [they should] tell Stone and Kelsey [that] both horses were stolen. No one agreed. . . .

While this debating was going on the hired or servant boys and girls of Stone's and Kelsey's were told by Shuk and Xasis to carry out all the guns. Bows and arrows, knives and everything like weapons were taken out of the house by these girls and boys, so the two white men were helpless in defense. . . .

So the five men went to the house where Stone and Kelsey were living, at daylight in the place where Stone always built a fire under a large pot in which he boiled wheat for the Indian herders, about sixteen of them. These five men waited around this pot until Stone came out to build the fire. Stone came out with a pot full of fire which was taken from the fireplace. And said to the Indians: "What's the matter, boys? You came early this morning. Some thing wrong?" The Indians said: "Oh, nothing. Me hungry, that's all."

Qka-Nas—or Cayote Jim as he was known by the whites—Qka-Nas said to the men: "I thought you men came to kill this man; give me these arrows and bow." He jerk[ed] the bow and the arrows away from Shuk and drew it, and as he did, Stone rose quickly and turned to Qka-Nas and said, "What are you trying to do, Jim?" And as Stone said it, the Indian cut loose. The arrow struck the victim [in the] pit of the stomach. The victim immediately pulled the arrow out and ran for the house. Fighting his way, he broke one man's arm with the pot he had. And succeeded in getting in the house and locked the door after him.

A little later Kelsey came and opened the door and noticed the blood on the doorstep. The Indians advanced. Kelsey saw that the Indians meant business. He said to them: "*No matar* [Don't kill] Kelsey. Kelsey *bueno hombre para vosotros* [a good man for you]." The Indians charged and two of the Indians caught Kelsey and the fight began. In this fight Kelsey was stabbed twice in the back. . . .

And then they called all the people to come and take what wheat and corn they could pack and go to a hiding place, where they could not be found by the whites. So the Indians of both villages came and took all the wheat and corn they could gather in the place, and then went to hide themselves. Some went to Fishel's Point and some went to Scotts Valley. The men went out to kill cattle for their use, and every man who was able to ride caught himself a horse. In around the valley and upper lake and Bachelor Valley, there were about one thousand head of horses and about four thousand head of cattles. So the Indians lived fat for a while. . . .

Two or three weeks had passed. No white men were seen on either trail. One day Qka-Nas and Ma-Laq-Que-Tou saw two white men on horseback come over the hill. They stopped on top of the hill. They saw nothing staring around Stone and Kelsey's place. No Indians in the village. Qka-Nas and Ma-Laq-Que-Tou went around behind a small hill to cut the white men off. The white men saw the Indians trying to go around behind them. The whites turned and went back before the Indians got in back of them. So three or four days went by. No more white man was seen. . . .

For three days they watch[ed] the lake. One morning they saw a long boat came up the lake with [a] pole on the bow with [a] red cloth. And several of them came. Every one of the boats had ten to fifteen men. The smoke signal was given by the two watchmen. Every Indian around the lake knew the soldiers were coming up the lake. And how many of them. And those who were watching the trail saw the infantry coming over the hill from [the] lower lake. These two men were watching from Ash Hill. They went to Stone and Kelsey's house. From there the horsemen went down torge [toward] the lake and the soldiers went across the valley torge Lakeport. They went on to Scotts Valley. Shoot a few shoots with their big gun and went on to Upper Lake and camped on Emerson Hill. From there they saw the Indian camp on the island. The next morning the white warriors went across in their long dugouts. The Indians said they would meet them in peace. So when the whites landed, the Indians went to welcome them but the white man was determined to kill them.

Ge-Wi-Lih said he threw up his hands and said, "No harm, me good man." But the white man fired and shot him in the arm, and another shot came and hit a man standing along side of him and was killed. So they had to run and fight back; as they ran back in the tuleys [bulrushes] and hid under the water; four or five of them gave a little battle and another man was shot in the shoulder. Some of them jumped in the water and hid in the tuleys. Many women and children were killed on [or] around this island.

One old lady, a Indian told about what she saw while hiding under a bank in under a cover of hanging tuleys. She said she saw two white men coming with their guns up in the air and on their guns hung a little girl. They brought it to the creek and threw it in the water. And a little later two more men came in the same manner. This time they had a little boy on the end of their guns and also threw it in the water. A little ways from her she said lay a woman shot through the shoulder. She held her little baby in her arms. Two white men came running torge [toward] the woman and baby. They stabbed the woman and the baby and threw both of them over the bank in to the water. She said she heard the woman say, "O my baby"; she said when they gathered the dead, they found all the little ones were killed by being stabbed, and many of the women were also killed [by] stabbing. She said it took them four or five days to gather up the dead: And the dead were all burnt on the east side of the creek. . . .

The next morning the soldiers started for Mendocino County. And there killed many Indians. The camp was on the ranch now known as Ed Howell ranch. The soldiers made camp a little ways below about one half mile from the Indian camp. The Indians wanted to surrender. But the soldiers did not give them time. The soldiers went in the camp and shot them down as if they were dogs. Some of them escaped by going down a little creek leading to the river. And some of them hid in the brush. And those who hid in the brush most of them were killed. And those who hid in the water was overlooked. They killed mostly women and children. . . .

One old man told me about the soldiers killing the Indians in this same camp. He must have been about 18 or 20 years of age. He said he and another boy about the same age was taken by the soldiers and he said there were two soldiers in charge of them. One would walk ahead and one behind them. . . . They both were barefooted, he said, when they began to climb the mountain between Mendocino and Lake County. He said they were made to keep up with the soldiers. When they were climbing over the Bottlerock Mountain, their feet were cut up by the rocks and their feet were bleeding and they could not walk up with the soldiers. The man behind would jab them with the sharp knife fixed on the end of the gun. . . .

Two or three days later the chief soldier told them they could go back. They was then given meat and bread. All they could pack. He said they started back on their journey. He said it was all most difficult for them to walk but [they] wrapped a lot of cloth around their feet and by doing so made their way all right. . . .

Now and then they would side track, and look back to see if the soldiers were following them. After seeing no soldiers following them, they would start out for another run. He said they traveled in such manner until they got to their home. He said to himself: Here I am not to see my mother and sister but to see their blood scattered over the ground like water and their bodies for coyotes to devour. He said he sat down under a tree and cryed all day.

WILLIAM BENSON, *Pomo*

4

YOUNG MEN, GO OUT
AND FIGHT THEM

*T*he gold rush of 1874, which lured thousands of white prospectors into the Black Hills of South Dakota, was a crucial factor in provoking a major confrontation between the United States and the Plains Indians. To the powerful Sioux nation these mountains were sacred terrain, and also properly protected by the Fort Laramie Treaty of 1868, signed by the Sioux and the United States government. It was Lieutenant Colonel George Armstrong Custer who originally violated that treaty. In July 1874, ostensibly to locate a site for a new fort, but covertly to hunt for mineral resources, Custer led the expedition into the Black Hills and reported that there was gold "from the grassroots down."

So it was poetic justice that in late June 1876 Custer's small command should blunder into the largest gathering of Plains Indian fighters ever assembled—an estimated twelve to fifteen thousand Indians, with at least four thousand fighting men, drawn from the Teton, Santee and Yankton Sioux, Assiniboine, Cheyenne, Arapaho, and Gros Ventre, camped together along three miles of the bank of the Little Big Horn River in central Montana. Under the leadership of the Sioux war chiefs Sitting Bull and Crazy Horse and the Cheyenne headman Two Moons, the natives comprised die-hard hostiles and recent reservation runaways come together momentarily as a united front.

Wooden Leg

Here is one warrior's memory of the tumultuous day of "many soldiers falling into camp," the battle of the Little Big Horn. Wooden Leg, the narrator, was about eighteen years old when Custer disastrously divided his Seventh Cavalry forces, ignored warnings from his Crow scouts, and was cut down along with all 225 of his officers and men. The battle was a freakish victory for the Indians, stunning the victors along with the vanquished. The tribes did not have sufficient unity or ammunition to follow it up with a broader offensive. Their forces quickly scattered, with Sitting Bull and his followers hiding out in Canada until 1881.

IN MY SLEEP I dreamed that a great crowd of people were making lots of noise. Something in the noise startled me. I found myself wide awake, sitting up and listening. My brother too awakened, and we both jumped to our feet. A great commotion was going on among the camps. We heard shooting. We hurried out from the trees so we might see as well as hear.

The shooting was somewhere at the upper part of the camp circles. It looked as if all of the Indians there were running away toward the hills to the westward or down toward the village. Women were screaming and men were letting out war cries. Through it all we could hear old men calling: "Soldiers are here! Young men, go out and fight them."

We ran to our camp and to our home lodge. Everybody there was excited. Women were hurriedly making up little packs for flight. Some were going off northward or across the river without any packs. Children were hunting for their mothers. Mothers were anxiously trying to find their children. I got my lariat and my six-shooter. I hastened on down toward where had been our horse herd. . . .

My father had caught my favorite horse from the herd brought in by the boys and Bald Eagle. I quickly emptied out my war bag and set myself at getting ready to go into battle. I jerked off my ordinary clothing. I jerked on a pair of new breeches that had been given to me by an Uncpapa Sioux. I had a good cloth shirt, and I put it on. My old moccasins were kicked off and a pair of beaded moccasins substituted for them.

My father strapped a blanket upon my horse and arranged the rawhide lariat into a bridle. He stood holding my mount. "Hurry," he urged me.

The air was so full of dust I could not see where to go. But it was not needful that I see that far. I kept my horse headed in the direction of movement by the crowd of Indians on horseback. I was led out around and far beyond the Uncpapa camp circle. Many hundreds of Indians on horseback were dashing to and fro in front of a body of soldiers. The soldiers were on the level valley ground and were shooting with rifles. Not many bullets were being sent back at them, but thousands of arrows were falling among them. I went on with a throng of Sioux until we got beyond and behind the white men. By this time, though, they had mounted their horses and were hiding themselves in the timber. . . .

Suddenly the hidden soldiers came tearing out on horseback, from the woods. I was around on that side where they came out. I whirled my horse and lashed it into a dash to escape from them. All others of my companions did the same. But soon we discovered they were not following us. They were running away from us. They were going as fast as their tired horses could carry them across an open valley space and toward the river. We stopped, looked a moment, and then we whipped our ponies into swift pursuit. A great throng of Sioux also were coming after them. A distant position put them among the leaders in the chase. The soldier horses moved slowly, as if they were very tired. Ours were lively. We gained rapidly on them.

I fired four shots with my six-shooter. I do not know whether or not any of my bullets did harm. I saw a Sioux put an arrow into the back of a soldier's head. Another arrow went into his shoulder. He tumbled from his horse to the ground. Others fell dead either from arrows or from stabbings or jabbings or from blows by the stone war clubs of the Sioux. Horses limped or staggered or sprawled out dead or dying.

Our war cries and war songs were mingled with many jeering calls, such as: "You are only boys. You ought not to be fighting. We whipped you on the Rosebud. You should have brought more Crows or Shoshones with you to do your fighting."

Little Bird and I were after one certain soldier. Little Bird was wearing a trailing warbonnet. He was at the right and I was at the left of the fleeing man. We were lashing him and his horse with our pony whips. It seemed not brave to shoot him. Besides, I did not want to waste my bullets. He pointed back his revolver, though, and sent a bullet into Little Bird's thigh. Immediately I whacked the white man fighter on his head with the heavy elk-horn handle of my pony whip. The blow dazed him. I seized the rifle strapped on his back. I wrenched it and dragged the looping strap over his head. As I was getting possession of this weapon, he fell to the ground. I did not harm him further. I do not know what became of him. The jam of oncoming Indians swept me on. . . .

I returned to the west side of the river. Lots of Indians were hunting around there for dead soldiers or for wounded ones to kill. I joined in this search. I got some tobacco from the pockets of one dead man. I got also a belt having in it a few cartridges. All of the weapons and clothing and all other possessions were being taken from the bodies. The warriors were doing this. No old people nor women were there. They all had run away to the hill benches to the westward.

I went to a dead horse, to see what might be found there. Leather bags were on them, behind the saddles. I rummaged into one of these bags. I found there two pasteboard boxes. I broke open one of them. "Oh, cartridges!"

There were twenty of them in each box, forty in all. Thirty of them were used to fill up the vacant places in my belt. The remaining ten I wrapped into a piece of cloth and dropped them down into my own little kit bag. Now I need not be so careful in expending ammunition. Now I felt very brave. . . .

The shots quit coming from the soldiers. Warriors who had crept close to them began to call out that all of the white men were dead. All of the Indians then jumped up and rushed forward. All of the boys and old men on their horses came tearing into the crowd. The air was full of dust and smoke. Everybody was greatly excited. It looked like thousands of dogs might look if all of them were mixed together in a fight. All of the Indians were saying these soldiers also went crazy and killed themselves. I do not know. I could not see them. But I believe they did so. . . .

I took one scalp. As I went walking and leading my horse among the dead, I observed one face that interested me. The dead man had a long beard growing from both sides of his face and extending several inches below the chin. He had also a full mustache. All of the beard hair was of a light yellow color, as I now recall it. Most of the soldiers had beards growing, in different lengths, but this was the longest one I saw among them. I think the dead man may have been thirty or more years old. "Here is a new kind of scalp," I said to a companion. I skinned one side of the face and half of the chin, so as to keep the long beard yet on the part removed. I got an arrow shaft and tied the strange scalp to the end of it. . . .

I waved my scalp as I rode among our people. The first person I met who took special interest in me was my mother's mother. She was living in a little willow dome lodge of her own. "What is that?" she asked me when I flourished the scalp stick toward her. I told her. "I give it to you," I said, and I held it out to her. She screamed and shrank away. "Take it," I urged. "It will be good medicine for you." Then I went on to tell her about my having killed the Crow or Shoshone at the first fight up the river, about my getting the two guns, about my knocking in the head two soldiers in the river, about what I had done in the next fight on the hill where all of the soldiers had been killed. We talked about my soldier clothing. She said I looked good dressed that way. I had thought so too, but neither the coat nor the breeches fit me well. The arms and legs were too short for me. Finally she decided she would take the scalp. She went then into her own little lodge. . . .

There was no dancing nor celebrating of any kind in any of the camps that night. Too many people were in mourning, among all of the Sioux as well as among the Cheyennes. Too many Cheyenne and Sioux women had gashed their arms and legs, in token of their grief. The people generally were praying, not cheering. There was much noise and confusion, but this was from other causes. Young men were going out to fight the first soldiers now hiding themselves on the hill across the river from where had been the first fighting during the morning. . . .

I did not go back that afternoon nor that night to help in fighting the first soldiers. Late in the night, though, I went as a scout. Five young men of the Cheyennes were appointed to guard our camp while other people slept. These were Big Nose, Yellow Horse, Little Shield, Horse Road and Wooden Leg. One or other of us was out somewhere looking over the country all the time. Two of us went once over to the place where the soldiers were hidden. We got upon hill points higher than they were. We could look down among them. We could have shot among them, but we did not do this. We just saw that they yet were there.

Five other young men took our duties in the last part of the night. I was glad to be relieved. I did not go to my family group for rest. I let loose my horse and dropped myself down upon a thick pad of grassy sod.

WOODEN LEG, *Northern Cheyenne*

||||||||||||||||||||||||||||||||||||||||||||||||||||||||||||||||| **5** |||||||||||||||||||||||||||||||||||||||||||||||||||||||||||||||||

GERONIMO PUTS DOWN THE GUN

G eronimo, whose Native American name, Goyathlay, means "One Who Yawns," was a Chiricahua Apache. In 1858 he returned to his home in southeastern Arizona to discover the dead bodies of his mother, wife, and three children; they had been killed by Mexican troops. From then on, Geronimo took every opportunity to terrorize Mexican settlements. As a warrior during the so-called Cochise wars of the 1860s, he fought against American soldiers. In the 1870s Geronimo was in charge as his Chiricahua band fled from the distasteful San Carlos reservation in southwestern Arizona to the wild, free backlands of Chihuaha and Sonora in Mexico and began marauding against Mexicans and Americans alike.

Frequently taken prisoner, Geronimo kept escaping until a major search by General George Crook and his Indian scouts led to his capture in 1883 in the Sierra Madre of Mexico. For two years Geronimo seemed to be settling into a quiet life of growing vegetables on the San Carlos Apache reservation. Then came the burst to freedom that is related here by Jason Betzinez, Geronimo's cousin, who was twenty-five years old at the time.

Geronimo's final surrender in 1887, described by Betzinez, put an end to significant Indian guerrilla action in the United States. The weary fighter and over three hundred of his fellow Chiricahuas were shipped under heavy guard to Fort Marion, Florida. Among the prisoners of war were Apaches like Betzinez, who had never joined Geronimo, and even Apache scouts who had taken sides against him.

AFTER SETTLING on the Fort Apache reservation [San Carlos], Geronimo and many others made a beginning in the effort to change from warriors to farmers. Nevertheless turbulent days still lay ahead. . . .

In the spring of 1885 Geronimo, Chichuahua, Mangas (son of the old chief Mangas Colorado), and a number of others got to making and drinking Indian beer in violation of orders from the authorities. This homebrew made the Indians drunk and quarrelsome. They were brought before Lieutenant Davis who threatened to report them to General Crook. At this the Indians got the idea that they might be sent off to prison [to Alcatraz]. . . . Having been placed in irons once before, when the band was shipped to San Carlos, some of the leaders determined not to undergo such treatment again. They plotted to leave the reservation, taking their immediate families as well as some other Apaches whom they induced to go with them. . . .

As told you, I learned of all this as I was coming home from planting the barley field which Geronimo and I had been farming together. My brother-in-law having met me on the road, we discussed the whole situation. It appeared to us that we would have to go with our family group leader, Geronimo. Some of the young men who were our close friends and blood relatives had already joined him that very afternoon. Late that night I started off southward accompanied by my mother and sister. Then I told them to go on ahead, I wanted to return for my brother-in-law, who had not come with us. We would catch up with them later.

Unable to find my brother-in-law, I hastened to overtake my own family. As I hurried along the main road through the dark moonless night, my thoughts were very troubled. I came to the conclusion that it would be foolish to throw away what I was just beginning to learn of a better way of life. So when I came up with my mother and sister I informed them of this decision and told them to return to our camp. . . .

According to what we learned later, [those who left the reservation] crossed the Black River, climbed the mountains to the south, and camped on the summit where they could observe any pursuit. After resting there the remainder of the night they took off straight south toward the border, not stopping to camp again until they had covered 120 miles. After reaching Mexico they separated into several small groups each under its own chief. . . .

Two troops of the Fourth Cavalry together with some Indian scouts under Lieutenants Gatewood and Davis promptly followed but were unable to catch the runaways. People who have been in this rugged country can well understand how easily the Apaches, with their superior speed and endurance, and their willingness to take to the rocks and the mountain tops, were able to evade their pursuers.

Another habit of the Apaches contributed largely to their success in keeping out of reach. . . . It was a mysterious manner of vanishing completely when the soldiers and scouts had just caught up with them or were about to attack their camp. Each day the chief designated an assembly point. . . . Then when the troops would find them or were about to launch an attack the Indians would scatter, keeping their minds firmly fixed on the assembly

Geronimo (front row, third from right) *and other Chiricahua Apaches in 1886,*
outside a prison train bound for Florida

point far away. The scouts, who were experienced warriors themselves, had
a hard time tracking down the hostiles, as they were forced to follow the
many diverging trails, most of which disappeared in the rocks anyway.

The hostiles would converge on their predetermined rendezvous point
but instead of camping there would make an imitation camp. They would
build several small campfires and tie an old worn-out horse to a tree to
make it look as though the camp was occupied. Then they would move on

for several miles and establish their real camp elsewhere. The scouts knowing that their fellow tribesmen, the hostiles, would assemble at nightfall, would lie in wait all through the night ready to attack at daybreak. The attack would land upon a fake camp. The scouts were of course disgusted and disappointed but presently they would laugh, saying, "Oh, my! We were fooled!" They took it as a great joke on themselves. . . .

General Miles came to Fort Apache in the summer of 1886 to plan a campaign for running down the Apaches who still remained out. He held a meeting at the agency at which I was present. He explained that he wanted to form a large expedition to corral Geronimo's band and thus bring all the Apache troubles to an end. Though most of the Indians present were Chiricahuas and Warm Springs Apaches, many of them related to Geronimo and his men, great enthusiasm was shown. The Indians were excited and happy over the prospect of going out on another campaign. Hardship and danger meant nothing, adventure was what they wanted and it didn't seem to matter that they were going to fight their own people. . . .

Meantime Geronimo and his warriors were moving slowly toward the U.S. border. It was August 1886. They had not been suffering but were driving some stolen cattle.

One day the scouts told Captain Lawton it would be a good idea to camp along the creek while Lieutenant Gatewood, Mr. George Wratten, Kayitah and Martine [Apache scouts], and ten soldiers should go out to find the hostiles. From the tracks and signs of old camps Kayitah thought that Geronimo was in the mountains to the east of this camp.

So this small party moved toward a long peak which the Apaches called Mountain Tall. At one point the ridge rose in a steep bluff. The keen eyes of the two Indians spotted something on top of the escarpment. Soon they realized that it was Geronimo's band. Motioning to Lieutenant Gatewood to stop his advance, the two Apaches moved up to the foot of the bluff. Kayitah shouted in a loud but quavering voice, "I am Kayitah. Let me come up. I have a message for you."

Geronimo called down, "All right. Come on. We'll listen."

Leaving the other men behind, the two scouts climbed up the steep mountain. Arriving at the summit, on legs trembling with fear, they saw Geronimo and his men there with ready guns. Up to that moment Kayitah and Martine didn't know whether they would be permitted to live. But the outlaws greeted them warmly. They really were glad to see each other, as close associates among the Apaches always were after a considerable separation.

After much friendly chatter and a recounting of what had occurred since Geronimo had left, Kayitah delivered General Miles' message. The General wanted them to give themselves up without any guarantees.

For a few moments there was silence. The Indians seemed stunned. Finally Geronimo's half-brother White Horse [Leon Perico] spoke out. "I am going to surrender. My wife and children have been captured. I love them, and want to be with them."

Then another brother said that if White Horse was going, he would go too. In a moment the third and youngest brother made a similar statement.

Geronimo stood for a few moments without speaking. At length he said slowly, "I don't know what to do. I have been depending heavily on you three men. You have been great fighters in battle. If you are going to surrender, there is no use my going without you. I will give up with you."

JASON BETZINEZ, *Southern Chiricahua Apache*

THE TREATY
TRAIL

A Prairie Indian leader negotiates with white officials. Two of his fellow tribesmen (seated)
wear medallions probably given to them during earlier diplomatic conferences.

Although the drama of Indian-white warfare has always captured the popular imagination, Native Americans lost far more of their land and independence by the bloodless process of signing treaties than they ever did on the battlefield. Indeed, most of the violence between Indians and whites flared up because Native Americans were being deprived of the very land promised them in earlier treaties. "You give us presents, and then take our land," complained the Cheyenne spokesman Buffalo Chief at the famous Treaty of Medicine Lodge in 1867. "That produces war."

To the Indians the practice of drafting a written agreement to settle political and territorial disputes was alien and unfamiliar, and as a result, it was used against them to great advantage. As Red Cloud, the Oglala Sioux leader, recalled, "In 1868 men came out and brought papers. We could not read them, and they did not tell us truly what was in them. . . . When I reached Washington the Great Father explained to me what the treaty was, and showed me that the interpreters had deceived me."

At first the European powers drew up treaties to cement relations with influential tribes, to "bury the tomahawk"—to use the famous phrase found in an early southern Plains treaty—with hostile Indians, and to formalize trading partnerships. During the period of New World colonization, the warring European nations used treaties to bolster their forces with Indian auxiliaries. As the white population grew, however, and Indian power waned, the documents became thinly disguised bills of sale, transferring ancient tribal lands into white hands.

In the fine print, these treaties usually called for Indians to move to the least fertile corner of their existing lands, to abandon their homes altogether and move elsewhere, or to slice up their holdings into single-family allotments, which the Indians were supposed to cultivate while selling off the rest to white land speculators. In some cases, whites reserved the right to run their wagon trails or railroad tracks across Indian land. Inevitably this brought trouble as settlers homesteaded and prospectors mined in country they were supposed to be only passing through.

The legal basis for making treaties with the Indians was established as early as the sixteenth century by lawyers for the Spanish court. Although vast portions of the New World were claimed by the conquistadores, Spain still felt that the Indians enjoyed some vague "aboriginal title" to the country. Ideally the king's envoys were to obtain the "voluntary consent" of Native Americans before usurping their lands. Other European and American legalists also granted Indians a "right of occupancy." Behind these manipulative phrases and contradictory postures lay the white man's vacillation between greed and conscience. He was determined to take possession of the territories he "discovered," but he needed to feel he was acquiring them fairly and legally. The muddled, controversial saga of Indian land loss shows the white man alternately behaving as the fair-minded negotiator trying to strike an honest bargain for the lands he had to have, and then as the ruthless land grabber employing any pseudo-legal scheme and threat of military power to drive the Native American from his home. By the mid-eighteenth century, treaty making was standard operating procedure for getting what one wanted from the Indians.

The young United States government negotiated its first Indian treaty during the Revolutionary War, wringing from the Delawares a 1778 pledge to help in the resistance to the British. (In return the Delawares were promised statehood, should they some time in the future desire it. This never materialized, and over the next century the Delawares signed a series of eighteen treaties that would leave them entirely powerless and dispersed from Canada to Oklahoma.)

In the Northwest Ordinance of 1787, in which Congress set forth principles for governing its landholdings west of the Appalachian Mountains, the United States promised that "utmost good faith shall always be observed towards the Indians; their land and property shall never be taken from them without their consent." But after 1800, treaties were contracted more in haste than good faith. Between 1800 and 1812, for instance, William Henry Harrison, superintendent of the Northwest Indians and governor of Indiana Territory, negotiated and speedily signed fifteen treaties with tribes who thereby yielded all of present-day Indiana, Illinois, a sizable chunk of Ohio, and portions of Michigan and Wisconsin—at the price of about a penny an acre. Farther west, between 1853 and 1857, Congress ratified fifty-two treaties by which tribes living in Idaho, Oregon, and Washington lost 157 million acres.

By this time, treaty making had degenerated into a hollow formality for inexpensively obtaining what would otherwise have cost a military expedition to seize, and for conveniently removing Indians to backwater reservations, where once confined, they could be schooled in the ways of white American civilization. The last of the 374 treaties with Native Americans was signed in 1868, forcing Chief Joseph and his Nez Percé followers to move from their beloved Wallowa Valley in Oregon because gold had been discovered there. It also precipitated the short-lived Nez Percé War.

On March 3, 1871, Congress formally ended what Andrew Jackson had dismissed as "the farce of treating with Indian tribes." In passing that year's Indian Appropriation Act, it tacked on the stipulation that from then on, "No Indian nation or tribe within the territory of the United States shall be acknowledged and recognized as an independent nation, tribe, or power with whom the United States may contract by treaty." At the same time

Congress took pains to reiterate the government's responsibility to honor all "lawfully made" treaties already in force. This decision was backed both by reformers, who denounced the corruption that had riddled such negotiations, and by anti-Indian politicians, who wanted to bury any suggestion that the tribes were sovereign nations. Thereafter the United States government made "agreements" and passed laws—about five thousand by 1940—for dealing with Indians.

Over the centuries Native American attitudes toward treaties changed from bewilderment to indignation to outrage. By the time Indians had grown aware of the opportunities for deception behind the diplomatic exercise of treaty signing, it was usually too late. Lamented Black Hawk, the Sauk chieftain, "I touched the goose quill to the treaty, not knowing, however, that, by that act, I consented to give away my village."

A pervasive form of abuse throughout the centuries was to rush tribesmen into affixing their X marks or name pictographs to treaty agreements before they had had time to discuss the matter, either among themselves or in formal council. Often those who approved the treaty were any agreeable Indians the negotiators could hastily collect for a meeting, or a clan leader who was unauthorized to speak for the entire tribe. (One American emissary was overheard to brag that he would bring a treaty with the Sioux to a successful conclusion even if only two warriors signed.)

Government officials also exploited schisms within Indian communities, playing one side against the other. They often neglected to explain that presents lavished upon their Native American guests during treaty negotiations were actually partial payment for lands soon to be gone forever. They transformed treaty sessions into colorful, multitribal affairs, inviting those Indians who participated to make speeches, sport their brilliant costumes, and accept specially minted medallions before signing away their homelands. The Native American talent for accurate recollection of the wording of ancient treaties sometimes, however, stymied white negotiators who wished to reinterpret their content. A common complaint among Indians was that government officials failed to make clear at the outset all the ramifications of the treaties they were signing. In the end, tribe after tribe was cajoled and threatened into renegotiating old agreements that had outlived their usefulness. In this respect the Potawatomi and Chippewa set the record; at the end of the treaty-making era, both tribes had signed forty-two successive treaties, each of them supposedly ironclad.

The durability of the promises contained in these treaties continues to be an explosive issue between Native Americans and the United States government today. Most of the documents included "in perpetuity" clauses, guaranteeing forever government outlays of food and clothing, aid and protection. More critically, the treaties were transacted on the premise that both parties were equal, sovereign nations. The government wants to avoid debating that premise and instead clear up all outstanding treaty disputes through its Indian Claims Commission and by means of cash settlements. A growing number of Native American nationalists are, however, highly critical of cash payoffs. And they want to preserve the unique, political status that distinguishes their tribal communities from other ethnic groups. They want to resurrect the political premise of the old treaties and demand that vows of aid and protection be observed, in the words of an old trade agreement, "For as long as the grass shall grow and the rivers run."

The following accounts show Native Americans struggling to preserve their rights within the alien context of the white man's diplomatic game and its strange rules.

1

LET US EXAMINE THE FACTS

Corn Tassel, an elderly Cherokee statesman, delivered this stinging reply to the United States commissioners who had come to sign a peace treaty with his tribe. The time was July 1785. The Cherokee had become well versed in the intricacies of power politics through their long dealings with France and England. They had actively sided with the British at the outbreak of the Revolutionary War, and as Corn Tassel makes clear they still felt themselves the equal of the Americans on the battlefield. The first part of this talk is a rebuttal to any claims to Cherokee land on the basis of right of conquest. Corn Tassel ends his remarks by insisting, as Indian orators frequently did, that whites must simply accept the irreconcilable differences between the two ways of life, and cease trying to transform Indians into white people.

IT IS A LITTLE SURPRISING that when we entered into treaties with our brothers, the whites, their whole cry is *more land!* Indeed, formerly it seemed to be a matter of formality with them to demand what they knew we durst not refuse. But on the principles of fairness, of which we have received assurances during the conducting of the present treaty, and in the name of free will and equality, I must reject your demand.

Suppose, in considering the nature of your claim (and in justice to my nation I shall and will do it freely), I were to ask one of you, my brother warriors, under what kind of authority, by what law, or on what pretense he makes this exorbitant demand of nearly all the lands we hold between your settlements and our towns, as the cement and consideration of our peace.

Would he tell me that it is by right of conquest? No! If he did, I should retort on him that *we* had last marched over his territory; even up to this very place which he has *fortified* so far within his former limits; nay, that some of our young warriors (whom we have not yet had an opportunity to recall or give notice to, of the general treaty) are still in the woods, and continue to keep his people in fear, and that it was but till lately that these identical walls were your strongholds, out of which you durst scarcely advance.

If, therefore, a bare march, or reconnoitering a country is sufficient reason to ground a claim to it, we shall insist upon transposing the demand, and your relinquishing your settlements on the western waters and removing one hundred miles back towards the east, whither some of our warriors advanced against you in the course of last year's campaign.

Let us examine the facts of your present eruption into our country, and we shall discover your pretentions on that ground. What did you do? You marched into our territories with a superior force; our vigilance gave us no timely notice of your maneuvers; your numbers far exceeded us, and we fled to the stronghold of our extensive woods, there to secure our women and children.

Thus, you marched into our towns; they were left to your mercy; you killed a few scattered and defenseless individuals, spread fire and desolation wherever you pleased, and returned again to your own habitations. If you meant this, indeed, as a conquest you omitted the most essential point; you should have fortified the junction of the Holstein and Tennessee rivers, and have thereby conquered all the waters above you. But, as all are fair advantages during the existence of a state of war, it is now too late for us to suffer for your mishap of generalship!

Again, were we to inquire by what law or authority you set up a claim,

I answer, *none!* Your laws extend not into our country, nor ever did. You talk of the law of nature and the law of nations, and they are both against you.

Indeed, much has been advanced on the want of what you term civilization among the Indians; and many proposals have been made to us to adopt your laws, your religion, your manners and your customs. But, we confess that we do not yet see the propriety, or practicability of such a reformation, and should be better pleased with beholding the good effect of these doctrines in your own practices than with hearing you talk about them, or reading your papers to us upon such subjects.

You say: Why do not the Indians till the ground and live as we do? May we not, with equal propriety, ask, Why the white people do not hunt and live as we do? You profess to think it no injustice to warn us not to kill our deer and other game from the mere love of waste; but it is very criminal in our young men if they chance to kill a cow or a hog for their sustenance when they happen to be in your lands. We wish, however, to be at peace with you, and to do as we would be done by. We do not quarrel with you for killing an occasional buffalo, bear or deer on our lands when you need one to eat; but you go much farther; your people hunt to gain a livelihood by it; they kill all our game; our young men resent the injury, and it is followed by bloodshed and war.

This is not a mere affected injury; it is a grievance which we equitably complain of and it demands a permanent redress.

The great God of Nature has placed us in different situations. It is true that he has endowed you with many superior advantages; but he has not created us to be your slaves. *We are a separate people!* He has given each their lands, under distinct considerations and circumstances; he has stocked yours with cows, ours with buffalo; yours with hog, ours with bear; yours with sheep, ours with deer. He has, indeed, given you an advantage in this, that your cattle are tame and domestic while ours are wild and demand not only a larger space for range, but art to hunt and kill them; they are, nevertheless, as much our property as other animals are yours, and ought not to be taken away without our consent, or for something equivalent.

CORN TASSEL, *Cherokee*

2

OSCEOLA DETERMINED

This is an edited transcript of a three-day meeting that took place in October 1834 between Seminole chieftains and General Wiley Thompson. Under dispute in the talks were two earlier treaties: the 1823 agreement at Camp Moultrie, Florida, signed by only a single faction of the tribe, under which the Seminole agreed to live on a reservation of four million acres, receiving annual payments of food and money in exchange; and the 1832 treaty at Payne's Landing, Florida, where again only a portion of the Seminole agreed to the treaty, requiring them to move to territory west of the Mississippi.

At the time of this meeting, Seminole leaders had already been taken to look over their prospective new home adjoining Creek Indian lands in Oklahoma. Thus the scene was set for the kind of classic confrontation—experienced by tribe after tribe—between Indian holdouts and impatient white officials anxious to have their way. Where the chiefs appear to be wavering, it was often because they were attempting to discover the consensus in their own group as it took shape before their eyes, and because, even in their beleaguered position, they shied away from showing open hostility toward a visitor. Notice the subtle role played by Osceola, at that time a young subchief, as he adamantly opposes removal, then sits back to let the words of his elders fly until, at the end, he decisively reenters the discussion.

A year after this clash of words, General Thompson was shot from ambush by a war party led by Osceola, and that same afternoon Jumper, Miconopy, and Alligator attacked two military companies, leaving only three soldiers barely alive. This marked the beginning of the Second Seminole War which lasted well after its recorded closing date of 1842, resulted in the deaths of fifteen hundred American troops, and cost the government twenty million dollars. Osceola was tricked into capture when he agreed to meet a group of soldiers under a flag of truce. Three months later, he died in prison. Many of the Seminoles eventually did remove, but several maverick bands clung to their stronghold in the Everglades where their descendants remain to this day.

Seminole Agency, Florida Territory
October 23, 1834, 11:00 A.M.

GENERAL THOMPSON: Friends and Brothers: I come from your great father, the President of the United States, with a talk: listen to what I say.

On the 9th of May, 1832, you entered into a treaty at Payne's Landing. I come from the President to tell you that he has complied with all his promises to you in that treaty that he was bound to do before you move, and that you must prepare to move by the time the cold weather of winter shall have passed away. . . .

The proposition which I present for your decision is:

1st. Will you accept the invitation of your brothers of the western Creek nation?

2nd. Do you prefer cattle or money, when you arrive at your new home, for the cattle, which, under the treaty, you must give up here?

3rd. Will you petition to go by water, or do you prefer to go by land?

4th. How will you have your next annuity paid to you, in money or in goods?

[*At this point one of the Seminole delegates, Holata Amaltha, announced that his group wanted to talk in private first, and would reconvene with Thompson the next morning. But Thompson must have planted a spy, for the talks that afternoon were "reported confidentially" and the following remains part of the official record.*]

OSCEOLA: My Brothers! The white people got some of our chiefs to sign a paper to give our lands to them, but our chiefs did not do as we told them to do; they done wrong; we must do right. The agent tells us we must go away from the lands we live on—our homes, and the graves of our Fathers, and go over the big river [the Mississippi] among the bad Indians. When the agent tells me to go from my home, I hate him, because I love my home, and will not go from it.

My Brothers! When the Great Spirit tells me to go with the white man, I go: but he tells me not to go. The white man says I shall go, and he will send people to make me go; but I have a rifle, and I have some powder and some lead. I say, we must not leave our homes and lands. If any of our people want to go west, we won't let them; and I tell them they are our enemies, and we will treat them so, for the Great Spirit will protect us.

The signature pages of the 1832 treaty at Payne's Landing

HOLATA AMALTHA: My Brothers and Friends! You want to hear my talk. When we made a treaty at Payne's, some of us said if the land was good for us, we would go across the great Mississippi. We were told, it would be better for the red people and the red people would be happy there; that if we stayed here the bad white men would wrong us; so we went to see the land our great father said we must have, and it was good land. We told the agents, whom our father sent with us, that we would do as our father bade us. My Brothers! I don't want to talk like a foolish child. My talk is good for my people; and I say we must act honest and do as our great father at Washington tells us.

JUMPER, "THE SENSE-KEEPER": My Brothers! You have listened to the talk of our brothers; now hear mine. I do not make talks today to break them tomorrow. I told the agent I was glad to see the lands which our great father said we must have, and I told him that I and my people would go, and we have no excuse. If we don't go, our father will send his men to make us go, and we will lose many of our tribe. . . .

October 24, 1834, 11:00 A.M.

[*General Thompson asks the Seminoles for their reply.*]

HOLATA MICO: God made all of us, and we all came from one woman, sucked one bubby; we hope we shall not quarrel; that we will talk until we get through.

MICONOPY: When we were at Camp Moultrie we made a treaty, and we were to be paid our annuity for twenty years. That is all I have got to say.

JUMPER: At Camp Moultrie they told us all difficulties should be buried for twenty years, from the date of the treaty made there; that after this we held a treaty at Payne's Landing, before the twenty years were out; and they told us we might go and see the country, but that we were not obliged to remove. The land is very good; I saw it, and was glad to see it; the neighbors there are bad people; I do not like them bad Indians, the Pawnees . . . the Indians there steal horses, and take packs on their horses; they all steal horses from the different tribes; I do not want to go among such people; your talk seems always good, but we don't feel disposed to go west.

HOLATA AMALTHA: The horses that were stolen from us by the Cherokees we never got back [*the horses had been stolen from the Seminoles while they were looking over their proposed new land*]. We then told the agent that the people were bad there. . . .

CHARLEY AMALTHA: My family I love dearly and sacredly. I do not think it right to take them off. . . . Should I go west, I should lose many on the path. As to the country west, I looked at it; a weak man cannot get there, the fatigue would be so great; it requires a strong man. I hardly got there. . . .

GENERAL THOMPSON: My talk to you yesterday must and will stand, and you must abide by it. . . . And I want, when you meet me again in council, that you give a correct account of the number of your people, that the government may provide for you comfortably while on your journey, whether by land or by water. . . . When you come here again, come prepared to act like chiefs, and honourable men; don't bring to me any more foolish talks. Men do not listen to the talks of a child; and remember that the talk I gave you must and will stand.

October 25, 1834, 11:00 A.M.

GENERAL THOMPSON: I am ready to receive your answers to the questions I submitted to you.

HOLATA MICO: I have only to repeat what I said yesterday, and to say that twenty years from the Moultrie treaty has not yet expired. I never gave my consent to go west; the whites may say so, but I never gave my consent.

JUMPER: We are not satisfied to go until the end of the twenty years, according to the treaty at Camp Moultrie. We were called upon to go to the west, beyond the Mississippi. It is a good country; this is a poor country, we know. We had a good deal of trouble to get there; what would it be for all our tribe?

MICONOPY: I say, what I said yesterday, I did not sign the treaty.

GENERAL THOMPSON: Abraham [the interpreter], tell Miconopy that I say he lies; he did sign the treaty.

CHARLEY AMALTHA: The agent told us yesterday we did not talk to the point. I have nothing to say different. . . . At Payne's Landing the white people forced us into the treaty. I was there. I agreed to go west and did go west. I went in a vessel, and it made me sick. I undertook to go there; and think that, for so many people, it would have been very bad. . . .

GENERAL THOMPSON: The Creeks, Choctaws, Chickasaws, and Cherokees, who live in the states, are moving west of the Mississippi River, because they cannot live under the white people's laws. . . . Suppose, what is however impossible, that you could be permitted to remain here a few years longer, what would be your condition? This land will soon be surveyed, sold to, and settled by the whites. . . . Thus, you may see, that were it possible for you to remain here a few years longer, you would be reduced to hopeless poverty, and when urged by hunger to ask, perhaps, of the man who thus would have ruined you (and is perhaps now tampering with you for the purpose of getting your property) for a crust of bread, you might be called an Indian dog, and be ordered to clear out.

[*Osceola, seated beside Miconopy, urges the chief to be firm against removal.*]

GENERAL THOMPSON: Your father, the President, sees all these evils, and will save you from them by removing you west; and I stand up for the last time to tell you, that you must go; and if not willingly, you will be compelled to go. I should have told you that no more annuity will be paid to you here.

[Osceola interrupts, saying he does not care whether any more money is paid his people.]

GENERAL THOMPSON: I hope you will, on more mature reflection, act like honest men, and not compel me to report you to your father, the President, as faithless to your engagements.

[Osceola says that the decision of the chiefs has been given; they will make no other answer.]

MICONOPY: I do not intend to remove.

GENERAL THOMPSON: I am now fully satisfied that you are wilfully disposed to be entirely dishonest in regard to your engagements with the President, and regret that I must so report you. . . .

OSCEOLA ET AL., *Seminole*

3

MY SON, STOP YOUR EARS

On January 14, 1879, a remarkable Indian was given a rare opportunity. Chief Joseph, the great Nez Percé leader, journeyed to Washington, D.C., to tell a full house of Congress why his people had gone on the warpath two years earlier.

His speech opened with a description of his forebears' amicable meeting with the explorers Lewis and Clark. In the excerpted selection presented below, Joseph focuses on the treaties that the United States government signed with his tribe. His own band boycotted the signing of the most critical of these treaties—that of 1863, in which the tribal lands in the Wallowa area were supposedly ceded and which

Joseph highlights here. Each year he and his loyal followers refused to leave their Oregon homes, and each year agents tried to remove them. In 1877 Joseph was about to relent when local cowboys stole several hundred Nez Percé horses. The Indians' pent-up anger exploded. During the next four months Joseph conducted an amazing guerrilla campaign, outwitting the pursuing troops led by General O. O. Howard over a distance of thirteen hundred miles, punctuated by desperate hand-to-hand fighting. The chase culminated in Chief Joseph's surrender almost within reach of freedom in Canada.

The congressional speech fell on deaf ears. Joseph was held prisoner in Kansas for a while; five of his children perished of disease there. He never again saw his homeland and died in 1904 on the Coleville Reservation in the state of Washington.

IT HAS ALWAYS been the pride of the Nez Percés that they were the friends of the white men. When my father was a young man there came to our country a white man [the Reverend Mr. Spaulding] who talked spirit law. He won the affections of our people because he spoke good things to them. At first he did not say anything about white men wanting to settle on our lands. Nothing was said about that until about twenty winters ago, when a number of white people came into our country and built houses and made farms. At first our people made no complaint. They thought there was room enough for all to live in peace, and they were learning many things from the white men that seemed to be good. But we soon found that the white men were growing rich very fast, and were greedy to possess everything the Indian had. My father was the first to see through the schemes of the white men, and he warned his tribe to be careful about trading with them. He had suspicion of men who seemed so anxious to make money. I was a boy then, but I remember well my father's caution. He had sharper eyes than the rest of our people.

Next there came a white officer [Governor Stevens], who invited all the Nez Percés to a treaty council. After the council was opened he made known his heart. He said there were a great many white people in the country, and many more would come; that he wanted the land marked out so that the Indians and white men could be separated. If they were to live in peace it was necessary, he said, that the Indians should have a country set apart for them, and in that country they must stay. My father, who represented his band, refused to have anything to do with the council, because he wished to be a free man. He claimed that no man owned any part of the earth, and a man could not sell what he did not own.

Mr. Spaulding took hold of my father's arm and said, "Come and sign the treaty." My father pushed him away, and said: "Why do you ask me to sign away my country? It is your business to talk to us about spirit matters, and not to talk to us about parting with our land." Governor Stevens urged my father to sign his treaty, but he refused. "I will not sign your paper," he said; "you go where you please, so do I; you are not a child. I am no child; I can think for myself. No man can think for me. I have no other home than this. I will not give it up to any man. My people would have no home. Take away your paper. I will not touch it with my hand."

My father left the council. Some of the chiefs of the other bands of the Nez Percés signed the treaty, and then Governor Stevens gave them presents of blankets. My father cautioned his people to take no presents, for "after a while," he said, "they will claim that you have accepted pay for your country." Since that time four bands of the Nez Percés have received annuities from the United States. My father was invited to many councils, and they tried hard to make him sign the treaty, but he was firm as the rock, and would not sign away his home. His refusal caused a difference among the Nez Percés.

Eight years later (1863) was the next treaty council. A chief called Lawyer, because he was a great talker, took the lead in this council, and sold nearly all the Nez Percés' country. My father was not there. He said to me: "When you go into council with the white man, always remember your country. Do not give it away. The white man will cheat you out of your home. I have taken no pay from the United States. I have never sold our land." In this treaty Lawyer acted without authority from our band. He had no right to sell the Wallowa [*winding water*] country. That had always belonged to my father's own people, and the other bands had never disputed our right to it. No other Indians ever claimed Wallowa.

In order to have all people understand how much land we owned, my father planted poles around it and said: "Inside is the home of my people— the white man may take the land outside. Inside this boundary all our people were born. It circles around the graves of our fathers, and we will never give up these graves to any man."

The United States claimed they had bought all the Nez Percés' country outside of Lapwai Reservation, from Lawyer and other chiefs, but we continued to live in this land in peace until eight years ago, when white men began to come inside the bounds my father had set. We warned them against this great wrong, but they would not leave our land, and some bad blood was raised. The white men represented that we were going upon the war-path. They reported many things that were false.

The United States Government again asked for a treaty council. My father had become blind and feeble. He could no longer speak for his people. It was then that I took my father's place as chief.

In this council I made my first speech to white men. I said to the agent who held the council: "I did not want to come to this council, but I came hoping that we could save blood. The white man has no right to come here and take our country. We have never accepted any presents from the Government. Neither Lawyer nor any other chief had authority to sell this land. It has always belonged to my people. It came unclouded to them from our fathers, and we will defend this land as long as a drop of Indian blood warms the hearts of our men."

The agent said he had orders, from the Great White Chief at Washington, for us to go upon the Lapwai Reservation, and that if we obeyed he would help us in many ways. "You *must* move to the agency," he said. I answered him: "I will not. I do not need your help; we have plenty and we are contented and happy if the white man will let us alone. The reservation is too small for so many people with all their stock. You can keep your presents; we can go to your towns and pay for all we need; we have plenty of horses and cattle to sell, and we won't have any help from you; we are free now; we can go where we please. Our fathers were born here. Here they lived, here they died, here are their graves. We will never leave them." The agent went away, and we had peace for a little while.

Soon after this my father sent for me. I saw he was dying. I took his hand in mine. He said: "My son, my body is returning to my mother earth, and my spirit is going very soon to see the Great Spirit Chief. When I am gone, think of your country. You are the chief of these people. They look to you to guide them. Always remember that your father never sold his country. You must stop your ears whenever you are asked to sign a treaty selling your home. A few years more, and white men will be all around you. They have their eyes on this land. My son, never forget my dying words. This country holds your father's body. Never sell the bones of your father and your mother." I pressed my father's hand and told him I would protect his grave with my life. My father smiled and passed away to the spirit-land.

I buried him in that beautiful valley of winding waters. I love that land more than all the rest of the world. A man who would not love his father's grave is worse than a wild animal.

For a short time we lived quietly. But this could not last. White men had found gold in the mountains around the land of winding water. They stole a great many horses from us, and we could not get them back because we were Indians. The white men told lies for each other. They drove off a great many of our cattle. Some white men branded our young cattle so they could claim them. We had no friend who would plead our cause before the law councils. It seemed to me that some of the white men in Wallowa were doing these things on purpose to get up a war. They knew that we were not strong enough to fight them. I labored hard to avoid trouble and bloodshed. We gave up some of our country to the white men, thinking that then we could have peace. We were mistaken. The white man would not let us alone. We could have avenged our wrongs many times, but we did not. Whenever the Government has asked us to help them against other Indians, we have never refused. When the white men were few and we were strong, we could have killed them all off, but the Nez Percés wished to live at peace.

If we have not done so, we have not been to blame. I believe that the old treaty has never been correctly reported. If we ever owned the land we own it still, for we never sold it. In the treaty councils the commissioners have claimed that our country had been sold to the Government. Suppose a white man should come to me and say, "Joseph, I like your horses, and I want to buy them." I say to him, "No, my horses suit me, I will not sell them." Then he goes to my neighbor, and says to him: "Joseph has some good horses. I want to buy them, but he refuses to sell." My neighbor answers, "Pay me the money, and I will sell you Joseph's horses." The white man returns to me, and says, "Joseph, I have bought your horses, and you must let me have them." If we sold our lands to the Government, this is the way they were bought.

CHIEF JOSEPH, *Nez Percé*

4

WE ARE NOT CHILDREN

I nviting Native American chiefs to journey to the national capital to meet the "Great White Father," as they termed the President, was a ritual as old as the Republic itself. Ever since George Washington asked the Iroquois leaders Corn-

planter, Red Jacket, Farmer's Brother, and Captain Joseph Brant to visit Phila-delphia in 1792, the excursion had appealed to the Indians' respect for pomp and protocol. The visits also gave the government a fine opportunity for impressing Indians with the might, wealth, and overwhelming numbers of white people before they sat down at the conference table.

In the fall of 1873, a delegation of Otoe chiefs from Nebraska held discussions with the Commissioner of Indian Affairs and their own agent in Washington, D.C. Foremost on the minds of the Otoes was permission for a final buffalo hunt and approval to relocate their tribe in Indian Territory in Oklahoma. Two of the chiefs, Medicine Horse and Stand By, had been in the city nineteen years earlier, when the Otoe signed one of many treaties they negotiated with the government of the United States between 1808 and 1865.

Just before this second trip, the superintendent of the Otoe reservation in Nebraska had written to his colleagues in Washington: "I cannot account for the ardent desire of all Indians with whom I have had business relations to visit the City of Washington. It appears to be the Mecca of their hopes. The Otoes have been particularly anxious to go there."

As the following condensation of a handwritten transcript of the conversations dramatizes, Washington was no Mecca this time around. The Otoe chiefs came away from the talks fully aware of the helpless status earlier treaties had placed them in. The commissioner, Edward P. Smith, shocks them with his reading of a paragraph in the treaty reserving to the President the right to decide how the Otoes are to use the money owed them for the land they had agreed to sell. The frustrating exchange also communicates the flavor of official attitudes toward Native Americans at this time.

A year after these conversations Medicine Horse attempted to lead fifty families on a flight to freedom from their Nebraska reservation into Kansas Territory, but he was shortly captured and imprisoned.

October 31, 1873, First Day

COMMISSIONER: I am glad to see you, my friends, as representatives of your tribe in Nebraska and hear what you have to say and render of your desires. Your tribe is an important one. You are elderly men, and probably have children, and what you say today will not only be for today, but will live after you.

MEDICINE HORSE: Grandfather, I have wanted to see you. We did not come for nothing, but we are tired. We just came. We want to ask one thing,

Medicine Horse

whether you have done it or not. Before I left my tribe wanted to go on a buffalo hunt, and waited for permission from their Grandfather. We want to know if it has been sent.

COMMISSIONER: Your Agent asked a short time ago for permission for you to go on a hunt, and he stated that it was necessary, for you to get something to eat. We thought a long time before we decided what to do, as it is bad for Indians to go on a hunt. This strikes you as very strange. It is because we must do one thing or the other. Either let you continue wild as you now are, or make you like white men; and nothing keeps up this wild living like hunting. No white man could hunt as you do, and farm. No one can take care of himself and do it. Now because we are not ready to help you and put you where you can help yourself, it is decided to let you go on the hunt. Now is there something else?

MEDICINE HORSE: Grandfather, I have to say the same I said before. Grandfather should listen to what we said before. He has been living here all the time. We just came. Give us time.

COMMISSIONER: We will not talk anymore today then. You will think a long time and then you will talk well.

November 1, 1873, Second Day

COMMISSIONER: Yesterday when we met you were tired and could not talk. I hope you have had a good sleep and can talk well now.

MEDICINE HORSE: My tribe has sent me down here to do the talking for them. I spoke to our Agent about it and I suppose you have heard about it, that we would sell our land. All our white brothers have big pieces of land, and get along much better than we do. We want the same. Some of the chiefs went with me to see another country. I like it and want to go there.

COMMISSIONER: There are two kinds of Indians there. Some are good and work, and others are very wild and bad. I should be very sorry to have you go from Nebraska so as to be able to go wild again like some now in Indian Territory. What you ought to do is get ready as fast as you can to be like white people, and know as much as they do. There are white men who live by roaming about, but they do not amount to much.

STAND BY: I made a Treaty and sold our lands—a large piece of it. We did not sell it for paper money but for hard money.

COMMISSIONER: I will tell you now for what purpose this money was promised to you. The Treaty says that all this money [the Commissioner picks up a volume of treaties and reads] is to be "expended for your use and benefit under the direction of the President of the United States who may from time to time (that means from year to year) determine at his discretion what proportion of the annual payments shall be paid in money and what portion shall be spent in your education, for such beneficial objects as in his judgment shall advance them in civilization, for building, opening farms, fencing, breaking land, providing stock, agricultural implements, seed, clothing, etc." That is what the money is given for. The President decides whether to give the money or other things which he considers better for you. I will not take your money away but will spend it so as to do you good. Four hundred dollars will feed your tribe a month. It will fence a farm that will feed you and your children a hundred years. Is it not better for us to send money to your Agent to fence your farms than to send it to you to pass over to traders for trinkets?

STAND BY: We always raised something from the ground to support our families before we ever saw white men. But sometimes we get a good many furs and they bring us more money than we can get from what we raise. My Father told me if I wanted anything I should come here and get it. I know what kind of a treaty we made. I have it in my head.

COMMISSIONER: Things last longer on paper than they do in your head. Your grandchildren will be able to take from this paper what was agreed to be done with the money. When they couldn't tell at all from your head better than you can now.

STAND BY: How would these white men feel to have their property used in this way?

COMMISSIONER: If the white men are children and you are their guardian, you can do what you please with their money—provided you do what is good for them.

MEDICINE HORSE: We are not children. We are men. I never thought I would be treated so when I made the Treaty.

COMMISSIONER: I have no way of knowing what was said at the time of the making of the Treaty, but to read what is written on the paper on which you have put your mark. If this course I propose was injuring you I should not propose it. But it is for your own good.

MEDICINE HORSE: Father, look at me and not at the table.

COMMISSIONER: I am busy writing.

MEDICINE HORSE: Those black curly-haired people I have always heard were made free. I thought I was always a free man. I am free yet. It hurts me badly what you read in the book. I did not know it was there.

COMMISSIONER: Did the Great Father promise always to do all you wanted him to do?

MEDICINE HORSE: We will not talk anymore now. We will think about it.

November 4, 1873, Third Day

COMMISSIONER: You have had a good long time to think about what we are to talk of today.

MEDICINE HORSE: Father, what you said to us the other day hurt our feelings very much and we could not sleep since. When we made a trade, they did not tell us we must use our money, as you told us the other day. Our Great Father owes us a great deal of money. I always thought I should draw my money. Your talk the other day takes our rights away. I will be ashamed to take home this news.

STAND BY: I can not say anything different from what this fellow has been saying. I have been living a long time up there on the reservation, but we have got dissatisfied. Before we started, we had a council between ourselves. Our plan suited us. Your plan does not suit us at all.

COMMISSIONER: Our Great Father likes his children and does what is best for them when sometimes his children do not like it. You have received these annuities for nearly twenty years. You have had the best land in Nebraska. Just such land as your white brothers have made such good homes out of. Now why is it you have no houses, oxen, cows, horses, and homes like the white man? You have not been brought up that way. But there is a change coming over your life and it is hard for an old man to change his ways, but unless you change sometime, and it is hard for some old ones, it will be hard for the children to change.

STAND BY: We don't want to settle this business now. We want to go home and study about it. When white men want to make a plan, they get together and study about it two or three days. You want to put it all through at once, like drowning me in the river. We are not the only chiefs. There are some more at home. We will take the news home, and if it suits all, we will have to do so.

COMMISSIONER: There is no use to talk about half the land for that is settled. Congress passed a law and you all agreed to it, and men have been sent out to appraise the land, and if there is anyone to buy it, the land will be sold.

STAND BY: If you have a piece of land and I sell it, you would not like it.

COMMISSIONER: If you are my Agent and sell it, it is all right. You must remember there is a difference. You are the child of Government, and it must take care of you.

STAND BY: If you have children and they want money, they have it. They do as they want to.

COMMISSIONER: No, they do not. My child does as I want to have her. If any child wants anything and I want her to have it she gets it. But if I don't want her to have it she don't get it and she does not turn around and ask me how I would like it if she had my money and would not let me have it.

BIG BEAR: We work all the time. We like to work. You want to bind us right down, and we don't like it. I have raised wheat, corn, potatoes, and pumpkins. We all work. But you cannot make white men of us. That is one thing you can't do.

MEDICINE HORSE: I don't want to sell part of the reservation.

COMMISSIONER: Half of your reservation will be sold and tell your people so when you go home or you will tell them a falsehood. Now we have talked enough today.

STAND BY: You must not get tired of us. We have much to say.

COMMISSIONER: You are rightly named Stand By.

STAND BY: The Railroad gave us money for the right of way through our Territory and it is here, and we would like it.

AGENT: They sold the right of way through the Reservation for nineteen hundred dollars and the Agent before me arranged for one thousand dollars to be spent for provisions which he turned over to me, and I expended that amount last summer. And there must be some one thousand dollars still on hand.

MEDICINE HORSE: We did not order you to buy any cattle or horses for us.

COMMISSIONER: You did not need to. You are my children, and I had a right to buy what I wanted to for you. It takes you a long time to find out that I am going to do what I think best for you.

MEDICINE HORSE: There is such a thing as children being whipped too often.

COMMISSIONER: There is a little over nine hundred dollars left you on the account of the railroad lands.

INTERPRETER: They want to keep that for provisions this winter. They are afraid they will not have a good hunt.

COMMISSIONER: I will send it to the Agent to spend for you in pork and flour.

MEDICINE HORSE: When I came here to visit the Great Father, he always gave us money to buy presents for our children.

COMMISSIONER: The Great Father never did that. The first time he ever did was to those Crows, and he is not going to do so anymore. But I will give you some presents to give the chiefs who did not come. I want you to go and see the President tomorrow at his house and in the afternoon go to the Navy yard and see the guns and shops and ships if you would like to.

MEDICINE HORSE ET AL., *Otoe*

5

PLENTY COUPS TRAVELS TO WASHINGTON

To Indians from the Far West much of the adventure of an official visit to Washington lay in the long journey. The first Crow Indian delegation to visit the city left central Montana in 1872, rode on horseback to Salt Lake City, then embarked on the train. In 1880 a second group headed east to discuss a railroad that was to cut across Crow lands. Among the chiefs was a rising young leader named Plenty Coups, who later described the trip.

THEY SAID THEY were going to take me to Washington. I thought it over for a while. I thought it was a wise thing. I told them I would go. This was my first trip east. I also told them that I wanted some other chiefs to go with me. I asked Two-Belly. At first he didn't want to go, but finally he said he would. The others were Old Crow, Pretty Eagle, Long Elk, and Medicine Crow. Three white men also accompanied us: A. M. Quivey, Tom Stewart, and J. R. Keller.

It was during the spring. There was no railroad yet in our country, and we had to travel by stagecoach which carried a light at night. We traveled in two coaches. Snow was still lying on the ground. We set out from the old agency, near Flesh Scraper Mountain. The horses were relayed, but we had no rest during these changes of horses. We traveled toward Butte [Montana], which took us four nights and five days. The further we came into the mountains, the deeper lay the snow. At Butte we rested for the first time. We slept a whole day and night. And I combed my hair for the first time since leaving our camp.

The 1880 Crow delegation to Washington. Plenty Coups is seated in the front row (second from right).

Early the next morning we were told to dress quickly and eat. The teams were ready and we traveled down the mountain, following Flathead River. Again we were relayed. We continued until we came close to another mountain, and we saw an Indian driving some horses. We called him to us. He was a Bannock. We asked him where the Bannocks were. He told us that they were on the other side of the mountain, in the valley. He also told us that their chief, Comes Out of the Grease, had gone to Washington. . . .

Early the next morning we took a sweatbath with the Bannocks. They told us that the road from their camp to the next station was hard and rough, and that it was better to travel by daytime. At that station, however, we should see the Fast Wagon [train]. They described it as a big black horse with his belly nearly touching the ground. This horse had a big bell on his back. He ran so fast that everytime he stopped, he puffed.

We left about noon and came to a big barn after dark where we slept. Early the next morning we started again and found the snow deep. Soon it started to rain which made the roads even worse. It was again after dark before we stopped at a dugout town, where they were building the railroad. Here we had supper. A white man with us pointed to a clock and told us that when the hands should be in a certain position we should start again. We did not know what he meant. Next morning we were awakened, took our bundles, and were taken to the train. We walked into the cars and sat down. We placed our bundles on shelves and looked out of the window. The train followed the river. Through the windows we could see many horses, game, and mountains. Stewart, who was traveling with us, acted as interpreter. We arrived at the Bannock Agency, and many Indians were there. As soon as the train stopped, we wanted to get off, but we were told to stay. That black horse was panting so hard that the bell on his neck was ringing.

We thought the train journey was grand. I realized, however, that it was not a horse that pulled it, and I wondered what made it go so fast. Birds would fly along outside our windows. They were swift, but before long we outdistanced them.

We had often been told that the Sioux were a numerous tribe. But it seemed to me that the Bannock was even larger. We halted at a junction, and another train passed going in a different direction. I saw a lake with a mountain rising from its center. We saw many white man's places, and passed many freshly skinned elk and buffalo carcasses. . . .

We came to a big forest and passed it and finally we arrived at the Missouri. Here we met a white man called Wood Frost who had been our agent. He invited us to dinner and gave us some red paint and shells. We had not even finished our meal when we had to leave for the train. We crossed the Missouri and were told that we were going to Chicago.

It was the first time that I had seen so many white people together. It was strange to see so many tall black houses. Here we left the train. There was a big lake and we spent much time there watching the ice bump against the shore and break into pieces. It was the biggest ice breakup I had ever seen, and the waves were very high.

There was more travel by train and finally we arrived in Washington. Here wagons were ready waiting for us. They took us to our lodging, and we were told to sleep until the next morning when we should be taken to President Hayes. The next day we were escorted to the President, who shook hands with us and told us that he was glad to see us. The President said that he had sent for us to talk concerning the future of our people. He said that he wanted us to send our children to school and that they would build a house and barn for each of us. He wanted us to learn how to farm. He said they were going to build a railroad through the Yellowstone Valley, but that they wanted us to make peace with the other tribes in our part of the country.

My companions told me to make some reply so I said that we were also glad to see him and that we wished to speak with him too. I said that he had asked us to do many things, but that before we could give him our answer, we would like time to talk it over among ourselves. The President gave us two days to consider his requests. Two days later we returned and again met with him. I said that we agreed to send our children to school and to let the Government build houses for us. I said that as far as stopping the fighting with other tribes, we wanted to fight them for about two more years and then we would reconsider this question. I added that we did not want a railroad built through our country because it was our hunting ground.

When we said this, the President kept us in Washington for over a month. We had several conferences with him in which he tried to overrule our objections, but he failed. The President suggested giving us another hunting ground, in North Dakota, but I refused because we did not wish to leave our country. When the President asked my reasons I said that in North Dakota the mountains are low and that I wanted to live where the mountains are high and where they are many springs of fresh water.

Then the President asked how we had treated the soldiers, and I said that we had been friendly to them. When their horses' feet were sore, so were ours. When they had to drink alkali, we shared their misfortune. When they suffered, we suffered, and I said we would continue to have friendly relations. Then the President said that he would grant our request to remain in the country where we lived, but that in return he expected us to let them build a railroad through the valley of the Yellowstone.

I said that when I returned to my people I would talk with them and hear their objections. I said then he could send us one of his servants and we would hold a council with him and he would tell the President of the results.

We were in Washington a long time. I became anxious to return home and see my people again. The President told us that we could return home in two Sundays. Although we dreaded the long journey, we were glad.

When the day arrived, we again walked into the cars and traveled for a long time. It was late summer when we finally reached home, but the trees were still in full leaf.

Soon after we returned, we had a conference with the railroad and Government officials. We finally agreed to let them build the railroad through our country, and they agreed to give us free transportation. This was done at first, but soon this agreement was not lived up to and since then we have had to pay for our own transportation. A few years later the Government began to build homes for the Crows on the Big Horn River. I then went to Pryor [the westernmost town on the Crow Indian reservation]. I donated the use of four head of horses and had a log house built on the land where I live today.

PLENTY COUPS, *Crow*

EXILES IN THEIR OWN LAND

L ong before they were driven from their homes by an expanding white society, many Native American peoples could have told of tribal resettlements. In the fourteenth century some Siouan-speaking groups are believed to have undertaken an epic journey from what we know today as the Carolinas to Minnesota, where they established themselves as the eastern Sioux. Sometime before the fifteenth century, bands of Athapascan-speaking people from northwestern Canada entered present-day New Mexico; they quickly adopted aspects of Pueblo culture and are known today as the nation's largest tribe, the Navajo. In the seventeenth century a branch of Missouri River Hidatsa broke away and traveled west-ward to become the Montana Crow. Not many decades later the Kiowa began an odyssey that took them from the northern to the southern Great Plains where they adopted new cultural patterns. These and many other large migrations generally occurred over a sufficient period of time so that the emigrants could gradually adapt to their new surroundings and new neighbors.

But the relentless spread of white culture throughout America allowed no such periods of grace. The series of convulsive tribal displacements that began soon after Native American contact with whites seriously disrupted Indian life everywhere. Generation after generation of Native American families came to know only the sorrows and terrors of exile. All their worldly goods on their backs, the Indian refugees suffered harassment from un-friendly whites along the way. Starvation and disease were their constant companions as they walked along unfamiliar roads to country they had never seen. Sometimes friendly Indians gave them shelter; sometimes enemy tribes took the opportunity to attack them.

Although these tribal uprootings reached their peak in the 1830s, they had acquired a customary pattern long before, and they continued until the end of the nineteenth century. "I think you had better put the Indians on wheels," a Sioux named Red Dog bitterly complained to treaty commis-sioners in 1876. "Then you can run them about whenever you wish."

The story of this erratic shifting of Native American populations accelerated in the mid-seventeenth century, when the Iroquois, making the most of

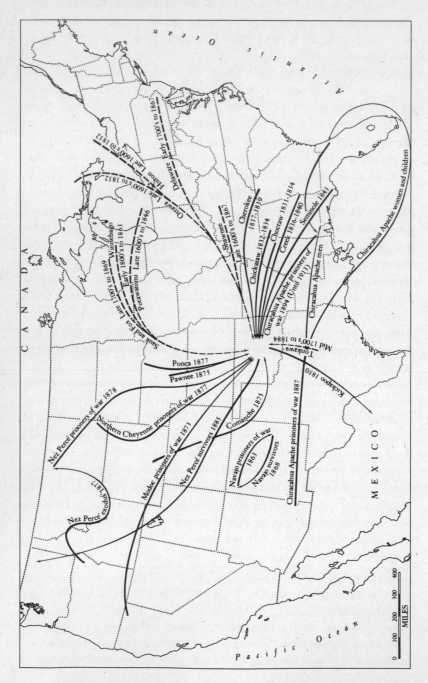

their strategic balance-of-power position between England and France, routed the Hurons westward. They then forced the Sauk and Fox, Osage, and Potawatomi into the uninhabited, northern Mississippi Valley. In the Southeast, white settlement compelled tribes to abandon their riverbank camps and seek refuge in the deep woods. In 1704 the English rampage against the Indians in Florida contributed to the formation of a new Native American tribe: the fleeing Creek regrouped as the Seminole Indians of the Everglades—the name Seminole means "runaway."

Between 1750 and 1850 the Osage averaged a hundred miles of westward movement every ten years. And in 1886 the Delaware chief Journeycake mournfully recollected his people's reluctant transformation into nomads: "We have been broken up and removed six times. We have been despoiled of our property. We thought when we moved across the Missouri River and paid for our homes in Kansas we were safe, but in a few years the white man wanted our country." Eventually nearly every Indian nation would be reduced to frontier flotsam by this push-and-shove movement toward the setting sun.

In the latter part of the eighteenth century, once the victorious American colonists no longer felt obliged to woo Indian allies in their struggle against England, they began eyeing Indian lands, particularly in the Southeast where settlers were shortly crowding as "thick as grass"—as the Indians phrased it. After 1790 the United States government faced four options in shaping its overall policy toward Indians: (1) exterminate them; (2) protect them in zoolike enclaves while towns rise around them; (3) assimilate Indians by encouraging them to become crop-raising, church-going, school-attending model citizens; (4) transplant them to that inhospitable, unwanted wilderness west of the Mississippi, known as Indian Territory.

President Thomas Jefferson had argued that assimilation was the only moral course. But in 1803, the year the United States acquired the Louisiana Purchase from France, thus gaining that vast expanse of land stretching from

⁣|⁣|⁣|⁣|⁣|⁣|⁣|⁣|⁣|⁣|⁣|⁣|⁣|⁣|⁣|⁣|⁣|⁣|⁣|⁣|⁣|⁣|⁣|⁣|⁣|⁣|⁣|⁣|⁣|⁣|⁣|⁣|⁣|⁣|⁣|⁣|⁣|⁣|⁣|⁣|⁣|⁣|⁣|⁣|⁣|⁣|⁣|⁣|⁣|⁣|⁣|⁣|⁣|⁣|⁣|⁣|

(Facing page) *Many Native American peoples were displaced from their ancestral homelands through wars, treaties, and takeovers of their lands by white settlers. The map shows the approximate routes and dates of some of these removals; the broken lines indicate a few of the more gradual displacements that took place over a period of time. Indian Territory, which consisted of most of the present-day state of Oklahoma, became a gigantic resettlement camp for tribes from every corner of the United States.*

the Mississippi River to the Rocky Mountains, even Jefferson suggested that perhaps the Indians might be "safer" if relocated in this new territory.

Over the next forty years, largely due to clamor from the citizens of Georgia, and of the newly created states of Tennessee, Alabama, and Mississippi, this policy of removal would reign. Of all the treaties signed with the Indians, none had such anguishing consequences as the seventy-six prescribing wholesale emigration as the final solution to the Indian problem. During the period of intensive removals—from 1816 to 1850—over a hundred thousand Native Americans from twenty-eight tribes would be deported west of "the Great Waters" (the Mississippi). As the waves of these and later groups came westward, the newcomers sometimes met with resentment from the culturally different Indian peoples in their way. Warfare between them and the western Indians over shrinking food supplies broke out as early as 1816.

The southeastern removals began about 1811 when a trickle of Cherokee from Tennessee were persuaded to resettle. But that exodus did not satisfy the southern states, especially Georgia where gold had been discovered. White cotton growers were also impatient to cultivate the fertile Indian fields. Homesteaders in Arkansas and Missouri began haranguing the federal authorities to quit stalling and clear all Indians from the area. Abruptly the southern states outlawed the new tribal governments. This was painfully ironic since at least four of the South's so-called Five Civilized Tribes— Cherokee, Choctaw, Chickasaw, and Creek—had responded to President Jefferson's earlier advice to assimilate. Proud of their recently drafted laws and constitutions, their trimly tilled fields, and well-bred herds, their slaves, grist mills, and missionary schools, they were successfully emulating white culture while giving it an unmistakably Indian cast. Yet no matter how well the Civilized Tribes blended white and Indian worlds, the federal government began caving in to state pressure to remove them all. Before long the once vast "Indian Territory" would be reduced to the confines of the present-day state of Oklahoma.

Shortly after his inauguration in 1829, President Andrew Jackson, who had never hidden his scorn for Native American rights, publicly refused to honor federal treaty obligations to protect the southern tribes from harassment by vigilantes or from trespass by squatters on their ancestral lands. In the spring of 1830, Jackson's Indian Removal Act was finally passed by Congress. Now, the President (whom the Indians had named "Sharp Knife") had both the power to select the tribes that were to be removed and the money—half a million dollars—to finance the giant exodus. To present an illusion of tribal consent, Jackson's secret agents bribed, deceived, and intimidated individual Indians, falsified records, squelched open debate, and finally persuaded some tribesmen to sign in favor of removal.

Digging in against removal, the Cherokee quarrel with the state of Georgia went all the way to the United States Supreme Court. In 1831 the tribe finally won an unequivocal acknowledgment of their status as an independent sovereign nation. In the historic opinion of Chief Justice John Marshall, the "acts of Georgia are repugnant to the Constitution. . . . They are in direct hostility with treaties [which] . . . solemnly pledge the faith of the United States to restrain their citizens from trespassing on it [Cherokee territory]. . . ." But Chief Justice Marshall's significant decision notwithstanding, President Jackson and Georgia officials were determined to oust the tribe.

The Cherokee resistance to removal was tirelessly led by a part-Cherokee named John Ross. Ross and his followers refused in 1835 to sign the illegal Treaty of New Echota, in which a fraction of the tribe agreed to go west. The debate over removal caused bloody disputes within the Cherokee community. Opponents of Ross said his stand was unrealistic, and later charged that the position he had taken caused greater hardship for the Cherokee when removal ultimately came. A leading advocate of Cherokee rights for more than forty years, Ross continued to defend his people when they resettled in Indian Territory and successfully rebuilt their dislocated lives and institutions.

The Choctaw were the first to make the hard journey. Leaving their Mississippi farms in the winter of 1831, several groups began the long trek westward under guard only to meet a blizzard of snow and below-zero weather; many of the Choctaw were barefoot and starving, one blanket being allotted to each family. The Creek began leaving Alabama in 1836—"drove off like wolves," as they described it—many of them in chains. A rotting, overloaded steamboat bearing one group sank, drowning 311 men, women, and children. Nearly half the Creek nation died either en route or during their first years in the harsh, unfamiliar climate of Oklahoma. In 1837, the first of the Cherokee began their nation's two-year-long removal, a time the Cherokee still refer to as "the drive-away."

Rebecca Nuegin was a three-year-old Cherokee child when her family's ordeal began. "When the soldiers came to our house," she recalled as an

John Ross in a photograph taken in 1862, four years before his death

old woman, "my father wanted to fight, but my mother told him that the soldiers would kill him if he did, and we surrendered without a fight. They drove us out of the house to join other prisoners in a stockade."

Traveling west in three separate parties, the Cherokee lost an estimated quarter of their tribe to sickness and exposure through the removal ordeal. As many as thirty thousand Native Americans perished either on these tragic journeys or shortly thereafter during the lawless period of readjustment in Indian Territory where the surviving members of more than sixty dislocated tribes eventually came to live.

Still another series of removals occurred in the Ohio Valley, where tribes who had already undergone at least one uprooting were pressured to sign new agreements to travel yet again to alien soil. In the 1850s and 1860s, the removal idea lay behind the displacement of tribes in the Far West as well. Indeed the sufferings of exile were experienced by Native Americans as far apart as California, the Great Lakes, and the Southwest.

The Choctaw still tell a story that poignantly sums up the profound sense of loss felt by the many Native Americans who were forced to leave their homelands. As one Choctaw community was about to move from its ancestral Mississippi forest and start the westward trek to Indian Territory, the women made a formal procession through the trees surrounding their abandoned cabins, stroking the leaves of the oak and elm trees in silent farewell. In each of the episodes that follow, we see tribal worlds threatened with the next-worst calamity to extermination.

1

PLEA FROM THE CHICKASAW

When *United States government officials suggested in 1826 that the Chickasaw swap their Tennessee Valley hamlets for unseen territory west of the Mississippi River, the Chickasaw leaders responded as follows.*

Actually the Chickasaw had quietly begun moving west as early as 1822. After agreeing to the removal treaties of 1832 and 1834, the remainder of the tribe followed, taking along five thousand of their highly prized horses. Although they had to slog their way through swamps and continually fight off horse thieves, their journey was better planned and financed than the other Southeast Indian removals. The Chickasaw arrived in Indian Territory considerably less damaged in body and spirit than the Creek, Cherokee, and Choctaw.

WE NEVER HAD a thought of exchanging our land for any other, as we think that we would not find a country that would suit us as well as this we now occupy, it being the land of our forefathers, if we should exchange our lands for any other, fearing the consequences may be similar to transplanting an old tree, which would wither and die away, and we are fearful we would come to the same. . . .

We have no lands to exchange for any other. We wish our father [the President] to extend his protection to us here, as he proposes to do on the west of the Mississippi, as we apprehend we would, in a few years, experience the same difficulties in any other section of the country that might be suitable to us west of the Mississippi. . . .

Our father the President wishes that we should come under the laws of the United States; we are a people that are not enlightened, and we cannot consent to be under your Government. If we should consent, we should be likened unto young corn growing and met with a drought that would kill it.

LEVI COLBERT ET AL., *Chickasaw*

2

TUSHPA CROSSES THE MISSISSIPPI

Between 1800 and 1830, white men tried on more than forty occasions to force the Choctaw to sell their Mississippi homeland. By 1830 the tribe had given up more than thirteen million acres. Nonetheless, pressure to yield their remaining ten million acres continued. Finally, when the Treaty of Dancing Rabbit Creek was signed in September 1830, most of the Choctaw agreed to move west.

Tushpa, who was later to provide his son, James Culberson, with the following account of the band's ordeal, was then about twelve years old. Their journey began in early spring 1834, and took them to Skullyville Agency, established the year before, in eastern Oklahoma. During the entire Choctaw removal, two thousand out of the twenty thousand who left their homes in Mississippi died. Intimate reminiscences of the removal period, such as Tushpa's story, are extremely rare, as if even the memories were too painful to recall.

THIS PARTICULAR BAND consisted of about one hundred persons, men, women, and children, and were all full-blood Choctaw Indians of very small means, and in fact had nothing of value to help them make this trip. The captain or headman of this band arranged the order of travel. One man was selected to carry choice seed corn for the planting of new fields; another to choose and select seeds from choice peach and apple trees so that new orchards might be planted; another to choose and select choice beans and melon seeds for the new gardens. . . .

Only a partial list of those who went in this band is necessary for us to know: Tushpa, the bare-footed lad; Ishtona, the deliverer, the mother of Tushpa; Kanchi, the seller, the father of Tushpa; Ishtaya, the fire bearer; Halbi, the kicker, second chief; and Chilita, the wise daughter of Halbi. . . .

Kanchi, who had heard a missionary preach from what he told the Indians through interpretation was a book from God, called his brethren together in the camp, and while the news of the disaster of the burning of their homes was fresh on their minds, and some swearing vengeance and others for giving up all and resigning to fate, bade them listen to him.

He said: "My own kin and blood brothers, I know how you feel about what has happened to you; I too have felt the same and looked about for comfort from this wretchedness into which we have been brought. . . . Why are we surrounded by foes and cast out of our homes . . . ? Some time back beyond our old homes I heard a man preach from a book that he called a Bible [*Holisso Holitopa*], and although that book was read by a white man, I believe there is something better in it than the way the white man acts. . . . We are in much trouble now, but don't want to kill or destroy, so give us hearts that we hear about in this book and let us be good, and if we live to see this new country to which we travel, help some of us to do good to those we meet. Perhaps we will not bring shame upon the land."

It was now early spring of 1834, and the Mississippi River was carrying a larger amount of headwater this spring than usual so it was necessary to wait until the river had fallen in its flow so that it could be crossed.

The party put up some shelter and arranged temporary camps and prepared to stay on the banks of the river until they might cross it. On the second night of their stay a runner had announced that a fire had destroyed their former homes and everything that had been left in them, so that the last hope of remaining in this homeland was rudely snatched away. . . .

Chief Baha ordered that arrangements be made for the crossing; so a plan to use a raft made of logs to carry over a part of the baggage and make a quicker crossing was agreed upon. . . . The point at which the party crossed is in the southeastern part of Arkansas in Desha County at the mouth of Cypress Creek south of Friars Point. The river here is about one mile wide and has a pretty stiff current at low tide. . . . An island known as Bihi or Mulberry Island was near the middle of the stream and broke the swift current of the main river and was used as a place to rest and straighten the cargo. . . .

Baha, the chief headman, had often made this crossing to visit some Indians who lived over the river near the Big Mound, and told his people they could make an easy crossing as he knew all the currents and landing places. During the two weeks' delay a number of small canoes and one large raft of logs were made by the men. . . .

Four canoes with four men in each were used to pull the raft loaded with household goods, clothing, and other things to be carried or used in the journey, and also some persons, men, women and children, were shipped over as each raftload made the crossing. . . . an accident happened when it appeared that the success in crossing would be complete. The raft was being towed across on its fifth trip laden with people and goods, when it was struck by a swiftly moving submerged tree. . . . In the excitement, Kanchi, who was on duty as a guard, after rescuing two children and balancing the raft, in some manner became entangled in the swirling, twisting mass of brush, trees, and refuse, and caught in the undertow, never came to the surface again. . . . Some thought of going no farther on the journey but realized it was impractical now as half of the party had already crossed over the river. Others recalled the prayer that Kanchi had made for them. . . .

The final crossing was made after a week of hard work, and the party decided to rest for a few days before attempting the westward journey and accordingly made a temporary camp upon the high ground away from the river bank. It had been six weeks since leaving their homes, and a greater part of the time there had been occasional rains, and not having had proper shelter, the aged people and young children had begun to show signs of the exposure which they had encountered. As a result of the weather an old lady and three small children died. . . .

A few days after these funeral rites were performed the headman, Baha, issued orders. . . . The march was resumed and much hard work was done to overcome the difficulties they now encountered. The trail now led through a dense forest. . . . Something had to be done about it, so Baha called the headmen in a council, and it was finally decided to have a gang of men under a subchief go ahead and clear the trail about one day in advance of the marching clan.

This proved a wise plan as this gang also prepared rafts on the bayous and rivers, and no time was lost when the clan reached these streams . . . the march was continued and persisted in once they had left the high grounds near the Mississippi River, as the headmen had been informed that dry grounds and an open country was theirs to enjoy if once they could get through these swamps. Ten miles was ordered for a day's journey, and all, young and old alike, set their program to make the ten miles at any cost.

The first three days were the most disagreeable they were to experience as it was nearly all swamps, sometimes knee-deep in muck, and added to that, camp had to be made in these swamps and on damp grounds, and they often had to sleep in wet clothes.

Brush was piled up and made a very comfortable place to sleep. If only a good fire had been built and a good meal cooked, their bodies would have been revived in condition to carry on. But the emergency was urgent, and no conveniences were to be had. . . .

Having crossed the most dense swamps, the marchers located on dry ground and prepared a camp, where they remained a few days looking after the sick. . . . By slow, painful marches they at last reached Little Rock, Arkansas, on the fifteenth of May, 1834, having been on the road two and a half months already and only about one-half of the journey complete. . . .

Many complaints of sickness were heard in the camp, and Baha thought it best to move camp as it might renew the spirit of the people. So after having been at the Post [Little Rock] one week, they began the march on the Post road towards their final destination, Fort Smith, Arkansas, and Skullyville, in Indian Territory, fifteen miles west of Fort Smith, Arkansas. . . . Three days out of Little Rock an Indian boy, named Shunka, died from a sort of dysentery and it quickly spread in camp among the weakened ones, and in the course of a week, before the disease could be checked, three others died. . . . They were laid away near one of the camps and the funeral rites performed over their lovely resting places. . . . [Then] good progress was made towards Dardenelle on the Arkansas River, which they reached on the 30th of May.

A ferry boat was used here in crossing the river by the post service, and after some parleying, the owners of the ferry consented to take all the company free of charge and ask the United States government to pay the bill at some future time. . . .

Having crossed the Arkansas River on the 31st day of May, the route of the company was over a somewhat traveled road, but there were many hills to climb and the road was so hard and dry that many suffered. . . . The number of sick increased and a forced camp was made in the hills ten miles out from Dardenelle, Arkansas. . . . The medicine men waited upon them as best they could, but two more died at this camp. . . .

If they could reach Fort Smith, Arkansas, or Skullyville, all their wants would be supplied by the United States agent, but they were fifty miles away now. A council of the headmen was called and a plan was agreed to make a camp for the sick and have members to remain and nurse them and the able-bodied ones to go on to their destination . . . [Baha] called off the names of twenty-five additional ones [people to join the twenty-five who already agreed to go on ahead] and insisted that they go. . . . Some of those who went at this time met friends of former days and settled in the various parts of the Indian Territory. . . .

Baha having conducted them safely into Indian Territory, returned at once with provisions to the sick camp. Conditions had become worse and some had died during his absence and so many were sick that a near panic had taken place. . . . In this extremity the deaths reached a total of eight, a staggering toll for such a small group of people. Ishtona died during a storm in the night with Tushpa, Chilita, and other friends by her couch. . . . On the last night of their stay at this camp, Tushpa, Chilita, and Ishtaya visited the grave of Ishtona for a last *ai-aksho* [cry of mourning]. . . .

The remnant of this devoted company, weary, emaciated, and penniless, reached the promised land, Indian Territory, on July 1st. At Skullyville they met real friends who took care of them and provided them with the necessary comforts for their immediate relief. Great rejoicing was experienced by them.

So ended a four-hundred-miles walk, one of the memorable migrations in the history of the native tribes in the United States. . . . After a few days' rest, the party so long together, separated to locate homes for themselves. Chilita remained near Skullyville with relatives. Ishtaya located a little further east of Skullyville near the Poteau River. He became a preacher. Later he and Chilita were married and moved across on the east side of the river, making a home at Pecola, where he was known as the famous preacher and evangelist—Willis Folsom. Their descendants occupy many places of trust in the state today. . . .

This, my fellow reader, is a true story of the life of John Culberson, or Tushpa, my father, a full-blood Choctaw Indian. . . . And who, on his death bed enjoined me to keep the family together and give them some chance for an education; to be a good citizen, and write the history of the journey if I thought it of benefit to mankind.

JAMES CULBERSON, *Choctaw*

3

CORRALLING THE NAVAJO

*I*n the early years the Navajo of the Southwest marauded against the Spanish, Mexicans, and Pueblo Indians. Their first "peace and friendship" treaty with the government of the United States, signed in 1846, was supposed to quell any harassment of American settlers. But the Navajo were a widely spread people; there was no central authority over their independent, roaming clans. Fifteen years, three unsuccessful military campaigns, and six treaties later, the word went out from Washington to round them all up.

Christopher "Kit" Carson headed the ruthless hunt in 1863 and 1864, with ready help from the Ute and other Navajo enemies. His troops slaughtered Navajo sheep and cut down every Navajo cornstalk and fruit tree they came across. At last eighty-five hundred starving men, women, and children were collected for the infamous "Long Walk," a 250-mile march to Bosque Redondo, near Fort Sumner, in eastern New Mexico. Here the Navajo were held in semiconfinement for four long years. Following their 1868 treaty with the United States they were, however, told they could return to their homeland near Fort Defiance, in Arizona; there they recuperated faster than most uprooted Indian tribes.

The events leading up to the Navajo removal are recollected here by Chester Arthur, clan relative of the most famous Navajo statesman of this century—Henry Chee Dodge.

ABOUT 1863, a Captain in the United States Army, called Red Shirt by the Indians, came to Red Lake, fifteen miles north of Fort Defiance, to make a treaty with the Navajos. He brought forty fat wethers for the feast and four big wagons loaded with calico, men's shirts and brass wire, to give away when the treaty was signed.

Red Shirt made a talk through his interpreter. He told the Indians they would have to stop stealing from the Mexicans, and from the neighboring tribes and each other. He told them they had made other treaties and broken them, but if they broke this one, it would be the last. He and the head chiefs sat down together on a blanket and they said they would sign the treaty.

When they had all made their mark on the paper, he gave each of the ten chiefs a pair of pants, a big silver medallion of George Washington to be hung around their necks and a fine gold-headed cane. Then he told the rest of the Navajos to line up, and he would give them all presents from the wagons. They lined up, and he and his men began to issue the calico and wire and shirts, but when he looked behind him, he found the rest were stealing from the backs of the wagons.

The Indians grabbed the ends of bolts of calico and ran them out, cutting off long strips with their knives, and they took the brass wire and shirts until they stole all he had and were unharnessing the mules to steal them. These were all young men that the chiefs could not control and Red Shirt made another speech.

"I thank you, my friends," he said, "for accepting my gifts as a sign that you make this treaty. Now if you will leave me the empty wagons I will go back to Santa Fe and bring you four more loads of presents."

The Indians let him go with his mules, but after a while, Nahtahlith, the orator, got up and began a speech, in which he scolded them for their thievery. All the time they had been taking the calico and blankets he had covered his face for shame, and while he sat there he had a vision, for he was a prophet. He told the young men that when they died they would not go to join the spirits of their ancestors, those great warriors, but would become Indian devils and whirlwinds and blow about on earth. The white man would not come back with four wagons of presents to give them. He would return with many soldiers, and Mexicans and Zuñis and Utes and Moquis—all armed with guns to kill them.

The young Indians told him to shut up, they were tired of hearing him talk; but he told them he was making a prophecy. When they heard that, they kept still and he went on. For this stealing, he said, they would be punished by being driven out of the rich country where they were into the barren desert to the west, where there was no water and the land would not grow corn. They would run and hide, from place to place, and when they met some of their people they would say: "Where is my wife? Where is my father? Where are my children?"

The "Long Walk" of the Navajo, as drawn by contemporary Navajo artist Raymond Johnson

But they would be hiding too, and the people would not know. Many would starve, many more would be killed, and in all that rich valley by Red Lake there would not be a single Navajo—not even a moccasin track. Only the footprints of coyotes.

That frightened the young men and they fled, but the soldiers did not come back. At first the Navajos were afraid and watched the trails, but as summer came on with lots of rain they went back to their old homes and planted corn. Even around Fort Defiance, which the Indians had burned down, they planted more wheat than ever before. But just as it was ready to cut, Red Shirt and the soldiers came back.

All the Navajos ran away as the soldiers moved in and camped at the fort, for besides them there were many of their enemies, the Mexicans; and also many Utes and Zuñis, all with guns. But the ten chiefs who had signed the treaty stayed on the cliff above the fort, and one day they saw Red Shirt with his escort riding north on the old Indian trail. So they ran down quickly to where he would pass and laid their canes and pants and medallions in the road.

When Red Shirt came and saw the presents, he knew why the chiefs had left them and he hollered for them to come down. They were ashamed at first, but at last they came down and he asked them what these things meant.

"War," they said. "You have come back with your soldiers."

"Yes, my friends," he said, "it is war. But at the same time I want you to stay. Sit down and smoke tobacco with me today, and tomorrow we will fight. My Government has given orders to kill you all unless you come in and surrender. So come in to the fort today or else take your families and flee to the wildest mountains."

They smoked together, and he said: "I thank you, my friends, for trying to restrain your people from stealing. But there is only one way to do that now and tomorrow we begin to kill them."

He shook hands and the chiefs went away, and the next day the soldiers began. They rode out in small parties in every direction and killed all the Navajo sheep, goats, horses, and cows that they could find. They killed the herders with the sheep, little boys, and grown men, and chased them through the rocks. The soldiers took the wheat to feed their horses and mules and cut down all the corn. The Mexicans and Utes and Zuñis trailed the Navajos everywhere and robbed them and stole their women and children.

The Navajos went up into the Canyon de Chelly, but the Mexican soldiers followed them. They cut down their peach trees and corn and chased the Indians up over the rocks, so high that their bullets would not reach. Then they tried to starve them out. But the Navajos had taken many water bottles with them and had hidden lots of corn in the caves, and at night while the soldiers were asleep, they would slip down and bring back more water. It was very hot in the canyon, and the Captain of the soldiers died, so they took his body and went away.

Every day the Mexicans and Utes would ride out over the country, and whenever they found sheep or pony tracks, they would follow them and kill the herders. The rich Navajos who had many sheep and goats drove them west as far as Oraibi, where the Moqui [Hopi] villages are, and many went so far they took refuge in the bottom of the Grand Canyon. But now from every side other Indians came in to fight them. Even the Paiutes and the Apaches had been given guns to kill them and chased them clear into the wild mountains. All their crops were destroyed and when winter came the people began to starve.

But Nahtahlith, the prophet, did not wait to starve and die. When he left Fort Defiance he mounted his best horse and rode out to meet the Zuñis, who were marching up Wide Ruins Wash. They saw him coming and surrounded him. Then he rode down their line, shooting his arrows until he had killed four men. A Mexican hit him with a bullet, and as they ran in to finish him he said: "I thank you, my friends, for giving me a warrior's death."

"We thank you," they said, "for coming to be killed."

They filled him full of arrows and broke his arms and legs with rocks, taking the sinews out to make war medicine, for they had seen what a brave man he was.

The prophecy of Nahtahlith came true. Red Shirt was their good friend, but the young men would not listen to him. They were so bad that nothing could be done with them and so they were destroyed. Those who escaped were driven to the Grand Canyon and the Painted Desert, where they hid in the rocks like wild animals, but all except a few were rounded up and caught and taken away to Hwalte [Bosque Redondo].

CHESTER ARTHUR, *Navajo*

4

THE UPROOTED WINNEBAGO

*A*mong *the lesser-known stories of tribal removal is that of the Wisconsin Winnebago. By 1865, when a chief named Little Hill told a congressional investigating team about his people's most recent troubles, the Winnebago had been reluctant wanderers for some forty years. They had been pressured into signing seven land-turnover agreements and had changed location at least six times.*

Evicted from their lead-rich lands along the Wisconsin River in the 1820s, the Winnebago were jostled back and forth until they finally agreed to settle in Minnesota. But, in the opinion of their white neighbors, that land was far too good

Two Cheyenne artists, Howling Wolf and Soaring Eagle, collaborated on this drawing of the boat that in 1875 took them and other Plains Indian prisoners to Fort Marion in St. Augustine, Florida.

for them. Under duress, they were sent to Crow Creek Reservation in South Dakota, as Little Hill relates. But life there was so impoverished that most of the Winnebago either secretly returned to Wisconsin or sought refuge with the Omaha in Nebraska, where they were finally given a reservation that they occupy to this day.

FORMERLY I did not live as I do now. We used to live in Minnesota. While we lived in Minnesota we used to live in good houses, and always take our Great Father's advice and do whatever he told us to do. We used to farm and raise a crop of all we wanted every year. While we lived there, we had teams of our own. Each family had a span of horses or oxen to work, and had plenty of ponies. Now, we have nothing. While we lived in Minnesota another tribe of Indians committed depredations against the whites [the 1862 Sioux uprising], and then we were compelled to leave Minnesota. We did not think we would be removed from Minnesota. Never expected to leave, and we were compelled to leave so suddenly that we were not prepared, not many could sell their ponies and things they had.

The superintendent of [our] farm was to take care of the ponies we had left there and bring them on to us wherever we went. But he brought to Crow Creek about fifty, and the rest we do not know what became of them. Most all of us had put in our crops that spring before we left, and we had to go and leave everything but our clothes and household things. We had but four days' notice. Some left their houses just as they were, with their stoves and household things in them. They promised us that they would bring all our ponies, but they only brought fifty, and the hostile Sioux came one night and stole all of them away.

In the first place, before we started from Minnesota, they told us that they had got a good country for us, where they were going to put us. The interpreter here with me now was appointed interpreter, on the first boat that came round, to see to things for the Indians on the trip round. After we got on the boat we were as though in prison. We were fed on dry stuff all the time. We started down the Mississippi River, and then up the Missouri to Dakota Territory and there we found our superintendent, and stopped there. Before we left Minnesota they told us that the superintendent had started on ahead of us, and would be there before us, and that he had plenty of Indians, and would have thirty houses built for us before we got there. After we got there they sometimes gave us rations, but not enough to go round most of the time. Some would have to go without eating two or three days.

It was not a good country. It was all dust. Whenever we cooked anything, it would be full of dust. We found out after a while we could not live there. . . . There was not enough to eat. The first winter one party started down the Missouri River as far as Fort Randall, where they wintered. Before the superintendent left us (the first fall after we went there), he had a cottonwood trough made and put beef in it, and sometimes a whole barrel of flour and a piece of pork, and let it stand a whole night, and the next morning after cooking it, would give us some of it to eat. We tried to use it, but many of us got sick on it and died. I am telling nothing but the truth now. They also put in the unwashed intestines of the beeves and the liver, and, after dipping out the soup, the bottom would be very nasty and offensive. Some of the old women and children got sick on it and died. . . .

I will pass and not say more about the provision, and say of things since we left Crow Creek. For myself, in the first place, I thought I could stay there for a while and see the country. But I found out it wasn't a good country. I lost six of my children, and so I came down the Missouri River. When I got ready to start, some soldiers came there and told me if I started they would fire at me. I had thirty canoes ready to start. No one interceded with the soldiers to permit me to go. But the next night I got away and started down the river, and when I got as far as the town of Yankton, I found a man there and got some provisions, then came on down further and got more provisions of the military authorities and then went on to the Omahas. After we got to the Omahas, somebody gave me a sack of flour, and someone told us to go to the other side of the Missouri and camp, and we did so. We thought we would keep on down the river, but someone came and told us to stay, and we have been there ever since.

LITTLE HILL, *Winnebago*

5

STANDING BEAR'S ODYSSEY

This saga of removal, related by Standing Bear of the Ponca, represents the first Indian grievance to receive sympathetic attention nationally. In 1877, the Ponca were forced on the 500-mile journey retraced here. A third of their people died en route of disease and starvation; those who survived were left disabled. Afterward, Standing Bear told the account that follows to a disbelieving Omaha newspaperman, then repeated it to an overflow audience in an Omaha church. In the fall of 1879, he described the experience up and down the East Coast, provoking a storm of letters to Congress in protest.

Meanwhile Standing Bear's son had died in Indian Territory. Disobeying an edict against leaving the reservation without permission, the old chief carried his child's bones back to the ancestral Ponca burial grounds in Nebraska. Some time

*later, a Senate investigating committee confirmed the allegations in Standing Bear's
account of his people's suffering. Decent acreage was given to those Ponca who wished
to remain in Indian Territory. Recompense was made to those who had had their
property confiscated during the removal. Standing Bear and his followers were
permitted to return to their old Nebraska homeland. In 1908, the old chief died
and was buried on a hill overlooking the site of his birth.*

W E L I V E D on our land as long as we can remember. No one knows
how long ago we came there. The land was owned by our tribe as far back
as memory of men goes. We were living quietly on our farms. All of a
sudden one white man came. We had no idea what for. This was the
inspector. He came to our tribe with Rev. Mr. Hinman. These two, with the
agent, James Lawrence, they made our trouble.

They said the President told us to pack up—that we must move to the
Indian Territory.

The inspector said to us: "The President says you must sell this land. He
will buy it and pay you the money, and give you new land in the Indian
Territory."

We said to him: "We do not know your authority. You have no right to
move us till we have had council with the President."

We said to him: "When two persons wish to make a bargain, they can
talk together and find out what each wants, and then make their agreement."

We said to him: "We do not wish to go. When a man owns anything,
he does not let it go till he has received payment for it."

We said to him: "We will see the President first."

He said to us: "I will take you to see the new land. If you like it, then
you can see the President, and tell him so. If not, then you can see him and
tell him so." And he took all ten of our chiefs down. I went, and Bright
Eyes' uncle went. He took us to look at three different pieces of land. He
said we must take one of the three pieces, so the President said. After he
took us down there, he said: "No pay for the land you left."

We said to him: "You have forgotten what you said before we started.
You said we should have pay for our land. Now you say not. You told us
then you were speaking truth."

All these three men took us down there. The man got very angry. He
tried to compel us to take one of the three pieces of land. He told us to be
brave. He said to us: "If you do not accept these, I will leave you here alone.

Standing Bear

You are one thousand miles from home. You have no money. You have no interpreter, and you cannot speak the language." And he went out and slammed the door. The man talked to us from long before sundown till it was nine o'clock at night.

We said to him: "We do not like this land. We could not support ourselves. The water is bad. Now send us to Washington, to tell the President, as you promised."

He said to us: "The President did not tell me to take you to Washington; neither did he tell me to take you home."

We said to him: "You have the Indian money you took to bring us down here. That money belongs to us. We would like to have some of it. People do not give away food for nothing. We must have money to buy food on the road."

He said to us: "I will not give you a cent."

We said to him: "We are in a strange country. We cannot find our way home. Give us a pass, that people may show us our way."

He said: "I will not give you any."

We said to him: "This interpreter is ours. We pay him. Let him go with us."

He said: "You shall not have the interpreter. He is mine, and not yours."

We said to him: "Take us at least to the railroad; show us the way to that."

And he would not. He left us right there. It was winter. We started for home on foot. At night we slept in haystacks. We barely lived till morning, it was so cold. We had nothing but our blankets. We took the ears of corn that had dried in the fields; we ate it raw. The soles of our moccasins wore out. We went barefoot in the snow. We were nearly dead when we reached the Otoe Reserve. It had been fifty days. We stayed there ten days to strengthen up, and the Otoes gave each of us a pony. The agent of the Otoes told us he had received a telegram from the inspector, saying that the Indian chiefs had run away; not to give us food or shelter, or help in any way. The agent said: "I would like to understand. Tell me all that has happened. Tell me the truth. . . ."

Then we told our story to the agent and to the Otoe chiefs—how we had been left down there to find our way.

The agent said: "I can hardly believe it possible that anyone could have treated you so. The inspector was a poor man to have done this. If I had taken chiefs in this way, I would have brought them home; I could not have left them there."

In seven days we reached the Omaha Reservation. Then we sent a telegram to the President; asked him if he had authorized this thing. We waited three days for the answer. No answer came.

In four days we reached our own home. We found the inspector there. While we were gone, he had come to our people and told them to move.

Our people said: "Where are our chiefs? What have you done with them? Why have you not brought them back? We will not move till our chiefs come back."

Then the inspector told them: "Tomorrow you must be ready to move. If you are not ready you will be shot." Then the soldiers came to the doors with their bayonets, and ten families were frightened. The soldiers brought wagons, they put their things in and were carried away. The rest of the tribe would not move. . . .

Then, when he found that we would not go, he wrote for more soldiers to come.

Then the soldiers came, and we locked our doors, and the women and children hid in the woods. Then the soldiers drove all the people [to] the other side of the river, all but my brother Big Snake and I. We did not go; and the soldiers took us and carried us away to a fort and put us in jail. There were eight officers who held council with us after we got there. The commanding officer said: "I have received four messages telling me to send my soldiers after you. Now, what have you done?"

Then we told him the whole story. Then the officer said: "You have done no wrong. The land is yours; they had no right to take it from you. Your title is good. I am here to protect the weak, and I have no right to take you; but I am a soldier, and I have to obey orders."

He said: "I will telegraph to the President, and ask him what I shall do. We do not think these three men had any authority to treat you as they have done. When we own a piece of land, it belongs to us till we sell it and pocket the money."

Then he brought a telegram, and said he had received answer from the President. The President said he knew nothing about it.

They kept us in jail ten days. Then they carried us back to our home. The soldiers collected all the women and children together; then they called all the chiefs together in council; and then they took wagons and went round and broke open the houses. When we came back from the council, we found the women and children surrounded by a guard of soldiers.

They took our reapers, mowers, hay rakes, spades, ploughs, bedsteads, stoves, cupboards, everything we had on our farms, and put them in one large building. Then they put into the wagons such things as they could carry. We told them that we would rather die than leave our lands; but we could not help ourselves. They took us down. Many died on the road. Two of my children died. After we reached the new land, all my horses died. The water was very bad. All our cattle died; not one was left. I stayed till one hundred and fifty-eight of my people had died. Then I ran away with thirty of my people, men and women and children. Some of the children were orphans. We were three months on the road. We were weak and sick and starved. When we reached the Omaha Reserve the Omahas gave us a piece of land, and we were in a hurry to plough it and put in wheat. While we were working, the soldiers came and arrested us. Half of us were sick. We would rather have died than have been carried back; but we could not help ourselves.

STANDING BEAR, *Ponca*

THE NATION'S HOOP
IS BROKEN AND
SCATTERED

In the 1860s and 1870s, the slaughter of buffalo by professional hunters spelled disaster for Plains Indians. At this Dodge City, Kansas, depot, forty thousand buffalo hides have been collected by one shipper alone, the meat left uneaten on the Plains.

By the 1870s the western American Indian homelands of wagonless plains, ranch-free valleys, and untunneled mountains were becoming a memory. Each passing year brought more miles of rutted roads, wire fences, telegraph wires, and metal railroad tracks. At river crossings, near age-old springs, beside groves of trees or in far-off mountains one found new cattle ranches and farms, frontier towns and mining camps. For the U.S. government the question of how to handle tribes in the path of this expansion came down to the old options—wipe out Indians, segregate them, or somehow blend them into society at large. By 1870 President Grant was advised that it would "be cheaper to feed every adult Indian now living to sleepy surfeiting during his natural life, while their children are educated to self-support by agriculture, than it would be to carry on a general Indian war for a single year."

Isolating Indians onto separate tracts of land to provide cheap labor or be taught white ways was, by the mid-nineteenth century, a familiar idea. In Latin America the Spanish claimed everywhere they touched down for the crown, and in the early seventeenth century set aside *resquardos de indigenes* (Indian reserves) for local natives. Under Mexico's *encomienda* system Indians were assigned to colonial plantations, which paid taxes for the privilege; in exchange the owners were also expected to teach their native hands the basics of Spanish civilization, vocational arts, and Catholic worship.

Early agreements between Indians and European colonists earmarked parcels exclusively for Indians. In many of the thirteen American colonies, Christianized Indians were quarantined within "praying towns" to safeguard them from the vices of frontier life as well as from "hostile" Indians who still resisted white authority.

As the United States won its independence, the new nation's Indian reservations emerged haphazardly—through special acts of Congress, official treaties between tribes and the U.S. government, or by presidential decree. In the 1830s the removal treaties relocated southeastern tribes west of the Mississippi River. In what would shift from Indian Territory to the state of Oklahoma in 1907, native refugees found themselves in a lawless frontier alongside Indians who might be traditional enemies. The Indian reservation of the Jacksonian era was as much a holding tank for society's unwanted as the prison, the poorhouse, or the mental asylum.

In the 1850s forecasts for the Indian future included a number of possibilities: Indians dying out altogether, the breakup of the reservations into Indian family farms, or the transformation of free Indians into dependent "wards." In 1851 President Millard Fillmore advanced an experiment of interrelated reservations for California's diverse native population, with new clothing, food, education, and religious training as part of the package. Pressured by land interests, however, Congress refused to ratify treaties that had already been signed with eighteen California Indian groups.

As for evicting tribes by military roundups and resettlement programs, that cost too much. And anyway, as white settlers took over more and more Indian land, available territory for tribal relocations was shrinking away. Senator Justin Morrill of Maine wondered in 1867: "We have come to this point in the history of this country that there is no place beyond the population to which you can remove the Indian . . . and the precise question is, will you exterminate him, or will you fix an abiding place for him?"

His mention of killing Indians off was as impractical as it was rhetorical. Warfare cost as much as removal; some estimated that the U.S. government paid a million dollars for every Indian it had slain. In the opinion of most politicians, the only realistic solution to the "Indian Problem" was a standardized policy for old reservations and to collect freewheeling Indians on new ones as quickly as possible.

From the Indian perspective, of course, they had a massive "White Problem." For tribes just recovering from traumatic relocations to Indian Territory, the Civil War only worsened their plights. The removal debates of the 1830s had pitted family against family, weakening tribal solidarity; now the Cherokee, Choctaw, and others were compelled to choose up sides once again. At the onset of the war Indian Territory held almost a hundred thousand Indians. Already factionalized over slavery, the former southeastern Indians were wooed by Confederate representatives with promises of an all-Indian state after the war. About fifty-five hundred Cherokees, Choctaws, Chickasaws, and Creeks sided with the South, another four thousand were recruited to fight for the North. During the hostilities, Indian Territory was pillaged by irregular raiders from North and South, burning Indian homesteads and killing cattle. After the fighting, Confederate and Union Indians suffered equally through the so-called Reconstruction treaties, which requisitioned additional Indian land for railroad right-of-ways and ranches.

Western Indians responded to reservations and land loss in different ways. Warrior tribes defied fresh restrictions against freely hunting and raiding and worshiping their own spirits. Especially in the Plains and the Southwest, armed resistance flared up through the 1860s and 1870s. The year 1871 saw two aging Kiowas, Sitting Bear and White Bear, slip away from their reservation for a final strike at white settlements in Texas. Captured, the seventy-year-old Sitting Bear sang his death song: "O Sun, you remain forever, but we of the Ten Bravest must die. O Earth, you remain forever, but we of the Ten Bravest must die." Then he chewed his wrists to remove his handcuffs, grabbed an empty carbine, and was shot to death. White Bear endured confinement in Texas State Penitentiary for eight years. Then he sang his death song and threw himself off the prison hospital's roof.

Defiance also took religious form, drawing upon inner resources. To many tribespeople their reliable cosmos was collapsing in death and despair. The sense of an impending end to the world had already overcome natives in the East, with "nativistic" religious movements erupting among the Iroquois, Delaware, and Cherokee. Their prophets foresaw apocalyptic fires or floods, with native survivors enjoying a purged and renewed earth, like that before the white man. A few seers preached holy wars, concocting supportive rituals of hypnotic song, dance, and vision-seeking. More hopeful visionaries grafted Indian and white beliefs together to strengthen their peoples through the coming hard times.

Feelings of helplessness overwhelmed others as they faced the depressing realities of reservation life. The era of Black Hawk's forecast seemed at hand, when Indians "would become like white men, so you can't trust them, and there must be, as in white settlements, nearly as many officers as men, to take care of them and keep them in order."

In the vast refugee camp that was Indian Territory, tribal distinctions remained intact despite new religions (peyotism) and a new political sensibility. In 1870, representatives of thirty-four tribes gathered at Okmulgee, Oklahoma, to discuss a constitution for an all-Indian state.

In the Northeast, thanks to the late-eighteenth-century visionary named Handsome Lake, the New York Iroquois staved off cultural disintegration throughout these years. A shrewd amalgam of Christian Quaker and old-time Iroquois values, the strict code of Handsome Lake's "Longhouse Religion" frowned on drinking and strengthened family ties.

In the mesa homelands of the stable, southwestern Pueblo villages, most of their seventeenth-century land grants from Spain became their official U.S. reservations. Periodically their religious and political freedoms fell under government disapproval, but these agricultural city-states remained the least assimilated in Indian America. On the other hand, a patchwork of vulnerable *rancherias*—generally on the poor land ranging from two acres to twenty-five hundred acres—held California Indian peoples who barely survived the gold rush years.

Within the widely scattered networks of native communities across America, many Indians lay low to avoid the white man's meddling. On the surface, they seemed to comply with government programs; underneath they were poor, hungry, ill-housed, defenseless against disease, and passively resistant.

Older Plains warriors sometimes balked at tilling the soil, and quietly slipped into the wilderness to fast and pray. Northwest Coast tribes still held "potlatch" ceremonies in secret, defying the Canadian government's ban. Hopis hid their children in corncribs rather than send them to school. Descendants of Cherokees who slipped into the Great Smoky Mountains rather than remove to Oklahoma lied to census takers who visited their log cabins.

During these years of trial some tribespeople resisted the verdict of the Oglala Lakota holy man, Black Elk: "The nation's hoop is broken and scattered." Others were not so sure. The selections in this chapter evoke what Kiowa Indian novelist N. Scott Momaday terms the "closing in" years—a time of anxious transition, of a bottomless loneliness for the open lands, available animals, and lost relatives of happier days that were, as Buffalo Bird Woman says, "gone forever."

1

THE BUFFALO GO

*I*n the mid-nineteenth century, professional hunters severely thinned the herds *of buffalo on the Great Plains; a single hunter might kill as many as 150 animals a day. Carriage owners in the East had developed a rage for buffalo hide lap robes, and smoked buffalo tongue had become a delicacy. To Indian hunters the near extinction of the buffalo meant the disappearance of their way of life, as a Kiowa woman named Old Lady Horse describes in this folktale.*

EVERYTHING the Kiowas had came from the buffalo. Their tipis were made of buffalo hides, so were their clothes and moccasins. They ate buffalo meat. Their containers were made of hide, or of bladders or stomachs. The buffalo were the life of the Kiowas.

Most of all, the buffalo was part of the Kiowa religion. A white buffalo calf must be sacrificed in the Sun Dance. The priests used parts of the buffalo to make their prayers when they healed people or when they sang to the powers above.

So, when the white men wanted to build railroads, or when they wanted to farm or raise cattle, the buffalo still protected the Kiowas. They tore up the railroad tracks and the gardens. They chased the cattle off the ranges. The buffalo loved their people as much as the Kiowas loved them.

There was war between the buffalo and the white men. The white men built forts in the Kiowa country, and the woolly-headed buffalo soldiers [the Ninth and Tenth Cavalries, made up of black troops] shot the buffalo as fast as they could, but the buffalo kept coming on, coming on, even into the post cemetery at Fort Sill. Soldiers were not enough to hold them back.

Then the white men hired hunters to do nothing but kill the buffalo. Up and down the plains those men ranged, shooting sometimes as many as a hundred buffalo a day. Behind them came the skinners with their wagons. They piled the hides and bones into the wagons until they were full, and then took their loads to the new railroad stations that were being built, to be shipped east to the market. Sometimes there would be a pile of bones as high as a man, stretching a mile along the railroad track.

The buffalo saw that their day was over. They could protect their people no longer. Sadly, the last remnant of the great herd gathered in council, and decided what they would do.

The Kiowas were camped on the north side of Mount Scott, those of them who were still free to camp. One young woman got up very early in the morning. The dawn mist was still rising from Medicine Creek, and as she looked across the water, peering through the haze, she saw the last buffalo herd appear like a spirit dream.

Straight to Mount Scott the leader of the herd walked. Behind him came the cows and their calves, and the few young males who had survived. As the woman watched, the face of the mountain opened.

Inside Mount Scott the world was green and fresh, as it had been when she was a small girl. The rivers ran clear, not red. The wild plums were in blossom, chasing the red buds up the inside slopes. Into this world of beauty the buffalo walked, never to be seen again.

OLD LADY HORSE, *Kiowa*

TAKE CARE OF ME

U pon his surrender to United States Army officers in 1858, the Seminole chief
Wild Cat (Coacoochee) demanded spoils from the victors.

WHEN I WAS A BOY, I saw the white man afar off, and was
told that he was my enemy. I could not shoot him as I would a wolf or a
bear, yet he came upon me. My horse and fields he took from me. He said
he was my friend—He gave me his hand in friendship; I took it, he had a
snake in the other; his tongue was forked; he lied and stung me. I asked
for but a small piece of this land, enough to plant and live on far to the
south—a spot where I could place the ashes of my kindred—a place where
my wife and child could live. This was not granted me. I am about to leave
Florida forever and have done nothing to disgrace it. It was my home; I
loved it, and to leave it is like burying my wife and child. I have thrown
away my rifle and have taken the hand of the white man, and now I say
take care of me!

WILD CAT, *Seminole*

I AM ALONE

D uring a truce talk in 1866 with General Gordon Granger, the famous
Chiricahua Apache chief Cochise made this moving request to remain in
Arizona's Dragoon Mountains rather than be forced to live on the Tularosa Reservation. Granger agreed, but a few months later, Cochise and his followers were
ordered to move to Tularosa; they refused and resumed hostilities for another six
years. After he died in 1874, Cochise was secretly buried in his old Dragoon
Mountains hideout, known thereafter as Cochise Stronghold.

THE SUN HAS BEEN very hot on my head and made me as in a fire; my blood was on fire, but now I have come into this valley and drunk of these waters and washed myself in them and they have cooled me. Now that I am cool I have come with my hands open to you to live in peace with you. I speak straight and do not wish to deceive or be deceived. I want a good, strong and lasting peace.

When God made the world he gave one part to the white man and another to the Apache. Why was it? Why did they come together? Now that I am to speak, the sun, the moon, the earth, the air, the waters, the birds and beasts, even the children unborn shall rejoice at my words. The white people have looked for me long. I am here! What do they want? They have looked for me long; why am I worth so much? If I am worth so much why not mark when I set my foot and look when I spit? The coyotes go about at night to rob and kill; I can not see them; I am not God. I am no longer chief of all the Apaches. I am no longer rich; I am but a poor man. The world was not always this way. I can not command the animals; if I would they would not obey me. God made us not as you; we were born like the animals, in the dry grass, not on beds like you. This is why we do as the animals, go about of a night and rob and steal. If I had such things as you have, I would not do as I do, for then I would not need to do so. There are Indians who go about killing and robbing. I do not command them. If I did, they would not do so. My warriors have been killed in Sonora. I came in here because God told me to do so. He said it was good to be at peace—so I came! I was going around the world with the clouds, and the air, when God spoke to my thought and told me to come in here and be at peace with all. He said the world was for us all; how was it?

When I was young I walked all over this country, east and west, and saw no other people than the Apaches. After many summers I walked again and found another race of people had come to take it. How is it? Why is it that the Apaches wait to die—that they carry their lives on their finger nails? They roam over the hills and plains and want the heavens to fall on them. The Apaches were once a great nation; they are now but few, and because of this they want to die and so carry their lives on their finger nails. Many have been killed in battle. You must speak straight so that your words may go as sunlight to our hearts. Tell me, if the Virgin Mary has walked throughout all the land, why has she never entered the wigwam of the Apache? Why have we never seen or heard her?

I have no father nor mother; I am alone in the world. No one cares for Cochise; that is why I do not care to live, and wish the rocks to fall on me and cover me up. If I had a father and a mother like you, I would be with them and they with me. When I was going around the world, all were asking for Cochise. Now he is here—you see him and hear him—are you glad? If so, say so. Speak, Americans and Mexicans, I do not wish to hide anything from you nor have you hide anything from me; I will not lie to you; do not lie to me. I want to live in these mountains; I do not want to go to Tularosa. That is a long ways off. The flies on those mountains eat out the eyes of the horses. The bad spirits live there. I have drunk of these waters and they have cooled me; I do not want to leave here.

COCHISE, *Chiricahua Apache*

4

I HAVE SPOKEN

C razy Horse, the great Oglala Sioux leader and hero of the Battle of the Little Big Horn, never had his photograph taken, and was on his deathbed before his thoughts were ever recorded on paper. Bayoneted by a Sioux guard at Fort Robinson, Nebraska, in 1877, he is supposed to have said these final words to Agent Jesse M. Lee.

MY FRIEND, I do not blame you for this. Had I listened to you this trouble would not have happened to me. I was not hostile to the white man. Sometimes my young men would attack the Indians who were their enemies and took their ponies. They did it in return.

We had buffalo for food, and their hides for clothing and our tipis. We preferred hunting to a life of idleness on the reservations, where we were driven against our will. At times we did not get enough to eat, and we were not allowed to leave the reservation to hunt.

"Dangerous" war chiefs were kept under government surveillance until they died. Here is Geronimo (seated on cannon) at Fort Pickens, Florida, with fellow Chiricahuas, Nachise (center) and Mangus.

We preferred our own way of living. We were no expense to the government then. All we wanted was peace and to be left alone. Soldiers were sent out in the winter, who destroyed our villages. Then "Long Hair" [Custer] came in the same way. They say we massacred him, but he would have done the same to us had we not defended ourselves and fought to the last. Our first impulse was to escape with our squaws and papooses, but we were so hemmed in that we had to fight.

After that I went up on Tongue River with a few of my people and lived in peace. But the government would not let me alone. Finally, I came back to the Red Cloud Agency. . . . I came here with the agent [Lee] to talk with Big White Chief, but was not given a chance. They tried to confine me, I tried to escape, and a soldier ran his bayonet into me.

I have spoken.

CRAZY HORSE, *Oglala Sioux*

5

I WANT TO LOOK FOR MY CHILDREN

J*ust thirty miles from the Canadian border and the freedom he prized so dearly, Chief Joseph and his band of Nez Percé fugitives were finally caught by Colonel Nelson Miles and General O. O. Howard. On October 5, 1877, Chief Joseph made his now famous surrender statement.*

TELL GENERAL HOWARD I know his heart. What he told me before, I have in my heart.

I am tired of fighting. Our chiefs are killed. Looking Glass is dead. Too-hoolhoolzote is dead. The old men are all dead.

It is the young men who say yes and no. He who led on the young men is dead. It is cold and we have no blankets. The little children are freezing to death.

Old enemies meet in 1904: the Nez Percé chief, Joseph, and the general who pursued him to within sight of freedom in Canada, O. O. Howard.

My people, some of them, have run away to the hills, and have no blankets, no food; no one knows where they are—perhaps freezing to death.

I want to have time to look for my children and see how many I can find. Maybe I shall find them among the dead.

Hear me, my chiefs. I am tired; my heart is sick and sad.

From where the sun now stands I will fight no more forever.

CHIEF JOSEPH, *Nez Percé*

6

NO DAWN TO THE EAST

To one tribal elder, the end of the Indian world as he had known it felt like this.

MY SUN IS SET. My day is done. Darkness is stealing over me. Before I lie down to rise no more I will speak to my people. Hear me, for this is not the time to tell a lie. The Great Spirit made us, and gave us this land we live in. He gave us the buffalo, antelope, and deer for food and clothing. Our hunting grounds stretched from the Mississippi to the great mountains. We were free as the winds and heard no man's commands. We fought our enemies, and feasted our friends. Our braves drove away all who would take our game. They captured women and horses from our foes. Our children were many and our herds were large. Our old men talked with spirits and made good medicine. Our young men hunted and made love to the girls. Where the tipi was, there we stayed, and no house imprisoned us. No one said, "To this line is my land, to that is yours." Then the white man came to our hunting grounds, a stranger. We gave him meat and presents, and told him go in peace. He looked on our women and stayed to live in our tipis. His fellows came to build their roads across our hunting grounds. He brought among us the mysterious iron that shoots. He brought with him the magic water that makes men foolish. With his trinkets and beads he even bought the girl I loved. I said, "The white man is not a friend, let us kill him." But their numbers were greater than blades of grass. They took away the buffalo and shot down our best warriors. They took away our lands and surrounded us by fences. Their soldiers camped outside with cannon to shoot us down. They wiped the trails of our people from the face of the prairies. They forced our children to forsake the ways of their fathers. When I turn to the east I see no dawn. When I turn to the west the approaching night hides all.

ANONYMOUS, *tribe unknown*

7

GONE FOREVER

I*n the mid-nineteenth century, when she was a child, Buffalo Bird Woman of the Hidatsa tribe lived along a bend of the Missouri River named "Like a Fishhook." As an old woman she looks back on those faraway times.*

I AM an old woman now. The buffaloes and black-tail deer are gone, and our Indian ways are almost gone. Sometimes I find it hard to believe that I ever lived them.

My little son grew up in the white man's school. He can read books, and he owns cattle and has a farm. He is a leader among our Hidatsa people, helping teach them to follow the white man's road.

He is kind to me. We no longer live in an earth lodge, but in a house with chimneys; and my son's wife cooks by a stove.

But for me, I cannot forget our old ways.

Often in summer I rise at daybreak and steal out to the cornfields; and as I hoe the corn I sing to it, as we did when I was young. No one cares for our corn songs now.

Sometimes at evening I sit, looking out on the big Missouri. The sun sets, and dusk steals over the water. In the shadows I seem again to see our Indian village, with smoke curling upward from the earth lodges; and in the river's roar I hear the yells of the warriors, the laughter of little children as of old. It is but an old woman's dream. Again I see but shadows and hear only the roar of the river; and tears come into my eyes. Our Indian life, I know, is gone forever.

BUFFALO BIRD WOMAN, *Hidatsa*

Buffalo Bird Woman, in 1926

8

THIS AWFUL LONELINESS

These are the words of an old Omaha tribesman remembering the landscape as he and his people had once known it along the western bank of the Missouri River, between the Platte and Niobrara rivers, in present-day Nebraska.

W H E N I was a youth, the country was very beautiful. Along the rivers were belts of timberland, where grew cottonwood, maple, elm, ash, hickory, and walnut trees, and many other kinds. Also there were many kinds of vines and shrubs. And under these grew many good herbs and beautiful flowering plants.

In both the woodland and the prairie I could see the trails of many kinds of animals and could hear the cheerful songs of many kinds of birds. When I walked abroad, I could see many forms of life, beautiful living creatures which *Wakanda* [the Great Spirit] had placed here; and these were, after their manner, walking, flying, leaping, running, playing all about.

But now the face of all the land is changed and sad. The living creatures are gone. I see the land desolate and I suffer an unspeakable sadness. Sometimes I wake in the night, and I feel as though I should suffocate from the pressure of this awful feeling of loneliness.

ANONYMOUS, *Omaha*

9

A WISH

The virtual extinction of the buffalo on the northern Plains contributed to the death by starvation of some six hundred Blackfoot Indians in the winter of 1883–84. Before he himself died during that "Starvation Winter," a Blackfoot named Flint Knife expressed this thought.

I W I S H that white people had never come into my country.

FLINT KNIFE, *Blackfoot*

RESERVATION TO RESURGENCE

(Preceding page) *The revered Siskiyou Mountains of the Yurok Indians of north-western California, with sacred Doctor Rock looming in the distance. Controversy over this snow-banked road reached the U.S. Supreme Court in 1988, when local Indians lost their campaign to halt access by lumber trucks and campers into their heartland.*

THE VERY SMALL
ISLANDS

In this view of the Northern Cheyenne Reservation on Tongue River, Montana, the major institutions of a typical reservation are shown: church, offices, and warehouse for distribution of supplies.

I n spring 1865 a United States senator visited Sand Creek in Colorado Territory and picked up the jawbone of an Indian child "whose milk teeth had not been shed." The youngster was among two hundred Cheyenne Indians whose camp was flying an American flag when they were killed the previous autumn by U.S. soldiers.

Leading the assault was Colonel J. M. Chivington, whose reputed cry— "kill and scalp all, big and little, nits make lice"—expressed how many white westerners felt toward Indians. To other citizens back East, however, Sand Creek exemplified a cruel and outmoded way of handling Indians. Their alternative was compulsory assimilation into white society.

The senator, a conservative Republican named James R. Dolittle, was investigating "the conditions of Indian tribes and their treatment by the civil and military authorities of the U.S." All that summer Dolittle and six colleagues visited Indian settlements in the Plains, the Southwest, and the Pacific Coast. They interviewed government agents, frontier traders, and missionaries who dealt with Indians every day.

But they also heard horror stories from Indians themselves. The Yankton Sioux described corrupt Indian agents and vicious U.S. soldiers. The Santee Sioux at Crow Creek told of starving women and children beaten for scavenging the leftover heads and entrails of butchered cattle. The Winnebago of Dakota City talked of young and old alike dying from government-issue soups boiled from rotten beef liver.

President Abraham Lincoln was busy with the Civil War, but he had learned enough about the notorious "Indian system," with its unscrupulous officials and helpless Indians, to promise: "If we get through this war and I live, this Indian system shall be reformed." Lincoln was assassinated just as the Dolittle investigators departed for the West, however, and they were still out there when the Civil War ended.

Rebuilding a war-torn country became Washington's immediate concern. Meanwhile, the crusade to reform the Bureau of Indian Affairs and assimilate Native Americans into white society attracted many former opponents of slavery. They dreamt of transforming tribespeople into idealized white women and men. Indians would attend Sunday services, use English, learn practical skills, wear pants or long dresses, become self-sufficient farmers on single-family farms, and strive toward full American citizenship. This vision dominated Indian affairs for the next sixty years.

When Dolittle's report finally appeared in 1867, its Indian testimonies were buried in an appendix. As a Chippewa leader from the Great Lakes remarked years later, "Generally, our Great Father sends big men. They come up—find condition on Indians. Make many papers for benefit of Indians . . . when they go back papers never come up." While Dolittle accused the military of brutality and reservation agents of greed, he accepted the "Vanishing American" theory of his day, which assumed that Indians were becoming extinct due to warfare, disease, liquor, prostitution, and what he called "the natural effect of one race replacing another." As town-building and homesteading surged after the Civil War, reformers like Dolittle pled for the government to treat Indians compassionately during their declining years.

But this Vanishing Indian idea ignored the fact that, despite centuries of forced migration, debilitating warfare, rampaging epidemics, and psychological resignation, over three hundred thousand enumerated Indians were still alive in 1865. They survived in official reservations and in tiny, little-known enclaves with no federal recognition. They endured in shanty hamlets on the outskirts of newly settled western towns or they blended or intermarried into New England neighborhoods where they felt safer keeping their tribal identities to themselves. They were permanent dwellers in centuries-old southwestern adobe villages or they existed out of sight in cypress-shrouded encampments throughout the Florida swamps.

Also in 1865, insurgent Apaches, Nez Percé, Sioux, Cheyenne, Modocs, and Kickapoos along the Mexican border were threatening settlers, stealing livestock, and hunting and traveling at will. While the government overlooked the independence of reclusive Seminoles in Florida or isolated Cherokees in North Carolina, it took military action against Indians who were striking back. Meanwhile, Washington politicians and lobbyists turned their attention to reservation Indians who had already been coerced or beaten into submission.

In 1865 few would disagree with General William T. Sherman's sarcastic definition of an Indian reservation: "a parcel of land set aside for Indians, surrounded by thieves." Even before the Civil War, rumors reached Washington of how this thievery worked. Muckraking journalists railed against the "Indian Ring," conspiracies between rotten politicians, dishonest Indian personnel, and the manufacturers and traders who supplied food, clothing, and tools which treaties had promised the Indians. The Civil War only worsened this situation as funds for Indian welfare were cut back and fewer troops patrolled reservations against squatters, cattle rustlers, and liquor bootleggers.

A political appointee, the Indian agent clothed and fed "his" Indians and implemented whatever policy was currently popular back east. Far from Washington's eye, he wielded absolute power. He monitored the comings and goings of suspicious outsiders on "his" reservation, and discouraged Indians from "barbaric" old-time rituals and social gatherings. As buffalo and fur-bearing animals thinned out, reservation Indians became utterly dependent upon their agents.

Indian agent, as carved by Coast Salish Indian, North Vancouver Reserve

The situation was ripe for skulduggery. Politicians and bureaucrats who dispensed agent jobs as part of the patronage system skimmed off federal funds before they ever reached the reservation, then demanded kickbacks from agents they favored. Cattle dealers who contracted with agents to supply their reservations with beef received top dollar for poor-grade stock, split the profits with agents, rustled or repurchased the animals at lower prices, then drove the scrawny herd to the next reservation where they repeated the scam.

Agents sold off reservation resources, such as timber and mineral rights, to cronies or high bidders. Goods intended for Indians were stolen outright or replaced with shoddy substitutes manufactured expressly for the Indian market. By treaty, for example, the western Sioux were due tools, clothing, and dry goods. They received thin canvas suits instead of woolen garments, the boots were sloppily nailed with third-rate leather, and the iron shovels were so soft they bent like tin. Indians got resentful and cynical. "The Indian agent they have sent us is so mean," complained one Plains chief, "that he carries around in his pocket a linen rag into which he blows his nose, for fear he will blow away something of value."

To be sure, there were also high-principled agents and sympathetic military officers, who helped Indians during these trying times. Many traders and former frontiersmen, married into Indian tribes and knowledgeable in both Indian and white worlds, also spoke out on behalf of Indians. Whether or not an agent was a crook, a benevolent tyrant, or a fatherly administrator, however, he usually undermined the authority of the old-time chiefs.

Some agents bypassed traditional leaders to handpick Indians they could easily dominate. "If there had been an election, I would have been satisfied," recalled a Blackfoot chief from the Canadian Plains. "The big white chief sent orders for me to give up the chieftainship medal to Crow Eagle, but I refused to do so. . . . The chief of police gave the medal to the agent, and the agent gave it to Crow Eagle, so we heard, but no one saw him give it to him; it was done in the dark."

To police their own people the agent put selected Indians into uniform. Reservations created a new climate of surveillance and subservience, as the Navajo leader Chee Dodge later warned his followers, ". . . the President has a rope on every one of you . . . if you try to make trouble, he will pull on all the ropes . . . you disobey the agent's orders, you disobey the President's orders."

In 1869, when Ulysses S. Grant became president, he, like Lincoln, pledged reform of the Bureau of Indian Affairs. By and large the humanitarian "friends of the Indian" behind him were ignorant about the inner workings of Native American societies. They did not want Indians to continue to live as Indians, but they believed that as God's children they had every right to live as white people. If decent civilians became agents, they argued, reservations could be training grounds for Indians. While children picked up manual trades at boarding schools, their parents would cultivate crops and milk cows. Once Indian families learned to feed and clothe themselves, their reservation lands could be subdivided, or "allotted," into single-family homesteads. They would forswear tribal allegiances and dissolve into American society.

At this stage Indians were not asked what they thought about this program. In actuality, just being fenced in was hard enough for many to take. As Sioux chief Sitting Bull put it, "I do not wish to be shut up in a corral. It is bad for young men to be fed by an agent. It makes them lazy and drunken. All [reservation] agency Indians I have seen are worthless. They are neither red warriors nor white farmers."

Nor were most Indians excited about giving up the kinship ties and religious traditions that lent joy and meaning to their lives. But the reformers were insistent about changing Indians for their own good. The centuries-old conflict between whites and Indians was shifting from open warfare for land to a struggle over hearts and minds. Not all white people supported this "Peace Policy" approach either. Many westerners blamed Indian uprisings on the laxity of military pressure and the mollycoddling of "Indian lovers." They agreed with the War Department: only a "Force Policy" kept meddlesome Indians in their place.

On the Indian question President Grant thus faced a divided nation. At first he sided with the reformers, promising only to deploy troops so that "Indians should be made as comfortable on, and uncomfortable off, their reservations as it was in the power of government." To recruit honest agents he looked to religious organizations, such as the Society of Friends. By 1872 the Grant administration had installed men from thirteen separate religious groups to oversee seventy-three Indian agencies across the country.

Heeding Dolittle's advice, Grant also named ten volunteer philanthropists to a new Board of Indian Commissioners. This civilian, largely ceremonial body, which lasted until 1933, tried to oversee Indian policy in Washington and monitored Indians' treatment out in the field. But outbreaks such as the Modoc Indian War of 1872–73 in northern California continued to spark military campaigns to smash Indians for good, while violence by settlers against Indians revived the outcry of reformers. And Grant could not eradicate illegal speculation on Indian lands, or selling licenses to trade on reservations to the top bidder.

This chapter offers Indian memories of life on what Sioux chief Red Cloud described as "very small islands"—the Indian reservations of the post–Civil War period.

1

TREATED BETTER BY WOLVES

When congressional investigators traveled west in 1865, they heard of Indian misery in Dakota Territory. The following accounts were recorded by the Dolittle Commission from Struck By The Ree of the Yankton Sioux and Passing Hail of the Santee Sioux.

In the first, Struck By The Ree offers a litany of grievances against Indian agents and soldiers assigned to keep the peace on his reservation. Struck By The Ree was born in August 1804. That very week the explorers Lewis and Clark were guests in his village; it was said that Captain Meriwether Lewis had swaddled the baby in the national flag, baptizing him publicly "an American." Much later, during the 1862 outbreak of the eastern Sioux, Struck By The Ree reportedly cordoned his warriors so as to protect white settlements from hostile Indians.

In the second piece of testimony, Passing Hail tells how his subtribe of the Dakota nation suffered at the hands of white officials.

THE FIRST AGENT was Redfield; and when he came there he borrowed blankets from me to sleep upon, and agreed to return them, but never did, though I asked for them. Goods have been stored up stairs in the warehouse, and have all disappeared; perhaps the rats eat them; I don't know what became of them. If they bring any goods for the Indians to eat and put them in the warehouse, the agents live out of them, and the mess-house where travellers stop has been supplied from the Indians' goods, and pay has been taken by the agents, and they have put the money in their pockets and taken it away with them. I have seen them take the goods from the storehouse of the Indians and take them to the mess-house, and I have had to pay for a meal for myself at the mess-house, and so have others of our Indians had to pay for meals at the mess-house, prepared from their own goods. . . .

When Redfield left the agency, a steamboat came in the night and took away fifteen boxes of goods, so that the Indians would not know it; but the Indians were too sharp for him. . . . Mr. Redfield said to me, "when I am gone you will meet with a great many agents; but you will never meet one like me." I think I never want to see one like him. . . .

The reason the whites have trouble with the Indians is on account of the agents. When the goods come they are not according to the treaty; they never fulfill the treaty. When the agent goes away he says he is going to leave these things to be done by his successor. When Agent Burleigh came he made fine promises of what he would do. I asked for my invoice, but he would not let me have it; and I told him what my grandfather told me. I think the agents are all alike. The agent puts his foot on me as though I were a skunk. And the agents are all getting rich and we are getting poor. . . .

When Burleigh brought the goods the first time he put the goods on the bank of the river; and there was one bale of fine goods with them, and Burleigh said the goods belonged to the Indians; and one of my young men come and told me about the fine bale of goods, and I went and examined it, and it was fine goods, and would have made nice breech-clouts; but we received none of it, and don't know what become of it. This was the second year Burleigh was there. . . .

A steamboat arrived with our goods, and the goods were put out; Burleigh said they were our goods, and they were marked for us; there were five boxes. There were some officers and soldiers there. The boxes remained there on the bank until the next day. At night somebody scratched the marks off and put on other marks. . . . I think the way the white men treated us is worse than the wolves do. We have a way in the winter of putting our dead up on scaffolds up from the ground, but the soldiers cut down the scaffolds and cut off the hair of the dead, and if they had good teeth they pulled them out, and some of them cut off the heads of the dead and carried them away. . . .

Another time when General Sully came up he passed through the middle of our field, turned all his cattle and stock into our corn and destroyed the whole of it. . . . The soldiers set fire to the prairie and burnt up four oi our lodges and all there was in them, and three horses. . . .

The soldiers are very drunken and come to our place—they have arms and guns; they run after our women and fire into our houses and lodges; one soldier came along and wanted one of our young men to drink, but he would not, and turned to go away, and the soldier shot at him. Before the soldiers came along we had good health; but once the soldiers come along they go to my squaws and want to sleep with them, and the squaws being hungry will sleep with them in order to get something to eat, and will get a bad disease, and then the squaws turn to their husbands and give them the bad disease. . . .

I think if you come up to our agency you will laugh in the first place, and then be mad to see our storehouse in the same building with the trader's store. I want the store moved away a mile, so that it won't be so handy to our goods; I want you to have this changed. I hope my grandfather will see that the store is moved away from my warehouse, because the trader's store is under the floor where my goods are stored. I sometimes have bad dreams; I feel that there may be cracks that my goods may fall through.

STRUCK BY THE REE, *Yankton Sioux*

WHEN THE PROVISIONS were brought here the agent told us the food was to be divided between us and the Winnebagoes, and only five sacks of flour were given us per week through the winter; they were issued to us each Saturday.

They brought beef and piled it up here; they built a box and put the beef in it and steamed it and made soup; they put salt and pepper in it, and that is the reason these hills about here are filled with children's graves; it seemed as though they wanted to kill us.

We have grown up among white folks, and we know the ways of white folks. White folks do not eat animals that die themselves; but the animals that died here were piled up with the beef here and were fed out to us; and when the women and children, on account of their great hunger, tried to get the heads, blood, and entrails, when the butchering was being done, they were whipped and put in the guard-house.

It is not right for me to omit anything. The heads, entrails, and liver were piled about here in the stockade, and the agent would keep watch of them, and when he wanted some work done he would pay for the work with the most rotten part of it. He employed the Indians to work, and paid them with the most rotten part, as above stated.

Last fall the agent told us to go out on a hunt, and while they were out on the hunt the goods came, and we suppose the reason he wanted us to go on the hunt was that he did not want us to see what was done with the goods.

Last fall the agent called the chiefs and said he would give us the goods. The next day we came up, and the agent, from the top window of the warehouse, threw out the goods; he threw out a dress for each woman and a blanket for each family. I think there were over one hundred blankets given out at that time.

They brought us here to a windy country, and we supposed the wind had blown the goods away; but we heard afterwards that there were some found in the houses in the stockade. We heard that the agent traded some of our goods away, and we suppose he traded them for robes and furs. We think if he had not have traded them away there would have been plenty to go round, and the women would not have been crying with cold. . . .

The President gave us some laws, and we have changed ourselves to white men, put on white man's clothes and adopted the white man's ways, and we supposed we would have a piece of ground somewhere where we could live; but no one can live here and live like a white man. I have changed my body to a white man's body. I have not told any lie.

PASSING HAIL, *Santee Sioux*

2
WE LOST EVERYTHING

Here a Navajo headman and silversmith named Herrero describes abysmal conditions among his people in southeastern New Mexico. Nearly the entire Navajo tribe was confined to a dreary military fort near a site known as Bosque Redondo, guarded by armed soldiers. Because of disease and depression, Herrero told Dolittle investigators, his people were "dying as though they were shooting at them with a rifle."

His own three sons and two daughters had just perished. "There is a hospital here for us," he said, "but all who go in never come out." In this selection, Herrero begs for relief from a land that won't grow corn, where his people can't raise sheep, and where poverty, loneliness, and prostitution are destroying their spirit.

Not until 1868 would the U.S. government finally conclude a peace treaty with these Navajo, letting them return to Arizona. Before taking that "Long Walk" home—to their new 3.5-million-acre reservation—nearly a quarter of the tribe would perish during the Fort Sumner ordeal.

IF WE HAD the wool we could make all the clothes for the tribe. All of us know how to cultivate by irrigation. There is plenty of land but somehow the crops do not come out well. Last year the worms destroyed the

Rounded-up Navajos under guard at Fort Sumner, New Mexico, mid-1860s

crops. There is plenty of land and when the ditches are all cut out there will be land enough. There is plenty of water. There is plenty of pasture for all our stock. Some have 25, 30, or 40 [sheep], but more have none. None have a hundred.

We try and keep our sheep for their milk, and only kill them when necessary, when the rations are short or smell bad. We depend on the milk of the sheep to live and to give to our little children. We are honest and do not kill each other's sheep. We own our animals ourselves, and not in common. . . .

Some officers at Fort Canby told us when we got here the government would give us herds of horses, sheep and cattle, and other things we needed, but we have not received them. We had to lose a good deal of our property on account of the war, and the Utahs stole the rest from us. We have been at war with the Utahs nine years, and about the same number of years with the Mexicans. Before the war with the Utahs and Mexicans we had everything we wanted, but now have lost everything. . . .

Some of the soldiers do not treat us well. When at work, if we stop a little they kick us or do something else, but generally they treat us well. We do not mind if an officer punishes us, but do not like to be treated badly by the soldiers. Our women sometimes come to the tents outside the fort and make contracts with the soldiers to stay with them for a night, and give them five dollars or something else. But in the morning they take away what they gave them and kick them off. This happens most every day. In the night they leave the fort and go to the Indian camps. The women are not forced, but consent willingly. A good many of the women have venereal disease. . . .

We would rather prefer to be in our own country, although we have lost everything we want here. We are all of this opinion and would like to have you send us back. And if you have any presents to give us we will distribute them among us. If we are sent back we promise never to commit an act of hostility. . . .

HERRERO, *Navajo*

3

THE WAY AGENTS GET RICH

Sarah Winnemucca always spoke her mind. A nationally known Paiute Indian critic of reservation policy in the late nineteenth century, she had been born in 1844 in present-day Nevada. Although her father, Chief Winnemucca, had guided Captain John C. Fremont to California, her childhood was relatively free from white influence.

After the Paiute War of 1860, however, tensions rose between her tribe and encroaching settlers. Sarah's own mother, sister, and brother died at white hands. In 1872 she experienced the removal of her tribe to a temporary reservation in Oregon, and then another forced move to a second reservation in Washington State, before they were allowed back to Nevada.

Sarah was scarred by these experiences. Her bitter chronicle, Life Among the Paiutes, published in 1883, described her eviction from a Catholic convent school because she was Indian, and a series of personal feuds with Indian agents in Oregon and Nevada. This selection opens with Paiute experiences on their earliest Nevada reservation. It ends with the story of her brother, a leader named Natchez, whose defiance of the Indian agent's power led to imprisonment at Alcatraz Island in California.

I N 1 8 6 4 — 6 5 there was a governor by the name of Nye. There were no whites living on the reservation at that time, and there was not any agent as yet. My people were living there and fishing, as they had always done. Some white men came down from Virginia City to fish. My people went up to Carson City to tell Governor Nye that some white men were fishing on their reservation. He sent down some soldiers to drive them away. Mr. Nye is the only governor who ever helped my people,—I mean that protected them when they called on him in this way.

In 1865 we had another trouble with our white brothers. It was early in the spring, and we were then living at Dayton, Nevada, when a company of soldiers came through the place and stopped and spoke to some of my people, and said, "You have been stealing cattle from the white people at Harney Lake." They said also that they would kill everything that came in their way, men, women, and children. . . .

After the soldiers had killed all but some little children and babies still tied up in their baskets, the soldiers took them also, and set the camp on fire and threw them into the flames to see them burn alive. I had one baby brother killed there. My sister jumped on father's best horse and ran away. As she ran, the soldiers ran after her; but, thanks be to the Good Father in the Spirit-land, my dear sister got away. This almost killed my poor papa. Yet my people kept peaceful. . . .

I will tell you the doings of the agents in [that] agency. The first six who came I did not know. In 1866, after my poor mother and sister Mary died, I came down from Virginia City to live with my brother Natchez, while there were some white men living on the agency. They had a great many cattle on the reservation at the time. My people did not know how to work as yet.

The agent was living there, and had a store of dry goods which he sold to my people. I staid [sic] with my brother all winter, and got along very poorly, for we had nothing to eat half of the time. Sometimes we would go to the agent's house and he would get my sister-in-law to wash some clothes, and then he would give us some flour to take home.

In the month of May the agent sold an Indian man some powder. He crossed the river, when he was met by one of the agent's men, who shot him dead on the spot, because he had the powder. My brother and I did not know what to do. All our people were wild with excitement. Brother and I thought he did wrong to sell the powder to one of our men, knowing it was against the law. . . . this is the way all the Indian agents get rich. The first thing they do is to start a store; the next thing is to take in cattle men, and cattle men pay the agent one dollar a head. In this way they get rich very soon, so that they can have their gold-headed canes, with their names engraved on them. . . .

While Batemann was agent, I was asked to act as interpreter to the Shoshones by a man called Captain Dodge, agent for the Shoshone Indians. He was going to issue clothing to them at a place called Battle Mountain. My brother Natchez went all about to summon the people there. . . . It took three days for the people to come up. Oh, such an issue! It was enough to make a doll laugh. A family numbering eight persons got two blankets, three shirts, no dress-goods. Some got a fishhook and line; some got one and a half yards of flannel, blue and red; the largest issue was to families that camped together, numbering twenty-three persons: four blankets, three pieces of red flannel, and some of blue, three shirts, three hooks and lines, two kettles. It was the saddest affair I ever saw. . . .

Then came another agent by the name of Spencer. He was a better one than we had ever had. He issued some blankets to some old men and women and blind people, and gave brother some pieces of land to work upon. He then gave my people wagons,—about ten altogether; and he had his daughter brought as a teacher, at the rate of fifty dollars a month. But he soon died, and then came our present agent.

He was not married at the time, but he very soon learned that there was money to be made, so he went back and got married. Of course he put his wife in as teacher. Mr. MacMasters, for that is his name, has his own method of making my people divide the produce. If they raise five sacks of grain, they give one sack for the Big Father in Washington; if they have only three sacks, they still have to send one. Every fourth load of hay goes to the Big Father at Washington, yet he does not give my people the seed.

The head-farmer, who is called Mushrush, never shows my people how to work. This is why they said, "Why does the Big Father want us to pay him when he does not give us the seed? We have to pay for the seed ourselves." Both the agent and farmer told my people they would have to pay it or the Big Father would take away their wagons. So my people talked it over and said, "We will pay it."

Later they got up a paper, which the agent and the farmer wanted my people to sign. The subchief would not put his hand to the pen. He said to the agent,—"I have been working for so many years, and I have never

Outspoken Paiute activist Sarah Winnemucca (left). *She often found herself in conflict with reservation officials, such as Agent W. V. Rinehart* (right), *whose treatment of Paiutes she protested in the 1870s.*

received anything as yet. You say it is supplies you are sending me and my people; but I am sick and tired of lies, and I won't sign any paper."

Of course our agent, Mr. MacMasters, told him to leave the reservation. His wagon was taken from him. At this my people sent me down to San Francisco to tell the commanding officer. I did so. I gave Gen. McDowell a full account of the doings, and he reported him to the authorities.

The following spring my poor brother Natchez went to the agent and asked him to help him to a plough, and to give him a set of harness. He told my brother to go away. "You and your sister," he said, "talk about me all the time. I don't want you and your sister here."

At this my poor brother got angry and said to him, "This is my reservation, not yours. I am going to stay here just as long as I like. My poor father and

I never got so much as an old rag from any agent that ever came here." At this our minister got angry, and telegraphed to the soldiers to come and take brother and carry him to the Acotrass [Alcatraz] Islands.

He wrote a letter, saying all my people wanted him to send my brother away where they could never see him any more. After he had written it, he called up all the head men of our people, and told them he had written to their father in Washington for good clothing for them, and wished them to sign the paper. Of course, they did not know any better; they put their names to the paper, and signed their chief away! So the soldiers came and took brother to San Francisco, Cal.

SARAH WINNEMUCCA, Paiute

4

THE CAREER OF ELY PARKER

Ely Parker was not the sort of man to express his feelings in public. In these two selections, however, he does reflect about Indian and white relations and his own unusual career. Ely Samuel Parker was a Seneca and Huron leader from northern New York State. As a youth he assisted the anthropologist Lewis Henry Morgan, and planned on a legal career. His people and white supporters expected great things of him. But upon passing his exams, Parker was denied certification because he was an Indian—and, hence, not a U.S. citizen.

Without protest, Parker shifted his profession to civil engineering, but then was caught up in the Civil War. As personal secretary to General Ulysses S. Grant, he drafted the surrender agreement at Appomattox. As president, Grant named his trusted aide as the country's first native commissioner of Indian affairs.

Great things were again expected of Parker, but he was in a political hot seat. Grant's opponents charged him, among others, with defrauding the government. Although an investigation cleared Parker's name, he had had enough of racial intolerance and resigned. Later he ruminated about his experiences in a letter to a white writer named Harriet Converse.

FOR MANY YEARS I was a constant visitor at the State and Federal capitals either seeking legislative relief or in attendance at State and

Federal courts. Being only a mere lad, the pale-faced officials with whom I came in contact, flattered me and declared that one so young must be extraordinarily endowed to be charged with the conduct of such weighty affairs. I pleased my people in eventually bringing their troubles to a successful and satisfactory termination. I prepared and had approved by the proper authorities a code of laws and rules for the conduct of affairs among themselves and settled them for all time or, for so long as Hawenneyo should let them live. . . .

The War of the Rebellion had broken out among the pale-faces, a terrible contest between the slaveholding and non-slaveholding sections of the United States. I had, through the Hon. Wm. H. Seward, personally tendered my services for the non-slaveholding interest. Mr. Seward in short said to me that the struggle in which I wished to assist, was an affair between white men and one in which the Indian was not called on to act. "The fight must be made and settled by the white men alone," he said. "Go home, cultivate your farm, and we will settle our own troubles without any Indian aid."

I did go home and planted crops and myself on the farm, sometimes not leaving it for four and six weeks at a time. But the quarrel of the whites was not so easily or quickly settled. It was not a wrangle of boys, but a struggle of giants and the country was being racked to its very foundations. . . .

Then came to me in my forest home a paper bearing the great red seal of the War Department at Washington. It was an officer's commission in the Army of the United States. . . . I went from the East to the West and from the West to the East again. They heard of me in great battles and they knew of my association with the great commander of all the Union armies and how I upheld the right arm of his strength, and they said, "How great and powerful is our chief!"

The quarrel between the white men ended. The great commander with his military family settled in Washington, where the great council-fire of his nation was annually lighted and blazed in all its glory and fury. As an humble member of this military family I was the envy of many a pale-faced subordinate embryo-general who said in whisper, "Parker must be a genius, he is so great and powerful."

In a few years my military chieftain was made head and front of the whole American people, and in his partiality he placed me at the head of the management of the Indian Affairs of the United States. I was myself an Indian and presumably understood them, their wants and the manipulation of their affairs generally. Then again went out among the whites and Indians the words, "Parker must be a genius, he is so great and powerful."

The Indians were universally pleased, and they were all willing to be quiet and remain at peace, and were even asking to be taught civilization and Christianity. I put an end to all wars either among themselves or with their white brothers, and I sent professed Christian whites who waxed rich and fat from the plundering of the poor Indians, nor were there teacherships enough to give places to all the hungry and impecunious Christians. Then was the cry raised by all who believed themselves injured or unprovided for, "Nay, this Parker is an Indian genius; he is grown too great and powerful; he doth injure our business and take the bread from the mouths of our families and the money from out of our pockets; now, therefore, let us write and put him out of power, so that we may feast as heretofore."

They made their onslaught on my poor innocent head and made the air foul with their malicious and poisonous accusations. They were defeated, but it was no longer a pleasure to discharge patriotic duties in the face of foul slander and abuse. I gave up a thankless position to enjoy my declining days in peace and quiet.

ELY S. PARKER, *Seneca-Iroquois*

5

ANNIE MAKES HER CHOICE

Born in 1867, just after the Civil War, the young girl Annie Lowry faced a painful choice. Her father was a well-to-do white cattleman near Lovelock, Nevada; her mother was a northern Paiute Indian. Every Indian community had its mixed-blood members, who had to make similar decisions over which side of their parentage and ethnic identity to emphasize.

As described in her poignant autobiography, Annie never really overcame the major crisis in her life, which is sketched in this excerpt. For mixed-bloods, the conflicts between Indian and white ways of life were waged first at home.

. . . I AM A HALF-BREED. That means I live on the fringes of two races. My white friends think I am just a plain old Paiute, while the Indian say I think I am better than they because my father was a white man.

When the time came to make a choice between the Indians and the white race, I made up my mind to be an Indian. At that time I felt resentful toward my white father because he was not fair to my mother. I was determined that no white man would ever make me suffer as Jerome Lowry, my father, a white man, made my little Indian mother suffer. I know I was right to choose the Indians for my people because I love them more. Anything Indian I learned quickly, but to the white teaching my mind was closed. . . .

In the vague hope that I would grow into an intelligent, attractive "Indian Princess" whom he could parade before his hated stepmother back in Virginia, my father took me from our dugout home to begin my education in a one-teacher school.

My father named me "Annie" for his sister and with patience saw to it that I spoke my first words in English rather than the Indian tongue. He had run away from home when he was thirteen or fourteen, and while he was clever, well-read, and a wonderful businessman, he did not reckon with the forces of Indian training and tradition. His vain, silly ambition would have had more chance of coming true if his work had kept him home after I was four or five years old. Then he could have attended to my education. Instead, when he was at Blue Wing on the cattle range and at Lowry Wells, which he dug from a spring, he would be gone for six weeks at a time. However, when he was home, he insisted that I speak good English and discouraged all Paiute talk.

During the time that my father was away Toodles and Mother, my little brother, Robert, and I would see no one but Mike McGovern, the hired man. Then we would revert to Indian life. Toodles and I would race over the plowed fields and play in and out of the sage and rabbit brush. Sometimes Mother would put brother Robert on her back and we would go out and hunt wild berries and seeds. We ate the wild berries and learned to grind the seed between the rocks to make Indian meal that tasted real good. . . .

One Sunday after I had been in school several months, Susie Lumkin, a relative . . . was combing my hair and said, "Annie, did you know that your Papa was going to put your Ma out and take you away from her?"

I did not answer because I thought this could not be true. But the next day after school when I was changing my apron up in my room, I heard voices below. Listening, I recognized Mrs. St. Clair's voice. Remembering her black, shiny hair and how Papa used to make over her, I lay down on the floor, put my ear to a crack, and heard her say, "Yes, Lowry, I would take those children and put them where people would never know they were Indians."

She went on, "You're a nice-looking man, Jerome Lowry. I wouldn't live with that old squaw."

"Yes, you're right, I'll go," I heard my father's voice. "As soon as the boys are old enough. I'll put Annie in a convent and take them with me. I've already bought a place in Oregon."

It was hard to believe that my father was talking about leaving my poor mother. I got off the floor and went down into the back yard. Feeling lonely and distressed. I was looking through a crack in the back yard fence when I saw my mother. She carried a pack of groceries on her back and a little boy, my brother Jack, on her shoulder. I stood a box on top of a keg of nails, climbed up, jumped over the fence, and followed her. When I was about two hundred feet behind, Jack turned and saw me. Of course he kept looking back at me.

"Be still, Jack," Mother told him. "You are heavy when you wiggle so." But Jack kept turning to look at me.

"What are you looking at?" she asked Jack. Then she turned and saw me behind her.

"Daughter, dear," she said to me, "what are you doing here?" I tried to tell her what I had heard.

"Maybe he was just talking," she said. She turned to go and I walked along with her. . . .

. . . Thus it was again that I found myself in my old room, my ear to the floor, listening to my father tell the women downstairs that he had sold his ranching interests here and was moving his stock to his acreage in Oregon. He began to tell his plans for me. He had made all arrangements for me, not only to enter the convent but to keep me there until I graduated. Then he would come and take me to his home in Virginia, and from there I was to enter an eastern women's college. I didn't know where and I didn't care. I could only think, "He's breaking up our home. He is leaving my poor broken-hearted mother to shift for herself, and I won't go with him. He can't make me go." Later he pleaded with me, he cajoled, even threatened my very existence, but I would not go with him. . . .

When my father realized that I was determined not to leave my mother, he promised me after he got settled he would come back for Susie and me. Later while we were waiting for his return at the dugout, Scarface Charley came back and told the Indians that my father had married a white woman in Idaho. When this information reached us, I knew that he had no intention of living with my mother again.

After a few more weeks had passed, we heard that he was on his way back. Fearing that he would force me to leave my mother and return with him, we ran away and hid. The country at Big Meadows is level and covered with sage and rabbit brush, so anyone walking there could be seen for miles. To keep him from finding us we stayed under cover of brush in the daytime and came out after nightfall to rummage for food which was so scarce we nearly starved. When we found out that Lowry had given up looking for me, and had left Lovelock for good, we returned to our dugout home on the ranch.

ANNIE LOWRY, *Paiute*

6

WE HAD EVERYTHING TO LEARN

Not all reservations were hellholes, as the Arapaho Indian Carl Sweezy remembers in this affectionate reminiscence from his autobiography, The Arapaho Way, A Memoir of an Indian Boyhood. Sweezy attributed the pleasant reservation of his youth to the high caliber of agents chosen during the Grant administration. Indian Territory was fortunate in obtaining empathetic men like Thomas Battay among the Kiowa and Comanche, Laban Miles among the Osage, and John Seger, Brinton Darlington, and John Miles among Sweezy's own people.

Carl Sweezy was born around 1880 and orphaned as a boy. After attending mission schools he eventually returned to Oklahoma. When his watercolors came to the attention of anthropologist James Mooney, Sweezy was hired to illustrate Arapaho custom and ritual. Until his death in 1953, he divided his time between art and dairy farming. Here Sweezy remembers helpful agents, and the exciting day of "Wohaw" (meaning beef), known simply as the "issue" to many tribes, when cattle distribution evoked fond memories of buffalo hunts on the open plains.

PRESIDENT GRANT was the Great White Father in Washington when we came to the Reservation. Before that time he had been a great warrior, just as our chiefs Left Hand and Powder Face had been, but he had left the warpath and he wanted us to leave it. So he saw to it that good men were sent to take charge of our Agency, and good officers and soldiers to Fort Reno when it was built across the river from the Agency in 1875. There was more than one white man's road that we might take, and President Grant wanted us to take the right one.

He sent Brinton Darlington to be our first Agent. Mr. Darlington belonged to the Society of Friends, the Quakers, and we could tell that he believed many of the things that we believed. He knew, as we did, that there was a good Man-Above and an evil Man-Below, and he worshipped and prayed to the Man-Above. And although he never spoke to my people about his belief in Mother-Earth, he must have believed in her as we did. . . .

He brought assistants there, many of them Quakers like himself, who built good buildings and started schools and opened trading posts and laid out farms. He planted an orchard and a garden, so that our people might learn how fruits and vegetables grew. He was patient and kind; he managed like a chief; he prayed to the Man-Above when he was thankful and when he needed power. So although he was a white man and did not speak our language, we could understand him.

He died in 1872, some years before I was born, and when he was buried in the cemetery on the hill near the road that ran between the Agency and Caddo Spring, there were Cheyenne and Arapaho chiefs, as well as white men, who wept over his grave. And when John D. Miles came to be our next Agent, we kept to the new road that we had taken under Brinton Darlington. Even today, when the Arapaho think of Darlington we think of a place where life was once happy and good.

We had everything to learn about the white man's road. We had come to a country that was new to us, where wind and rain and rivers and heat and cold and even some of the plants and animals were different from what we had always known. We had to learn to live by farming instead of by hunting and trading; we had to learn from people who did not speak our language or try to learn it, except for a few words, though they expected us to learn theirs. We had to learn to cut our hair short, and to wear close-fitting clothes made of dull-colored cloth, and to live in houses, though we knew that our long braids of hair and embroidered robes and moccasins and tall, round lodges were more beautiful. . . .

We had never made brick or sawed lumber or had a wooden door to open and shut. Although some of us had visited the forts and the trading posts before we came to the Reservation, and a few of us had seen the white

Carl Sweezy, Arapaho artist

man's towns and cities, hardly any of us had ever been in houses where families lived. We thought windows were put in the walls so that we might look in to see how white people did their work and ate their meals and visited with each other. We pulled up some of the first little trees that were planted at Darlington, to see why the white people had put sticks in the ground in rows. There is a story that one of our men, given a little pig to raise so that when it grew up he could have pork and bacon, returned it to the Agency to be kept for him until it grew too big to get through the holes in his fence. He did not realize that he could repair the fence to suit the size of his pig.

We knew nothing about how to harness a work horse or turn a furrow in a field or cut and store hay; and today I suppose there are men living in cities who know no more about these things than we did. Our women did not know how to build a fire in a cook-stove or wash clothes in a tub of water. It was a long time before we knew what the figures on the face of a clock meant, or why people looked at them before they ate their meals or started off to church. We had to learn that clocks had something to do with the hours and minutes that the white people mentioned so often. Hours, minutes, and seconds were such small divisions of time that we had never thought of them. When the sun rose, when it was high in the sky, and when it set were all the divisions of the day that we had ever found necessary when we followed the old Arapaho road. When we went on a hunting trip or to a sun dance, we counted time by sleeps.

My people had everything to learn about the white man's road, but they had a good time learning it. How they laughed when a war pony, not understanding what it was supposed to do when it was hitched to a plough or a wagon, lunged and jumped away and threw them flat on the ground, with the plough or the wagon riding high in the air.

How puzzled they were when they found that old men and women, among the white people, had teeth they could take out of their mouths and put back in again. They gave Brinton Darlington the name "Tosimeea," "He Who Takes Out His Teeth," when he showed them that he could do this, and they wondered how he had come by that strange power. But when Mr. Miles came, he could do the same thing. It must be, they thought, something all Agents had the power to do; so the movement of taking out and putting back a set of teeth became the word for Agent in our sign language. And stair steps, built to take people up to a house built on top of another house, still amused us. We had never expected to have such things for our own use, on our Reservation. . . .

By the terms of the treaty at Medicine Lodge, the United States Government was to furnish us what we needed to live on, after we sat down on the Reservation, until we had time to learn to provide for ourselves. It was also to give us schools and teachers, and farm implements and blacksmiths and Agency farmers, to start us on the corn road. All this was paid for out of the fund credited to us for our claim to lands that we surrendered when we moved to the Reservation. Each winter, under this plan, we received an issue of what was called annuity goods.

Issue days were big times for all of us. The men who were to do the killing painted their faces and rode their fastest horses and brought along their best bows and arrows, or their guns. The women followed along, usually with a pony travois to carry the smallest children and to bring home the beef. People all put on some of their finery, and braided some colored cloth into the manes and tails of their horses, and made a holiday out of the work they had to do. All across the prairies, on Monday mornings, people in bright colors and high spirits came riding to the issue station. There were visiting and excitement and work and feasting ahead for everyone. One by one, as the clerk stamped the ration tickets of the heads of families, the men in the corral drove a beef from the pen and sent it down the chute. Yelling and racing his pony and with his family coming along behind as close as they could manage to do, the man rode after his wohaw as it bellowed and plunged and tore across the prairie, trying to escape. Wohaw could run almost as fast and bellow and turn almost as wildly as the buffalo once did. For a few hours, the Arapaho knew once more some of the excitement of the old buffalo hunt. And when at last the beef was shot down, the women moved in with their knives and kettles, skinning the hide off and cutting up the meat to take back to their lodges. Everybody had a piece of the raw liver, fresh and warm, before the families set out for home. Then, in the tipis or outside, fires were kindled; some of the beef was cooked, and the feasting began. Lodge walls were lifted at the sides if the weather was good, and the skins at the entrance were propped up overhead, so that several lodges could be thrown together during the feast. It was a time of plenty and of hospitality for everyone.

Next day the women were busy outside the tipi, cutting into strips whatever meat was left and hanging it from poles to dry. We had never heard of refrigerators in those days, but the sun and the wind soon cured the meat so that it did not spoil. The cattlemen who leased pastures on our Reservation called this jerked meat, or jerky. But usually there was little left of our wohaw for drying. When there was anything to feast on in our villages, we feasted well.

After 1896, the method of issuing beef was changed. To shorten the time required for the issue, and to do away with the celebrating that went with it, live beeves were no longer given out. Instead, the cattle were slaughtered, and issued from the block. At first all the men objected to the change, and the chiefs protested to the Agent. Many a Cheyenne family went hungry until the proud chiefs of that tribe decided they must bow to authority and accept slaughtered beef. The sport that had been as important as the feasting on issue days was ended with that change from beef on the hoof to beef on the block. Progress was catching up with us.

CARL SWEEZY, *Arapaho*

TO LEARN
ANOTHER WAY

Thanksgiving pageant acted by North Dakota Indian teenagers

Once groups of Indians were consolidated onto chunks of reservation land, they often faced contradictory interests of outsiders
in their culture. On the one hand, children were sent to school
and adults were pressured to abandon their traditions. On the other hand,
pioneer scholars began to visit the new reservations to record the same old
customs for posterity.

The crusade by white society to educate and indoctrinate American Indian
children had actually been going on for centuries. As early as the 1560s the
Spanish had established a special school for Indian children on the island
of Cuba. Farther north, the Virginia Company earmarked financial assistance
for white families to shelter and tutor young Indians.

But Indians were not so eager to abandon their ways of child-rearing. As
early as the mid-1700s some well-intentioned whites urged Iroquois parents

from Upper New York State to turn over their sons to be taught "in the best manner." This had been tried already, the Iroquois responded, but the youngsters had come home "absolutely good for nothing, being neither acquainted with the true methods of killing deer, catching beaver, or surprising an enemy." However, they would be willing to rear some English lads "in what really was the best manner and make men of them." The colonists declined.

In many treaties between Indians and colonists (drafted but not always honored), funds were set aside for Indian education. Harvard College was dedicated in 1636 to "the education of English and Indian youth . . . in knowledge and godliness," but only one tribesman received a degree. Dartmouth College opened in 1769 to offer "all parts of learning which shall appear necessary and expedient for civilizing and Christianizing children of pagans." Initially, Dartmouth's founder, an educator named Eleazar Wheelock, was thwarted by Indian disinterest; later on Dartmouth attracted more native students, and graduated many prominent Indians.

By the late nineteenth century, however, native parents had little say in

Learning to sweep at Riverside Indian School, Anadarko, Oklahoma, 1901

their children's education. Indian reformers insisted that if the young were taught white habits of hygiene, diet, clothing, work by the clock, and worship on Sunday, then paganism and savagery, poverty and dependency would eventually die out. After 1869, the government encouraged Christian missionary societies to manage the far-flung Indian school system.

In response, some tribes in the Southeast designed their own school systems. Before their peoples were forced out of present-day Oklahoma in the 1830s, the Choctaw and Cherokee established a network of over two hundred classrooms. Tribal literacy among their youth rose by ninety percent. The long tradition of Indian journalism was also launched around then with the *Cherokee Phoenix* published in both native and English languages in Georgia. The motive behind such initiatives was spelled out in a Cherokee elder's words to younger Indians, "Remember that the whites are near us. With them we have constant intercourse, and you must be sensible, that unless you can speak their language, read and write as they do, they will be able to cheat you and trample on your rights."

After 1819, the U.S. Congress set aside a so-called Civilization Fund so church groups could "put into the hands of their [Indian] children the primer and the hoe . . . and they will grow up in the habits of morality and industry." By 1838, about three thousand Indian students were "going to see some writing"—a Winnebago phrase for schooling—at over eighty government boarding schools in the eastern United States.

About this time a new methodology came to dominate Indian education. In 1837 Colonel Richard M. Johnson, a veteran of the Indian wars, established a "Choctaw Academy" in Indian Territory. This "manual" or "industrial" school adopted militarylike uniforms and discipline and stressed practical skills—mechanics, printing, and agriculture. In Virginia, the Hampton Normal School, serving blacks as well as Indians, was likewise founded upon this pull-yourself-up-by-your-own-bootstraps philosophy.

The most durable of these academies opened its doors in 1879 in Carlisle, Pennsylvania. Four years earlier another former Indian fighter, Colonel Richard Pratt, was given custody of seventy-two Plains Indian war prisoners at the gloomy old Spanish fort of San Marcos in St. Augustine, Florida. When Pratt removed their irons and put them in class, most became model students. This led to Pratt's U.S. Training and Industrial School at Carlisle, which opened with eighty-two Sioux and forty-seven Pawnee, Kiowa, and Cheyenne students. "I believe in immersing the Indians in our civilization," Pratt proclaimed in fund-raising speeches across the country, "and when we get them under, holding them there until they are thoroughly soaked." Institutions patterned after Carlisle sprang up at Haskell and Chilloco in Kansas.

Earlier boarding schools usually lay within visiting distances of the students' villages. These sterner educators separated Indian children from their roots, transporting them halfway across the continent. The Sioux writer Luther Standing Bear remembered being a homesick kid on a train speeding across the plains to a distant school in the east. Some of his buddies were so frightened they began to sing the death songs of Sioux warriors approaching battle.

Once they arrived, the new students entered a regimented environment. Often their introduction began with a new name, as the Omaha writer Francis La Flesche recalls in *The Middle Five*, a classic memoir of Indian school life: ". . . the aboriginal names were considered by the missionaries heathenish . . . in the place of Tae-noo-ga-wa-zhe, came Philip Sheridan; in that of Wa-pah-dae . . . Jonathan."

Their long hair was clipped to the skull, sometimes as part of a public ritual in which they renounced Indian origins. They were forbidden to speak native languages, often under threat of physical punishment. Daily routine followed a strict schedule of academic and vocational studies, mealtimes, intervals for prayer, housekeeping chores, and recesses. The costs of keeping up the buildings and grounds and food was defrayed by student labor. Learning by working was the creed.

Some youngsters flourished under these regimes and grew into eminent Indian spokespeople who would credit their success to this training. A few seized every opportunity to dash for freedom, and were captured only to run away again. Still others, only half indoctrinated, became what the Stony Indians of Canada called their returned students, *aintsikn ustombe*, "the lost people." One Iroquois elder taunted students just back from school: "What have we here? You are neither a white man nor an Indian. For heaven's sake, tell us, what are you?"

An unexpected outcome of intermixing children from diverse tribes was a special camaraderie that usually developed among them. Thrown together into these alien, scary environments, with only each other for emotional support, youth from contrasting cultures discovered that they had attitudes and experiences in common by virtue of simply being American Indians. When these students became adults, friendships formed at these institutions blossomed into marriages, intertribal visiting, and political alliances. The birth of the phenomenon that would be labeled "Pan-Indianism"—a sense of shared identity as Indians that transcended tribal boundaries—can be traced, in some measure, to the boarding school experience.

For parents worried about perpetuating local tribal heritages, however, such schooling presented a distressing dilemma. When their young were absent from crucial festivals in their community's religious calendar, or from the initiation rituals that transformed the young into tribal adults, the persistence of their culture was in jeopardy. One Kickapoo father told a school recruiter at his wigwam door, "Take that axe and knock him on the head. I will gladly bury him. I would rather you do that than take him to school. . . ."

Cruelty toward children was another concern. In one famous incident, a white agent was captured by a Navajo headman who was furious over the forced recruitment and mistreatment of students at the Fort Defiance boarding school in Arizona. "When we put our children in school it is like giving our hearts up," said a Navajo parent, "and when the Superintendent abuses our children it hurts us very much. The name we have given this superintendent is Billy Goat. A billy goat is always butting all the rest of the sheep and imposing on them."

All across Indian America the ancient social customs and religious rituals of Indian parents were falling under new regulations. On the Great Plains, Indian agents were instructed to halt the Sun Dance, a major yearly ritual for more than twenty different tribes, because it was considered "brutal" and "pagan." Hence the last old-style traditional Oglala dance was held in 1881, while the Kiowa observed their final Sun Dance in 1887.

Up and down the coast of British Columbia the Canadian government banned a key feature of native religious and social ceremonialism. This was the "potlatch," a complex ceremony through which prestigious families or whole tribes competed with one another in giving away immense amounts of accumulated goods. But despite the efforts of white soldiers and their Indian police, many tribes continued to hold the outlawed rituals in secret.

During this same period of cultural suppression a number of scholars, explorers, and sympathetic army officers began documenting on paper the very customs that were falling under official disfavor. Earlier, while settlers were still fighting Indians and the government was relocating them, men such as Henry Rowe Schoolcraft, George Catlin, and Lewis Henry Morgan were already studying the Indians' social organization, folklore, and ways of dress and hunting. In their eyes this research contributed to science as well as to greater sympathy for Indians. After 1879, this scholarly interest won official sanction, as the famous explorer of the Grand Canyon, John Wesley Powell, inaugurated the government's new Bureau of American Ethnology to collect cultural information directly from Indians.

But even these scholars disagreed about administrative policy toward Indians. Alice Fletcher, for instance, who wrote beautifully about beliefs and rituals of the Pawnee and Omaha tribes, enthusiastically promoted assimilation. Frank Hamilton Cushing, however, who had immersed himself in Zuñi Indian culture to the extent of becoming a priest of their sacred Bow Society, died without divulging its secrets and believed Indians should be left alone. James Mooney, another Bureau anthropologist, even fought for the rights of Indians to create new traditions. He wrote a moving account of the Plains Indian Ghost Dance, and lobbied on behalf of Indian religious freedom.

For the most part Indians accepted or rejected these cultural interlopers on an individual basis. The Zuñis adopted Cushing as one of them, but found anthropologist Matilda Coxe Stevenson too aggressive. "You cannot believe how arrogant she was," said a Zuñi woman. "She entered the kivas [ceremonial chambers] without asking permission of the high priests." Thereafter the Zuñis carefully monitored anthropologists in their midst, and were among the first to forbid photographs of their sacred dances.

The following accounts cover Indian reactions to new kinds of cultural assault, the efforts to replace, but sometimes to understand, their native habits of thought and behavior.

1

RESPONSIVE AND RESISTANT STUDENTS

Indian children responded very differently to learning the white man's way. In the first selection, Ellis B. Childers, a Creek Indian boy, writes enthusiastically for his Carlisle Indian School newspaper in 1882 about a visit by some older, assimilated Indians to the school.

In the second, Lone Wolf, part Blackfoot, tells his adopted son, the painter Paul Dyck, of bitter memories of school. Following this episode Lone Wolf went after his teacher with his fists. Transferred to a different school, he was jailed for defending a fellow student against a white disciplinarian. Lone Wolf's father was the writer James Willard Schultz, author of My Life as an Indian. *After Lone Wolf's release from jail, Schultz decided that his son and schools did not mix.*

INSPECTOR HAWORTH with a large delegation of Indians visited us on Easter week on their way back home from Washington. We were sorry that the school-room work and shops were all closed. Although they went through the shops and saw what the boys have been making but they did not see them at work.

The same evening when they arrived the boys had dress parade. At 7 o'clock the school had an entertainment in the chapel. After it was over Inspector Haworth asked some of the delegates to say something to the school. Kihega the father of Charles Kihega the Editor of the SCHOOL NEWS made the first speech. He made a very nice speech.

And among other things he said to the children: "Here are people trying to teach you. You must try to learn and when you come back home your people will be glad to see you and what you learn will be a benefit to them." When he said, "Here are people" he meant our kind teachers who are trying their best to teach us to live a civilized life.

There were four others made little speeches to us. They all spoke so good that Capt. Pratt said at the close. "I could sit and listen all night to such good speeches as these." Henry Jones the interpreter said something before it was closed. He is an Indian but he has learned enough English so as to interpret for his people.

Among other things he said, "If we Indians are willing to learn we can learn. We can learn as well as our friends, the whites. We can do just as well as the white people. If we try. We have muscles, brains and eyes just the same as the whites. If we cultivate our brains and muscles and eyes we can do just the same as they."

And then closed his speech by saying. "Don't look back, all that is passed away. This country through here is all improved. You saw when you were coming, cities, railroads, houses, manufactories.

"Boys, this was once all our country, but our fathers had not their eyes open as we have; our pale face brethren told us to move a little further and a little further, until now we are on our least stepping ground. Now, the only way to hold that even is to get educated ourselves."

We have had many Indian delegates, but those were the best delegates we have had.

ELLIS B. CHILDERS. *Creek*

S C H O O L W A S N ' T for me when I was a kid. I tried three of them and they were all bad. The first time was when I was about 8 years old. The soldiers came and rounded up as many of the Blackfeet children as they could. The government had decided we were to get White Man's education by force.

It was very cold that day when we were loaded into the wagons. None of us wanted to go and our parents didn't want to let us go. Oh, we cried for this was the first time we were to be separated from our parents. I remember looking back at Na-tah-ki and she was crying too. Nobody waved as the wagons, escorted by the soldiers, took us toward the school at Fort Shaw. Once there our belongings were taken from us, even the little medicine bags our mothers had given us to protect us from harm. Everything was placed in a heap and set afire.

Next was the long hair, the pride of all the Indians. The boys, one by one, would break down and cry when they saw their braids thrown on the floor. All of the buckskin clothes had to go and we had to put on the clothes of the White Man.

If we thought that the days were bad, the nights were much worse. This was the time when real loneliness set in, for it was then we knew that we were all alone. Many boys ran away from the school because the treatment was so bad but most of them were caught and brought back by the police. We were told never to talk Indian and if we were caught, we got a strapping with a leather belt.

I remember one evening when we were all lined up in a room and one of the boys said something in Indian to another boy. The man in charge of us pounced on the boy, caught him by the shirt, and threw him across the room. Later we found out that his collar-bone was broken. The boy's father, an old warrior, came to the school. He told the instructor that among his people, children were never punished by striking them. That was no way to teach children; kind words and good examples were much better. Then he added, "Had I been there when that fellow hit my son, I would have killed him." Before the instructor could stop the old warrior he took his boy and left. The family then beat it to Canada and never came back.

LONE WOLF, *Blackfoot*

2

HE IS NOT ONE OF US

*S**un Elk was the first boy from the pueblo of Taos in northern New Mexico to attend Carlisle. In 1883, four years after the institution's founding, he joined its demanding program of study and work. Among other skills, he learned to set type on the school newspaper.*

After seven years in Pennsylvania without a break, Sun Elk returned home. Although his highly conservative tribe put him through a harsh reentry ordeal in their sacred ceremonial chamber, or "kiva," they still kept him at arm's length. He grew his hair back to its traditional length, and cut the seat out of his trousers so he could wear the Indian-style breechcloth, but only marrying back into the tribe made him "an Indian again."

WHEN I WAS about thirteen years old I went down to St. Michael's Catholic School. Other boys were joining the societies and spending their time in the kivas being purified and learning the secrets. But I wanted to learn the white man's secrets. I thought he had better magic than the Indian. . . . So I drifted a little away from the pueblo life. My father was sad but he was not angry. He wanted me to be a good Indian like all the other boys, but he was willing for me to go to school. He thought I would soon stop. There was plenty of time to go into the kiva.

Then at the first snow one winter . . . a white man—what you call an Indian Agent—came and took all of us who were in that school far off on a train to a new kind of village called Carlisle Indian School, and I stayed there seven years. . . .

Seven years I was there. I set little letters together in the printing shop and we printed papers. For the rest we had lessons. There were games, but

I was too slight for foot and hand plays, and there were no horses to ride. I learned to talk English and to read. There was much arithmetic. It was lessons: how to add and take away, and much strange business like you have crossword puzzles only with numbers. The teachers were very solemn and made a great fuss if we did not get the puzzles right.

There was something called Greatest Common Denominator. I remember the name but I never knew it—what it meant. When the teachers asked me I would guess, but I always guessed wrong. We studied little things—fractions. I remember that word too. It is like one half of an apple. And there were immoral fractions. . . .

They told us that Indian ways were bad. They said we must get civilized. I remember that word too. It means "be like the white man." I am willing to be like the white man, but I did not believe Indian ways were wrong. But they kept teaching us for seven years. And the books told how bad the Indians had been to the white men—burning their towns and killing their women and children. But I had seen white men do that to Indians. We all wore white man's clothes and ate white man's food and went to white man's churches and spoke white man's talk. And so after a while we also began to say Indians were bad. We laughed at our own people and their blankets and cooking pots and sacred societies and dances. I tried to learn the lessons—and after seven years I came home. . . .

It was a warm summer evening when I got off the train at Taos station. The first Indian I met, I asked him to run out to the pueblo and tell my family I was home. The Indian couldn't speak English, and I had forgotten all my Pueblo language. But after a while he learned what I meant and started running to tell my father "Tulto is back. . . ."

We chattered and cried, and I began to remember many Indian words, and they told me about an uncle, Tha-a-ba, who had just died, and how Turkano, my old friend, had finished his year's fast and was joining the Black-eyes to become a priest and delight-maker.

Two little sisters and many little cousins had come along with the family to meet me. All these children liked me and kept running up and feeling my white man's clothes and then running away laughing. The children tried to repeat the English words I said, and everyone was busy teaching me Pueblo words again. We sat down on the grass and talked until it became very dark. . . .

I went home with my family. And next morning the governor of the pueblo and the two war chiefs and many of the priest chiefs came into my

The transformation of Tom Torleno, Navajo, after three years at the Carlisle Indian Industrial School, c. 1880s

father's house. They did not talk to me; they did not even look at me. When they were all assembled they talked to my father.

The chiefs said to my father, "Your son who calls himself Rafael has lived with the white men. He has been far away from the pueblo. He has not lived in the kiva nor learned the things that Indian boys should learn. He has no hair. He has no blankets. He cannot even speak our language and he has a strange smell. He is not one of us."

The chiefs got up and walked out. My father was very sad. I wanted him to be angry, but he was only sad. So I would not be sad and was very angry instead.

And I walked out of my father's house and out of the pueblo. I did not speak. My mother was in the other room cooking. She stayed in the other room but she made much noise rattling her pots. Some children were on the plaza and they stared at me, keeping very still as I walked away.

I walked until I came to the white man's town, Fernandez de Taos. I found work setting type in a printing shop there. Later I went to Durango and other towns in Wyoming and Colorado, printing and making a good living. But this indoor work was bad for me. It made me slight of health. So then I went outside to the fields. I worked in some blacksmith shops and on farms.

All this time I was a white man. I wore white man's clothes and kept my hair cut. I was not very happy. I made money and I kept a little of it and after many years I came back to Taos.

My father gave me some land from the pueblo fields. He could do this because now the land did not belong to all the people, as it did in the old days; the white man had cut it up and given it in little pieces to each family, so my father gave me a part of his, and I took my money and bought some more land and some cattle. I built a house just outside the pueblo. I would not live in the pueblo so I built outside a house bigger than the pueblo houses all for myself.

My father brought me a girl to marry. Her name was Roberta. Her Indian name was P'ah-tah-zhuli (little deer bean). She was about fifteen years old and she had no father. But she was a good girl and she came to live with me in my new house outside the pueblo.

When we were married I became an Indian again. I let my hair grow, I put on blankets, and I cut the seat out of my pants.

SUN ELK, *Taos Pueblo*

3

WHAT HARM IS IN OUR SUN-DANCE?

*I*ndian *children could be forced to attend school and adopt white dress, but what about their parents? The answer for government officials, once Indians were confined on reservations, was to make traditional expressions of religious belief and social organization a crime.*

Here a Blackfoot spokesman from the Canadian Plains argues against suppressing their Sun Dance to ethnographer Walter McLintock, who recorded it in his book The Old North Trail. *What repulsed missionaries and officials in the United States and Canada was the self-torture practiced by fasting Sun Dancers. They penetrated their flesh with skewers as a personal offer to strengthen their prayers.*

Sanctions against the Sun Dance were not lifted until the 1930s, although young men still stole away into the mountains to offer flesh to their spirits and seek visions.

YOU HAVE BEEN among us for many years, and have attended many of our ceremonials. Have you ever seen a disturbance, or anything harmful, that has been caused by our Sun-dance? . . .

We know that there is nothing injurious to our people in the Sun-dance. On the other hand, we have seen much that is bad at the dances of the white people. It has been our custom, during many years, to assemble once every summer for this festival, in honour of the Sun God. We fast and pray, that we may be able to lead good lives and to act more kindly towards each other.

I do not understand why the white men desire to put an end to our religious ceremonials. What harm can they do to our people? If they deprive us of our religion, we will have nothing left, for we know of no other that can take its place.

We do not understand the white man's religion. The Black Robes (Catholic Priests) teach us one thing and the Men-with-white-neckties (Protestant Missionaries) teach us another; so we are confused.

We believe that the Sun God is all powerful, for every spring he makes the trees to bud and the grass to grow. We see these things with our own eyes, and, therefore, know that all life comes from him.

ANONYMOUS, *Blackfoot*

4

WE WILL DANCE

The greatest custom of Northwest Coast Indians was the potlatch, an elaborate ritual in which huge amounts of arts, foods, and even slaves passed hands. Sometimes, in grand gestures, the goods were even destroyed as leaders of clans or great "houses" outdid each other in conspicuous displays and magnanimous give-aways of wealth. Recipients at one potlatch were obligated to balance accounts

In the late nineteenth century, the Canadian government banned the Northwest Coast Indian ceremony popularly known as the "potlatch," in which vast amounts of gift goods changed hands. The festive gatherings, accompanied by masked dancing, were considered anti-Christian and contrary to the white man's ideals of frugality and private property. These dance masks were "voluntarily surrendered" to Canadian authorities by Kwakiutl Indians of British Columbia after they were convicted of breaking the law against holding potlatches.

during the next. One's reputation depended on how much one gave or owed, and elaborate accounts kept people linked to extended kin who helped them prepare for potlatches as well as to their "adversaries" whom they sought to "shame" at the next giveaway.

In the late 1850s an influential missionary named William Duncan, who worked among the Tsimshian tribe, argued that potlatches were barbaric. Despite the Canadian government's 1884 anti-potlatch law, however, clandestine ones were held right up until 1951, when the archaic edict died a natural death. Here the famous anthropologist Franz Boas is warned in 1886 by the Kwakiutl Indians of British Columbia to leave such traditions alone.

WE WANT TO KNOW whether you have come to stop our dances and feasts, as the missionaries and agents who live among our neighbors try to do.

We do not want anybody here who will interfere with our customs.

We were told that a man-of-war would come if we should continue to do as our grandfathers and great-grandfathers have done. But we do not mind such words.

Is this the white man's land? We are told it is the Queen's land; but no! It is mine! Where was the Queen when our God gave the land to my grandfather and told him, "This will be thine"? My father owned the land and was a mighty chief; now it is mine.

And when your man-of-war comes let him destroy our houses. Do you see yon woods? Do you see yon trees? We shall cut them down and build new houses and live as our fathers did.

We will dance when our laws command us to dance, we will feast when our hearts desire to feast. Do we ask the white man, "Do as the Indian does"? No, we do not. Why then do you ask us, "Do as the white man does"?

It is a strict law that bids us dance. It is a strict law that bids us distribute our property among our friends and neighbors. It is a good law. Let the white man observe his law, we shall observe ours.

And now, if you are come to forbid us to dance, begone; if not, you will be welcome to us.

ANONYMOUS, Kwakiutl

5

DR. FEWKES PLAYS LIKE A CHILD

I n 1898 Dr. J. Walter Fewkes, a fieldworker for the Bureau of American Ethnology, abruptly halted his study of the sacred winter ceremonies of the Hopi Indians. He left their village of Walpi in northern Arizona, never to return.

Why exactly Fewkes made his sudden departure was never clear. Officially it was explained as stemming from his fears over a recent outbreak of smallpox. But the Hopi give a more mysterious reason, as related by Edmund Nequatewa from the Hopi village of Shongopovi on Second Mesa.

ONE OF THE MOST important of the Hopi winter ceremonies is the Wuwuchim which comes in November. At a certain time during the ceremony the One Horned and the Two Horned Societies hold a secret rite in a certain part of the pueblo, and all the people who live on that plaza go away and close their houses. No one may witness this ceremony, for Masauwu, the Earth God, is there with the One Horned Priests who do his bidding in the Underworld and the Spirits of the dead are there and it is said that anyone who sees them will be frozen with fright or paralyzed or become like the dead.

Masauwu owns all the Hopi world, the surface of the earth and the Underworld beneath the earth. He is a mighty and terrible being for he wears upon his head a bald and bloody mask. He is like death and he clothes himself in the raw hides of animals and men cannot bear to look upon his face. The Hopi say he is really a very handsome great man of a dark color with fine long black hair and that he is indeed a great giant. When the Hopi came up from the Underworld and looked about them in fear, the first sign which they saw of any being of human form, was the great footprints of Masauwu. Now Masauwu only walks at night and he carries a flaming torch. Fire is his and he owns the fiery pits. Every night Masauwu takes his torch and he starts out on his rounds, for he walks clear around the edge of the world every night.

Dr. Fewkes had been in the kiva all day taking notes on what he saw going on there. Finally the men told him that he must go away and stay in his house for Masauwu was coming, and that part of the ceremony was very sacred and no outside person was ever allowed to see what was going on. They told him to go into his house and lock the door, and not to try to see anything no matter what happened, or he would be dragged out and he would "freeze" to death. So he went away into his house and he locked the door just as he had been told to do and he sat down and began to write up his notes.

Now suddenly he had a queer feeling, for he felt that there was someone in the room, and he looked up and saw a tall man standing before him, but he could not see his face for the light was not good. He felt very much surprised for he knew that he had locked the door.

He said, "What do you want and how did you get in here?" The man replied, "I have come to entertain you."

Dr. Fewkes said, "Go away, I am busy and I do not wish to be entertained."

And now as he was looking at the man, he suddenly was not there any more. Then a voice said, "Turn your head a moment," and when the Doctor looked again the figure stood before him once more, but this time its head was strange and dreadful to see.

And the Doctor said, "How did you get in?" and the man answered and said, "I go where I please, locked doors cannot keep me out! See, I will show you how I entered," and, as Dr. Fewkes watched, he shrank away and became like a single straw in a Hopi hair whisk and he vanished through the key hole.

Now Dr. Fewkes was very much frightened and as he was thinking what to do, there was the man back again. So he said once more to him, "What do you want?" and the figure answered as before and said, "I have come to entertain you." So the Doctor offered him a cigarette and then a match, but the man laughed and said, "Keep your match, I do not need it," and he held the cigarette before his horrible face and blew a stream of fire from his mouth upon it and lit his cigarette. Then Dr. Fewkes was very much afraid indeed, for now he knew who it was.

Then the being talked and talked to him, and finally the Doctor "gave up to him" and said he would become a Hopi and be like them and believe in Masauwu, and Masauwu cast his spell on him and they both became like little children and all night long they played around together and Masauwu gave the Doctor no rest.

And it was not long after that Dr. Fewkes went away but it was not on account of the smallpox as you now know.

EDMUND NEQUATEWA, *Hopi*

6

JUDGE WOODEN LEG KEEPS ONE WIFE

F or an Indian to be appointed as tribal judge under the reservation system, the job could be more of a problem than an honor. That was the experience of a Cheyenne Indian from Montana named Wooden Leg, as he relates here in a selection from his autobiography.

Deputizing the opposition was a cunning way for the government to indoctrinate adult Indians in the rules of white society and to inexpensively keep order at the same time. Indians were paid to wear uniforms and police their own reservations, and were appointed to judge minor offenses among their own kind. Being a tribal policeman made one a target of community criticism, and judges were sometimes accused of being cultural traitors.

A veteran of the famous battle of Little Big Horn against the U.S. Cavalry,

Wooden Leg was a tall, handsome man and a respected warrior. To become a tribal judge, however, he had to abandon the old Cheyenne custom of polygamy, where a man had more than one wife—who were preferably sisters. To keep their spouses, Indians learned to tell missionaries and agents half truths, explaining, for instance, that it was tribal custom for a sister-in-law to live under the same roof. In Wooden Leg's case, however, he decides to play by the new rules.

A POLICEMAN CAME to my place, one time, and told me that Eddy wanted to see me at the agency office. He did not say what was wanted. I thought: "What have I done?" I went right away. I never had been much about the agency, and I did not know Eddy very well. But the people all the time were saying he was a good man, so I was not afraid. When I got there, a strange white man was at the office. The interpreter told me this man was from Washington. Eddy and the other man talked to me a little while, about nothing of importance. Then Eddy said:

"We want you to be judge."

The Indian court was held at the agency. My home place was where it now is, over a divide from the agency and on the Tongue River side of the reservation. I accepted the appointment. I was paid ten dollars each month for going to the agency and attending to the court business one or two times each month. Not long after I had been serving as judge, Eddy called me into his office. He said:

"A letter from Washington tells me that Indians having two or more wives must send away all but one. You, as judge, must do your part toward seeing that the Cheyennes do this."

My heart jumped around in my breast when he told me this. He went on talking further about the matter, but I could not pay close attention to him. My thoughts were racing and whirling. When I could get them steady enough for speech, I said to him:

"I have two wives. You must get some other man to serve as judge."

He sat there and looked straight at me, saying nothing for a little while. Then he began talking again:

"Somebody else as judge would make you send away one of your wives. It would be better if you yourself managed it. All of the Indians in the United States are going to be compelled to put aside their extra wives. Washington has sent the order."

I decided to keep the office of judge. It appeared there was no getting around the order, so I made up my mind to be the first one to send away my extra wife, then I should talk to the other Cheyennes about the matter. I took plenty of time to think about how I should let my wives know about what was coming. Then I allowed the released one some further time to make arrangements as to where she should go. The first wife, the older one, had two daughters. The younger wife had no children. It seemed this younger one ought to leave me. I was in very low spirits. When a wagon came to get her and her personal packs I went out and sat on a knoll about a hundred yards away. I could not speak to her. It seemed I could not move. All I could do was just sit there and look down at the ground. She went back to her own people, on another reservation. A few years later I heard that she was married to a good husband. Oh, how glad it made my heart to hear that!

I sent a policeman to tell all Cheyennes having more than one wife to come and see me. One of them came that same afternoon. After we had smoked together, I said:

"The agent tells me that I as the judge must order all Cheyennes to have only one wife. You must send away one of yours."

"I shall not obey that order," he answered me.

"Yes, it will have to be that way," I insisted.

"But who will be the father to the children?" he asked.

"I do not know, but I suppose that will be arranged."

"Wooden Leg, you are crazy. Eddy is crazy."

"No. If anybody is crazy, it is somebody in Washington. All of the Indians in the United States have this order. If we resist it, our policemen will put us into jail. If much trouble is made about it, soldiers may come to fight us. Whatever man does not put aside his extra wife may be the cause of the whole tribe being killed."

Many of our men were angered by the order. My heart sympathized with them, so I never became offended at the strong words they sometimes used. Finally, though, all of them sent away their extra wives. Afterward, from time to time, somebody would tell me about some man living a part of the time at one place with one wife and a part of the time at another place with another wife. I just listened, said nothing, and did nothing. These were old men, and I considered it enough of change for them that they be prevented from having two wives at the same place.

WOODEN LEG, *Northern Cheyenne*

THE FLOOD
HAS COME

Oklahoma reservation lands, formerly owned by the Cheyenne and Kiowa, among other tribes, were "opened" for white homesteaders in the 1890s and early 1900s. Here, at noon, on September 16, 1893, non-Indians on horses and wagons race to stake their claims to what was until recently Cherokee Indian territory.

A t the heart of the post–Civil War movement to reform Indian policy was a new threat to native lands. In the 1860s the phrase "allotment in severalty" was heard from Indian sympathizers and landgrabbers alike. It meant the plan to chop up reservation lands that tribes had been assigned in former treaties, and to distribute ("allot") the parcels to individual Indian families ("in severalty"). To most Indian peoples this was their worst nightmare, the ultimate threat to religious, social, and political identity. It would obliterate their rights to lands which, for the most part, they still owned and occupied in common.

In practice the concept worked like this: the government conducted a census of an Indian tribe that had once signed a treaty and accepted a reservation with its finite land base. Each Indian family was then granted a certain number of acres—usually 160, or the amount commonly considered a "homestead." The sum of these allotments was subtracted from the total acreage on the reservation. Leftover lands were sold to the highest bidder, even though they might comprise as much as half the original reservation. Some whites supported the plan because they thought it was the fastest way for Indians to enter the dominant society; others backed it to increase their own farms, ranches, mines, or towns.

To white reformers the reservation was always considered a stopgap solution anyhow, a temporary haven where government-appointed "boss farmers" taught Indians how to plow and sow (ignoring the fact that many of the Plains Indians, in particular, had been raising vegetables for centuries). As rapidly as possible they expected Indian settlements to split up, with families raising cattle or growing crops like everyone else.

In the final years of President Grant's administration the property deed was described as essential to this assimilation program as a school diploma, a Bible, or citizenship papers. "The common field is the seat of barbarism," proclaimed an Indian agent; "the separate farm [is] the door to civilization." A Commissioner of Indian Affairs explained in 1886, "[the Indian] must be imbued with the exalting egotism of American civilization so that he will say 'I' instead of 'We,' and 'This is mine' instead of 'This is ours.' "

Allotment threatened Indians for many reasons. Although the majority of tribes were barely surviving on government-issue foods and government-issue blankets, at least they were suffering together and sharing land as they had always done. Even though their political independence was undermined, abiding ties of family and society still wove most of them tightly together. Despite official efforts to forbid their religious practices, medicine men still practiced behind closed doors and traditional ceremonies were conducted secretly. From family to clan to religious or warrior society to tribe, the individual usually came last. The prospect of single people and nuclear families looking out for their own interests was new and frightening.

Many Indian traditions also drew the surrounding landscape and its animals into their wider web of relations. For Indians who had avoided removal, their homelands often held sacred significance as actual locations for their myths, places where their rituals were born, and sites where their ancestors had lived and were buried. Much as families, clans, and religious societies must not be fragmented, it was inappropriate to cut up the land into separately owned plots.

Some Indians also suspected that allotment was not for their benefit but just another scheme for destroying their solidarity and stealing their last resource—the land their treaties granted them as semisovereign tribes and which most still held collectively. In the view of Ely S. Parker, the Seneca who had been President Grant's Commissioner of Indian Affairs, "Our wise legislators at Washington, the Indian Aid and Indian Rights Associations are all advocating with a red hot zeal the allotment and citizenship schemes . . . [but] the Indians as a body are deadly opposed to the scheme for they see too plainly the certain and speedy dissolution of their tribal and national organizations."

Still, as with "removal" in the 1830s, "allotment" aroused divisiveness throughout the late-nineteenth-century tribal world. Some Indians were persuaded that in a nation where individual success and property titles were valued over group well-being, a land deed was their only protection. Others agreed with an old Omaha warrior who yelled out when he saw government surveyors mapping his reservation prior to carving it up, "Friends, the flood has come."

Like the strategies of removal, establishing reservations, and schooling native children, the allotment idea had actually been around a while. Granting Indian families their own piece of ground was discussed in colonial times, and the General Court of Massachusetts argued that without property deeds Indians would be defenseless. And that is largely what eventuated in New England, where few northeastern tribes managed to retain any land base.

In the mid-nineteenth century about sixty treaties signed between the U.S. government and western Indian tribes included provisions for parceling land to heads of households. But by 1880 few of those Indian homesteaders still had their house and garden. For tribes such as the Chippewa of the Great Lakes, the Catawba of South Carolina, and the Shawnee of Indian Territory, allotment proved disastrous. After their reservations were cut up, non-Indian speculators purchased the surplus acreage at bargain prices. Indian families floundered on their minuscule allotments, and sold their deeds for bottom dollar, leaving them destitute, landless, and with no tribal structure to back them up.

Despite these early alerts, East Coast lobbyists stepped up their allotment campaign. Among them were the new Indian Rights Association (formed in 1882), the National Indian Association (organized in 1885), various church groups, spokespeople for the Indian boarding school system, and

After the allotment process on the Pine Ridge Reservation of the South Dakota Sioux took place from 1904 to 1916, what had been a tribal-owned area of more than 2.5 million acres was reduced to less than 150,000 acres for the tribe as a whole. The balance was assigned to individual Indians or sold off as surplus. Pine Ridge chief American Horse, shown here with allotment officials at the time, was one of the 8,725 heads-of-households who received his personal allotment from the original acreage.

the Lake Mohonk Conference, which was first convened in 1883 by many of the same people who had fought slavery. Until 1916, their annual meetings at an elegant retreat in Upper New York State focused upon Indians' needs, especially "self-sufficiency." Said the president of Amherst College at a Lake Mohonk gathering, "We must make the Indian more intelligently selfish. . . . By acquiring property, man puts forth his personality and lays hold of matter by his own thought and will."

As a national allotment policy gained advocates, the Grant administration boasted that over ten thousand Indian children were in boarding schools, over forty-two thousand Indian men were undertaking some form of "self support," and that some two hundred thousand acres were under cultivation on the seventy-eight reservations around the country. However, Grant's liberal approach toward Indians fell on hard times. Rebellious Indians were not interested in reservations becoming safe places for transforming themselves; the wipeout of General Custer's command in 1876 fueled protests against his administration. "Who slew Custer?" asked the *New York Herald* newspaper. "The celebrated peace policy of General Grant, which feeds, clothes, and takes care of their noncombatant force while the men are killing our troops . . . [and] the Indian Bureau, with its thieving agents and favorites as Indian traders, and its mock humanity and pretense at piety—that is what killed Custer. . . ."

When Rutherford B. Hayes replaced Grant as president in 1877, he swore to get tough again. Throughout the Hayes, Garfield, and Arthur administrations political patronage returned to the Bureau of Indian Affairs; the civilian agents appointed by Grant were replaced once again by political appointees. Claiming that "village life" was slowing Indian progress, Hayes's interior secretary, Carl Schurz, vociferously endorsed allotment.

Further eroding Indian independence was a series of new laws and court cases. In 1871 the U.S. Congress forbade any more treaty-making with Indians. As piecemeal laws and presidential edicts replaced treaties, their implication that tribes and government interacted as sovereign powers was considered best ignored. In courts the Indians won one famous fight, but lost the rest. The Supreme Court resolved the *Ex Parte Crow Dog* case by deciding in 1883 that it could not challenge Indian jurisdictions that had been affirmed in treaties, even when an Indian had committed murder. This drew such instantaneous outcry from state authorities that Congress rushed through laws assuring the government absolute authority over capital offenses—murder, rape, burglary, and the like—committed by Indians.

A year later the Supreme Court declared that even Indians who forswore tribal affiliation and lived like white men were not citizens unless they had been allotted lands under the Dawes Act or had special documentation. [Indeed, it would not be until 1924 that Indians would be granted citizenship.] Finally, in 1886, the *U.S.* v. *Kagema* case saw the Court demoting Indian tribes still further, as "wards of the nation" and "communities dependent upon the United States."

Throughout the 1880s an unlikely coalition pressed Congress for allotment—eastern assimilationists standing alongside western politicians. Opposing them were a minority of U.S. congressmen who warned that "the real aim [of allotment]," in Senator Henry M. Teller's words, "is to get at the Indians' lands and open them up for resettlement."

Most Indians agreed with the New York Senecas, who argued in 1881 that "Under [the traditional, communal] system no Indian, however improvident or thriftless, can be deprived of a resort to the soil for his support and that of his family." That same year, however, pro-white Omahas of Nebraska won passage of a special allotment plan tailored to their tribe.

Debate was particularly intense among the so-called Five Civilized Tribes of Indian Territory. A pro-allotment spokesman, the Cherokee leader Elias Boudinot, petitioned Congress to give his people individual deeds because "it is proven beyond question that our title in common is insecure." Contesting allotment were such Indians as the Creek who argued that "the United States Congress has just as good a moral and legal right to take from its owners a farm in Maine or Kansas as to take away the home of a Creek or Cherokee."

Congress made the momentous decision in February 1887; the General Allotment Act passed by a unanimous voice vote. Throughout Indian country it was known as the Dawes Act, for its sponsor, Senator Henry L. Dawes of Massachusetts. Now the President could impose 160-acre deeds on Indian families; if they refused, the local agent accepted for them. Originally, Indian title was to be protected: Indians were not to sell their allotments for twenty-five years to safeguard them from the lure of quick cash. Surplus lands went on the auction block. Allottees who succeeded in the "habits of civilized life"—standards never really defined—could receive U.S. citizenship.

Surveying teams spread throughout the West. When the Yakima of Washington State encountered Dawes agents on their rangelands, they yanked out their marker stakes. In Wyoming, Arapaho horsemen drove their mounts through the surveyors' measuring tapes. When a U.S. commissioner praised the virtues of single-family vegetable gardens to old Washakie of the Shoshoni, the Plains chief exploded, "God damn a potatoe."

In this atmosphere of change and coercion, Indians were drawn by new, defiant prophets who opposed farming, schooling, Christianity, and allotting lands. "You ask me to plow the ground," said Smohalla, a Wanapum visionary from the Northwest, in an oft-quoted statement. "Shall I take a knife and tear my mother's bosom? You ask me to cut grass and make hay and sell it and be rich like white men. But dare I cut off my mother's hair?"

In following accounts we hear Indian reactions to this era of political and territorial upheaval, concluding with a native version of the movement that was its symbolic climax, the Plains Ghost Dance.

1

A HOUSE OF OUR OWN

In 1881 some progressive, English-speaking Omaha Indians from Nebraska asked the U.S. Congress to allot their lands and give each family a deed to its property. The explanations by four Omaha men in this selection accompanied that request. Actually, the Omaha tribe was split over the issue, the group known as "make-believe white men" wanted allotment and U.S. citizenship; the conservative "those who live in earth lodges" group was opposed to schooling and allotment.

With energetic lobbying by anthropologist Alice Fletcher, a special Omaha Allotment Act passed the following year. As it turned out, the Omaha were not prepared for the burdens of taxation, heirship, budgeting, and land-leasing that came along with owning your own land under the Anglo-American system. Eventually two-thirds of the acreage allotted to Omaha farmers was lost, as individual Indians found themselves selling to neighboring cattlemen and farmers their 160-acre allotments in order to make ends meet.

XITHA GAXE: I have worked hard on my land so that I should not go round begging. I thought the land was my own, so I went to work and cultivated it. Now I have found out it is not my own, and this makes me stop. I am afraid if I should build a house and spend money on it I would lose it if the Government should move the Indians from this land. Three times I have cut wood to build a house. Each time the agent told me the Government wished to build me a house. Each time my wood has lain and rotted, and now I feel ashamed when I hear an agent telling me such things. . . . I want a title to my land; I want a house that is my own.

WA THISHNADE: Before I began to farm I was just a wild Indian doing as I pleased, going round the country looking for death. . . . We have no government on the reserve. We have trouble which we would not have if we had government and law. We want these. We are right among the white people, and as we have no law we can't get along very well. There are persons living on the reserve who have certificates of allotment; they believe that the land is theirs and that they can always keep it. I know differently.

. . . I went on my farm with a certificate. I believed the land was mine. I have found out the land is not mine; that the Government can take it away. We are going to ask for our titles. As long as the Government does not give them, we will ask until the Government gets tired. We won't stop asking until we get our titles.

DU BAMO THI: . . . The road our fathers walked is gone, the game is gone, the white people are all about us. There is no use any Indian thinking of the old ways; he must now go to work as the white man does. We want titles to our lands that the land may be secure to our children. When we die we shall feel easy in our minds if we know the land will belong to our children and that they will have the benefit of our work. There are some Omahas who do not yet care for titles. We desire the Government to give titles to those who ask for them. . . . We are willing the others should do as they please but we are not willing that they should keep us from getting titles to our lands. Our children would suffer even a greater wrong than would befall us. Give us who ask titles to our lands. . . . do not let us be held back and our children be sufferers because of the inaction of those who do not seem to care for our future.

JOSEPH LA FLESCHE: . . . I was born in this country, in Nebraska, and I have always lived among the Indians. There was a time when I used to look only at the Indians and think they were the only people. The Indians must have been long in this country before the white man came. . . . In the spring they would take their seed and farm their 1 or 2 acres. There were no idlers, all worked in the spring. Those who had no hoes worked with pieces of sticks. When they had their seed in, they went on the hunt. They had nothing to worry them; all they thought of was their little garden they had left behind. . . .

Then it was I used to see white men, those who were going around buying furs. Sometimes for two or three years I would not see any white men. At that time the country was empty, only animals to be seen. Then after a while the white men came, just as the blackbirds do, and spread over the country. Some settled down, others scattered on the land. The Indians never thought that any such thing could be, but it matters not where one looks now one sees white people. These things I have been speaking about are in the past and are all gone. We Indians see you now and want to take our steps your way. . . .

It seems as though the Government pushes us back. It makes us think that the Government regards us as unfit to be as white men. The white man looks into the future and sees what is good. That is what the Indian is doing. He looks into the future and sees his only chance is to become as the white man. When a person lives in a place a long time he loves the place. We love our lands and want titles for them. When one has anything he likes to feel it is his own, and belongs to no one else, so we want titles; then we can leave our land to our children. You know, and so do we, that some of us will not live very long; we will soon be gone into the other world. We ask for titles for our children's sakes. For some years we have been trying to get titles but we have never heard from the Government. . . .

We are not strong enough to help ourselves in this matter, so we ask you to help us. In the past we only lived on the animals. We see that it is from the ground that you get all that you possess. The reason you do not look upon us as men is because we have not law, because we are not citizens. We are strangers in the land where we were born. . . . We know that in asking for titles we are asking for that which will bring responsibility. We are ready to accept it and to strive to fulfill its requirements. It seems as though in the past the Government had not listened to the words of the Indians. We know our own needs, and now we speak to you directly.

JOSEPH LA FLESCHE ET AL., *Omaha*

2

LUTHER'S FATHER STANDS ALONE

Luther Standing Bear *was an Oglala Sioux Indian writer whose books about his people's lifeways and interactions with whites were rich in autobiographical detail. In the first of three volumes intended to introduce readers to his tribe,* My People, The Sioux *(1928), he recalls when his father, a South Dakota storekeeper, was at odds with a traditional chief named Yellow Horn over the allotting of lands.*

Eventually Luther became part of the first class to attend Captain Pratt's Carlisle Indian School, and his tribe was compelled to follow his father's position and accept allotment.

SOON AFTER THIS, the Government sent some commissioners out to our reservation. The object was to investigate allotments. All the chiefs were against the allotment proposition. They figured that they were to be given a piece of land, fenced in like a white man, but they were to have no openings to and from the land, and would starve.

The agent sent out word for all the Indians to come to the agency. Soon they came trooping in from all directions and made their camps, waiting for the council to open. Of course all the chiefs who imagined they knew something about this allotment proposition had spoken to the other Indians about it, and they all agreed that there was to be no more signing of any more papers for the white man.

But my father was in favor of the allotment. He had listened while I explained it to him. So he paid no attention to either the commissioners or the agent, but went alone to the council held by the Indians while they were waiting. Here several of the old chiefs arose to talk. My father also arose, and as he faced the others, they waited to hear first what he had to say. He spoke as follows:

"My friends, there are some white men here from the Great Father at Washington. They have come to see us about an agreement concerning an allotment of land. Now, my son has explained the proposition to me, and I consider that it is a very good one. We are to receive a piece of land, three hundred and twenty acres, which will be surveyed. This is for farming. We are also to get a team of horses, a farm wagon, a milk cow, farming implements, and fifty dollars in cash toward building a house. This land we live on is not good for farming, because the seasons are not right for it. So I am going to ask the commissioners for a full section of land, six hundred and forty acres. If they will give us this, in addition to the other things mentioned, we should sign the paper. Our tribe is to receive three million dollars for this land, half of which is to be used to educate our children, and the balance is to be paid to us within twenty-five years. If we take a piece of land it will be ours forever. If any of you old men die, under present conditions, you have nothing you can leave your children. But if you have a piece of land, it will be theirs when you are gone. No one can take it from them. So I am in favor of accepting this land."

Then Chief Hollow Horn Bear arose. He was against the allotment. He was the husband of my oldest sister Wastewin, the daughter of my mother by her first husband. He liked my father, but he was the head of his own band, and had a right to his opinion. He spoke as follows:

Among non-Indians who supported allotment was Alice C. Fletcher, a government anthropologist. After helping Omaha and Winnebago Indians receive deeds to their own homesteads, she assisted in the survey of Idaho's Nez Percé Indian Reservation in the early 1890s, as shown here.

"My friends, you have all heard what my father-in-law says, but I do not think he is right. He believes what the white people tell him; but this is only another trick of the whites to take our land away from us, and they have played these tricks before. We do not want to trust the white people. They come to us with sweet talk, but they do not mean it. We will not sign any more papers for these white men."

All the Indians grunted "Hau!" ("How!"), which meant that they agreed with what Hollow Horn Bear said. Then other chiefs arose and spoke. So many of them were against the allotment that it seemed we were not to get it. But these councils which the Indians held among themselves were not recorded, as there were no white persons present.

Finally the Indians became so determined not to favor the allotment that they agreed that the first Indian who signed any more papers for the white men would be shot down. While many of the Indians really agreed with my father, they were afraid to say so for fear of the consequences.

At last the day arrived for the meeting at the agency. All the chiefs and headmen, as well as all the Indians, were gathered together to listen to what the white men had to say. General George Crook, the famous army officer, was the first man to talk. He explained all about what the Indians were to receive, how the children were to be educated, etc. He mentioned the Carlisle School, and the good being accomplished there by Captain Pratt. He was followed by other white men, who asked the Indians if they did not think this was a good thing for them.

Then one of the Indians arose and said they did not fully understand things yet, but if the agent would furnish them with food, they would hold another council, and then they might consider what to do, to which the agent agreed. As soon as the Indians reached their tipis, they held another council.

The following day everybody was at the agency again. The commissioners again spoke, and were followed by several of the other Indians. Chief Hollow Horn Bear, who was against the allotment, spoke as follows:

"You white men have come to us again to offer something to us which we do not fully understand. You talk to us very sweet, but you do not mean it. You have not fulfilled any of the old treaties. Why do you now bring another one to us? Why don't you pay us the money you owe us first, and then bring us another treaty?"

Other chiefs followed and expressed their opinions of the treaties that had not been fulfilled. They argued that if they signed this treaty, then the old treaties would be forgotten. The commissioners tried to explain that the new treaty would be on the same footing with the others—that they were to receive their annuity goods just the same, as well as what was now being promised. However, the Indians did not believe this, so they said they would go home and think it over. They left, and then held another council between themselves alone. My father attended all these councils among the Indians, as well as those held with the commissioners. But he had already told the Indians what his own opinion was about the matter, and what his decision was, and he never spoke of it again; the Indians knew his decision was final.

LUTHER STANDING BEAR, *Rosebud Sioux*

‖‖‖‖‖‖‖ ‖‖‖‖ ‖‖‖‖ ‖‖‖‖ ‖‖‖‖ ‖‖‖‖ ‖‖‖‖ ‖‖‖‖ ‖‖‖‖ **3** ‖‖‖‖ ‖‖‖‖ ‖‖‖‖ ‖‖‖‖ ‖‖‖‖ ‖‖‖‖ ‖‖‖‖ ‖‖‖‖

HALF WHITE AND HALF INDIAN

*T*he vaunted goal of allotment policy was self-sufficiency among Indians. This meant raising livestock and growing vegetables. In fact, many western tribes had been cross-breeding and racing horses for over a century; for even longer many had bred dogs for both transportation and food.

Like quite a few buffalo-hunting Plains Indian tribes, the ancestors of northern Cheyenne storyteller John Stands In Timber lived much differently before the horse. During the summers his people cultivated corn, beans, and squash along the floodplain of the Missouri River and its tributaries, occupying large round lodges framed with cottonwood and roofed with earth. As they moved westward and acquired horses, they put farming behind them. Thus, when the government began to promote metal plows and the raising of unfamiliar crops in the 1880s, the Cheyenne were taking up agriculture all over again.

In his autobiography, Cheyenne Memories, *Stands In Timber remembers how earnestly his people tried to heed the government-appointed agricultural instructors with amusing results. By this time the northern Cheyenne had finally settled on the central Montana reservation they occupy today.*

THE GOVERNMENT started the Indians raising gardens as soon as they surrendered. Some had gardens of corn and other crops at Fort Keogh. They had forgotten how, though they all used to garden in the old days before they hunted buffalo. Now they were learning about new crops as well, things they had never seen before. The Dull Knife people got to Oklahoma in 1877 about the time the watermelons ripened, and when the Southern Cheyennes gave them some they cut them up and boiled them like squash. They did not know you could eat them raw. But later when they planted their own they put sugar with the seeds. They said it would make them sweeter when they grew.

When they reached Tongue River every man was supposed to have a garden of his own. A government farmer went around to teach them. And many of them worked hard, even carrying buckets of water from the river by hand. One man, Black White Man, wanted to raise cotton. He had seen it in Oklahoma. He plowed a piece of ground and smoothed it up, and when it was ready he took his wife's quilt and made little pieces from the inside and planted them with a garden hoe. When his wife missed the quilt, she got after him. He was afraid to tell her, but finally he said, "I got it and took out the cotton and planted it. We will have more quilts than we need, as soon as it grows."

When they first learned to plow in Oklahoma the farmer told them to get ready and come to a certain place and he would show them. They did not understand. They thought "Get ready" meant fancy costumes and not their new pants and shirts. So everybody had feathers on their heads and necklaces and leggings and fancy moccasins. It looked like a dance, not a farming lesson. And all the women and children went along to see them.

The farmer told one man to grab the handles while he started ahead with the team. But the plow jumped out of the ground and turned over, and the Indian fell down. But he tried again, and by the time they got back around he was doing pretty well. Then they all tried. At last they came to one man who had been watching closely. When he started off the dirt rolled right over and he went clear around that way, and the criers started announcing, "Ha-aah! See that man!" The women made war cries and everybody hollered just as if he had counted coup. . . .

From 1890 on the Cheyennes were getting wagons as well as plows. Some of them had quite a lot of trouble learning to drive, like Big Foot and Tall White Man, in Ashland.

The Ashland District farmer was named Heywood. When these two got their wagons he came to teach them how to put the harness together and get it onto the horses. Then he hitched them up and explained how to drive and work the brakes. He told them to grease the wheels if they squeaked. Then he went on to the next place.

As soon as he left, these two got up on the seat. But they did not like the farmer's way of holding the lines. They seemed too long for one man to have both. They were used to guiding saddle horses with little ropes around the jaw. So Big Foot took one line and Tall White Man took the other. They decided if they wanted to turn, one could pull and the other let go.

They started out toward the hills and had a fine ride. But soon the wheels began to squeak. The farmer had told them about the grease, but they did not understand where to put it, so they just rubbed it on the spokes and rim of the wheel, and the squeaking kept on. "Well, the farmer can fix it," they said.

They came to a little hill, and locked the brakes as they had been taught. But at the bottom they could not get the brakes loose again. The team could not move the wagon at all. At last Big Foot went back to get an ax and chopped the blocks off.

The next hill was steeper and they were afraid to go down. Tall White Man remembered how he had seen a white man holding his buggy wheels back with his hands on a steep hill. So they decided to try it. But the wagon was too heavy to hold. It jumped forward and hit the horses, and threw Tall White Man over the top of the wheel and down in front of it, and ran over his legs. Big Foot could not stop the horses, so he just hung on. They went faster and faster down the hill and finally crashed into an ash tree at the bottom. The horses ran on either side of it.

Tall White Man came down and chopped the horses loose. They went home without any more trouble, and took the harness all apart and put it back in the box. And they waited for the farmer. He laughed and laughed. He showed them what to do again, and made them understand where to grease the wheels, and fixed new blocks, and told them not to take the harness apart next time but hang it up. And he gave them some hats and overalls and told them to try again.

The next day they went on holding one line apiece, and nearly tipped the wagon over when they met someone on a narrow trail and tried to get out of his way. But they were doing better so they decided to go visiting in Ashland and show off their new outfit. The only trouble was the clothes. They had gotten too hot, so they cut the tops out of the hats, and the fronts and backs of the pants. They still had their breech clouts on. They felt very stylish. They met the farmer on the way and he almost died laughing at them. "You have ruined the pants," he said. "No," said Big Foot, "not for us. We are mixed, half white and half Indian."

JOHN STANDS IN TIMBER, *Northern Cheyenne*

4

WE WANT TO TELL YOU SOMETHING

Here Albert Yava, a Hopi Indian from First Mesa in Arizona, tells how his people confronted the land-division menace in the early 1890s. They dispatched this little lecture on the Hopi way of life, family organization, and traditional farming to the "Washington chiefs."

Unlike the gulf within the Omaha over allotment, the more conservative Hopi Pueblo villages of Arizona were fairly unified against it. Interestingly, they still desired some "paper" clarifying their special land rights. Their request was quite bold, for they were requesting approval for the very native, communal system the entire assimilation program was targeted to destroy. As Yava describes, this involved inheriting lands through the female line and working together so that no villagers were left wanting.

I DON'T KNOW where [Senator] Dawes got his knowledge of Indian ways, but he was dead set against a tribe or clan owning communal lands. The 1890 law said that clan lands and tribal lands should be abolished and every individual given a plot for himself. A couple of years after that the Government began to survey the Hopi lands to divide them up, and they did all this without any consultations with responsible Hopi leaders. They started around Oraibi and ran into difficulties when they tried to allot one clan's land to individuals outside that clan. They only stirred up confusion and resentment by what they were doing.

Old Tom Keam was very concerned about the whole land question, the lack of an officially designated Hopi reservation and the carving up of the clan lands as well. He thought that the Hopis had better get together and do something to keep their lands and landholding system intact. In 1894 he went around urging the village and ceremonial leaders to unite and write a petition asking that the Government protect the Hopi claims. He talked with the leaders a good long time before he convinced them that it was important to put up a solid front. The villages had never had a tradition of working together. Each one considered itself to be an independent group. The Hopis had never seen themselves as a single tribe that could act in a unified way, but rather as separate village communities, you might say separate political entities.

Tom Keam persuaded them to send an appeal from the Hopi people to Washington. He drew up the letter in his own handwriting and had it taken to all the important men in the villages and read to them. After that they signed. On First Mesa, representatives of Walpi, Sichomovi and Tewa Village signed. On Second Mesa he got signatures of people living in Shongopovi, Shipaulovi and Mishongnovi, and on Third Mesa from Oraibi. Practically every clan and family was represented. One hundred and twenty-three men in all signed by making their clan marks.

The petition went into great detail explaining the traditional system of

Last page of the 1894 Hopi petition protesting allotment, with Indian officials indicating their approval by drawing symbols of their clans clan landholding, and why so much land was required by a family to keep it alive in this desert country. Although the petition was received in Washington, there never was a reply to it, and on the Hopi side there was no follow-up. The Government continued to carve up the clan lands, but finally, about fifteen or sixteen years later, it gave up on this because there was so much confusion and resistance. However, there are still some fields over in Oraibi and Moencopi that are known as allotment lands.

Moqui Villages
Arizona March 27 & 28, 1894

To the Washington Chiefs:

During the last two years strangers have looked over our land with spy-glasses and made marks upon it, and we know but little of what it means. As we believe that you have no wish to disturb our Possessions, we want to tell you something about this Hopi land.

None of us wer[e] asked that it should be measured into separate lots, and given to individuals for they would cause confusion.

The family, the dwelling house and the field are inseparable, because the woman is the heart of these, and they rest with her. Among us the family traces its kin from the mother, hence all its possessions are hers. The man builds the house but the woman is the owner, because she repairs and preserves it; the man cultivates the field, but he renders its harvest into the woman's keeping, because upon her it rests to prepare the food, and the surplus of stores for barter depends upon her thrift.

A man plants the fields of his wife, and the fields assigned to the children she bears, and informally he calls them his, although in fact they are not. Even of the field which he inherits from his mother, its harvests he may dispose of at will, but the field itself he may not. He may permit his son to occupy it and gather its produce, but at the father's death the son may not own it, for then it passes to the father's sister's son or nearest mother's kin, and thus our fields and houses always remain with our mother's family.

According to the number of children a woman has, fields for them are assigned to her, from some of the lands of her family group, and her husband takes care of them. Hence our fields are numerous but small, and several belonging to the same family may be close together, or they may be miles apart, because arable localities are not continuous. There are other reasons for the irregularity in size and situation of our family lands, as interrupted sequence of inheritance caused by extinction of families, but chiefly owing to the following condition, and to which we especially invite your attention.

In the Spring and early Summer there usually comes from the Southwest a succession of gales, oftentimes strong enough to blow away the sandy soil from the face of some of our fields, and to expose the underlying clay, which is hard, and sour, and barren; as the sand is the only fertile land, when it moves, the planters must follow it, and other fields must be provided in place of those which have been devastated. Sometimes generations pass away and these barren spots remain, while in other instances, after a few years, the winds have again restored the desirable sand upon them. In such event its fertility is disclosed by the nature of the grass and shrubs that grow upon it. If these are promising, a number of us unite to clear off the land and make it again fit for planting, when it may be given back to its former owner, or if a long time has elapsed, to other heirs, or it may be given to some person of the same family group, more in need of a planting place.

These limited changes in land holding are effected by mutual discussion and concession among the elders, and among all the thinking men and women of the family groups interested. In effect, the same system of holding, and the same method of planting, obtain among the Tewa, and all the Hopi villages, and under them we provide ourselves with food in abundance.

The American is our elder brother, and in everything he can teach us, except in the method of growing corn in these waterless sand valleys, and in that we are sure we can teach him. We believe that you have no desire to change our system of small holdings, nor do we think that you wish to remove any of our ancient landmarks, and it seems to us that the conditions we have mentioned afford sufficient grounds for this requesting to be left undisturbed.

Further it has been told to us, as coming from Washington, that neither measuring nor individual papers are necessary for us to keep possession of our villages, our peach orchards and our springs. If this be so, we should like to ask what need there is to bring confusion into our accustomed system of holding corn fields.

We are aware that some ten years ago a certain area around our land, was proclaimed to be for our use, but the extent of this area is unknown to us, nor has any Agent, ever been able to point it out, for its boundaries have never been measured. We most earnestly desire to have one continuous boundary ring enclosing all the Tewa and all the Hopi lands, and that it shall be large enough to afford sustenance for our increasing flocks and herds. If such a scope can be confirmed to us by a paper from your hands, securing us forever against intrusion, all our people will be satisfied.

[The above Hopi petition was signed in clan symbols by 123 principals of kiva societies, clan chiefs, and village chiefs of Walpi, Tewa Village, Sichomovi, Mishongnovi, Shongopovi, Shipaulovi, and Oraibi.]

ALBERT YAVA, *Hopi*

5

HE-NA TOM, THE HOODWINKER

Spiritual movements to resist the intrusions of white culture cropped up throughout the nineteenth century all over Indian America. Sometimes their charismatic leaders asked their followers to reject the white man's goods and skills. That would purify them for the day when outsiders would disappear or be destroyed and traditional Indian life would return.

In the following story a Yurok woman, Lucy Thompson, describes a seer who appeared around 1865 among the Smith River Indians of northern California, but whose prophet's garb hid a con man's heart.

THIS INDIAN was a Smith River, and the Klamath Indians in their tongue, called him, He-na Tom. In the year about eighteen hundred and sixty five, this He-na Tom, while living at his home on Smith River, which is north from the Klamath River, his wife became sick and died, and he mourned her loss greatly. In the fall he had a prophetic dream, which caused him to commence a sort of revival among the Smith River Indians, telling them to destroy everything they had ever received from the white people, discard all the clothing, houses and in fact, burn all and everything, and go back to their old Indian way of living entirely, and in a short time all the dead Indians would come back to life, to this world. . . .

So in the fall, after the Klamaths had finished putting in the fish dam, and the Indians from all parts of the country had been invited to come and see the ceremony, and the White Deer Skin Dance was going on, He-na Tom made his appearance among them with his sayings, telling them to destroy all their white man's goods, burn all the houses that were made in the white man's way, and tear down all their Indian houses, but not to burn the lumber of the Indian houses, thus leaving a clear opening, and for all of them to bring all their Indian money and wealth of all kinds, and hang it up in plain view, around him where he was lying, covered with Indian blankets made of deer skin.

He told them to go ahead with the White Deer Skin Dance, so when the dead ones appeared, they would all dance with them and make a big jubilee, and all of them who failed to comply with his holy orders, and not bring their valuables, that it would all turn into rock or rocks, and those that disbelieved and did not come, would themselves turn to rock.

He had a great many of the Klamath Indians of the wealthy class, all of the poor class, and a few of the high class that was wild and willing to follow, and there was a lot of valuable property and things destroyed, while the shelves or tables were loaded with provision for the dead when they came, so they could eat, dance and all be joyful, while all the white people were to turn to rocks.

Some of the wise ones of the high class, that were versed in the secret mysteries, hung back saying no, that they wanted to see. While they were claiming that He-na Tom had gone to meet the dead Indians, and that he would be back with them that night, three or four of the doubtful ones went over to where the large piles of Indian blanket were by a fire, and on lifting up the blankets behold, there was He-na Tom. They spoke to him, calling him by name, but he did not answer, his followers claimed that his body was there, but that his spirit had gone to meet the dead ones.

When the old ones who were so highly versed in the mysteries as not to be hoodwinked, had seen enough to convince them that there was no truth in it, they shook their heads, quietly moved back and retired to their camps or homes, saying that He-na's prophesies were a fake, and that he was a humbug. As it turned out, that night He-na Tom slipped down the Klamath River, to the mouth, and up the coast, back to Smith River, his home.

LUCY THOMPSON, *Yurok*

6

THE DEAD DID NOT RETURN

When he was a boy, this sixty-year-old oral historian remembers, he snuck out of his school dormitory to join Sioux Indians performing the Ghost Dance. As he told anthropologist Ella Deloria, herself a Sioux, they danced and sang for the return of their dead relatives and their disappearing way of life.

Inspired by a Paiute visionary named Wovoka, the Ghost Dance was taken up by disheartened tribes across the Plains and beyond in the 1880s. Its tragic end came shortly before Christmas Day, 1890. A bedraggled band of starving Ghost Dancers was camping along Wounded Knee Creek. They had been pursued by U.S. Cavalry soldiers who feared an outbreak. Discovering the Indians, they trained howitzer cannons on their tipis. When soldiers searched for weapons, one Sioux was thought to reach for a hidden gun. Within an hour more than two hundred Indian men, women, and children lay dead or dying in the snow.

IT WAS over fifty years ago. A big new government school had been put up at Pine Ridge, and we were kept there, boys and girls *together*—an unheard-of thing. We wore *Wasicu* clothes, which neither fitted nor felt right on us. In fact, we looked terrible in them, but we had to wear them or be punished.

The rumor got about: "The dead are to return. The buffalo are to return. The Dakota people will get back their own way of life. The white people will soon go away, and that will mean happier times for us once more!"

That part about the dead returning was what appealed to me. To think I should see my dear mother, grandmother, brothers and sisters again! But, boylike, I soon forgot about it, until one night when I was rudely wakened in the dormitory. "Get up, put on your clothes and slip downstairs, we are running away," a boy was hissing into my ear.

Soon fifty of us, little boys about eight to ten, started out across country over hills and valleys, running all night. I know now that we ran almost thirty miles. There on the Porcupine Creek thousands of Dakota people were in camp, all hurrying about very purposefully. In a long sweat lodge with openings at both ends, people were being purified in great companies for the holy dance, men by themselves and women by themselves, of course.

A woman quickly spied us and came weeping toward us. "These also shall take part," she was saying of us. So a man called out, "You runaway boys, come here." They stripped our ugly clothes from us and sent us inside. When we were well purified, they sent us out at the other end and placed sacred shirts on us. They were of white muslin with a crow, a fish, stars, and other symbols painted on. I never learned what they meant. Everyone wore one magpie and one eagle feather in his hair, but in our case there was nothing to tie them to. The school had promptly ruined us by shaving off our long hair till our scalps showed lighter than our faces!

The people, wearing the sacred shirts and feathers, now formed a ring. We were in it. All joined hands. Everyone was respectful and quiet, expecting something wonderful to happen. It was not a glad time, though. All walked cautiously and in awe, feeling their dead were close at hand.

The leaders beat time and sang as the people danced, going round to the left in a sidewise step. They danced without rest, on and on, and they got out of breath but still they kept going as long as possible. Occasionally someone thoroughly exhausted and dizzy fell unconscious into the center and lay there "dead." Quickly those on each side of him closed the gap and went right on. After a while, many lay about in that condition. They were now "dead" and seeing their dear ones. As each one came to, she, or he, slowly sat up and looked about, bewildered, and then began wailing inconsolably.

One of the leaders, a medicineman, asked a young girl, "My kinswoman, why do you weep?" Then she told him tearfully what she had just seen, and he in turn proclaimed it to the people. Then all wailed with her. It was very dismal.

I remember two of the songs:

> Mother, hand me my sharp knife,
> Mother, hand me my sharp knife,
> Here come the buffalo returning—
> Mother, hand me my sharp knife!

> Mother, do come back!
> Mother, do come back!
> My little brother is crying for you—
> My father says so!

The visions varied at the start, but they ended the same way, like a chorus describing a great encampment of all the Dakotas who had ever died, where

Anthropologist James Mooney took this photograph of the Sioux Ghost Dance shortly before the massacre of followers of the religious movement at Wounded Knee, South Dakota, in December 1890.

all were related and therefore understood each other, where the buffalo came eagerly to feed them, and there was no sorrow but only joy, where relatives thronged out with happy laughter to greet the newcomer. That was the best of all!

Waking to the drab and wretched present after such a glowing vision, it was little wonder that they wailed as if their poor hearts would break in two with disillusionment. But at least they had seen! The people went on and on and could not stop, day or night, hoping perhaps to get a vision of their own dead, or at least to hear of the visions of others. They preferred that to rest or food or sleep. And so I suppose the authorities did think they were crazy—but they weren't. They were only terribly unhappy.

ANONYMOUS, *Pine Ridge Sioux*

HEARTS ON
THE GROUND

Forcibly relocating tribes was a practice that carried over into the early twentieth century. Here the small Cupeño tribe of southern California is shown en route to its new Pala Reservation in 1903, having been evicted from its traditional village beside the hot springs at Agua Caliente after several years of unsuccessful legal resistance.

I t took more than a decade for allotment to penetrate all corners of Indian America. When an Oklahoma Creek heard that Dawes officials were heading his way, he fumed, ''Egypt had its locusts, Asiatic countries their cholera, France had its Jacobins, England its black plague, Memphis had the yellow fever . . . but it was left for unfortunate Indian Territory to be afflicted with the worst scourge of the nineteenth century, the Dawes Commission."

As the specter of land redistribution reached these so-called Five Civilized Tribes in present-day Oklahoma, Indians braced themselves. Representatives of some twenty tribes met to form an all-Indian state. Congress responded with the Curtis Act of 1898, abolishing with one stroke their tribal governments and leaving Indians no legal say in the matter. Nine years later their territory became the state of Oklahoma (from the Choctaw, meaning "Red People," a name suggested by Choctaw historian Allen Wright).

Before a tribe could be allotted, however, some semblance of Indian acceptance was called for. Old agreements were brushed aside and dirty tricks were common in a replay of the removal era seventy years before. As described by one Cherokee, "The Indian people don't want their allotments . . . but at the same time some of them take them, for they scared them into it. They are like children with the white man. The white man can come among us and give us whiskey and get us drunk and he can get us to do anything . . . they would send half-breeds around . . . and hunt for the names of the full-bloods without their consent, and they would take the names down and present them before the Dawes Commission . . . and take an oath on it . . . [then, the full-bloods] would find a certificate of allotment sent to them at the post office."

Among the Cherokee the threat of losing tribal lands revived a secret society called the Ketowahs, or "Nighthawks." During the chaotic Civil War years this brotherhood defended Cherokee families against pillaging by both North and South. Now a forty-year-old traditionalist named Redbird Smith rallied its full-blood membership against allotment, and was harassed by white authorities in return. The rebels even hired lawyers to argue their cause during congressional debates. In 1905, when general Cherokee resistance to allotment crumbled, Smith formed a renegade enclave of Cherokees in the Cookson hills of eastern Oklahoma to preserve their sense of tribal unity.

Among Oklahoma Creeks the anti-allotment fight was led by Chitto Harjo, a full-blood whose name meant "Recklessly Brave" but who was popularly called Crazy Snake. Realizing that allotment spelled doom for Creek independence, he founded a "Snake" government, and selected a settlement called Hickory Ground for its capital. Five thousand Creeks rallied to his cause before Harjo was jailed by U.S. lawmen for insurrection. When he was freed, Harjo returned his supporters to the backwoods, sparking the last major insurrection in Indian Territory. In 1912, Harjo died of gunshot wounds when government troops tried to capture him. By then, however, all of Indian territory was allotted. On the map, at least, the Five Civilized Tribes were no more.

When Theodore Roosevelt became president in 1901 he praised allotment as "a mighty pulverizing engine to break up the tribal mass." Yet after the Dawes Act was passed in 1887, it took a while for that engine to gain full steam. First to be affected were the Iowa Indians. After their reservation was surveyed, only about ten percent of its original territory was required for 160-acre plots to be distributed to every Iowa Indian family. That left ninety percent, or about 207,000 acres, for prompt purchase by the U.S. government for white homesteaders. Practically every tribe lost land this way. The Cheyennes and Arapahos of Indian Territory, Plains Indians who

Salish Indians selling baskets to white passersby in Seattle, Washington, c. 1900

were forcibly relocated from ancestral homelands far to the north, likewise had no choice but to accept allotments. Their surplus land amounted to eighty-one percent of the country that they had been told, only twenty years before, was theirs forever.

The cash that Indians received from these sales temporarily replaced government rations, which, according to the Dawes Act, they would enjoy no longer. Many purchased cattle and took up ranching; others tried small-scale farming. Tribes like the Blackfeet and Assiniboine, for instance, showed a knack for running successful cattle operations. But frequently, they discovered their 160-acre future homes were located in isolated corners of the old reservations without streams or underground water. "Gumbo with greasewood on it," was how an Assiniboine from Montana described his allotment. "There were cracks in it so big you could almost see China."

Other Indians either lacked the capital to carry their operation over the long seasons before cattle or crops could be sold, or else could not get used to plowing and harvesting with unfamiliar equipment. In 1890, 1894, and 1897 Congress passed laws that freed Indians to lease for a pittance their acres to larger, better organized white outfits. This often turned Indians into impoverished, absentee landlords on the fringes of white settlements, dependent on the government for food once again. This was precisely the opposite of what Dawes Act advocates had intended. Now Indian grass fed white men's cattle, which in turn were sold to fill white men's pockets.

Another unforeseen twist thwarted the grand design of the Dawes Act. A factor that was central to the "Can't Go Beyond"—the translation of an Osage Indian phrase for allotment—was the old "Vanishing Indian" idea that native population was on the wane. It was true that the overall American Indian population hit an all-time low around the turn of the century. From an estimated 1.5 million native people at the time of first white contact, the number of Indians was down to 237,000 by 1900. Much to everyone's surprise, however, in another few years the population curve swung up again.

If recovery of Indian numbers continued, before long the original 160-acre parcels of allotted land would be subdivided into smaller and smaller homesteads for the increasing heirs. This also meant that descendants of the original Indian would have to eke out a living on plots smaller than an acre, or be forced to lease to non-Indians who could afford to patch together a large pasturage.

In 1902 the U.S. Congress let heirs in this predicament get rid of inherited parcels before the twenty-five-year protective period was up. Over the next three years hungry, impatient, or confused Indians sold over a quarter-million acres for quick cash. In 1906 the Burke Act gave the Bureau of Indian Affairs the power to decide when Indians could handle their own affairs. Deemed "competent," an Indian could then sell to the top bidder. On the Coeur d'Alene reservation in Idaho this law hastened the loss of more than sixty percent of all allotments.

In Oklahoma, particularly, shady deals were common. Fraudulent wills were drafted for dead Indians. Deeds were forged for tribespeople who never existed. White opportunists were appointed as "guardians" for Indian children soon to inherit land from their parents. Allottees were bribed or murdered to steal their property.

Although tribal uprisings were now a thing of the past, the helplessness of Indians during these turn-of-the-century decades resulted in outlawry by angry, isolated young Indians with no outlet for their warrior heritage. In Canada a Cree named Almighty Voice slaughtered another man's steer, launching a manhunt that made him a folk hero after he was killed by Royal Canadian Mounted Police in 1897. In the fall of 1909 a Paiute named Willie Boy, who murdered another Indian, became the object of a widely publicized manhunt. Around 1910 an Indian rustler named "Shoshone Mike" harassed white settlers in northern Nevada. The last official Indian "wars" fought by the U.S. Army were actually outbursts by Navajo (in 1913) and Ute (in 1915) individuals whose powerless leaders could not control them.

During these years a new religion from the Southwest took the place of shorter-lived messianic movements such as the Ghost Dance. Its rites revolved around consumption of a sacred, hallucinogenic cactus known as peyote (*Lophophora wiliamsii*). Peyote meetings expressed a blend of Indian and Christian spirituality. Instead of preaching defiance to the white man's ways, they endorsed family cooperation and pan-Indian unity. Incorporated as the Native American Church in 1918, peyotism attracted many in Oklahoma, and soon spread among tribes as far away as the northern Plains and the Great Lakes.

It is ironic that while Indians themselves were lectured about abandoning old customs and intertribal warfare, "savage" Indian life was exploited in popular Wild West shows that toured the United States and overseas. In the most renowned of these performances, lasting from 1883 to 1916, William "Buffalo Bill" Cody hired Indians to chase covered wagons and sign autographs. White reformers and educated Indians alike decried these "circuses" as barbaric throwbacks to a primitive past that was best forgotten. To counter stereotypes of "wild" Indians, their "agricultural fairs" promoted the New Indian as a financially independent, reading and writing Christian farmer. At the same time, America's early anthropologists produced more educational exhibitions of old Indian arts and culture. Tribespeople built authentic housetypes and danced in traditional dress at the 1893 Chicago World's Columbian Exposition, the 1898 Trans-Mississippi Exposition in Omaha, and the 1904 Louisiana Purchase Exposition in St. Louis.

With so many mixed messages in the air, it is not surprising that on the reservation, discussions were often tense between natives who retained the old ways and those who adopted the white man's road. Rather than using the simplistic word "factionalism" to characterize such intra-tribal dissension, anthropologist Loretta Fowler describes it as an abiding debate between "shared symbols" and their "contested meanings." The value of her phrases is that they remind us how, even in these powerless years, Indians were still struggling to determine their destiny.

To some degree, however, every tribesperson had to face the question of how white to become. Whether the opposite poles of opinion within Indian communities were described as Conservative or Progressive, "Old Bear" versus "Young Bear (among the Omaha), or "hostiles" and "friendlies" (among the Hopi), within many tribes this debate caused grievous splits that reverberated down to the family level.

In 1900 the Indian population in the United States was barely surviving on 171 steadily shrinking land areas scattered throughout twenty-one different states and territories. Along with shock waves of land loss, crippled tribal authority, and internal disagreements, they were suffering from malnutrition and new outbreaks of tuberculosis, influenza, and trachoma. This chapter covers one of the bleakest epochs in Indian history, the turn of the century, when, as a Crow elder phrased it, "our hearts were on the ground."

1

LIFE ON THE CHECKERBOARD

T he *"Jim Runningwolf"* of the following anecdote is fictional, but his problem
is not. He was invented by Oklahoma Indian writer Ruth Muskrat Bronson
to dramatize the consequences of land allotment.

A fatal weakness in the concept was its assumption that Indians were dying out.
Instead, their numbers gradually picked up after 1910. How the original 160-acre
allotments were to support successive generations of Indian children was a question
the Dawes advocates never addressed.

As Bronson illustrates in this sketch from Indians Are People, Too, the parcels
soon became so diced up among descendants that no single heir could possibly
sustain a family. With some allotments sold and others retained in Indian hands,
a *"checkerboard"* of land ownership blanketed many reservation maps. A non-
Indian with enough money and know-how could lease adjoining squares from
Indians to create a big, promising cattle operation—a practice on many reservations
today.

JIM RUNNINGWOLF is typical of much of the Indian population. He doesn't know how to farm. His people were hunters. But he sits
on his allotment wishing someone would come along and show him what
to do. The Indian Agent comes along.

"You are not using your land," he says to Jim. "Why don't you let me
lease it for you to that white farmer who was looking it over the other day?"
All right with Jim. The government has always insisted it knew best anyway.
So Jim Runningwolf and many others like him become petty landlords living
in idleness on an annual rent barely sufficient to hold off starvation—never
enough to lift the shadow of malnutrition from their households.

Then there is the problem of heirship. When Jim Runningwolf dies there
will be four daughters and one son to inherit his one hundred and sixty
acres. No one of the five heirs has enough money to buy out the other four.
The usual way a white family handles such a situation is for the family
member who wants to keep the farm to mortgage the land for enough to
buy out the other heirs. The Runningwolf heirs can't do this for this land
cannot be sold because Jim Runningwolf is a ward. So, in the absence of a
will, the only thing to do would be to partition his land among the five

heirs. In a country ill adapted to agriculture, thirty-five acres are not worth much money, so the land will probably not be partitioned. Instead, the government will go on leasing the land, dividing the lease money among the heirs down through the generations.

There are pieces of land on the books of the Indian Office so divided among heirs that the annual lease income therefrom to any one heir is less than one cent. Yet the annual cost to the government to administer the estate is estimated at approximately fifty times as much as the annual lease the heir receives.

RUTH MUSKRAT BRONSON, *Cherokee*

2

BIG MAN'S RULES AND LAWS

*I**n his regular column for the native Oklahoma newspaper* Indian Journal, *the Creek Indian poet and journalist Alexander Posey regularly poked fun at the white man's greed. He satirized attempts to change Indian ways through new names, short haircuts, and slogans such as "long stride," by which Washington meant "civilized." Posey's native readers enjoyed his puns, inside jokes, and the pidgin English dialect of his recurring cast of characters—especially the wry old-timer, Hotgun. Posey helped Indians regain through shared humor some of the self-respect they were losing with their lands.*

Posey was born in 1873 and graduated from Bacone Indian University in Tah-lequah, Oklahoma. There he learned to set type and to write. Before his premature death at the age of thirty-four he gained renown as an author, and prepared his people for statehood. This piece, from his weekly "Fux Fixico's Letters," appeared on April 24, 1903. Sofky is the traditional southeastern Indian corn soup; "Big Man" refers to white officials; "Crazy Snake" is the Creek Indian rebel against allotment, Chitto Harjo.

WELL, SO BIG MAN at Washington was made another rule like that one about making the Injin cut his hair off short like a prize fighter or saloon keeper. Big Man he was say this time the Injin was had to change his name just like if the marshal was had a writ for him. So, if the Injin's name is Wolf Warrior, he was had to call himself John Smith, or maybe so

Alexander Posey

Bill Jones, so nobody else could get his mail out of the postoffice. Big Man say Injin name like Sitting Bull or Tecumseh was too hard to remember and don't sound civilized like General Cussed Her or old Grand Pa Harry's Son.

Hotgun he say the Big Man's rule was heap worse than allotment, and Crazy Snake he say he was hear white man say all time you could take everything away from a him but you couldn't steal his good name.

Guess so that was alright 'cause they was nothing to a name nohow if you can't borrow some money on it at the bank. Tookpafka Micco he say he was druther had a deed to his land than a big name in the newspaper. When I ask him what he do after he sell his land, he say he don't know, like Bob Ingersoll. Then he say he was let the future take care of its own self like a calf when it was get too old to suck. Guess so Tookpafka Micco was made up his mind to drink sofky and eat sour bread and be glad like a young cat with a ball a yarn before the fire place in the winter time.

Well, so we hear lots a talk about big progress in Creek nation and read about it in the newspaper before breakfast time. They was good news all time about long stride and development and things like that till you can't make a crop and get out of the hole if you was try to hear all of it. Hotgun he say he think he was had to put beeswax in his ears like Few Leases (Ulysses) in olden time.

But look like you don't hear nothing about fullblood Injins 'way back behind the hills that was had they sofky patch and cabin on land that was done filed on by some half-breed or maybe so white man that was had a right. We don't hear nothing about them kind a Injin at all. But we hear all time about some fellow that was find a coal mine with a post auger, or maybe so some other fellow that was strike oil that was shoot up like a squirrel gun soon as he touch it.

Must be the Big Man that was look out for Injin was look out for himself too much. Hotgun he say it was natural for the Big Man to do that way 'cause he was had the chance. Maybe so, Hotgun he say, that was the only law civilized man don't want to break.

ALEXANDER POSEY, *Creek*

3

THE OUTRAGE OF ALLOTMENT

T*he life of DeWitt Clinton Duncan, a part-Cherokee from Vinita, Oklahoma, spanned the key events of Cherokee history in the nineteenth century. As a boy he experienced the mass eviction of southeastern Indian tribes to lands west of the Mississippi. In 1906, when he was seventy-six years old, Duncan told a Senate committee about trying to survive on a small allotment.*

Duncan graduated from Dartmouth College in 1861, returning to Indian Territory just after the Civil War. He taught English, Latin, and Greek, became prominent in Cherokee tribal politics, and was known under the pen name Too-Qua-Stee. Yet when allotment arrived, none of this prestige exempted him from the fate of every other Cherokee.

SUPPOSE THE Federal Government should send a survey company into the midst of some of your central counties of Kansas or Colorado or Connecticut and run off the surface of the earth into sections and quarter sections and quarter quarter sections and set apart to each one of the inhabitants of that county 60 acres, rescinding and annulling all title to every inch of the earth's surface which was not included in that 60 acres, would the State of Connecticut submit to it?

Would Colorado submit to it? Would Kansas brook such an outrage? No! It would be ruin, immeasurable ruin—devastation. There is not an American citizen in any one of those States would submit to it, if it cost him every drop of his heart's blood. . . .

Under our old Cherokee régime I spent the early days of my life on the farm up here of 300 acres, and arranged to be comfortable in my old age; but the allotment scheme came along and struck me during the crop season, while my corn was ripening in full ear. I was looking forward to the crop of corn hopefully for some comforts to be derived from it during the months of the winter. When I was assigned to that 60 acres, and I could take no more under the inexorable law of allotment enforced upon us Cherokees, I had to relinquish every inch of my premises outside of that little 60 acres. What is the result? There is a great scramble of persons to find land—the office was located here in our town—to file upon. . . .

What a condition! I have 60 acres of land left me; the balance is all gone. I am an old man, not able to follow the plow as I used to when a boy. What am I going to do with it? For the last few years, since I have had my allotment, I have gone out there on that farm day after day. I have used the ax, the hoe, the spade, the plow, hour for hour, until fatigue would throw me exhausted upon the ground.

Next day I repeated the operation, and let me tell you, Senators, I have exerted all my ability, all industry, all my intelligence, if I have any, my will, my ambition, the love of my wife—all these agencies I have employed to make my living out of that 60 acres, and, God be my judge, I have not been able to do it. I am not able to do it. I can't do it. I have not been able to clear expenses.

It will take every ear of the bounteous crop on that 60 acres—for this year is a pretty good crop year—it will take every bushel of it to satisfy the debts that I have incurred to eke out a living during the meager years just passed. And I am here to-day, a poor man upon the verge of starvation— my muscular energy gone, hope gone. I have nothing to charge my calamity to but the unwise legislation of Congress in reference to my Cherokee people. . . .

I am in that fix, Senators, you will not forget now that when I use the word "I" I mean the whole Cherokee people. I am in that fix. What am I to do? I have a piece of property that doesn't support me, and is not worth a cent to me, under the same inexorable, cruel provisions of the Curtis law that swept away our treaties, our system of nationality, our every existence, and wrested out of our possession our vast territory. . . .

DEWITT CLINTON DUNCAN, *Cherokee*

4

FARMING AND FUTILITY

C *ontrary to public opinion, many western Indians demonstrated that they could transform from hunters to ranchers or farmers if given half a chance. But as Martin Charlot from Montana describes here, their efforts to live as whites wanted were often sabotaged by white homesteaders eyeing their land base or by half-hearted government support.*

Martin was the son of Old Charlot, chief of the Flathead-Salish who occupied prime agricultural land in the Bitterroot Valley. By the early 1890s, pressure to leave became intolerable and they resettled in the Pend d'Oreille Indian reservation to the north. After that, they were on their own.

IN THE BITTERROOT when my grandfather, Victor, was chief, we Salish started farming. The government told us to do it and we did. We had no equipment except the few things the agent gave us, such as harness and plows. We made fenceposts in the mountains and hauled them home by packing them on our horses. Each of the Indian families fenced small acreages and protected their grain. Then time went on and my grandfather died. My father, Charlot, became chief.

We continued farming. The agent told my father to tell the people they would receive wheat and oat seed. My father told the tribesmen to do more farming and get the seed. They did. We got more plows and harness. We helped each other with the farm work. One Indian farmer had two or three plows going at the same time. Everyone helped everyone else in the harvest. We didn't have any threshing machines. We put the grain on buffalo hides that the women had sewed together. Then we led horses over the grain to separate it. Several of the men would lift the robes and shake them to let the wind blow the chaff out. We also had two mills going and we used to fetch the grain to the mill on pack horses. The mill was about 12 miles from where we lived.

Everything was going along fine. We were making a good living and learning the White man's way. Then Garfield came to see us. He came to visit my father, for Charlot was the head man among the Salish. Garfield told my father that we would have to move out of the Bitterroot and go to the Jocko.

"I am doing some farming," my father said. "I am getting good crops and my people and I are living here as the agents and priests have taught us to do. I am not going to move."

"If you don't move you will be treated like a fish in dirty water," Garfield said.

"This is my home," my father answered. "By the 1855 treaty, we don't have to move. We will stay in the Bitterroot."

A general who was with Garfield spoke up and told my father that he would send an army in there and kill us if we didn't move. Still my father would not agree to go. Some of the other tribesmen pulled out and went to the Jocko. Arlee led them.

About a year later, the general came back and told my father that we had to move. He said that my father was no longer the head man of the tribe now that Washington considered Arlee the head man. That made my father mad because Arlee was not a full-blooded Salish. He was mostly Nez Percé. So every year for about three years this same general came back and asked us to go, and every time my father said he wouldn't do it. Finally, my father said that he would move to the Bannock tribe or the Shoshoni tribe and

Skookum Wallihee, a Klickitat Indian, farming his spread in Oregon, April 1911

live with them on their reservation, but that he would not go to the Jocko to live. The government men would not agree to that so we stayed in the Bitterroot.

We tried to keep on farming, but Whites came in and homesteaded our land. We could not keep the little patches where we had fenced and had raised our crops. The wild game kept getting scarcer and scarcer. Nearly 20 years went by. We had no money or supplies from the government. Our young men were getting lazy, my father said. Also, many of them wanted to move to the Jocko. One of the leaders of the Salish, Vanderberg, asked my father to take us over. He said that the time had come for us to go. My father sent word that we would move.

A man from the government came to see us. He promised that we could have some livestock. Every family would get one cow and one calf of their own. Besides that, the government would have a herd of steers for us so that every Saturday seven head of steers would be butchered and distributed to us. My father knew some White men in the Bitterroot who had good cows, so he asked if the government would buy the cows and calves from him. The agent said "no," because the cattle would drift away and we would lose them coming over.

We were told also that we should leave behind our belongings such as furniture and equipment, for we would get new things once we got to the Jocko. Some of the people really owned some good machinery and some pretty good household equipment, and they hated to leave it but thought they would get new things, so they just left it. The government man also told my father that the government would buy him a new team and buggy to make the trip over in.

"When you go through Missoula," the government man said, "you look at the residences and see the best-made house that you like. Our carpenters will make one for you just like it."

But when we got to the Jocko, things were not the way they were promised. Whatever we got, we had to work for. There was no new machinery nor household stuff for those people who had left theirs behind. We never saw or heard of the seven head of steers that were to be butchered every Saturday. We never got the cow and the calf apiece like we were promised. My father did not get his new house. Instead, we cut logs and had to haul them to the mill to make lumber for our houses. Then we built our cabins, some near the Agency and more of them along Jocko Creek in the timber. Then, we were told to fence off the land we wanted. Only a few people did that. The next instruction we got was to start farming. Again, only a few people did that. My father refused to do it, although he had put in an irrigation system.

The men in the tribe did all that work digging ditches without getting much pay for it. After the irrigation system was in, many more people started farming. They were successful in farming on both sides of the Jocko River. In time, we even had a threshing machine. Just as we had done in the Bitterroot before the trouble began, we started helping each other out and got quite a bit of farming done. After the harvest, we took the grain to the flour mill and had it made up into flour for our winter provisions. The surplus grain we sold. All in all, we made a good living.

But those days didn't last either. Pretty soon, maybe in 15 years, engineers surveyed the reservation. When my father asked why they were doing it, they told him that the government was just making a survey to determine the acreage. But it wasn't long before we were allotted and the Whites moved in. Then, the government took hold of the irrigation system. They made it bigger, all right, but the Indians didn't get the water when they wanted it and needed it. Their crops burned up. Some of them went in debt. Pretty soon, most of them quit farming. The White man took over everything.

MARTIN CHARLOT, *Flathead-Salish*

5

THE HOPI PUSH OF WAR

T*his Hopi account, describing tragic division within one of the oldest Indian villages, resulted from the campaign to "Americanize" Indian societies through forced schooling and land division. It is an example of how such issues wound up pitting Indian against Indian.*

The event occurred during the peak of the allotment era. It remains vivid in twentieth-century Hopi memory, for it led to the splitting of Oraibi village and the establishment of a new Hopi settlement, the village of Hotevilla. The conflict began in the 1880s, and climaxed in 1906. By this time Oraibi Pueblo had become divided between Hostiles, who opposed sending their children to white schools, led by a priest named Yokeoma, and Friendlies, under a leader named Tewaquaptewa. Their struggle turned to violence, but then a peaceful contest, a pushing match, was proposed. A line was drawn in the sand; the two camps lined up on either side. Finally the Hostiles were pushed back of the line. That same day all four hundred of them had to pack up and leave. They walked north, camping each night, until they settled at Hotevilla. In her autobiography, Helen Sekaquaptewa, whose parents were among the exiles, recalls that tense day.

F R E Q U E N T L Y reiterated during this time was a prophecy that there would come a time when the village would be divided and one of the groups would be driven off the mesa forever and that the decision of who should go and who should stay was to hinge upon the ability of one party to push the other over a line which should be drawn on the ground. . . .

The crisis was precipitated prematurely during the first week of September,

1906, when the two factions came to an actual physical struggle. Tewaquaptewa, whose following was slightly outnumbered by the Hostiles, received private information of a plot to assassinate him; indeed he understood that the Shungopovis, rather than the Oraibians, were the instigators of the plot. Tewaquaptewa called his council together that night at his house on the northern edge of the village, September 6, and they spent the night preparing for an attack on the Hostiles in the morning. During the night he sent word to Yokeoma and his followers, who were also in council, that the Shungopovis would have to leave at once and that anyone taking their part must leave with them. . . .

Thereupon, the Friendlies set about clearing the village of Shungopovis. They began at the very spot where they stood; but every Friendly who laid hold of a Shungopovi to put him out of doors was attacked from behind by an Oraibi Hostile, so that the three went wrestling and struggling out of the door together. There was great commotion as the Friendlies carried out the Hostiles, pushing and pulling, the Hostiles resisting, struggling, kicking, and pulling the hair of their adversaries. The Hostiles were taken bodily, one by one to the northern outskirts of the village, and put down on the far side of a line which had been scratched in the sandstone, parallel to the village, some time before.

After evicting the Hostile men, the Friendlies went into each home and forcibly ejected each family, driving them out to join their menfolk on the other side of The Line. A struggling stream of humanity—men, women, and children—poured out of their houses past Tewaquaptewa's house and out of the village, being shoved and dragged and pulled by Tewaquaptewa and his excited followers. Those resisting had their clothing torn and were bruised and scratched; the majority went passively, carrying burdens, the men with set faces and the women and children frightened and crying. . . .

My father, knowing that trouble was brewing, had told the boy who took his sheep out that day to drive them toward the Hotevilla spring that night. He spent the night in the Hostile council. My mother, hearing the rumor that we might be expelled from the village, had made ready some food, a jug of water, and blankets.

There was an underground little room in our house, our secret hiding place in case of war or trouble. The entrance was a hole in the floor, covered with a sheepskin on which my mother sat as she ground her corn. There was a little window to the outside for light and air. On this morning mother put her children into this hiding place—my married sister, Verlie, about sixteen; my brother Rincon, twelve; myself, seven; and my brother Henry, two. She watched and kept telling us what was happening, saying, "Don't be afraid. Nothing will happen to you." After a while she lifted the sheepskin and said for us to come on out. She started helping us up, as the sides were steep. Just at that moment, in came Tewaquaptewa's men, who started jerking us out. I was so little, I can't remember it all. One of the men said, "The time has come for you to go, so come on out of your hiding place. . . ."

We walked into the plaza and were driven out of the village with the others. Many of the Friendly women sat on the flat housetops clapping their hands and yelling at us, making fun of us as we walked away from our home and village. . . .

Around four o'clock Yokeoma finally yielded to the continued pressure from the Friendlies. He stood up, and with all eyes on him, took a sharp rock in his hand and drew a line on the sandrock. Taking his stand with his back to the line he said, "Well, it will have to be this way now. If you pass me over this line, then I will walk." (He meant that he and his people would leave.)

Tewaquaptewa immediately jumped to the challenge. The two chiefs faced each other, each with his hands on the shoulders of his opponent. Their men rushed into the conflict, each eager to add his weight and exert his strength. Yokeoma was tall and thin. He was pushed up above the heads of the mass, gasping for breath; then he disappeared, and eventually he was passed over the line. A shout went up as Yokeoma, badly disheveled and trampled, was helped to his feet, and his men made sure that he was not hurt. As soon as he could collect himself, Yokeoma left the knot of men around him and started walking the trail to the Hotevilla spring. We all gathered our bundles and followed him.

It was dark when we got to the spring, but soon there were forty or fifty campfires burning, and preparations for sleeping under the trees were under way. A few days later it rained, and the weather turned colder. A shelter of brush and trees was thrown up, reinforced with blankets, shawls, gunny sacks, and pieces of old canvas, anything for protection against the cold. The dreary picture of the women and children crouching under this crude shelter persuaded Tewaquaptewa to further leniency. He gave four more days in which the Hostiles might go into the village, in groups of three, and bring out their belongings. Many Hostiles expressed themselves: "We don't want to go back to the village and get our food. We want to go back to our homes and live there as we have always done."

Superintendent Lemmon said to Yokeoma, "I am sorry that you are going away. I want you here for my friend." Yokeoma replied, "I do not want to go away from here." And the misery in the old man's face testified that the words came from his heart. . . .

It had been understood that the Mesa Verde area in Colorado was to be our destination. Some of the clans claimed to have originated there. But after about a week, Yokeoma stood by the spring one morning, looked out over the valley, and said, "I am staying here. Anyone who wants to, can go on." None were anxious, and none did go on. . . .

There are many big flat sandstones cropping out of the ground on the outskirts of Old Oraibi. One of them marks The Line. An inscription was scratched there by a young man named Robert Selena. Robert was a student at the Indian School at Keams Canyon and was home in the summer of 1906. He took it upon himself to mark the spot:

> WELL IT HAVE TO BE DONE
> THIS WAY NOW
> THAT WHEN YOU PASS ME OVER THIS LINE
> IT WILL BE DONE SEPT. 8, 1906

HELEN SEKAQUAPTEWA, *Hopi*

A TWENTIETH-
CENTURY
INDIAN VOICE

Society of American Indians holding Fourth Annual Meeting banquet, Philadelphia, Pennsylvania, 1914. Speakers seated against rear wall (left to right): Charles E. Dagenett (Peoria tribe), W. J. Kershaw, Commissioner of Indian Affairs Cato Sells, Rev. Sherman Coolidge (Arapaho tribe), Arthur C. Parker (Seneca tribe), Dr. Carlos Montezuma (Yavapai-Apache tribe), Carlisle Indian School founder Richard H. Pratt, and Gabe E. Parker (Choctaw tribe)

A new Indian elite emerged in the first decade of the twentieth century to advocate on behalf of Indians as a whole. The institutional expression of what scholars would label as modern "Pan-Indianism" began on October 12, 1911. On that occasion about fifty Indians convened for three days in a stately hotel in Columbus, Ohio, to launch the Society of American Indians. These elegantly dressed men and women represented full-bloods and mixed-bloods, proponents of tribal values as well as advocates of complete assimilation, popular writers and artists, lawyers and doctors. Most of them were graduates of industrial or boarding schools; their common cause was social progress and a better image for Indians across the country.

During the Society's lifespan, from 1911 until 1923, it offered a meeting ground for Indians from different cultural and professional backgrounds. But unlike multitribal movements of the past led by the Pueblo rebel Pope, the Shawnee chief Tecumseh, or the Sioux leader Sitting Bull before them, their outlets for expressing Indian discontent and aspirations would be open debates and published articles.

The society was inspired in part by a white Ohio sociologist Dr. Fayette McKenzie, who believed it was high time for Indians to lead themselves. Most of the delegates at Columbus exemplified the middle-class, progressive-minded Indians who his reform movement had tried to mold. As Seneca Indian anthropologist and historian Arthur C. Parker described that first gathering: "The Indians at Columbus were truly a superior class of men and women and 'above the class of pale invaders' I heard one visitor say. . . . Columbus was discovered this time by the Indians and the town was surprised." After the Society's third annual gathering in Denver, Colorado, Parker remarked, "It [the press] groped around for feathers, for opinions on woman suffrage and on Col. Roosevelt. It missed [the Society's] great idea . . . the call of the leaders of the race to the race to strike out into the duties of modern life and in performing them find every right that had escaped them before."

The leaders included the lean, good-looking Dr. Charles A. Eastman. Reared as a long-haired boy on the Santee Sioux Indian reservation he graduated from Dartmouth, became a reservation doctor, and authored such best sellers as *Indian Boyhood* (1902) and *The Soul of the Indian* (1911).

Another pillar of the Society was a part-Preoria Indian from Oklahoma, Charles E. Dagenett, who, since 1894, had risen through the Bureau of Indian Affairs to become its highest-placed Indian. His dual role as government bureaucrat working within the system and Indian advocate associated with colleagues who harshly criticized the Indian Service sometimes placed Dagenett in a difficult position.

Henry Roe Cloud, a young Winnebago, chaired the meetings at Columbus. Born in a wigwam along the Missiouri River in 1884, he was Yale University's first Indian graduate. Cloud remained in the forefront of the Indian rights struggle longer than any of his fellow Society members. In the 1920s he was appointed to special committees investigating reservation conditions, joined the Indian New Deal of the 1930s and in the 1940s become a reservation superintendent.

There was also Angel Decora, a young Winnebago woman whose native name meant "Fleecy Cloud Floating Into Place." She was forcibly taken from home at age six and later sent to Hampton School in Virginia. Studying illustration with the famous artist Howard Pyle, she became a successful designer but quit to teach art at Carlisle. Until her death in the influenza epidemic of 1919, she remained a staunch Indian advocate and influenced the direction of new Indian art.

The Reverend Sherman Coolidge, an Arapaho minister, was the Society's humorist. Named as a boy "Runs Mysteriously On Ice," he had been captured by the U.S. Army and adopted by a white officer named Coolidge. Later he returned to the Arapaho and Shoshone reservations as an Episcopal missionary.

The easygoing Coolidge contrasted with the volatile personality of Dr. Carlos Montezuma, whose reputation as a fierce opponent of federal paternalism started in the Society. Born a Yavapai-Apache in central Arizona, as a boy Montezuma was captured by Pima Indians around 1872. They sold him for thirty dollars to an Italian photographer who adopted him and sent him to school. Montezuma became a prominent Chicago physician and was the Society's firebrand, often goading its moderates. "I can lick you. My tribe has licked your tribe before," he once bellowed at Coolidge during one of their incessant debates over the Bureau of Indian Affairs.

Many of the delegates at Columbus shared a deep bond as alumni of Carlisle Indian School. Of its founder, Colonel Richard Pratt, they spoke almost reverentially. Following principles espoused at Carlisle, most of them applauded assimilation into white society and frowned on "tribalism." They envisioned Indian citizens as full participants in America's economic, social, and political life.

For years they lobbied, without success, for a "National Indian Day," and fought derogatory terms like "buck" and "squaw." They praised young American Indian athletes, like the Olympic champion Jim Thorpe, who were trained at Carlisle and Haskell. They distinguished pride in being Indian from stereotypes that made whites think, in the words of the Society's magazine, "that the Indians are still wild savages . . . that every Indian of whatever tribe wears, or once wore, the Sioux war bonnet . . . that Indian women all wore a feather in their hair standing straight up."

An outspoken Society member, the Yanktonai educator Chauncey Yellow Robe, condemned William "Buffalo Bill" Cody for his movie about the infamous Wounded Knee massacre. "Women and children and old men of my people, my relatives," he wrote sardonically, "were massacred with machine guns by soldiers of this Christian nation. You will soon be able to see their bravery and hair-breadth escapes in your theaters."

Montezuma urged the Society to challenge the Bureau of Indian Affairs over their peoples' worsening health and housing conditions. But fellow members protested that their "association [was not] for the purpose of antagonizing or opposing the forces of government." Impatient with the Society's moderation, Montezuma founded his own organ, *Wassaja*, whose slashing editorials reflected his fury against Indian wrongs.

In principle the Society promoted Indian education, Indian citizenship, and a federal department to handle Indian court cases. In reality it offered a forum for sharing dreams and venting resentments, but little real redress for specific cases of injustice. The Society also was weakened by internal disputes over peyotism. Its important Omaha member, the Omaha attorney Thomas Sloan, and Francis La Flesche, an Omaha writer, endorsed the new Pan-Indian faith, claiming it was an Indianized sort of Christianity that served as a positive deterrent to alcoholism and family disintegration. But Sioux authors Gertrude Bonnin and Charles Eastman insisted that peyote was an addictive scourge, a destroyer of Indian character, and a throwback to paganism. Peyote worship was threatened until the late 1920s, when a new climate of Indian reform offered protection for all native religions.

While lack of a bold policy focus contributed to the Society's waning authority, the general American public was also distracted by industrialization, the growth of trade unions, and an imminent global war. A moderate and deferential Indian rights group could not capture its imagination or galvanize its politicans. Nonetheless, the Society of American Indians represented a milestone in Indian history. It was the first lobby of modern

Indian intellectuals to play the white man's game of debate, parliamentary procedure, and public relations. It opened discussion about problems of Indian health, self-determination, education, and civil rights. It established roots for stronger Indian protests to come.

Among the Society's more effective stands was quick and angry opposition to suggestions that Indian soldiers be segregated during World War I. The idea was quietly shelved. Indeed, it remains an irony of Indian and white relations that while Indians are first to criticize the U.S. government, they are also first to volunteer for military service. This almost religious sense of patriotism was apparent in World War I when twelve thousand young tribesmen, many of whose parents had fought against U.S. soldiers, joined the Army and Navy.

On the home front another ten thousand Indian women and men became Red Cross workers. Indians spent their checks from leased allotments on $25 million in war bonds. In Canada, too, Indians were enthusiastic about fighting the German Kaiser. One old warrior, refused recruitment because he would not cut his braids, admonished younger Indians, "Don't be foolish like these white soldiers. They call off the war every day at mealtime. You boys want to keep on shooting even if you see them sitting down to eat." There was the rare conscientious objector, such as the Warm Springs Indian pacifist from Oregon who wrote Carlos Montezuma, "this earth was not created to go and have a war on."

Newspapers at Carlisle, Haskell, and Chilocco Indian schools published letters from Indian servicemen about overseas combat and foreign life-styles. They took pride in Indian heroes, the Arikara Thomas Charles Alone, the Tulalip James Elson, and the Choctaw Joseph Oklahombi, who won the French Croix de Guerre for single-handedly capturing fifty machine guns and holding them for four days under artillery and gas barrage before bringing in 171 German prisoners. Indians were effective scouts, and Choctaws and Comanches spoke their tribal languages to frustrate German eavesdroppers. Back home from the war, however, veterans found conditions as bleak as ever. They could die in a foreign land, they realized, but they still could not vote. Indian soldiers also drew a parallel between the countries they had liberated and their reservations; Indian agents, wrote one veteran, "are enemies to us like the Germans."

From 1917 on, the Bureau of Indian Affairs was actively assisting white

Southern Plains Indian veterans of World War I

land interests through its power to declare Indians "competent" enough to sell their allotments. Homesteads allotted under the Curtis Act were still shifting ownership to non-Indians. In Oklahoma, asserted one U.S. senator, "There are only two classes of people, the Indians and those who live off Indians." The discovery of oil under Indian lands in northern Oklahoma incited a new crime wave. Indian leases were bought, stolen, and swindled. The Indian Rights Association sent the Society of American Indians' Gertrude Bonnin to investigate. Her *Oklahoma's Poor Rich Indians: An Orgy of Graft and Exploitation* exposed a pattern of Indian abuse.

Throughout Indian country the early twentieth century witnessed an upsurge in the white man's diseases. Influenza swept unchecked through entire communities in the West. Tuberculosis was also on the rise, while trachoma, an inflammation of the eyelid that often leads to blindness, infected over half of Wyoming's Indians and an estimated seventy percent of Oklahoma's natives.

While participation in World War I and accepting allotments earned citizenship for about two-thirds of America's Indians, citizenship still was not their birthright. Gertrude Bonnin had no success at placing the issue before the postwar World Peace Conference in Paris. At last, in 1924, progressive Indian lobbying and the outstanding Indian performance in the Great War forced Congress to pass the Indian Citizenship Act. But this did not assure voting rights for some untaxed reservations or for Indians whom government officials still declared "incompetent" to handle their own land dealings. "I thought as a citizen of the United States I could manage my own affairs," complained the Sioux Joseph Claymore, "but I found that the Indian Bureau still held on to seven sections of land I had by inheritance."

Then again, not all Indians supported citizenship. Clinton Rickard, a Tuscarora chief from Upper New York State, feared it would negate their status as a sovereign tribe. "We had a great attachment to our style of government," he wrote. "We wished to remain treaty Indians and preserve our ancient rights. There was no great rush among my people to go out and vote in white man's elections. Anyone who did so was denied the privilege of becoming a chief or a clan mother in our nation." Rickard and his supporters pioneered militant Indian protest, arguing at home and in Europe that treaties granted them the autonomy of a separate nation, that no dams could be built on their sovereign land, and that Tuscarora passports should be honored in the United States and Canada.

This chapter covers the origin of modern, multitribal movements and the problems of formulating a collective program for Indians as an ethnic group. It also highlights the contrasts in tribal concerns and temperaments that have always made that unity so elusive.

1

THE BEST AND THE BRIGHTEST

W hen the Society of American Indians held their historic inaugural convention in 1911, the Indian delegates represented divergent views on many issues confronting Indians, as suggested by the following excerpts from their back-and-forth discussions at the time. Some topics they opened up—tribal rights of eastern Indians, the question of whether Indian groups retained sovereign rights, and whether oral tradition was a valid mode of literature—would not be fully addressed for another fifty years.

In a time that otherwise represented the ebb of Indian well-being, this airing of concerns was very hopeful. As these men and women brainstormed together, they envisioned the fullest possible role for the Indian in America's future.

Discussion on Indian Education

DR. EASTMAN: One of the professors of Cambridge laid out a discussion on attainment, the capacity and power to attain. It was said that it has been proven scientifically that no race, as far as is known, is denied that power; that there have been members from each race known to have attained the highest success where they have had the opportunity . . .

MR. CHASE: I think that a great amount of the natural abilities of our people lie still dormant because of a lack of proper educational institutions. . . . Some of our Indian people at home, and some of our old people existing to-day, have just as good intellects as you or I have, who have been to the white schools, but cannot express their feelings to white men. (Applause.) There is an Indian education as well as a white education. (Applause.) I would just as soon sit down among our older men to-day and hear them talk and tell their old stories as I would to turn to my library and read Charles Dickens and such writers as that. . . .

MR. JOSEPH K. GRIFFIS: A short while ago I spent some time among the

Seminoles of Florida, in the Everglades, and they will not allow one of their members to learn to read or write. I said, "Why do you do this?" "Well," they said, "a good while ago some of our men learned to put their names on paper. That meant the signing away of our homes." To learn to write may be good for the white man, but it is not good for the red man, and so it is partly because of these prejudices that the Indian has not made better progress. And now, as has been emphasized by this Conference, the Indian, the young men, the boys and girls, should be taught that they belong here, that they must play a part in this civilization, and they should be given a chance to learn how they may adjust themselves to progress. . . .

MR. JOHN M. OSKISON: We must not run away from here with the idea that we alone appreciate Indian civilization. Some white people with whom I have talked are anxious to get together in some sort of organization that will help to perpetuate all ideas and organizations that are distinctly Indian, and which are worth preserving. It was suggested to me that the beginning might be made in the Puebloes of Mexico and Arizona. There a complete civilization has been worked out and a state of government which has been entirely successful is in vogue. There they say, "We would like to have the power to exercise a sort of censorship over our government, and not to let any teacher go to a Pueblo which is well organized, and which is prosperous—not to let a teacher go there who will not understand the necessity for perpetuating all the good that is represented in the government of that Pueblo, and prevent any trader going in there who is not sympathetic and will not try to understand us." . . .

REV. COOLIDGE: I wish to say in regard to the education of the Indian, that during the last forty years the process has been going on, and I think we have reached a time when the white people are pretty well educated to the fact that the Indian can be civilized, can be Christianized, can be a good man. We must also educate the white people to be careful not to make too many false statements about the Indians in general, or about some, perhaps, in particular. I know a white man among the Arapahoes who said, "You can't educate the Arapahoe any more than you can the Ethiopian," and I have heard friends of mine say I was educated because I was an Arapahoe smart enough to take all the studies and carry them through creditably, including the Latin and Greek languages; that the Arapahoe was the quickest to catch on; he had a quicker intellect than the Sioux and the Chippewa who were educated in the same schools. I believe there are many Chippewas, many Sioux just as smart as I am! (Laughter.) . . .

Discussion on Native Indian Art

MISS CORNELIUS: Mrs. Deitz spoke of the manufacturers now employing Indian designs in deteriorated forms. A while ago Mr. Doxon spoke along lines similar to this. It seems to me that there ought to be some organization come from this very meeting that ought to place a censorship on that manufacture, to prevent the use of these deteriorated forms, and to insist upon the manufacture of the real article.

DR. EASTMAN: . . . We have been drifting away from our old distinctive art. In Indian art originally, as Mrs. Deitz has described it, the geometric figures predominated. In most of the designs you will find the light background; it is, of course, intended to represent the bright blue heaven; and then you will find the sun effect shown by shafts. In others you will find the rays of the sun and the shadows dovetailed, symbolizing the Great Mystery of the day and night, summer and winter, life and death. . . . It all shows that one basic idea, but it has been very badly confused by our teachers who are white people, who have mixed the different characteristics of the different tribes, so that you cannot tell an Arapahoe from a Sioux now, and cannot tell a Cheyenne from a Crow.

REV. COOLIDGE: . . . the Arapahoes' sacred tipi—I have a picture of it,— I wish I had it here. I have used this tipi myself, but not in the cause of the old religion of our people, which was not so very bad after all. Why, when I was in New York, taking a special course in college, the rector asked me to take his place one Sunday in a very aristocratic church, and I addressed those people about something that was tender among them, and that was the pew-rent system. Those people paid so much for their pews, those in front, of course, paying a little more than those behind. There were only one or two pews, way back in a corner, for the poor people and for strangers, and I want to tell you that I did not feel as though I was in a religious house and in a religious atmosphere. When I went in there I felt that I could not sit down and worship God, and I told those people in that sermon that I would rather have the religion of the Arapahoes, of my fathers, and sit in their sacred tent, than a religion auctioned off in that way. There is art in their religion, not commerce. (Applause.) . . .

Discussion of the Indian
in the Professions

MISS EMMA D. JOHNSON: I cannot resist saying a few words upon this subject. I am no public speaker, except when I feel that I have to speak. I have been through the country quite a little in my work as teacher. I have seen our Indians in the professions and I have seen them with their higher education, and I have seen them in the camp, and I regret very much that *the majority of the people of the Caucasian race of the United States do not recognize the ability of the Indian to compete with the white race.* . . .

We are not all agriculturists,—we have our lands allotted to us, it is true, but we are not all agriculturists. I hope that the members of this Conference will herald it far and wide, not only by words but by example, and encourage our younger generation not to be afraid to step out and say: "I am not an agriculturist; I am a carpenter; I am a blacksmith; I am a physician," and go ahead and not be afraid after we get out to assert ourselves, not so much in speaking, as in acting and proving to the world that we are capable. (Applause.) . . .

CHAIRMAN CLOUD: . . . I like Mr. Oskison's definition of the Indian in the professions, "The man who lives by his wits," and that would include not only the Indians who have gone into the professions such as teaching, the law, medicine, and all that, but all Indian men and women who have gone out upon their own initiative and worked out their own salvation, perhaps in some line of business. Another speaker has spoken of the fact that the best way to overcome the prejudice that the white man has against us, is to go out in the professions and compete with them, and I want to speak upon this fact. I have noticed among the Indian people a certain prejudice against the Indian who is trying to strike out for himself. Here is an Indian who has started a store, and the Indian passing in the street says, "This man is trying to set himself above me, and I will go and trade with the white man next door," and the white man next door may be the greatest grafter in town, and that Indian who is starting out in business may have had a vision. . . .

Discussion on Reservation Administration

MR. CHASE: It is my opinion that the evils which we are now feeling are the result of the violation of common principles of justice, our treaties, and even the Constitution of the United States. The duty of investigating property rights belongs to the judicial department and not the executive, and the law which gives the Secretary of the Interior the right to decide questions with reference to ownership of land is unconstitutional and void, and we are not bound by the decisions of the Secretary of the Interior if he violates our rights and decides adversely to our vested rights. We have had innumerable cases of that kind on our reservation . . . I believe that the whole system of procedure should be changed and that the *rights that are guaranteed to every man under the Constitution should be given the Indian.*

MISS JOHNSON: I live upon a reservation now. I know nothing whatever about my rights as a citizen. I have been given a letter which reads as follows: "You may control your own land, providing you do thus and so," and what brought that letter to me, I am free to state, was this: The renting of my farm was in the hands of our Agent. I went to him, as is the custom with our Indians, and I saw to the making out of the papers. An agreement was made between myself and this renter, calling for the clearing of a certain number of acres of land. I allowed him his pay for this work out of the cash rent, consequently taking a very small sum of cash rent, and I received a very small sum. He had been paid in advance for doing this work. When the time came for him to do it, he did not do the work. I wrote to the Agent about it, and he said he would see about it. I have the letters downstairs. I wrote him again, and nothing was done. The man had not fulfilled his contract. The United States government was behind this Agent. . . .

My people do not know when they are citizens or when they are not. They send word to the Department, "We wish this and so." The Department sends word back, "You are citizens of the United States. We can't do that for you." They send in for something else. The word comes back, "Why you are wards of the government, we cannot grant you that." Where are we now?

Discussion on Legal Conditions

CHAIRMAN SLOAN: . . . there occurred to my mind a circumstance which I wish to relate: After the Omaha Indians had been citizens for a period of twenty-two years the superintendent or agent in charge of the agency requested authority from the Office of Indian Affairs to establish what was termed a Court of Indian Offenses. The authority was granted, and this agent selected as members of that court persons who were entirely subservient to his will. The result was that this court was the form through which he exercised the power of prosecutor, judge, and executioner. Indians were placed under arrest; their money was taken from them by so-called fines; they were required to work upon the streets and roadways around the agency; and a jail was built in which some of them were confined. This man who was in jail asked me to get him out. I proceeded to the city of Omaha, made application for a writ of habeas corpus to the United States Circuit Court for the District of Nebraska, and a temporary writ was allowed. It came on for hearing, and at that hearing the court said this:

"The utmost research on the part of the United States District Attorney and his assistant, supplemented by an effort on the part of the court, has failed to find any authority of law for the establishment of such courts or the exercise of such a power." . . .

Mr. Griffis: Legally and officially there are no Seminoles in Florida. You will remember that in 1855 they were all run down and sent to a reservation in the west; but 112 of them escaped, and the descendants of those 112 are now living in the Everglades, a place to which no white man can go; and they have been living there in their primitive condition since that time. They are hunters, farmers, fishermen, making a good living. They say, "We have nothing to do with the United States government. This home belongs to us according to the treaties made with our ancestors. No white man south of the Chattahoochee river has any business here. This is our home and our land, and we will never leave it. We have a right to govern ourselves."

And as an illustration of what the Indian might have been if the white man had kept his hand off of him, look at this very people. I spent a month with them. They gave me the best they had. I happen to speak their language. I found how those people govern themselves, and apparently there is no force in their government; yet there is no stealing; they leave their belongings laying around without any idea of protection. They are living just about as they did when the white man first came there. One day I went out with one of the men and he left his things laying around not locked up, and I said to him, "Why do you leave these things here in the wigwam?" "Why shouldn't I?" he said. "Well," I said, "they are valuable to you, and someone might steal them." He said, "Oh, no, there is no danger down here. A white man couldn't get into these Everglades." But it is a fact that there is no thievery among those Seminoles, because no white man can touch them. (Applause.)

MISS JOHNSON: That is my opinion of Oklahoma before it was settled.

DR. EASTMAN: . . . I was in Providence last Saturday, and a stranger came and talked to me. "Do you know so and so?" I said, "No." "Well, there is an Indian here who lives at Pawtucket; she just went by the street here; she claims half or nearly half of Rhode Island; her claim extended along the shore nearly fifty miles." And the people somehow conceded to give her so much a month. Now, this treaty, or whatever it was, was made a hundred or a hundred and fifty years ago. And there are so many things all over this country which stand out like that. . . .

MR. CHASE: The principle of international law that I have just stated in the paper there will solve many of the questions that have been propounded. Because the government of the United States is composed of certain of the higher intelligent people of the human race, philosophers, scientists, lawyers of great ability, and those skilled in all the arts and sciences—that fact does not warrant them in violating the treaty rights of our people. Our treaty rights with the government of the United States, in the language of that western judge, are just as sacred as the treaty made with England or any of the foreign powers; and the fact that we have been placed here by the All-Wise Creator gives us the right to enjoy this life after our own methods, our own ideas, our own religion; and that is what the officers of this government guaranteed to our people in the early treaties, the terms of which they violated in later times. . . . When our Indians become civilized and wish to quit the reservation and its mode of living, let them receive citizenship just as the Russian or the Frenchman or the Spaniard who comes over here to make this country his home. (Applause.)

SOCIETY OF AMERICAN INDIANS

2

LAUGHING AT THEMSELVES

The pages of the Society of American Indians' Quarterly Journal (1913–15) and its successor, The American Indian magazine (1915–20), usually contained somber, somewhat self-congratulatory articles and ringing slogans such as "call for racial and national advancement." On rare occasions, however, its proper tone was punctuated by anger and humor.

This anonymous column, entitled "Notes from Adario's Journal," used "Indian English" dialect to lighten up serious subjects: the rifts within the Indian home when schoolchildren consider themselves better than their parents, the irony of a white man branding an educated Indian a troublemaker for articulating his rights.

ME WORK 'UM on my farm. Wear um overalls. My boy com' 'long home. Been 'way Gov'ment school. Putum on overalls help ol' man plow um fields. Boston man come along in smell-bad-snort-wagon, no horse hitch um. Mebby so, horse inside talk heap honk. Boston man him say, 'um his wife-woman, "Really aborigines laboring! Most extraordinary!" Boston-heap-talk-man yell um, "Aw! come here my good fellow." My boy he go see um. Heap-talk-Boston-man him say um, "You got farm no? You been Carlisle? You no go back blanket? You paint face? You got heap squaw? You civilize, sure, eh? You get drunk all the time, no? You Carlisle failure, no? You got cough inside? You got high blood pressure? Me your friend. Understand me? I do you heap good. Believe me! Have a cigarette, no?"

My boy he stan' heap straight. Face hard, eye flash black fire. Him talk um pale face dictionary silly. Him say 'um, "Stranger I perceive you are afflicted with hallucinations concerning the present status of the portion of our country's population you are wont to designate Indians. In all probability a practitioner of psychopathic therapeutics would diagnosis your evidently microscopic intellect as due to some phase of cerebrocardiac neurosis producing paralsthesis and dysaethesis, if not atropathy of the entire cerebral tissue. As for your questions couched in stilted English, I have no inclination to answer them. May Cerberus bite you when you reach the Styx. Good day sir."

Boston man heap sick, yell, "Maimie fetch the smelling salts." Me say um, very anxious; "Boy, you kill um Boston talk-man, no?" Boy say um "No, Dad, I told him he was crazy and to go to blazes."

E L K   B O N E sen' his boy school. Cost um Uncle Sam 175 silva' dollars ev'ry year. Six year young Elk Bone he gettum vocational book educate. Byimeby young Elk Bone come along home dress all up collar, black shine war paint on shoe-moccasins. Ugh! Him heap meby-so Boston man. He say, "Ole man where's your allotment?" Old Elk Bone him say, "Cattle man got em 'lott-men." Young fella say, "Wher's the ductas, mazooma, simoleons?" Old Bone say, "Um, no savy ducks." Young Bone say, "I mean rental money." Ole man say, "No Catchem."

Young fella go to Agent. Bimeby he say, "Say, where my dad's 'Lottmen rental?" Agent say, "Shut down mouth." Young Fella button coat up an' he say, "I no shut up—you open up or I'll write Indian Wrongs Remedy Company." Agent he say, "you trouble maker, go away you bad feller." Bimeby, young Elk Bone heap mad—get letter from Washington. Letter all same he say—"Elk Bone, you have been reported as a trouble maker. Alas! that after all you expensive schooling you should be a failure! I advise you to be polite to the agent and endeavor to assist him deal with your people." Young Elk Bone mumble heap Boston cuss talk, and say "Bead Arned iffits any use to try." Me no catchem what he mean, but Young Elk Bone try again all time keep try. Mebyso he go jail bimeby.

This make me open eye look roun'. Me notic' ev'ry smart boy come back home try make good rights him people catch um. Supt. he say, "Heap no good." Me notic' Gov'ment no much care about boy he make um educate. When school kickem out. Boy out. Come back home and heap no good Indian: heap no good white man. Jus' trouble maker. Whass mattar Gov'-ment school make so many trouble makers?

ANONYMOUS

3

FROM WASSAJA TO MONTEZUMA

The career of Carlos Montezuma was strange and poignant. Born with the name Wassaja, he was captured by Pima Indians who dubbed him "Left Alone." They sold him to a photographer for thirty dollars, but his benefactor's business failed, and he was abandoned at age eleven. Montezuma worked his way through college and became a respected Chicago doctor and pharmacist. His passionate antagonism to the Bureau of Indian Affairs led him to clash with other members of the Society of American Indians. He epitomized the well-educated "troublemaker" referred to in the previous selection.

In 1906 Dr. Montezuma refused President Theodore Roosevelt's offer to head the Bureau of Indian Affairs; he wanted no part of the institution he had fought so long. Eleven years later he publicly opposed drafting Indians for World War I. When he came down with diabetes and tuberculosis in 1922, he returned to his Arizona birthplace. There, in a humble wickiup, attended by Yavapai-Apache medicine men, he died on January 31, 1923. In a magazine interview, Montezuma described his childhood, his later career, and his call for Indian emancipation.

I, LITTLE WASSAJA, was asleep in our grass hut. I woke to the sound of war cries, the echoes of guns, and the crackle of fires. I ran for my life, and soon overtook my two sisters, the older one carrying the younger on her back. I passed them, but presently stumbled and fell. Too frightened to go on, I crawled under a bush, smaller than myself, and curled up, hardly daring to breathe. I might have been safe there, but at that moment the moon rose above the rim of Iron Peak and revealed my hiding-place as if it had been mid-day. I caught sight of someone stealing toward me—a stranger, I knew, for he had a queer high hat on his head, and a cape around his shoulders. I had never seen anybody clothed, and I could think of nothing but this was some god coming after me. The figure came close, put out a swift hand and seized my arm. All the terror in me came out in a great yell.

My captor dragged me back the way I had come. I saw something lying in front of our hut. I took it for my mother. Never having seen a dead person, I shut my eyes and kept them closed till I was commanded to stand. I was crying all this time. The night was full of terrifying cries and death noises. After a while I thought I heard a familiar voice beside me. I opened my eyes a tiny bit, and saw one of my playmates. I looked around and saw another and another. More than a dozen of us were standing in a row in front of a great fire, which was blazing high above the treetops. I thought it had been built for our burning. I imagined I could hear my flesh sizzling. . . .

I tried then to think it was all a dream. It seems indeed like a dream still, after fifty years. But it was no dream. The massacre on the peak, and what followed, led on directly to what has happened to me. . . .

Our destination proved to be Adamsville, which in those days was the center of the commercial and social life of the territory for the whites; now it has vanished in the desert. In the town there was at that time, curiously, a photographer and artist named Gentile. As you can imagine, a photographer was a marvelous man to the Indians. He could take their faces away from them and put them on a piece of paper, and yet leave their faces unharmed. My three captors offered to sell me to Mr. Gentile. He did not have any good reason for wanting me, a dirty, helpless little savage (my captors by this time had supplied me with a pair of pants), but he bought me anyway. He gave each of the Pimas ten dollars. . . .

And there ends the story of WASSAJA. The rest is Montezuma. We reached Santa Fe eventually. Thence the stage took us to Trinidad; and from Trinidad we traveled by rail, first to Washington, then to New York, and then to Chicago. WASSAJA became Carlos, for the first name of the man who had bought him, and Montezuma for a relic of the Aztecs that Gentile had seen in Arizona. I began a new life. . . .

I started my schooling in a public school on the west side of Chicago. I went subsequently to various schools in that city and in Brooklyn, where Mr. Gentile took me. Later I got sickly and was put on a farm near Galesburg, Illinois, and there I used to walk two miles to a country school. Still later— for Mr. Gentile could not always look after me himself—I was put with a preacher in Urbana, Illinois. This preacher had five children of his own, and I made the sixth. But somehow he managed with me. A little money may have come to him from my friends; it could have not been much. My education up to that time had been rather hit-or-miss, so a number of students set to work and fitted me for the preparatory school for the University. . . .

I think that for some time a very great and good man had had his eye on me: another of those friends who have come my way. This one was General Richard Henry Pratt, a Civil War cavalry officer, later on frontier duty, who founded and for a long time headed the nation's first off-reservation Indian

Young Carlos Montezuma and Carlos Gentile

school, which developed into the Carlisle Indian School at Carlisle, Pennsylvania. At any rate, not long after graduation, I received a message from the Commissioner of Indian Affairs in Washington, asking if I would care to enter the Indian Service as a physician and surgeon. I suspect General Pratt whispered to the Commissioner about me.

That was my first service. I continued in it for more than seven years. The first year I worked at Fort Stephenson Indian School in North Dakota. Following that, I was at the Western Shoshone Agency in Nevada for three years. Then I went to the Colville Agency in the State of Washington. From there I was ordered for service to the Carlisle Indian School in Pennsylvania. I resigned from the last post in 1896. . . .

The guiding policy seemed to be that the Indian must be cared for like a little child. The feeling was general that if he were allowed to look out for himself, he would be cheated out of his property and would starve. I have never seen an Indian starve. He can dig dirt faster than a badger if he has to—and a badger, mind you, will dig a hole and hide in the ground in the time it takes you to reach the spot where you first saw him!

No, it is the same with Indians as with all other people. There is only one way to achieve: do things for yourself. This rule is not abridged for the Indian because his skin happens to be brown or red. It is perhaps easy to let someone else take care of you. I could have done it. Thousands of my people have been forced to do it. And what has it done for them? Go to the reservations. You will find them there, gamblers, idlers, vicious, committing crimes worse than I could tell you. Why? Because the Indian is taken care of. He does not have to do things for himself. The law of nature is subserved. The principles by which worthwhile achievement is realized are set aside. I defy you to do that for anyone and expect him to achieve things that are worth while.

Believing this, fully convinced that personal development consists in rubbing against the world without pampering, I resigned from the Indian Service to prove that I, a lone Indian born in savagery, could make my way by myself, unaided, in the world alongside white men. And if I could, so could my people. From that time, 1896, I have done it. My people can do it. Any man, black, red, yellow, brown—or white—can do it against obstacles, if he will. But he must do it himself; it cannot be done for him.

CARLOS MONTEZUMA, *Yavapai-Apache*

4

SUDDENLY A GATE

Michael Posluns is a Shuswap Indian from the interior plateau of British Columbia, Canada. Isolated, far western tribes like his experienced land loss and restricted access to old foraging grounds later than Indians in populous regions. In this memory of the late 1920s, Posluns recalls his grandparents' shocking discovery that their old life was over. When educated Indians met in urban settings, this was the sort of family memory they shared.

BERRY PICKING TIME. Late summer in my eighth year. The mountains were filled with life up to their snow-capped peaks. My grandmother had risen with the first sign of dawn that morning to get us ready for the long walk to our first berry-picking after the strawberries had ripened. Before she had stirred from her bed, I had already been awake long enough to walk the whole trail in my mind. Last year my grandfather had had to carry me the last part of the walk. This year I was determined to make it on my own and carry my filled basket home as well.

Now the sun was high and we had been on the trail for several hours. Soon we would reach the shady spot by the creek where we would have a bite of lunch. Then we would be a little less than two hours from the first bushes where we would pick.

I must have been thinking about that lunch and not looking straight ahead. Suddenly there was a gate blocking our way with a barbed-wire fence running away from it in both directions into the bushes. On the gate there was a lock and a white board with black letters. I could not read them then, but they are still clear in my mind's eye today.

My grandparents talked awhile in quiet voices. Then my grandmother held her skirts with one hand and lifted herself over the gate with the other hand. My grandfather looked at her strangely when he handed her the walking stick and baskets. But he followed her, and so did I.

We were not a hundred steps beyond the gate when a white man came around a bend in the trail. As soon as he saw us he began to shout and wave his arms at my grandfather. Grandfather talked back to him in Chinook. I did not need to understand the words to know that they were both angered.

Grandfather had put down his baskets when the man had begun to speak to him. He was just bending over to gather them up when my grandmother picked up her stick and began to chase the white man. She spoke only our own Shuswap language but she had made herself well understood. He left. We stayed.

That woman was quite convinced that our people owned the land and that we had a special right to the bushes for which we were heading. No one had a right to fence it off.

Her victory was very short-lived. We completed our walk to the berry bushes. It was a good crop. Three weeks later we came back to the village with our baskets filled with berries already dried for the long winter. But my grandparents had a heavy sadness about them I had never seen before. They did not speak the rest of that trip. When they had sung their voices had been very low, as if each one were alone and had to work hard just to remember the tunes they had sung each day of their lives.

MICHAEL POSLUNS, *Shuswap*

5

FOLLOWING THE MEDICINE

This story about peyote was related by a Washo Indian leader in the Native American Church. The sacred cactus plant is referred to as the all-seeing "medicine" of his tale, which emphasizes its special value to Indians. Here the plant's mystical power guides these Nevada Indian emmisaries to historical documents, helpful to their fight for their rights, which lie deep in the archives of the nation's capital.

In the controversy over whether to legalize or outlaw religious use of the hallucinogenic cactus peyote, Indian spokespeople and anthropologists lined up on both sides. By the mid-1920s, no medical study had proven it harmful to Indian health or morals, and the Native American Church, incorporated in Oklahoma in 1918, was a widespread fact of reservation life.

THERE WAS some Indians back East once. I don't know just where they was from, but it was at the time them Indian organizations was just beginning—like the League of North American Indians. I heard this the first time from a Member who used to come down from Fort Hall to our meetings here. He told us to be careful who we told it to because the government might get mad and call us saboteurs.

He said them Indians back there began to worry about their treaty because they were losing all their land and the government didn't do nothing to help them. They was poor. They could not fish or hunt even on their own land. Their bellies was flat and their children got sick and died.

So them Indians had a meeting to pray for what to do. They took the Medicine and prayed and used all their songs. That meeting kept up for a long time—four days, I heard—and the Members only stopped to eat real Indian breakfast and to sleep some during the day. Every night they prayed and sang with the help of the medicine.

On the fourth night, in the morning, just after Midnight Water Call, the leader said the Medicine is showing him something. He prayed and passed around more Medicine to the Members. He passed around smoke. Then some of them began to see it too. The Medicine helped them see good. They saw their treaty inside a big white building in Washington. They could see it plain right through the walls, just where them papers was. They could even see the number on the door of that room—444.

They knew what to do. They told the five members who had seen these things to go to Washington. They sent them there to get their treaty from that place where it was. Before they went the five Members took more Medicine. It helped them to see good so they knew just where to go. It was a long way, but they took nothing with them except a little Medicine to keep them on the track.

None of them Indians ever seen that Washington before. But they went right there and they found that big white building pretty quick. They went in there and they saw all them big shots standing around in there. They was wearing guns. Them government officers said, What are you Indians doing in here? And them Indians said, We come here to get our treaty . . . it's here. But them big shots said, No, them papers was gone a long time ago . . . burned up . . . not here.

Then them Indians said, We know them papers are in this building some place . . . we know that. But them officers said it wasn't so.

Finally one of them Indians—that leading Indian—said, You men took an oath to tell the truth when you got this job. Now I want each of you to take an oath that you will tell the truth in honesty about that treaty.

So them officers agreed and lined up to take the oath before that Indian.

Miwok Indians from California, protesting racial insults, prepare to burn the negative. *"Digger Indian" image in effigy.*

Each one took the oath and swore there was no treaty. Until the last one came along. That last man was shaking and sweating. He was too nervous to take the oath. Then the Indians looked straight at him and said, Where are them papers? And that officer could not look at him, and said, I'll show you . . . follow me.

Them Indians followed that officer down into the secret rooms of that building. Them other officers came along, too, because they didn't like what that one was doing. They came to a big iron door. The officer took out a bunch of big keys and found the one to open that door. It was so heavy they all had to push it open. Inside there was a room full of all kinds of boxes. But the officer did not stop. He opened six big doors and rooms full of stuff, and each time he locked the door behind him.

The sixth door was to the room where they keep all that money in Washington . . . piles of silver and gold and green bills. That whole room was piled with money. But them Indians wasn't interested in that money. They just kept on going.

Then they came to that seventh door. It was the biggest door of all . . . the last door. Them Indians saw the number on that door—444. They knew what door it was. When the door opened they saw it was the room where all the treaties was kept. That officer said, There is where your treaty is!

Them officers laughed because the papers was piled high to the top of that room and when they went inside everything started to fall down and get all mixed up. But them Indians all looked in one place. They climbed inside all them piles of Indian treaties and right away they found their own. They could see it in there just like it was all by itself. It was bright like a light was shining on it. They were glad, then, and they started to sing and go out through the door.

But then the officers took out their guns and said, You Indians will never take them papers back for your people to see!

The officer who was afraid to take the oath did not pull his gun. He said to the others, Let these Indians go. You can't fool them no more. They saw that you lied when you took that oath.

But them other officers pointed their guns at him, too, and when he saw that he didn't say nothing more.

Then them officers rounded up them Indians and chained them right there in that room. They went out and locked the door. Them Indians are still there. Sometimes when you take the Medicine and pray for them in a meeting, you can see them there. One time I saw them up close. Their eyes was wide open and looking out. I think they are still alive and waiting in there for someone to come.

Some day I think Indians will go there and let them out. They will find the treaties of all the Indians. We will find our treaty there, too. The lawyers and all the big shots say we never had no treaty. But it will be there. When that day comes, the Medicine will show us the next thing we must do.

ANONYMOUS, *Washo*

6

SCANDAL IN OKLAHOMA

I n the mid-1920s, Gertrude S. Bonnin, a founder of the Society of American
Indians, investigated corruption against Indians in Oklahoma. The discovery
of oil on Indian allotments had made Indians victims of unscrupulous men who
would stop at nothing to secure their leases.

The Society found it hard to take action as a group, but individual members
volunteered for assignments on behalf of their people. Dr. Charles Eastman, another
founder, was one of the first to provide eyewitness reportage on the massacre of
Wounded Knee in 1890. When the Indian Rights Association asked Bonnin to join
a team looking into the Oklahoma story, she immediately agreed.

Under the pen name of Zitkala-sa, Bonnin wrote short stories of reservation life.
She taught at Carlisle Indian School, was a violinist, advised the government's
Meriam Commission in the late 1920s, and remained prominent in Indian affairs
until her death in 1938. This excerpt from Bonnin's report tells of a Choctaw girl
who had inherited valuable reserves of oil. How she lost them is one of the tales
of exploitation that Bonnin and her colleagues uncovered in Oklahoma.

THE SMOTHERED CRIES of the Indians for rescue from
legalized plunder come in a chorus from all parts of eastern Oklahoma. . . .
And now follows another outrage perpetrated under cover of a County Court
in the southern part of eastern Oklahoma.

Little *Ledcie Stechi*, a Choctaw minor, seven years old, owned rich oil
property in McCurtain County. She lived with her old grandmother in a
small shack back in the hills about two and a half miles from Smithville.
They lived in dire poverty, without proper food or clothing and surrounded
by filth and dirt. Ledcie Stechi inherited lands from her mother, including
twenty acres which became valuable oil property. Other lands she inherited
were sold by her uncle, Noel Samuel, for a consideration of $2,000 which
was deposited in the bank subject to control by the County Judge, who
allowed $10 a month for the support of Ledcie Stechi.

After the discovery of oil on the twenty acres above mentioned, her uncle,
Noel Samuel, who was her guardian, was induced to resign through a
combination of various tactics, force, persuasion and offer of reward which
he never got. Mr. Jordan Whiteman, owner of the First National Bank of
Idabel, whose attorney was instrumental in Noel Samuel's resignation, was

Gertrude S. Bonnin, also known as the author Zitkala-sa

appointed guardian. At the time of Mr. Whiteman's appointment, July, 1921, Ledcie lived with her old grandmother in the hills, and until 1923 they were in semi-starving condition. Once a week the old grandmother walked to Smithville to buy food on the monthly credit of $15 allowed them by Mr. Whiteman, at Blake's store. They had no conveyance. Then she hired someone to take her home, which cost fifty or sixty cents. During this period from 1921 to 1923, the guardian did nothing to make them more comfortable or to educate the little Indian heiress.

In the fall of 1922 the guardian attempted to sell ten acres of Ledcie's oil land which was producing at the time, and appraised at $90,000, for a consideration of $2,000. This attempt was defeated, and with the result that Ledcie Stechi's monthly allowance was increased to $200, from which the guardian allowed the child and grandmother a credit of $15 monthly at a local store. Still, throughout the following year, Ledcie and her old grandmother fared no better than prior to the $200 allowance to the guardian. In April, 1923, they were brought to Idabel, the County seat. The rich little Choctaw girl, with her feeble grandmother, came to town carrying their clothes, a bundle of faded rags, in a flour sack. Ledcie was dirty, filthy, and covered with vermin. She was emaciated and weighed about 47 pounds.

A medical examination showed she was undernourished and poisoned by malaria. After five weeks of medical treatment and nourishment, Ledcie gained 11 pounds. Her health improved, and she was placed by an employee of the Indian Service in Wheelock Academy, an Indian school. Mr. Whiteman, evidently fearing to lose his grasp on his ward, demanded the child, and Ledcie Stechi, child of much abuse, was returned to the custody of her legal guardian 24 hours after she was taken to the school where she would have had good care. The last time the aged grandmother had seen Ledcie, and only for a few minutes, was on the 12th of July.

A month later, on the 14th of August, word was brought to the hills that Ledcie was dead. There had been no word of the girl's illness and the sudden news of her death was a terrible blow to the poor old grandmother.

The following day, at dawn before the corpse had arrived, parties of grafters arrived at the heretofore unknown hovel in the hills and harassed the bereaved old grandmother about the future disposal of Ledcie's valuable properties.

Rival speculators went over with the body of Ledcie Stechi. Some of them sent flowers to be placed on the grave of her, who though but a child, had known only of poisonous thorns. The floral offerings were too late for the child of sorrows, but they were made by hypocrites who hoped thereby to play upon the heart of the aged grandmother, who was now the sole heir to Ledcie Stechi's vast estate.

Greed for the girl's lands and rich oil property actuated the grafters and made them like beasts surrounding their prey, insensible to the grief and anguish of the white-haired grandmother. Feebly, hopelessly, she wailed over the dead body—its baby mouth turned black, little fingernails turned black, and even the little breast all turned black! In vain she asked for an examination of the body, believing Ledcie had been poisoned. "No use. Bury the body," commanded the legal guardian.

The Court has already appointed a guardian for the grandmother—against her vehement protest. She, too, will go the way of her grandchild, as sheep for slaughter by ravenous wolves in men's forms unless the good people of America intervene immediately by remedial Congressional action.

GERTRUDE BONNIN, *Sioux et al.*

INTERLUDE
OF HOPE

John Collier, commissioner of Indian affairs, conferring with Seminole Indian leaders in Florida, January 1940

In February 1934, a gaunt and spectacled man who looked more like a poet or professor than an administrator sat down before the U.S. Senate's Indian Affairs Committee. He was John Collier, the new chief of the Bureau of Indian Affairs. A year before, Collier had been named by President

Franklin D. Roosevelt to design a "New Deal" for the American Indian. Now he was ready to unveil his revolutionary program for returning land and culture to the country's 344,000 Native Americans.

By personality an idealist, Collier became fascinated with Indians during a Christmas stopover in Taos, New Mexico, in 1920. He was visiting Mable Dodge Luhan, a writer friend from New York who had married a Taos Indian named Antonio Luhan. Collier was thirty-six years old and had recently finished a decade of organizing New York City's poor emigrants.

As "Tony" Luhan led Collier through the narrow streets of Taos Pueblo, showed him the Red Deer dance, and described his tribe's world view, Collier was spellbound. He felt he was witnessing a model for all mankind, a "Red Atlantis" as he later called it, a community that successfully integrated the needs of the individual with those of the group. Even after Commissioner Collier's entanglements with the less-than-ideal politics of daily reservation life and Indian bureacracy, he would rhapsodize of Indians: "They had what the world has lost. They have it now. What the world has lost, the world must have again lest it die . . . the ancient reverence and passion for the earth and the web of life. . . ."

In the early 1920s the lands and rights of the Pueblo Indians of the Southwest, which barely escaped allotment, were suddenly at risk. This began after 1913, when the U.S. Supreme Court ruled that lands granted to southwestern Indian groups by the Spanish crown three centuries before were now classified as U.S. reservations. Over three thousand non-Indian families who were then living illegally on Pueblo lands would be evicted.

To counter the ruling, in 1921 New Mexico senator Holm O. Bursum drafted a bill to validate the claims of anyone who had squatted on Pueblo land since 1902 or earlier. The eighteen or so different Pueblo tribes stood to lose at least sixty thousand acres, along with their old form of self-government due to an appended clause that put domestic quarrels under the control of white man's courts. In the Indian mind the Bursum bill was linked to revived campaigns by the Bureau of Indian Affairs and various missionary organizations to condemn ceremonies for making the rains come and the crops grow as "heathenish" and "immoral."

Collier and other friends of the Pueblo Indians rallied against these anti-Pueblo measures, forming the American Indian Defense Organization. With Collier at their side, the highly independent Pueblo tribes convened at Santo Domingo Pueblo in 1922, united against a common enemy for the first time since their rebellion against the Spanish in 1680. The Indians sounded a public alarm: "This [Bursum] bill will destroy our common life and will rob us of everything which we hold dear—our lands, our customs, our traditions. Are the American people willing to see this happen?" As a result of ardent lobbying, the Bursum bill was defeated. New sentiments and policies on behalf of Indians were in the air.

In 1923, the secretary of the interior, Hubert Work, was prodded by rumors of widespread mismanagement of Indian affairs to delegate a "Committee of One Hundred" prominent citizens to "review and advise on Indian policy." Their report instigated a more wholesale study for which the Interior Department contracted a private firm, the Institute of Government Research.

Nine specialists, including Henry Roe Cloud—who was also one of the "One Hundred"—crisscrossed the nation for seven months over 1926–28, interviewing Indians and officials and reviewing a century's worth of statistics on population, health, and social conditions. Their 800-page "Meriam Report," published in 1928, detailed dire poverty, inadequate housing and diet, disastrous epidemics, poor schooling, and incompetence by reservation personnel. Although the existing administration of President Herbert Hoover made some improvements, the need for structural change was still unmet when Collier found himself appointed by the pro-Indian secretary of the interior, Harold Ickes, in spring 1933.

Eleven months later, Commissioner Collier disclosed his legislative package for revolutionizing U.S. Indian policy before the senators. His avalanche of facts left no doubt that the Dawes Act was a catastrophe. Instead of granting Indians the "dignity of private property," Collier reported that allotment "has cut down Indian land holdings from 138,000,000 [the acres Indians owned when the Dawes Act was passed in 1887] to 47,000,000 [the acres they had left in 1934]"—roughly two-thirds of their land base was gone.

Furthermore, allotment had "rendered whole tribes totally landless. It has thrown more than a hundred thousand Indians virtually into the breadline . . . [and] put the Indian allotted lands into a hopelessly checkerboarded condition." The sweeping cure for fifty years of vacillating, disastrous government policy was contained in his 52-page Indian Reorganization Act (to be known popularly by its initials, the IRA).

This was the most daring proposal in the history of U.S. Indian affairs. Among Collier's more radical items were (1) the reorganization of Indian tribes so they might enjoy self-governing powers similar to those of any American town, (2) an immediate end to the allotment concept, (3) a multimillion-dollar credit fund to foster Indian farms and businesses, (4) stepped-up recruitment of Indians for Bureau of Indian Affairs jobs, (5) an Indian court system with native judges handling non-federal crimes, and (6) a mechanism for Indians to pool allotted lands and buy additional acreage that Indian tribes would own as corporate entities.

In addition, Collier wanted to revamp the entire Indian health care system, to promote Indian arts and crafts, to shift from boarding schools to day schools for Indian children, and to institute a soil conservation and stock reduction programs on eroded Indian lands. He called for restoring Indian cultural freedoms, so Native Americans need not fear government interference or the scorn of missionaries.

Politicians were taken aback by this utter refutation of a half-century of government policy. Collier's idea of "reform" flew in the face of the earlier Indian reform movement. In a series of open "congresses" held around the United States, Collier took his agenda to Indians themselves. These encounters in Indian communities, where they could speak their minds, revealed an unexpected diversity of tribal experiences and temperaments. Indians seemed as wary of Collier's idealism as politicians did. At a meeting of Northwest Indians in Chemawa, Oregon, one speaker predicted that if his people actually won the authority promised in Collier's bill they would "feel like a child who would get lost when his guide left him." At Rapid City, South Dakota, plains Indians suspected any scheme for retrieving allotted lands that excluded them from the planning process. Others were understandably nervous about turning over their few acres to any tribally owned program.

During a California forum Collier heard his program for reinstituting the tribal land base branded as "communistic," an accusation that would be echoed by a Seneca Indian, Alice Jemison, from New York State, who said, " . . . this talk of reviving [Indian] languages, this talk of Bureau education, this talk of more land and more land and more land for the Indians, it seems to me . . . that the agents of Russia are already busy in the field." At an Oklahoma gathering, the Creek Indian Jerome Bruner claimed that Collier's encouragement of old tribal values would return Indians to the "stone age."

Collier's advocacy for Indian religious freedom, including the use of peyote, was also attacked by Christian missionaries and the conservative Indian Rights Association. Others agreed that his notion of land repatriation was tantamount to "segregation," that promotion of traditional culture threw Indians "back to the blanket," and that rejecting the older emphasis on farming, schooling, and Christianity was "turning back the clock fifty years."

Collier was undaunted, and fought for his program in and out of Washington. When it became law in June 1934, the Indian Reorganization, or Wheeler-Howard, Act, officially named for its congressional supporters, was a shadow of his grand design. Gutted were the Indian court system and the major commitment to rebuilding tribal land bases. Retained was the halt to allotment, voluntary pooling of allotted lands to give Indians parcels large enough to ranch, and restoration of unsold "surplus" acreage. In an attempt to reconstruct tribal authority, tribes could charter themselves to be eligible to borrow from a ten-million-dollar credit fund. Now Indians could have their own elected tribal councils, and engage once more in a limited form of self-government.

For the second time Collier's field-workers traveled throughout Indian country to win or coerce native acceptance of his revised program. After much debate, 181 tribes out of 263 voted to join in the provisions of the Wheeler-Howard bill. Initially, the Five Civilized Tribes of Oklahoma, comprising the largest number of Indians in the United States, voted against it. But after they watched the IRA in operation, a second piece of legislation, the Oklahoma Indian Welfare Act of 1936, brought them under the umbrella of Wheeler-Howard as well.

Fifteen years later it was possible to assess the Collier program. By then approximately ninety-five tribes were self-governing bodies. In the troublesome area of land recovery for collective tribal management, it was a disappointment. Only enough money was allocated to restore four million acres to the tribes, less than half that "urgently needed," according to a government report.

From a revolving fund established by Wheeler-Howard, however, Indians from over seventy tribes had borrowed more than twelve million dollars to launch farming operations and salmon canning factories. By the end of 1946 none had failed and nearly all the loans were repaid. Native cattle ranches more than doubled. Thanks to improvements in health delivery programs, the Indian death rate was cut in half. New Indian education funds paid for the transfer of students from boarding schools (sixteen were closed) to day schools (eighty-four were opened), a move that was especially welcomed by Indian parents.

Another aspect of the Indian New Deal's impact fit less easily into statistics. It lay in a new pride that Indians expressed more publicly about their tribal heritages. Under the Collier administration, anthropologists were hired to

Leaders from Montana's Flathead Indian Reservation represent the first tribe to receive a new constitution and bylaws under the Roosevelt administration's revolutionary Indian Reorganization Act. Flathead chiefs Victor Vandenberg and Martin Charlo meet with Secretary of the Interior Harold Ickes, October 1935.

make reservation management more attuned to Indian ways of doing things. The Bureau of Indian Affairs published clearly written and well-illustrated pamphlets on Indian life and bilingual texts in native languages such as Lakota and Navajo. A new Indian Arts and Crafts Board aided traditional native artisans. While Indian youngsters began picturing their culture in school art classes, Kiowa, Pueblo, and other Indian painters contributed to the murals that adorned public buildings during the Depression-era work projects.

There remained keen disappointments and hot disputes. Land recovery was far too slow for Collier. There were also problems over his sense of urgency about Indian self-government. He wanted tribes to "keep their ancient democracy," and vowed at his swearing-in "not to make a white man" of the Indian. But he did not distinguish between the Indians' form of participatory democracy, in which all tribal members played a part and decisions were reached after struggle for group census, and the white man's representative democracy, where elected spokespeople quickly passed laws that affected everybody. This process might save time, but in the traditional Indian view that was not necessarily a virtue.

Many reservation Indians had known only a culture of dependency, living their entire lives with the Bureau of Indian Affairs making most of their survival decisions. They were thrown by the chance to exercise power in a world that was still run by non-Indians under non-Indian rules. On the other hand, the Navajos detested Collier for cutting their livestock herds precisely because he had dictated his outsider's solution to their soil erosion problems.

Another obstacle facing the Collier program was the growing danger of a second World War, which turned the nation's attention and finances toward military mobilization. As with World War I, Indians readily volunteered their services. About fifty percent of all able-bodied Indians became engaged in the military or war industries. Indian schools, hospitals, and reservations were stripped of personnel. After the war the winds of political attitude toward Indians shifted again. The new administration of President Harry S. Truman disowned much of Collier's philosophy and programs.

The selections in this chapter focus on a rare and radical moment in Indian affairs. What made it so unusual was that for the first time whites in authority tried to draw upon the traditional Indian past to create a more hopeful Indian future.

1

HARD TIMES IN SIOUX COUNTRY

I*ndian country experienced its Great Depression before the rest of America. Over the twentieth century's opening decades waves of pneumonia, influenza, tuberculosis, trachoma, and other health problems led to a skyrocketing Indian mortality rate.*

As recollected by an Oglala Sioux medicine man named John Fire Lame Deer, death and poverty were constant companions on his South Dakota reservation. Lame Deer was born in a twelve-by-twelve-foot log cabin in 1900. After he died in 1970, Lame Deer was remembered as a new sort of traditionalist, with a gusto for life no matter the odds, who always spoke his mind with a healthy dose of humor.

THERE WERE twelve of us, but they are all dead now, except one sister. Most of them didn't even grow up. My big brother, Tom, and his wife were killed by the flu in 1917. I lost my own little boy thirty-five years ago. I was a hundred miles away, caught in a blizzard. A doctor couldn't be found for him soon enough. I was told it was the measles. Last year I lost another baby boy, a foster child. This time they told me it was due to some intestinal trouble. So in a lifetime we haven't made much progress. We medicine men try to doctor our sick, but we suffer from many new white man's diseases, which come from the white man's food and white man's living, and we have no herbs for that.

My big sister was the oldest of us all. When she died in 1914 my folks took it so hard that our life was changed. In honor of her memory they gave away most of their possessions, even beds and mattresses, even the things without which the family would find it hard to go on. My mother died of tuberculosis in 1920, when I was seventeen years old, and that was our family's "last stand." On her last day I felt that her body was already gone; only her soul was still there. I was holding her hand and she was looking at me. Her eyes were big and sad, as if she knew that I was in for a hard time. She said, "*Onsika, onsika*—pitiful, pitiful." These were her last words. She wasn't sorry for herself; she was sorry for me. I went up on a hill by myself and cried.

When grandfather Crazy Heart died they killed his two ponies, heads toward the east and tails to the west. They had told each horse, "Grandson, your owner loved you. He has need of you where he's going now." Grandfather knew for sure where he was going, and so did the people who buried him according to our old custom. . . .

But in 1920 they wouldn't even allow us to be dead in our own way. We had to be buried in the Christian fashion. It was as if they wanted to take my mother to a white boarding school way up there. For four days I felt my mother's *nagi*, her presence, her soul, near me. I felt that some of her goodness was staying with me. The priest talked about eternity. I told him we Indians did not believe in a forever and forever. We say that only the rocks and the mountains last, but even they will disappear. There's a new day coming, but no forever, I told him. "When my time comes, I want to go where my ancestors have gone." The priest said, "That may be hell." I told him that I'd rather be frying with a Sioux grandmother or uncle than sit on a cloud playing harp with a pale-faced stranger. I told him, "That Christian name, John, don't call me that when I'm gone. Call me Tahca Ushte—Lame Deer."

With the death of my mother one world crumbled for me. It coincided with a new rule the Government made about grazing pay and allotments. Barbed-wire fences closed in on us. My dad said, "We might just as well give up." He went back to Standing Rock, where he was from. He left my sister about sixty horses, forty scrub cows and one bull. I had about sixty head of broken saddle horses and fifty cows. My dad turned me loose. "Hey, I give you these horses; do as you please. If you want to live like a white man, go and buy a car till you are broke and walk on foot." I guess Dad knew what was in my mind.

I started trading my stock for a Model-T Ford and bought things that were in style for the rodeo—fancy boots, silver spurs, gaudy horse-trappings, a big hat. I followed the rodeo circuit, but I wasn't too interested in competing as a rider. It was just an excuse to travel to different reservations. My life was changed and I myself was changing. I hardly recognized myself anymore. I was a wanderer, a hippie Indian. I knew nothing then. Right or wrong were just words. My life was a find-out. If somebody said, "That's bad," I still wanted to experience it. Maybe it would turn out to be good. I wasn't drinking then but soon would be. My horses and cows were gone. Instead I was the owner of a half-dozen wrecked jalopies. Yet I felt the spirits. Always at night they came down to me. I could hear them, something like the whistling from the hearing aid that I am wearing now. I could feel their touch like a feather on a sore spot. I always burned a little sweet grass for them. Though I lived like a hobo, I was visiting many old medicine men, trying to learn their ways.

I didn't need a house then or a pasture. Somewhere there would be a cave, a crack in the rocks, where I could hole up during a rain. I wanted the plants and the stones to tell me their secrets. I talked to them. I roamed. I was like a part of the earth. Everything had been taken from me except myself. Now and then, in some place or other, I looked at my face in a mirror to remind myself who I was. Poverty, hardship, laughter, shame, adventure—I wanted to experience them all. At times I felt like one of those modern declawed cats, like a lone coyote with traps, poisoned meat, and a ranger's gun waiting for him, but this did not worry me. I was neither sad nor happy. I just was.

I knew an old Indian at this time who was being forced to leave his tent and to go live in a new house. They told him that he would be more comfortable there and that they had to burn up his old tent because it was verminous and unsanitary. He looked thin and feeble, but he put up a terrific fight. They had a hard time dragging him. He was cursing them all the time: "I don't want no son-of-a-bitch house. I don't want to live in a box. Throw out the goddam refrigerator, drink him up! Throw out the chair, saw off the damn legs, sit on the ground. Throw out that thing to piss in. I won't use it. Dump the son-of-a-bitch goldfish in there. Kill the damn cow, eat him up. Tomorrow is another day. There's no tomorrow in this goddam box!"

JOHN FIRE LAME DEER, *Sioux*

2

NEGLECT ALONG THE KLAMATH

I*n the spring of 1926 Robert Spott, a Yurok Indian from northern California, addressed the Commonwealth Club of San Francisco. On Spott's mind were the straits of fellow Yurok along the Klamath River, whom he describes here as "almost at the end of the road."*

Spott was honored by the French government for bravery during World War I. Afterward he apprenticed with the California anthropologist Alfred L. Kroeber;

eventually they collaborated on publications of Yurok oral tradition. Kroeber himself was among the Committee of One Hundred, which, in 1923, documented the same sort of neglect covered by Spott in his talk.

I **DID** make up my mind in the war that I am American and I went overseas to fight for this country. Then the officers came to me while I was overseas and they told me, "You are all right. You fought for your country."

Robert Spott

I just gave them a smile and I thought to myself, "Where is my country when I get home?"

There are many Indian women that are almost blind, and they only have one meal a day, because there is no one to look after them. Most of these people used to live on fish, which they cannot get, and on acorns, and they are starving. They hardly have any clothing to cover them. Many children up along the Klamath River have passed away with disease. Most of them from tuberculosis. There is no road into there where the Indians are. The only road they have got is the Klamath River.

To reach doctors they have to take their children down the Klamath River, to the mouth of the Klamath. It is 24 miles to Crescent City, where we have to go for doctors. It costs us $25.00. Where are the poor Indians to get this money from to get a doctor for their children? They go from place to place to borrow the money. If they cannot get it, the poor child dies without aid. Inside of four or five years more there will be hardly any Indians left upon the Klamath River.

I came here to notify you that something has to be done. We must have a doctor, and we must have a school to educate our children, and we must have a road upon the Klamath River besides the bank of the river. Every creek in the winter time goes into the river, and when that river is high you only have a little path, and you cannot go behind the white man's homestead. We have to go some place else. Whenever the river is low we go back to plant a little, and we get maybe a bucket full of beans, but you know very well we cannot live on that little land that we have got.

My father was an Indian chief, and we used to own everything there. When the land was allotted they allotted him only ten acres, a little farm of land which is mostly gravel and rock, with little scrubby trees and redwood. My father was not satisfied with the land and he said, "We owned this land. We ought to pick out what we want." "Well," the surveyor said, "You cannot do it, because it is already taken up by homesteaders. I will tell you what I will do. I will have furnished to you a plow, also a cow and horse and everything so that you can improve your land." Then, of course, my father said, "All right. I am satisfied with that." Well, we are still waiting. My father passed away when he was ninety years old. I am his son, and I am waiting for it right now. If I ever will get the cows or the horses or the plow, I don't know.

So I am here to tell you how we are standing up along the Klamath River. Often we see a car go past. It is the Indian Service. Do you suppose the man driving that car would stop? Always he has no time for the Indians, and the car with some one from the U.S.A. Indian Service goes past just like a tourist. When he does come to his office, maybe he wants even an Indian woman to give up her allotment to put up a better house for the Government—a Government house, we call it—to help us. "You will have a man to help the Indians out." The poor Indian woman says, "All right. I will let you have it." That man only stops there four days and he leaves. Whenever he comes there, just the minute he sees an Indian coming in he meets him by the door, and he says, "I got business to do. I have not got any time for you. . . ."

ROBERT SPOTT, *Yurok*

3

THE TWENTIES AT SAN JUAN

*S*ituated alongside the Rio Grande in northern New Mexico, San Juan Pueblo weathered the Depression remarkably well. Probably this was because its tight-knit community existed outside the main rush of western progress; it was not caught up in a cash economy and was blessed with well-watered fields for growing ample food in hard times, and, for hundreds of years, its leaders defied outsiders' campaigns to tamper with their customs.

Here, a scholar who was born at San Juan in 1939, Alfonso Ortiz, describes everyday life back then. After attending both Indian day and boarding schools, Ortiz earned a Ph.D. in anthropology at the University of Chicago, and then directed the advocacy-minded Association on American Indian Affairs from 1973 to 1988. He used his MacArthur Fellowship, awarded in 1982, to return to San Juan to collect oral traditions in his native Tewa language, including the times his elders had lived through.

I N O R D E R to talk meaningfully about a period which began a decade before my birth, I asked my relatives and friends who were around in San Juan Pueblo, New Mexico, in the late 1920s and early 1930s to tell me what kind of world the Indian Reorganization Act (IRA) came into. I first asked what impact the Great Depression had on life at San Juan. The reply, to my surprise, was no impact at all. Some of you might think that reservation communities were so depressed that the fall in the stock market and subsequent economic crash would not have any effect on them. Actually, the reason was quite different.

There was really very little need for cash on a day-to-day basis. Sugar and coffee and then, occasionally, cheese and soap were the staples most often paid for with cash. Each family needed only to have one member working seasonally to have enough cash for the whole year. Typically, a family sent an older son, or in the absence of an older son the father went, to herd sheep in the mountains of northern New Mexico or southern Colorado to earn the needed cash. A few young women worked as maids on call twenty-four hours a day for well-to-do whites in Santa Fe. They earned, as they were eager to tell me, thirty dollars per month and were lucky to get one or two Sunday afternoons off per month to go home. A few other people worked for the BIA or in stores in nearby Espanola.

Those families that did not have wage earners traded corn, strings of red chili, and wheat in the nearby store for things they could not trade for with neighboring Spanish-Americans and other Pueblo Indians or which they did not grow themselves. This barter system was the major subsistence activity for things you did not have or grow yourself or gather or hunt. Otherwise, the people just used the occasions of ceremonies and festivals to exchange useful gifts, to sell surpluses, and to try to take advantage of the occasional tourists, with pretty ears of corn done up in braids or with pottery. The pottery that exchanged hands between Indian people and Hispanics, as well as anything else they made or grew, went in the form of gifts or trade.

Those who could eat canned foods were envied because it was a sign that they could afford to buy their food, rather than grow it or trade for it. In the past half century, this envy of the white man's processed food has diminished because worries about the high incidence of cancer and other relatively new diseases and their suspected link to processed foods have become established in the people's minds.

There was a federal extension agent. We had a Tewa name for this fellow. It was "he who knows how to farm." The extension agent was established in San Juan by the late 1920s, and he was busy growing things like carrots, spinach, radishes, and other foods which the people had not known. And he was trying to coax them to grow these new foods, as well, in their fields.

There were two other externally imposed institutions in the pueblo which were not so benign—the Catholic church and the day school. The church was regarded as disruptive by those who were not really true, completely devout believers. The resident priest regularly told the people that, if they did not stop dancing and praying to the sun, moon, and stars, they would all go to hell. A half a century later, the people there are still singing, dancing, and praying to the sun, moon, and stars, and so far as we know, no one has gone to hell. Everyone knows there are no Indians in hell. It is not a place designed for us.

Indeed if anything has changed at San Juan, it is the church itself. Today, the Mass is often said in Tewa by members of the community, and the bilingual, bicultural personnel have translated the entire Mass and, many prayers, hymns, and proverbs into Tewa. Traditional Tewa embroidery adorns the altar. It also often adorns the priest himself, replacing the priestly vestments of yesteryear.

The teachers at the school used less terrifying language, but they also told their charges that everything they were, heretofore, had to end and that they had to go away to boarding schools and learn to be progressive like whites. The BIA had not yet begun to distribute clothing in the 1920s, but by the 1930s, younger students began to get shoes.

In the San Juan of that time, people never locked their doors when leaving for the day, as a fear of theft was almost nonexistent. Neighbors looked out for one another's welfare and interests. Children could pop into any open door they saw when out playing if they got thirsty or hungry. Anyone who denied a gourd of water or a piece of tortilla to a kid soon got a reputation as being stingy and uncivil.

Similarly, parents never worried about where their children might be during the day. They knew in a most basic sense that their children would be safe, no matter where they were within or around the village. This little point about parents not worrying about their kids caused teachers no end of frustration. They interpreted this permissiveness, at least the culturally insensitive ones did, as a sign that the parents were not concerned about their kids. It was a sign of just the opposite. The parents cared; they knew in a more basic sense that the children were quite safe no matter where they were.

At night, after the day's chores were done, one could step outside and hear the music of flutes playing in different parts of the village. This was what musically inclined men did after the evening meal, especially in the summer when it was likely to be warm inside. They took their flutes and sat outside by the door on adobe benches and played. They also played for the women to entertain them when the women, in a communal ceremony, ground cornmeal.

There was also enough neighborliness that, when one needed a particular kind of medicine, he merely asked a neighbor or a relative. Traditional medical herbs and other remedies were freely given. Ben-Gay, Mentholatum, and aspirin were later added to the list of those things that could be given away to neighbors and relatives. When a midwife was called in to massage an expectant mother, she was paid twenty-five cents or fifty cents or given a shawl. When she attended a childbirth, she was paid in food and given several braids of blue corn. A favorite method of treating illness through the 1930s was by smoking the patient, smoking over the patient with someone else's hair, but not the patient's own hair. This practice gave rise to a common insult in those times in Tewa. The insult could be translated, "He was smoked with his own hair." This meant he was tricked or cheated. To be smoked with one's own hair was to be duped.

The government of that time was simple, unpretentious, and straightforward. There was a council of mostly religious leaders, elders who worked hard to keep things from changing. They appointed the secular officials. They picked men who would be like them, carry out their bidding, and uphold tradition when questioned. There were no budgets, there was no money, and there were no full time employees.

As far as religious life was concerned, this was a bad time for Indian religion. Everyone said that the dance lines were short because people were so desperately poor. They had good costumes for their dances only because they were well made at an earlier time. On the other hand, there were many more customs then for passing on cultural knowledge to the next generation, such as story-telling sessions in the autumn and winter months, traditional games, and pilgrimages to get religious items such as fruit up in the mountains.

I am not trying to paint an idyllic picture of life fifty years ago. There were also problems and hardships. Hauling wood and water were two of the severest hardships mentioned by people, especially in the winter. In order to bathe, people had to build fires outside to heat the water, because fire pits and corner fireplaces were not adequate for heating large quantities of water. The major health problems of the time were tuberculosis, trachoma, and cataracts. No one alive then was unaware of the great flu epidemic of 1918. This epidemic, for a time, killed people off so fast in San Juan that some days the church bell never stopped tolling, day and night. The most serious recurrent internal problems people recalled were domestic quarrels, charges of witchcraft, and land boundary problems.

All of the pueblos, with the exception of Jemez, supported the IRA. Only three of the pueblos in New Mexico adopted IRA constitutions; they were Santa Clara, Isleta, and Laguna pueblos. The Hopi in Arizona also initially supported the IRA. But the immediate impact of the IRA was not great, even though the Pueblos supported it. I suspect they did so because they regarded John Collier as a great and true friend because of his prominent leadership and support in the two great battles in which they were involved in the decade prior to the 1930s, the fight over the Bursum Bill and the fight over religious freedom.

Collier comes across as enigmatic because there is a fundamental contradiction in his thinking and his policies. Collier was content to uphold and celebrate and honor our expressive life, our cultural life, namely, the arts and religion. At the very same time, he was also content to deliver our more fundamental freedoms such as sovereignty and tribal self-government into the hands of the federal government. These two things seemed to work simultaneously in his life, and so both are true.

ALFONSO ORTIZ, *San Juan Pueblo*

4

COMMISSIONER COLLIER IS
ON OUR SIDE

I t was natural for John Collier, the new commissioner of Indian affairs, to ask Antonio Luhan to be his spokesman among the Pueblo Indians. A council member from Taos Pueblo, Luhan had introduced Collier to Pueblo culture more than ten years before. That visit kindled Collier's vision of a revitalized tribal world.

After Collier steered his new legislation through the U.S. Congress, he still had to sell it to the Indians. His field-workers dispersed throughout the country, persuading Indians to "come under the Wheeler-Howard bill." This meant that a tribe had to accept government by a duly elected tribal council and follow guidelines set forth, nonetheless, by the Bureau of Indian Affairs. For some Indians, stripped

Antonio Luhan

of their old forms of self-governing, this offered hope of some autonomy. Other groups, like the highly conservative Hopi, feared they had more to lose than to gain by joining Collier's program.

A Collier loyalist, Luhan did his best to persuade the various Hopi villages otherwise, as he writes in this personal letter to Collier in 1934. But the single-minded Collier was not prepared for the diversity of Indians he had to satisfy— from well-educated professionals to wary rural nationalists. Nor was he fully appreciative of the difficulties, as Luhan suggests, that existed even when one Indian was trying to persuade another.

LAST SUMMER when I went to the Snake Dance, I talked with Fred Kabotie of Chimopavi about the Wheeler-Howard Bill. He told me then, it was impossible to have an organization, on account of they're living far apart in separate pueblos. At that time, Fred said that all the old people were against that Bill, and did not believe in it.

This time when I went, on the 15th of November, I went first to Hotevilla and I asked how I could arrange to get a meeting to talk about the Wheeler-Howard Bill. They told me to go and see the Chief about it for that is all they have—just a Chief. I went to see the Chief to ask him to have the meeting and he asked me if I had any right to come there and do that kind of work. I hadn't the recommendation of the agent that day. I just said I had the Bill you sent me, signed John Collier, and I told him, "I am coming from John Collier and he signed this Bill," and I showed him the sign.

The Chief then told me he would call a meeting for the afternoon.

I went up at two o'clock and there was no sound of any meeting. I went again to the Chief and then he began to call the people.

The ones that were there that day came and I explained to them what the Bill meant, and all about Self-Government. . . .

And I told them to look ahead and see that, maybe sometime, some Secretary of the Interior could allot Indian land to separate Indians and pretty soon they would have nothing, but if they decide to have Self-Government under the Wheeler-Howard Bill, they are safe, forever. . . .

I told them that a lot of outsiders would tell them not to take this Bill, for this Bill is no good for white people.

I told them that in past times, the Government tried to make white people out of us, and force us into different ways by schools and things, but it looks now they have turned around and are giving us back to our own Indian ways and this Bill helps us to that. But there are still people in the Indian

Service who don't understand this yet, and there are some of those who are against the Bill. And I said, "I know no white man came here and told you this Bill is good, like I come to tell you, who am an Indian, myself.

"I do it because I know all our situation and our religious problem myself. I am not afraid to talk about that to you.

"I have property myself in my Pueblo and why should I come here and advise you to take this Bill if it wasn't any good? I am in the same place as you are. I would be foolish to come here and advise you to take it if it wasn't any good."

This is what I said at all the different villages and, of course, I said a lot more things. . . .

At Walapi, they were against the Bill when I got there. At the end of the meeting I had there, they said, "Before you came, we were against this Bill. Our white friends who told us about it, never explained as you have done. We didn't like this Bill but now we like it."

At Hotevilla, they just listened to me and said nothing. Then at the end of the meeting, the Chief said, "I am going to write to John Collier and ask him all about this." I said, "All right. Write carefully and make a petition and have your men sign it and John Collier will explain to you better than I do," I said.

I said, "We have got a real friend in John Collier. He really likes Indians. In past time, we had Commissioners against us who tried to stop our cer-emony dances and our dances-religious. They nearly destroy us; call our ways bad or immoral or something, and put in the paper they are going to stop us. But John Collier fight for us with the Indian Defense Association and he saves us. Now, he look far ahead and it is like he is putting a wall all around us to protect us—and this Wheeler-Howard Bill is this wall. And no white man or grafter can come inside and take away our land or our religion which are connected together."

I said, "Otherwise, if we don't take this Bill, our white neighbors are all round the edge of us, they always *look*, they always look what they going to see! And maybe, they see gold. The might see coal. And if we had the allotment, the white men might begin to loan money to some Indian boy or girl because they see something on their land. And the boy or girl might want to buy an automobile and will lose their land in a few years because they have borrowed on it. That is enough to finish the Indians. You have no place to hang your hat or shawl. No house, no home. And that all be destroyed."

I told them now we're lucky because the President, Mr. Ickes and the Commissioner are all on the side of the Indians. In times to come, maybe, another kind get in and want to go back to the old treatment. But if we have come under the Wheeler-Howard Bill, they cannot get at us and we are safe from them.

ANTONIO LUHAN, *Taos Pueblo*

5

RESISTING THE INDIAN NEW DEAL

Despite its glowing promise of new forms of self-rule, Indians were torn over Commissioner Collier's proposed Indian Reorganization Act. Many resisted his personal charisma and sincerity to question its underlying consequences. These reminiscences, by a bitter Collier opponent named Rupert Costo, cover some native arguments that Collier tried to satisfy, or if that was unsuccessful, to override.

Costo was a Cahuilla Indian scholar, educator, and lobbyist from a small reservation in southern California. Born in 1906, he was educated at Haskell Indian School in Kansas, worked two years for Indian causes in Washington, D.C., and often spoke out on behalf of his fellow Cahuilla and their neglected, southern California Indian neighbors. Together with his wife, Jeanette, Costo founded the American Indian Historical Society in 1950, and began publishing Indian-oriented books and magazines in 1970. These remarks are condensed from his participation, in August 1983, in a conference at Sun Valley, Idaho, which cast a retrospective eye on the Collier era.

THE IRA was the last great drive to assimilate the American Indian. It was also a program to colonialize the Indian tribes. All else had failed to liberate the Indians from their land: genocide, treaty-making and treaty-breaking, substandard education, disruption of Indian religion and culture, and the last and most oppressive of such measures, the Dawes Allotment Act.

The Quapaw of Oklahoma were bitterly opposed to the IRA. They said:

We have a treaty with the United States, describing by metes and bounds the size and shape of our allotments, and it states that its purpose is to provide a permanent home for the nation. And the United States agrees to convey the same by patent to them and their descendants, and this is according to article 2 of the Treaty of 1833.

In hearings before the House of Representatives, the Flathead made a similar statement. They agreed that the tribe might have the power to make contracts through the IRA, but instead of new legislation they believed it would be better to insist on sovereign rights and treaty rights.

On May 17, 1934, in hearings before the Senate, the great Yakima nation, in a statement signed by their chiefs and councilmen, said, "We feel that the best interests of the Indians can be preserved by the continuance of treaty laws and carried out in conformity with the treaty of 1855 entered into by the fathers of some of the undersigned chiefs and Governor Stevens of the territory of Washington."

But the commissioner of Indian affairs reported to the House of Representatives on May 7, 1934, that "I do not think that any study of the subject with all of the supporting petitions, reports, and referendums could leave any doubt that the Indian opinion is strongly for the bill." He then proceeded with this outright falsification of the facts, saying, "In Oklahoma I would say quite overwhelmingly they favor the bill."

During April 1934, the tribes that had bitterly opposed the IRA attended some of the ten meetings held by the commissioner of Indian affairs throughout the country. Here, as evidence shows, they were subjected to Collier's manipulations. In May, they came before the House of Representatives and completely reversed themselves. In fact, they gave a blanket endorsement to the Indian Reorganization Act. The congressmen, in shocked disbelief, prodded them again and again. Finally they asked, "If the proposed legislation is completely changed into an entirely different act would you then also endorse it?" The Indian delegates, according to many of their tribesmen and tribeswomen said, without any authority of their people, "Yes. Even then we would endorse it." How did this happen? I can tell you how it happened. They received promises that were never kept.

In California, at Riverside, forty tribes were assembled. All but three voted against the proposed bill. Collier then reported that most of the California tribes were for the proposed bill. It is a matter of record that in California Indians were afraid to come to meetings for fear of losing their jobs if they showed disapproval of the Collier proposed bill.

It is a curious fact that, in all the ten meetings held with Indians over the country, in not one meeting was there a copy of the proposed legislation put before the people. We were asked to vote on so-called explanations. The bill itself was withheld. We were told we need not vote but the meetings were only to discuss the Collier explanations. In the end, however, we were required to vote. And I suppose you would call all this maneuvering self-rule. I call it fraud.

The Crow rejected the IRA and stated for the record in a letter to Senator Burton K. Wheeler, one of the sponsors of the bill, "That under the Collier-chartered community plan, which has been compared to a fifth-rate *poor farm* by newspapers in Indian country, the Indian is being led to believe that they, for the first time in history, would have self-government." But according to the bill, any plans the Indians might have for such self-government would have to be first submitted to the interior secretary or commissioner of Indian affairs for supervision and approval.

A resolution by the Seneca in New York stated their opposition to the bill. It warned that the proposed bill absolutely revoked the right of free citizens enacted in 1924 by Congress. The objection was published in the Senate hearings on May 17, 1934. The Seneca scornfully dubbed the proposed Indian court, which did not pass, as "ridiculous." To this opposition was added the position of the Oneida at Senate hearings. They said, in a resolution to Senator Wheeler published on April 17, 1934, that

> The Oneida nation firmly adheres to the terms of the Treaty of Canandaigua between our nation, our confederacy, and the U.S. of November 11, 1794, that the laws of the U.S., the acts of Congress, and the customs and usages of the Oneida nation are the controlling provisions of Oneida basic law, and/or the federal officials, the exponents of such basic law and the guides for the sachems, chiefs, headmen and warriors.

And they added this statement: "Any acts of the state of Wisconsin through its officers, courts, or legislature contrary to the above are without sanction of law and repugnant to the nation of Oneida Indians." They had some courage then, you know.

RUPERT COSTO, *Cahuilla*

6

DEBATE OVER IRA

The two native points of view given here, from interviews conducted during the 1960s, also reflect divided opinion about the Indian "New Deal." To some of them, the individualism they had come ultimately to accept as the American way was lost in this "socialistic" vision of reborn tribes. Others worried that if they accepted the terms of the IRA they would lose their sovereign rights under old treaties.

Speaking on behalf of the IRA is Alfred DuBray, a Sioux Indian who, in 1970, was superintendent of the Winnebago Reservation. Arguing that the IRA caused more problems than it solved is Ramon Roubideaux, a Sioux and well-known South Dakota attorney.

Pro

I REMEMBER [when the Indian Reorganization Act was applied out at Rosebud, South Dakota]. I never had too much contact before with the agency. We always lived way out in the country, and our contacts with the Bureau at that time were what you would call farm agents, or boss farmers. These were abandoned districts in the outlying areas of the reservations. They would come around and keep us informed and deal with leases and things of this sort.

We lived in a community where there was quite a number of Indian families, many of whom were my relatives. They were quite politically minded—tribally, politically minded. I remember them talking about this New Deal that was coming out at that time. Of course, this was in administration of a Franklin D. Roosevelt, and his new Commissioner, John Collier, who immediately proposed to Congress a new era for the American Indian people. He proposed to Congress this legislation.

This was a new deal for the Indians. Nobody really understood it. They knew that they were going to have to vote on whether they wanted it or not. Of course, it was very difficult many times to get things accurately to them. It was a matter of communication—very difficult because they would interpret in many ways the minor things. They had all kinds of stories going about the new program. Many were against, and many were for it. From what they understood of it, it was very difficult because it was such a radical change from their way of life. Really, their customs and practices up to that point—most of all their governing procedures in the tribe—were handled through tribal leaders, designated by the chiefs, the leaders from one generation to another. They looked to the tribal chiefs, or leaders, to guide them in their procedures. They had no formal government of any kind, though they were fairly well organized.

Anyway, this was quite a radical change to bolt on. I think many of them looked at this as another way for Government to take over more of their controls. But, finally, the Bureau got going on this and organized themselves fairly well, and established some positions as to the responsibilities of employees. They would go around to explain the Reorganization Act to the people on all the reservations as best they could. I remember the one on Rosebud—the reorganization man they called him—was Mr. Ben Reifel. He was a man who had been in Washington working for the Bureau and was very capable. He was selected as one of these men to go out in the Rosebud area and explain this—sell it, in other words. So he did. He spent quite a lot of time out there. Then, finally, they were given deadlines or dates to vote. I don't remember all the details on that, but I think they had a rather close vote, as I recall, on adopting the Reorganization Act on the Rosebud Reservation.

Of course, the point of interest was it had a lot of advantages, in that many of the people would have loan funds available—huge amounts. Farm programs were developed through this; cattle-ranging programs were initiated. Educational loans were beginning to be made available for the Indian youngsters who had never had any opportunity before to attend higher institutions. There was a new feeling there in education. And, of course, mainly the tribal governing body got busy there and established the governing body, voted on their representatives and their council meetings. It was, I think, difficult for the people to recognize what they were doing for probably several years, until they got into the change.

ALFRED DUBRAY, *Sioux*

Con

AS FAR AS the Indian Reorganization Act is concerned, I think this is possibly one of the best intentioned but unfortunate happenings that could have possibly taken place as far as the Indian people are concerned. Although it did stop the sale of Indian lands and did stop the allotment system, it created a socialistic society and set the Indian people apart from the main-stream of American life and made them a problem. It has substituted in place of the governing system that the Indians had prior to the Indian Reorganization Act a white man's idea of how they should live—rather a paternalistic type of government which has as its object the socializing of all activities of the Indian people. While the framers of this act and the ones who are responsible for the idea of formulating it probably had the best intentions in the world, I cannot help but think that there was, maybe not an overt conspiracy, but one on the back of the mind of these bureaucrats to really perpetuate their own existence. . . .

To make myself a little clearer, I want to elaborate a little on the effects of the Indian Reorganization Act insofar as it has deterred the development and the independent thinking of the Indian people. In the first place, it set the Indian aside as a problem. The Indian was told that he was a problem from the very day he was born under this system, and as he grew older, by the presence of these so-called experts in ranching and agriculture and other activities they were paying lip service to teaching the Indians, he was some-how made to feel that he was inferior, that he wasn't able to compete. So that the whole system emphasized the activities of the Indians as a whole for the benefit of the whole, rather than the individual private enterprise system of our American system. He wasn't taught to be a capitalist, which he must be taught in order for him to survive in this country. . . .

And I think the main thing that was wrong with the whole thing was that the setting of the Indian aside on a different place in the state, designating him as a problem, making him feel he was a problem, beating down rebels, beating down Indians who expressed any independent thinking, rewarding collaborators, rewarding them with positions of importance and completely stifling independent and creative thinking from the Indian people, having different laws apply to him, setting up a different kind of government. . . .

It's not self-government, because self-government by permission is no self-government at all. Everything that the Indian Reorganization Act brought in under the guise of self-government was subject to the approval or the concurrence of the Secretary of the Interior or his authorized rep-resentative—the superintendent. These Indians have never made policy de-cisions; they have never been able to use creative thinking. Everything they've done has been under the wing of the Government; it's just like the rich kid with the rich father. Everything is planned for him, he never develops this mind of his.

RAMON ROUBIDEAUX, *Sioux*

7

REDUCING NAVAJO SHEEP

I n Arizona, Commissioner of Indian Affairs John Collier faced a unique and volatile dilemma. The cultural resurgence for which he fought, represented among Navajos by the symbolic and economic importance of sheepherding, clashed with ecological realities.

After the Navajo resettled on their reservation in 1868, pasturage seemed limitless. The former hunters settled into animal husbandry; breeding and exchanging sheep became a matter of family prestige as well as a source of income (from wool) and food. As early as the 1890s overgrazing was eroding their arid landscape; summer rains washed away the topsoil from slopes stripped bare by livestock.

By the late 1920s the Navajo were warned that they must cut back their sheep, horses, goats, and cattle, but the hapless task of persuading them fell to the Collier period. Between 1934 and 1944 his sheep-reduction policy eliminated about half of the Navajo stock, but earned Collier the reputation of "devil" and "Hitler" throughout the tribe. Here a woman named The Blind Man's Daughter describes its impact on her family.

WHEN I HAD A HUSBAND and a lot of sheep I was happy. Then when it came my sheeps' turn to be acted upon, they were all driven away from me. They were driven into a corral and I was told to select the ones that were the best. That hurt me and I just bowed my head. I just sent my children over and they selected some.

We became despondent over it. My husband became sick from worry, and these officials went about in their cars even at night. Early in the morning one would be going about. They even interrupted our sleep. They did this on account of our sheep and our way of life. When we drove our sheep to the dipping vat some more were taken away.

It was there that my husband said, "You people are indeed heartless. You have now killed me. You have cut off my arms. You have cut off my legs. You have taken my head off. There is nothing left for me. This is the end of the trail," he said. This happened, and it wasn't long before my husband fell ill. It was no doubt the worry that sickened him. He was sick all winter, and at the beginning of spring he died.

These two events, the loss of my sheep and and the loss of my husband, made me feel terribly unhappy. I was despondent, and I am still so today.

I had five sons then, and seven daughters. We were all dependent on the small amount of stock granted to us on the permit (lit. we all climbed onto this tiny permit). We could not always make ends meet (lit. some of us would fall off it and would grab about for something to reestablish our balance and get us back onto it). In the course of getting one back onto it, another would fall off, so we really had to work closely together in order to stay on this permit. We suffered from everything, from hunger, from lack of meat and from despondency. The Special Grazing Regulation is like a killing disease from which one can not sleep.

THE BLIND MAN'S DAUGHTER, *Navajo*

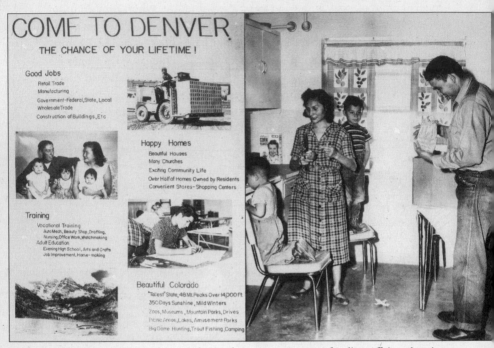

Indians are encouraged to resettle in urban areas—Bureau of Indian Affairs relocation promotion poster

T he Indian veterans who came back to their reservations after World War II were different men. They felt worldly, returning with awareness of lands and peoples beyond America. They had been brothers-in-arms with non-Indians, and had learned more about their own nation in the process. On the battlefield their courage had earned the respect of their white officers. They felt proud, and equal to the white man, and ten thousand of them had died to prove it.

Twenty-five thousand Indians had joined the Navy, Army, or Marine Corps. Another forty thousand between ages eighteen and fifty worked in the war support industry at home. Of the thirty-six hundred Navajos who went overseas, some were recruited into the Marines' crack 382d Platoon where they became the famous "code talkers." Using transmissions derived from phrases in the Navajo language, they regularly outwitted Japanese eavesdroppers in the South Pacific. The Congressional Medal of Honor went to the Cherokee Jack Montgomery, and to the Creek Ernest Childers, for action against the forces of dictators whom the Navajo called "mustache-smeller" (Hitler), "big gourd chin" (Mussolini), and against the "narrow-eycds" (Japanese).

But a hero's reputation in a foreign battle bore little relation to his sense of self and status in America, as the sad tale of the Pima Indian soldier Ira Hayes vividly demonstrated. Hayes helped hoist an American flag on Mount Suribachi at Iwo Jima, a moment immortalized in the war's most publicized photograph, by Joe Rosenthal. Back home in Arizona, he couldn't handle the acclaim, and began drinking. He tried jobs in various cities, but died of acute alcoholism and exposure in a cotton field on his own reservation.

Discrimination was something they fought overseas, but they had forgotten their second-class citizenship at home. In New Mexico and Arizona state law still did not allow Indians to vote. They could not take out GI loans. "Look," a veteran said, "I have a false eye, cheekbone, a silver plate in my head, but I can't buy liquor in a bar like any American."

Many came back primed to live and work within the wider American scene beyond the reservation, but realized that the military had not taught them marketable skills. A few carved out new roles in their old reservations. Some were only too glad to find work with the Bureau of Indian Affairs. Others turned into discouraged outsiders, wandering the skid rows of reservation border towns in torn army field jackets.

The vets also discovered a Bureau of Indian Affairs once again in a state of upheaval. After eleven years of resistance to his reforms, John Collier resigned as commissioner of Indian affairs in 1945. By then the political climate had clearly turned. The new slogan reminded old timers of allotment days: "government should get out of the Indian business."

Home-coming Indian GIs also found that the Collier years had created a new body of elders, the National Congress of American Indians. It was organized in Denver in 1944 by Indian officials who were optimistic about the Collier style of self-government. In the coming years, the NCAI played a central role in mobilizing Indians against unwelcome legislation.

A step toward concluding traditional ties between tribes and the federal government was the establishment, in 1946, of the Indian Claims Commission. This court of last resort was a clearinghouse for an accumulation of unresolved grievances—disputes over old treaties, restitution for wrongful use of Indian trust funds, loss of hunting and fishing rights. Within its first five years, however, the commission found it could not dispense with the past so hastily, as 588 complicated claims were submitted by Indian tribes across the country. The life span of the commission was extended; by 1963, only 122 claims had been settled, and new cases were still coming in.

In 1950 Dillon S. Myer was named commissioner of Indian affairs. During the war Myer directed the detention program for Japanese-Americans in the United States. To him Indian reservations were akin to concentration camps from which Indians should be "freed" as soon as possible.

The buzzword for Myer's new Indian policy was "Termination." It meant a second, decisive stroke to sever relationships between the U.S. government and Indians, which had grown out of 372 treaties, more than 5000 laws, and presidential edicts. It meant liquidating the special "ward" status of Indians and the "trust" responsibilities of government to look after their best interests—especially their lands. It started a countdown for eliminating the Bureau of Indian Affairs altogether.

Myer also wanted to phase out health, economic, and educational benefits provided by the Indian Reorganization Act. He saw a return to boarding schools to draw children away from the ties of home and reservation; he ordered classes to stop stressing native culture, to emphasize instead "the preparation of these children for permanent off-reservation employment." When Myer put to some native leaders the rhetorical question "What can we do to Americanize the Indian," an elder responded that Indians were more concerned with "how we can Americanize you. We have been working at that for a long time. . . . And the first thing we want to teach you is that, in the American way of life, to have respect for his brother's vision."

Due to the credit fund established by Collier's IRA, Indians had shown they were acceptable financial risks. Myer cited this fact to argue for commercial banks to fund Indian sawmills, cattle ranches, and small businesses; the lands that Indians had regained under IRA could be collateral. When the Bureau stopped loaning them money in 1952, this seemed to Indians to turn their achievements toward self-sufficiency into an opportunity to steal their lands through foreclosures, since often they could not afford the higher interest payments imposed by commercial banks.

This about-face from the Roosevelt and Collier era's emphasis on revived

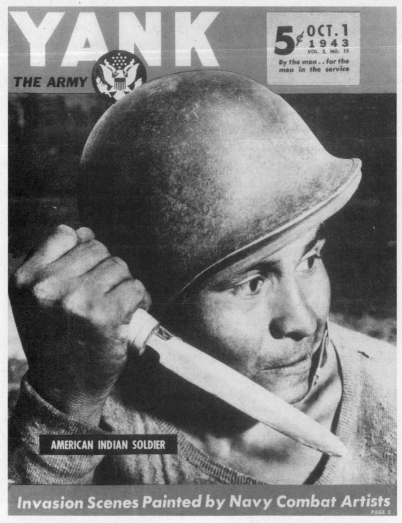

During World War II Army publicity promotes image of Indian as guerrilla fighter.

tribalism and restored lands was summarized in ten bills placed before Congress in 1954. At an emergency session in Washington the National Congress of American Indians, comprising most of the country's elected tribal chairmen, began lobbying intensely against the legislation, but six bills passed anyway.

Related to this "Termination" package was a Bureau of Indian Affairs strategy to persuade reservation Indians to resettle in big cities across the country, especially Seattle, Denver, Los Angeles, and Chicago. Actually, Indian families had been migrating between rural and urban centers since the turn of the century. After the White Earth Chippewa of Minnesota sold their timberlands in 1906, there was a significant exodus to the "twin cities" of St. Paul and Minneapolis. For years the Mohawks of Upper New York State had driven to work on skyscrapers in Manhattan and establish Indian neighborhoods in Brooklyn.

"Relocation" was the catchword for the Bureau's plan to help Indians to find apartments and jobs and schools for their children. In 1955, thirty-four hundred Indians were already living in low-rent apartments or housing developments in Chicago, Los Angeles, Seattle, St. Louis, and Detroit. By 1957 close to ten thousand more Indians had been lured away from home and kinfolk to work in construction sites and light industries in the "cement prairies." In reality the U.S. government delivered minimal psychological support during this trying cultural and economic change of life-style. For many Indians relocation meant an anguishing dislocation. Stories filtered back to the reservation of loneliness, alcoholism, depression, police harassment, unemployment, and crime.

Indians found it hard to fit in, and weren't sure they wanted to. "Why is it so important that Indians be brought into the 'mainstream of American life?' " asked the Blackfoot tribal chairman, Earl Old Person. "What is the 'mainstream of American life?' I would not know how to interpret the phrase to my people in our language. The closest I would be able to come to 'mainstream' would be to say, in Indian, 'a big, wide river.' Am I then to tell my people that they will be 'thrown into the Big Wide River of the United States'?"

Soon the very word "Relocation" shot anxiety into the hearts of Indians, much as "Removal" had more than a century before; it was dropped in favor of the milder "Employment Assistance." By 1960 the process had rearranged the map of Indian America, as the U.S. Census counted nearly a third of the country's 525,000 Native Americans as "urban Indians."

The termination program of the 1950s sought to reestablish tribes as going concerns that no longer needed Bureau of Indian Affairs financing. So it began with Indians who had shown they could manage their natural resources and make a profit. Termination meant, officially, that they would no longer be treated as tribes but as corporations, which would now have to pay taxes on their businesses and their lands. Most were not prepared for that.

Between 1954 and 1962 Congress imposed Termination upon sixty-one tribes, groups, bands, and communities, thereby severing their federal services, protections, and sense of sovereignty. Many of these would eventually have to have their old status restored, however, because their fortunes plummeted almost immediately. The Klamath of Oregon were a prime example, since at the outset they were one of the best bets to make it on their own. Over the past few decades their tribe of 2,133 enrolled members had built up a successful ponderosa and sugar pine lumber business. The average Klamath family earned nearly four thousand dollars a year from the tribally owned and run lumber mill.

Since the 1930s some of the Klamath themselves had called for an end to federal supervision. But the majority opposed it, and the tribal chairman, Seldon Kirk, echoed their suspicions that "the Secretary [of the Interior] wants the white man to get our land." Their resistance irritated Senator Arthur Watkins of Utah, a principal designer of what he called the "Indian freedom program." To him the Klamath were shirking their responsibility as financially independent Americans.

The termination ultimatum finally imposed on the reluctant Klamath gave them two ways to face it. They had three years under government support to learn to operate their $100-million tribal holdings totally on their own, tutored by a management corporation, or they could sell their assets and distribute the lump sum throughout the tribe on a person-by-person ("per capita") basis.

In either case, the Klamath would no longer be officially a distinct political entity. They would have to fend for themselves without special health, welfare, or education benefits. Some observers foresaw disaster; Chairman Kirk worried that, "If a man has enough children [who would each receive part of the lump sum payoff], he is demoralized by per capita payments and lays around."

Ultimately the tribe chose to sell. Payments to minors and other special cases were supposedly safeguarded in trusts, but within a year nearly half of them were closed out. "It was like throwing steak to the dogs," remembered one Klamath. "Too few of us are prepared. . . ." In less than two years the sudden wealth—fifty thousand dollars per person—had demoralized the community. Men no longer worked at the mills, alcoholism and family problems rose markedly, and the money was not reinvested.

As a Senate investigation concluded in 1969, "The termination of the Klamath Reservation in Oregon has led to extreme social disintegration of that tribal group. Many of them can be found in state mental and penal institutions." The Menominee of Wisconsin also underwent Termination and told a similar story. Only they corrected matters by petitioning successfully to restore their tribal status.

As for the new Indian city dwellers, some were those veterans who had not found acceptance at home, and now were in conflict with older tribal leaders. They wanted more from America than menial jobs, yet they wanted to remain proud of being Indian. This chapter covers the experiences of Indians during and after the Second World War, their reactions to postwar government policies, and the rise of the new Urban Indian.

1

COUNTING COUP IN WORLD WAR TWO

J oseph Medicine Crow was a regular Indian GI when he shipped out of New York City for Europe in fall 1943. First he was a clerk-typist, but when America casualties got heavy he was assigned to "K" Company of the "Cactus" division. Soon he was no longer an ordinary soldier and no longer on foot, as he described to me in 1972.

Medicine Crow got a chance to relive the days when his Crow Indian ancestors were horse-riding raiders on the Montana plains. Remarkable as an example of particular tribal continuity, his account also represents the thousands of Indian soldiers whose bravery against the Germans and the Japanese was part of an inherited warrior code. Medicine Crow safely returned home to become an anthropologist, a land assessor, and a respected historian of his people.

WHEN I WENT to Germany I never thought about war honors, or the four "coups" which an old-time Crow warrior had to earn in battle. Those days were gone. But afterwards, when I came back and went through this telling of the war deeds ceremony, why, I told my war deeds, and lo and behold I completed the four requirements to become a chief.

The first one happened when we started to push across this little creek about like Lodge Grass Creek, that separated France and Germany, the Siegfried Line. That was the first time any American units reached the German line, and the *Stars and Stripes* photographers were there for the historic moment.

I was a platoon runner, carrying messages back and forth, and the CO said, "All right, Chief, let's see you jump over the creek here to Germany." We got into Germany and before long we ran into foxholes loaded with Germans. We got to the top of this hill that was a network of trenches every which way, and the top was kinda steep and muddy and by the time about thirty guys were there it was just slippery. A guy in front of me, fat and heavy, kept falling back on top of me and when the Germans opened fire I think that was the only reason I didn't get killed that day—the guys on top were all wiped out. We stayed in the side trenches all night and threw hand grenades.

Come daylight the message came to send some men to get dynamite to blow up the big guns and the CO says, "Well, Chief, if anybody can get through, you can get through. Get six men and go up there." Boy, it was a high hill, loaded with mines. So the guns from the American side started throwing these smoke screen shells. Pretty soon that whole hillside's just one white mass of smoke. We didn't know where the mines were, we just took off. The Germans knew something was happening and began throwing in mortar shells and sometimes they'd get awfully close.

We finally reached our platoon center and they gave us the boxes of dynamite and fuses and we threw them on our shoulders and started down through that smoke again. I tell you, that was a terrible thing, but we came back without a scratch and they went ahead and dynamited two or three big guns. That earned me the war honor of being assigned to lead a war party and come back safely.

The next ones came in March 1944 when the big push was on and we came to a little German town about the size of Hardin, Montana. We came from behind while the other outfits made a straight attack. There was still snow and we came through this slough with it up to our chests. I was a corporal then and took about five or six guys up a back alley. There was a lot of fighting in the main street but it was kind of quiet in the alley. There was a stone fence about ten feet high and a gate and I was heading for that gate to look around. A German had the same idea and he was running on the other side but with all this firing going on I couldn't hear him, and he couldn't hear me. So we were running and here he came around and by golly I somehow knocked him down, knocked his rifle down. He landed on his back and I was on top of him. And he was reaching for his rifle, but I kicked that out of the way and sat on his chest and grabbed his throat and started choking him.

The rest of the guys showed up ready to blow his brains out but I had my hands there. This German guy had tears running down and hollered, "Hitler kaput, Hitler kaput, Hitler nicht gut." I felt sorry for him and let him go. And that was two coups, the first German we ran into and by knocking him down and touching him I counted two in one whack. They did that too, in the olden days.

The fourth one was in May, just about the time the Germans gave up. We were following a group of SS officers on horse—they were the worst ones, who had started all this, so we had to get them. We followed them all night. They stayed on the asphalt highway and you could hear the horses clonking away.

Toward daybreak they went off the road and we found their tracks in the mud. They came to a farmhouse and turned all their horses into a small pasture, sort of a good-sized corral. Then they went into this house and probably bedded down. So we decided to get them when it was light enough to see what you're shooting at.

I said to the CO, "You know," I said, "in the meantime I'll chase their horses away." I was looking out for myself. They got the attack all mapped out and when it was time beforehand he said, "All right, Chief, you're on." So I took one guy with me, one of my partners. "Come on, you open the gate for me." We sneaked down in there. We didn't know there was a guy down in the barn sitting on guard.

These horses were tired and standing around. I came up to one and said in English, "Whoa, whoa, now, whoa now." Kind of snorted a little bit and stopped. I usually carry this little rope to tie my brown army blanket. So I took that rope, about six feet long, and tied his lower jaws the way the old-fashioned Crow warriors do. I tried to get on but it was a tall horse and my boots were caked with mud and I had a hard time. Finally I got on and said to the other guy, "I'll go toward the other end and as soon as I get there I'll give you a whistle and you open the gate."

I got back of the horses and gave a little whistle and then I started in and gave a war whoop. Boy, here they come. My partner took off and just about that time they opened fire over there at the house. There was some timber about a half-mile aways so I just headed there and then it was daylight and I looked them over. There were about forty to fifty head. I was riding a sorrel horse with a blazed forehead—real nice horse. So I did something spontaneously. I sang a Crow praise song, you know. I sang this song a little bit and I rode around the horses. The horses looked at me and finally I left them there and went back, staying on that horse bareback. I came back and all the firing was done.

Then our guys were walking along this old abandoned railroad tracks and I was still on my horse. It was good. Better to ride than walk. But about a mile or so the CO finally said to me, "Chief, you better get off. You'll make too good a target." So I got off the horse and walked.

I wrote a long letter to Bob Yellowtail, my uncle, and when I was writing, this capturing idea came to me. So I said, "I captured forty to fifty of officers' horses—my war deed," I said. And when he read that, boy, he ran out and told Jack Covers Up, Pup Plays, Jim Blaine, and Red, my grandfather, and said, "My nephew has captured a bunch of horses." So by the time I came back they asked me to recite my war deed here at Lodge Grass in spring of 1947. I went through the ritual of telling them in detail and that's when the idea came to me of completing those four things. And they said, "That's right. So you've completed all the old four military requirements, so you are a chief."

JOSEPH MEDICINE CROW, *Crow*

2

A CODE TALKER COMES HOME

The secret language that was used by more than four hundred Navajo communications specialists in the Pacific during World War II associated Navajo words, broken into code, with military terms. Thus their word for "owl" meant an observation plane, "potato" was a hand grenade, "rabbit trails" were roads, "eggs" were bombs, and "iron fish" meant torpedo. An alphabet was also devised where the Navajo word for "ant" was the letter a, "bear" in Navajo meant b, and so forth.

Messages transmitted via this complicated code enabled U.S. Marines to take over the island of Iwo Jima. After the war these "code talkers" agreed to anonymity, in case their services were needed again. Here one Navajo code talker dwells less upon his wartime adventures than upon his return to culture and kin, an experience that was more stressful to other Indian veterans. For their success in evading Japanese intelligence and making secret landings possible, the Navajo code talkers were honored in 1982 with a presidential proclamation declaring August 14 as National Navajo Code Talkers Day.

I W A S 1 8 when I entered the service, on very short notice. I didn't even have time to go back to see my parents. All I did was write them a letter. I was working at the hospital in Fort Defiance when I suddenly made up my mind to join the Marines. I filled out my application, had my physical and was on my way. I had been exposed to the Catholic religion a little, but I admit I hadn't taken it very seriously.

I *did* pray many many times when I was exposed to danger on the main battleline, as a code talker and as a signalman. I prayed as my mother and father had taught me—to the Heavenly Being as well as to Mother Earth.

Now when I came back, surprisingly my mother told me, "Son, do you know that since you left, almost every morning, I have gone to my sacred hill and prayed, using my sacred corn pollen, that you would come back with your whole physical being and a good mind." Maybe that is the reason I came back all in one piece.

Now I did have a hell of a time with malaria; I got it on Guadalcanal. Out of about 6000 Marines over there, I was among the last 16 to get it. Some of the colonels and generals asked, "How is it with you Navajos? Are you so tough that you don't even need to take quinine?" I always said, "I don't know. I had a tough life when I was a little boy."

I came back to San Francisco, where they sent me to a rehabilitation center, then to a hospital, then home for a month's leave. I was skin and bones. I came back to Gallup where my father met me. He said, "Son, I'm glad you came back alive, I don't want you to go to town and try to have some fun; I want you to come home with me. I have something for you there." So I said, "O.K." Well, they had a medicine man there for me. They had a sing over me.

My mother and father were so happy to have me back that they killed a little nine-months pet goat; it was real tender. They wanted to feed me, I was so thin. But it didn't have any taste to it. I just couldn't eat it. I had to set it aside. There was something about the malaria, the things I had gone through, the difference in the wind and air . . . well, I just couldn't eat it.

But I got well. I think my mother's prayers on her sacred hill helped me through the war and after I got back home.

ANONYMOUS, *Navajo*

Indian interests and land claims often suffered during periods of government dam-building, such as occurred after the 1930s. Here, in 1950, Hidatsa Indian leader George Gillette breaks into tears as his people are pressured into signing away Missouri River frontage that these North Dakota tribes had occupied for more than a thousand years. The resulting Garrison Dam submerged most of the traditional Hidatsa and Mandan town sites.

‖‖**3**‖‖

THE MENOMINEES ARE
TERMINATED

Heading the list of tribes whom Bureau of Indian Affairs experts felt were ready for Termination in the 1950s was the Menominee of Wisconsin. Their timber business had done well enough, it was believed, that they could cut their lifeline to the government, and feed themselves, pay their taxes, and send themselves to school like every other American community. When Menominee Termination went into effect, what had been a tribe and a reservation was overnight a corporation with taxable holdings and profits.

The following chronology of their declining fortunes was prepared by an anti-termination group of Menominee activists called DRUMS. This group also advocated legislation that would restore their tribal identity. When this was passed in 1965, the U.S. government admitted, as it had with the allotment program, that Termination had been a big mistake.

EARLY IN 1953, we Menominee wanted a portion of our 1951 settlement—about $5,000,000—distributed among ourselves on a $1,500 per capita basis. Since Congressional approval was required for such disbursement of our assets, [then] Representative Melvin Laird and Senator Joseph McCarthy introduced in Congress on behalf of our Tribe a bill to authorize the payment of *our* money to us.

This bill passed the House, but in hearings before the Senate Committee on Interior and Insular Affairs, it ran up against an amendment sponsored by the late Senator Arthur V. Watkins (R. Utah) calling for "termination" of federal supervision and assistance to the Menominee. Watkins and the Committee refused to report the bill favorably, calling upon us Menominee to submit a termination plan *before* we would be given *our* money! "Termination!" What did *that* mean? Certainly at that time, none of us Menominee realized what it meant! . . . In June, 1953, we Menominee invited Senator Watkins to visit the Reservation and explain "termination" to us.

Senator Watkins badly wanted our termination. He was firmly convinced that factors such as our status as Reservation Indians, our tribal ownership of land, and our tax exemption were blocking our initiative, our freedom, and our development of private enterprise. He wished to see us rapidly assimilated into the mainstream of American society—as tax paying, hard working, "emancipated" citizens. . . .

On June 20, 1953, Senator Watkins spoke for 45 minutes to our General Council. He told us that Congress had already decided on terminating us, and that at most we could have three years before our "affairs would be turned over to us"—and that we would not receive our per capitas until *after* termination.

After he left, our Council had the opportunity to vote on the "principle of termination!" Some opportunity! What little understanding we had of what termination would mean! The vote was 169 to 5 in favor of the "principle of termination." A mere 5 percent of the 3,200 Menominee people participated in this vote. Most of our people chose to be absent from the meeting in order to express their negative reaction to termination. Many who did vote affirmatively that day believed that termination was coming from Congress whether the Menominee liked it or not. Others thought that they were voting *only* in favor of receiving their per capitas. . . .

We then set about preparing a termination plan, which the BIA subsequently emasculated, and we received word that Senator Watkins was pressing ahead with his *own* termination bill. *Another* general council meeting was called, one which is seldom mentioned, but at which the Menominee voted 197 to 0 to *oppose and reject* termination! But our feelings did not matter—and although the Watkins bill met a temporary defeat on technical grounds in the House in late 1953, Senator Watkins re-introduced it in 1954.

We became convinced that there was *no* alternative to accepting termination. Therefore, all we pleaded for was adequate time to plan this sudden and revolutionary change in our lives! On June 17, 1954, the Menominee Termination Act was signed into law by President Eisenhower. . . .

Termination represented a gigantic and revolutionary *forced* change in the traditional Menominee way of life. Congress expected us to replace our Indian way of life with a complicated corporate style of living. Congress expected immediate Menominee assimilation of non-Indian culture, values, and life styles. . . .

The immediate effect of termination on our tribe was the loss of most of our hundred-year-old treaty rights, protections, and services. No amount of explanation or imagination prior to termination could have prepared us for the shock of what these losses meant.

Congress withdrew its trusteeship of our lands, transferring to MEI [Menominee Enterprises, Inc., the corporation which was to supervise Menominee holdings after termination] the responsibility for protecting these lands, our greatest assets. As we shall explain, far from being able to preserve our land, MEI has been forced to sell it. And because our land is now being sold to non-Menominee, termination is doing to us what allotment has done to other Indian tribes.

Congress also extinguished our ancient system of tribal "ownership" of land (under which no individual had separate title to his home) and transferred title to MEI. Consequently, we individual Menominee suddenly discovered that we would be forced to buy from MEI the land which had always been considered our own, and to pay title to our homesites. Thus began the tragic process of our corporation "feeding off" our people.

We Menominee lost our right to tax exemption. Both MEI and individual Menominee found themselves saddled with tax burdens particularly crushing to a small tribe struggling to develop economically.

BIA health, education and utility services ceased. We lost all medical and dental care within the Reservation. Both our reservation and hospital were closed because they failed to meet state standards. Individual Menominee were forced to pay for electricity and water that they previously received at no cost. Our county found it had to renovate at high cost its substandard sewerage system.

Finally, with termination and the closing of our tribal rolls, our children born since 1954 have been legally deprived of their birthright as Menominee Indians. Like all other Menominee, they have lost their entitlement to United States Government benefits and services to Indians. . . . The only major Menominee treaty right which the government has allowed us to retain has been our hunting and fishing right. Wisconsin had tried to deprive us of this right, but in 1968, after costly litigation, the United States Supreme Court ruled that this treaty right had "survived" termination. . . .

We hope you can appreciate the magnitude of these treaty losses to us. Visualize a situation similar to ours happening in one of your home states. Imagine the outrage of the people in one of your own communities if Congress should attempt to terminate their basic property, inheritance, and civil rights. . . .

Today Menominee County is the poorest county in Wisconsin. It has the highest birthrate in the state and ranks at or near the bottom of Wisconsin counties in income, housing, property value, education, employment, sanitation and health. The most recent figures available (1967) show that the annual income of nearly 80 percent of our families falls below the federal poverty level of $3,000. The per capita annual income of our wage earners in 1965 was estimated at $881, the lowest in the state. . . .

This lack of employment opportunities, combined with our high birthrate, forced nearly 50 percent of our county residents to go on welfare in 1968. Welfare costs in the county for 1968 were over $766,000 and our per capita welfare payment was the highest in the state. The majority of Menominee who have left our county to seek work in the cities have become trapped in poverty there also.

With the closing of the BIA hospital, we lost most of our health services, and most Menominee continue to suffer from lack of medical care. There have been no full-time doctors or dentists in Menominee County since termination. Shortly after termination, our people were stricken by a TB epidemic which caused great suffering and hardship because of the lack of local medical facilities. . . .

The loss of the BIA school required that our youth be sent to Shawano County for their high school training. The Shawano school system had assumed that Menominee children possess the same cultural and historical background as [children from the] middle-class white community. . . . Since 1961, our high school drop-out rates have increased substantially, absenteeism has soared, and our children apparently are suffering a downward trend in achievement. . . .

We have told a story which is very tragic, yet it is a true story of the Menominee people since termination. We have told how termination has meant the loss of treaty benefits, has pushed our already poor community further into the depths of poverty, forced our sale of assets; and denied us a democratic community.

DRUMS COMMITTEE, *Menominee*

4

ON RELOCATION

For rural Indians who signed up for the government's Voluntary Relocation program, the big city could be a confusing place. Scary as it was, the experience drew enough families to Los Angeles, Chicago, and other cities to produce a new sociological category: the Urban Indian. These selections cover this new period, when thousands of Indian immigrants, many from the Southwest, adapted to Chicago. At first the government tried to assist them with housing and employment, but most relocatees wound up in substandard apartments and menial jobs; by 1955 at least six hundred of them left Chicago for home.

First, a young Winnebago from Nebraska describes to interviewer Studs Terkel the new skills and dangers of city survival. Then a Cherokee storyteller named Watt Spade explains why Relocation gained the reputation among Indians as a "missing persons factory."

GETTING URBANIZED. I like this term. It means you have to learn the ropes, just like a person moving out from prairie country into the woods. You know, there are certain dangers in such a transition, and it's the same way in a city. You have to learn the ropes. And once you become urbanized, this means to me that you're gonna settle down, and you have to have a goal to look forward to. Otherwise, I think it would drive you crazy.

I'll tell you the extent to which I'm urbanized, after being here for seventeen years. Some years ago, we went back to Nebraska, to my wife's parents' place. And for three or four nights in a row, I'd wake up in the middle of the night, feeling that there was something drastically wrong. And it puzzled me until I began to realize: it was quiet, that's what was wrong. There's no fire engines or police sirens passing by, no street noises. It's funny.

I was raised all the way from the Winnebago Indian reservation in northeast Nebraska, to Iowa, Minnesota, and Wisconsin. My father was a laborer. He moved his family whenever there was employment. So I got an early introduction to the melting pot.

In those days, I didn't give discrimination much thought. Since we moved around quite a lot. The one thing that stands out in my mind is that every new school we attended, we had to go through an ordeal. The toughest fellas wanted to see how tough we were. So we got kind of oriented that way. And if we could whip the toughest kid, why then, we had it made from then on. We had a lot of friends. Of course, that didn't always happen that way, either.

I came to Chicago in 1947, after I had been married, and later on I sent for my wife and my one child and since that time we've lived here in the city. The most important reason was that I could at least feel confident that perhaps fifty paychecks a year here . . . and you can't always get that way. Even though it might be more pleasant to be back home, for instance, Nebraska.

I think this is one feature most Indians have in common. They have a deep attachment for the land. This has been so for a long, long time. Many different tribes of Indians are now residing in Chicago, but most of them maintain ties with the people back home. Even in cases where the older members of their families have passed away, they still make a point to go home. Many of them make the trip twice a year to go back to the place where they were born and raised.

Four of our children were born here in this city, and yet, I think, they're oriented as American Indians. I make it a point to take them on my vacation trips in the summer, always to a different reservation to get acquainted with the people of the tribe. We take photographs, we record the songs that are sung, we participate in dancing and compete for prizes. . . .

I have five now. My wife is a full-blooded Winnebago. I met her on the Nebraska reservation.

Oh, one time we had a little trouble with housing. In 1960 the work was kind of slack, there wasn't anything going on about that time. So I got together with three other boiler-makers, and we went up to Pierre, South Dakota, where the U.S. Army Corps of Engineers had this dam-construction project going on. While I was up there, the rents were raised where I had been living on the West Side. Well, my wife, with the help of the parish priest, found another apartment.

But I was kind of worried about being eight hundred miles from home, so I jumped on a train and came back to help her make the move. We made the move, and it happened that weekend the American Indian Center was holding a show. So after we got everything moved, we all went down to the theater. And after the show, we all went to the Center and had coffee and a good visit with everyone.

When we went back to the apartment on the West Side, the first thing we discovered that most of the windows were smashed. Well, I called the Chicago police. The police came out there, and we had a police car in front of the door for about two weeks, I guess.

I still don't know who did it, because it was done at night. They evidently thought we were Mexicans. Well, when the police asked me about this, I said I was sorry to disappoint anybody. As much as I admire Mexicans, I'm not a Mexican. I'm an American Indian.

And, well, during the following days, there were representatives of many different organizations who came out and talked to us. There was a man from the Chicago Commission on Human Relations, the Illinois Commission, from the National Conference of Christians and Jews, American Friends Service Committee, Bureau of Indian Affairs, Catholic Interracial Council. You know, there was very little that they could do.

If I didn't have any children to worry about—they would have to walk to school about four, five blocks—I think I would have stayed. It was one of those arrangements where the thing was operated by a trust. Even the newspapers couldn't find out who was the actual owner. But I found out later that this was right inside the battle lines that had already been established. It was an old Italian neighborhood, and just across the line east of us were Puerto Ricans, Southern whites, and to the South were Negroes. And since we were different, we posed a threat. They thought we were breaking the dike or something. It was kind of enlightening, really, after it was over.

The most amusing part of it was the Chicago *Defender* ran a cartoon. Yeah, there was a picture of an Indian family leaving a neighborhood in an old jalopy, and the people were all shouting. And then the label said, the caption said: These fellas just got off the boat. The fellas just got off the boat were running the first Americans out of the neighborhood.

BENNIE BEARSKIN, *Winnebago*

ONE TIME I went up there to Chicago where my brother lives. Rabbit is his name. He was right there when I got off the bus. We were a little hungry so we stopped to eat on the way across town. This restaurant we stopped at was all glass on the outside, like one big window. You could see all the people eating inside. They weren't sitting down either; they were all standing up at a counter that wound all around through the place. They were standing along both sides of this counter, but they didn't seem to be talking to each other or looking at each other. It was like they were all looking at the wall.

My brother and I decided to eat at a place called Wally's Bar over near where he lives at Fullerton and Green. There were a lot of people in that place and they were all very friendly. They all seemed to know my brother too, but they called him "Indian Joe." I hadn't ever heard him called that.

Rabbit told me he didn't have any place where I could stay. He had an apartment, but they'd had a fire there a few days before. We went over to look at it, and I guess he hadn't been there for a few days because there was a letter from Momma on the stairs right where you come in. There was black soot on the stairs all the way up to the fourth floor, where his apartment was; and there were some Puerto Rican guys up there cleaning the place up. They had the radio turned on real loud playing some kind of Puerto Rican music. The whole place smelled like charcoal and burnt furniture.

We went back to that place where they all called Rabbit "Indian Joe" and I told him about the news from home. Then he told me all about the city and about Chicago Rawhide, where he works. Finally I said I didn't think I was ready to settle down there just yet. We went on back to the bus station and waited around for the bus back to Oklahoma. There were a couple of Indian guys there, and they were telling this story. They said the government wanted to put a man on the moon and it could be done alright, but nobody knew how to get the guy home again after he landed on the moon. These guys said all the government had to do was put an Indian in that rocket ship and tell him he was being relocated and then, after he got to the moon, that Indian would find his own way home again and the government wouldn't have to figure that part out at all.

Rabbit and I sure liked that story. I wonder what ever happened to those two Indian guys.

WATT SPADE, *Cherokee*

After World War II, many Indian veterans found themselves unable to fit into either white or Indian society. Alcoholism became a major problem, as did harsh police treatment of Indians who frequented the skid row bars. In his realistic sketches, Indian artist Aaron Yava portrays life around what he calls the "border towns of the Navajo Nation."

⁙⁙⁙⁙⁙⁙⁙⁙⁙⁙⁙⁙⁙⁙⁙⁙⁙⁙⁙⁙⁙⁙⁙⁙**5**⁙⁙⁙⁙⁙⁙⁙⁙⁙⁙⁙⁙⁙⁙⁙⁙⁙⁙⁙⁙⁙⁙⁙⁙

STOPPING EROSION

By the beginning of the 1960s it was a reservation joke that whenever Indians seemed restive or poverty statistics made national news, someone would appoint a "task force," the "study" would come out, and things would simmer down again. Now, however, Indians were not taking it anymore, as suggested by the resentful tone of this Navajo reply to some land management experts.

THE FIRST TIME you came from Washington and brought with you your plans [indicating a very small written report] for conservation of the reservation we said there is an honest man who means well.

As time passed and nothing happened, we became suspicious. When you returned again with many more plans [indicating a stack of documents four or five feet high] and still nothing happened, we thought to ourselves, this man means well but is a fool.

Now you have returned after another interval with still more plans for controlling erosion [indicating a pile of reports reaching far in the distance], we are convinced that you are a liar and dishonest.

My advice to you is this; take your plans and wipe your rectum with them and throw them into the arroyo; that will stop the erosion.

ANONYMOUS, *Navajo*

LET'S RAISE
SOME HELL

*Most newsworthy of the militant Indian demonstrations during the turbulent 1970s
was the takeover of Wounded Knee, South Dakota, by armed American Indian Movement (AIM) members and Oglala Sioux opposed to the existing tribal council.*

By the late 1950s most experienced observers, even some Washington politicians, admitted that liquidating Indian reservations was
a very bad idea. "Like the miner's canary," wrote the eminent legal
scholar Felix S. Cohen in 1953, "the Indian marks the shift from fresh air
to poison air in our political atmosphere . . . our treatment of Indians, even

more than our treatment of other minorities, reflects the rise and fall of our democratic faith." Termination was clearly one of the down cycles. In a catastrophic reprise of the Removal and Allotment episodes in the previous century, between 1948 and 1957 Indians lost about 3.3 million acres.

Moreover, "terminated" reservations were disintegrating into rural slums; many "relocated" Indian families had a tough time adjusting to big-city life. To halt the policies, the National Congress of American Indians organized representatives from more than eighty tribes to pack the corridors of Washington's buildings for eight weeks of protest. What America at large did not appreciate was the combustible Indian discontent that had been building for years. Termination and Relocation were the fuse. The atmosphere of militant confrontation over civil rights and the Vietnam War of the sixties provided the match.

Although the new administration of President John F. Kennedy repudiated Termination after 1960, Indian anger was not assuaged. Secretary of the Interior Stewart Udall's call for Indian self-determination and new health, education, and welfare programs echoed the Collier reforms of the 1930s. But Indian doubts about government motives were too deep to be pacified by promises that they had heard before.

"As I look around at the Indian situation," warned the Cherokee scholar-activist Robert K. Thomas early in 1964, "it looks like one big seething cauldron about ready to explode." He was a prophet: between 1964 and 1974 a series of demonstrations, road blockades, land takeovers, and building occupations from coast to coast amounted to a firestorm of Indian outrage against wrongs past and present. Local dissatisfactions and generalized resentments against government and white society burst into the public eye.

Indian defiance was led by two new interest blocs: off-reservation and urban Indians on the one hand, and Indian students on the other. In 1960 more than thirty percent of America's Indians existed outside of any reservation; ten years later they totaled nearly half the U.S. Indian population. Suffering much the same racial discrimination, police violence, and unemployment as other minorities, Indians in the cities began fighting back. Joining them were the postwar generation of articulate, college-educated Indian youth. Both the streetwise Indians and sophisticated students often found themselves shut out of national decision-making by "old guard" tribal leaders who had risen to prominence during the Collier years.

This gap widened in the summer of 1960 when nearly five hundred Indians representing more than sixty-five tribes converged on the University

An early expression of Indian self-defense was the fight between the Lumbee Indians of North Carolina and the local Ku Klux Klan. After their successful rout of a Klan gathering in January 1958, Lumbee tribesmen Charlie Warriax and Simeon Oxendine proudly display the Klan banner they confiscated.

of Chicago campus in response to an invitation for Indian ideas extended by the Kennedy administration. The younger generation's energy and priorities rang throughout the symposium's "Declaration of Indian Purpose," which demanded Indian involvement at all levels of government policymaking. But youthful delegates still felt outnumbered by non-Indian experts and Collier-era Indian politicos, and stifled by an outmoded deference of Indians toward the power structure.

As a consequence, a few months later ten student leaders met privately in Gallup, New Mexico, to discuss more activist approaches. They were convened by Herbert Blatchford, a Navajo graduate from the University of New Mexico. As early as 1954 Blatchford began bridging the distance between Indian students and tribal elders by holding "Indian youth conferences" around the nation. That established a network of native talent upon which he drew for the Gallup sessions.

Clyde Warrior, a young Ponca who had recently joined the civil rights struggle in the South (instead of the Marine Corps), was particularly outspoken. Shirley Hill Witt, a Mohawk, Mary Natani, a Winnebago, and Mel Thom, a Paiute, also joined in. By the close of their sessions, Thom, a graduate student in civil engineering, was named spokesperson for a new voice in Indian affairs: the National Indian Youth Council (NIYC).

They were responding to grim realities of Indian life: an average death age of forty due to disease, alcoholism, and malnutrition; an infant mortality rate more than twice the national average; an unemployment rate ten times higher than the national average; the highest teen and pre-teen suicide rate in America; liver disease from alcoholism five times higher than the white population, and Indians under twenty-four years of age dying from alcoholism at a rate twenty-eight times the national average; more than fifty thousand Indian families living in unsanitary shanties or abandoned cars. Only now Indians themselves were thrusting these facts into the country's face.

As he surveyed the national scene in 1964, commentator Robert Thomas—himself also an NIYC member—underscored some hot spots where Indian patience had reached the breaking point: (1) in Upper New York State the Senecas were furious over the flooding of their valleys by the Kinzua Dam Project, a violation of one of the oldest U.S. treaties with Indians; (2) in Alaska both Eskimos and Indians were agitated over challenges to water rights; (3) in Washington State game wardens were stepping up arrests of Indian fishermen in a confrontation over fish and game laws; (4) in South Dakota Sioux groups were resisting the state's curtailment of the power of Indian reservation police; (5) in California the use of peyote cactus in rituals of the Native American Church came under new legal assault.

Although native outbursts over local crises were rarely nationally coordinated at first, they announced a Pan-Indian readiness to speak and act out. At the usually placid Isleta Pueblo in New Mexico, the village's Indian leader moved against a Catholic priest who cemented over the earthen dance plaza. Handcuffed and escorted out of his church, the priest was banished from the pueblo. On the Atlantic Coast the Passamaquoddies, one of many little-known eastern Indian tribes who were fighting for federal recognition, donned turkey-feather bonnets and halted traffic on Maine's Route One, exacting tolls from motorists to pay for food and medicine for needy tribal members.

In late winter of 1964 came the first of two takeovers by Indian activists of the closed-up prison on Alcatraz Island in San Francisco Bay. On the basis of an old Sioux Indian treaty that turned over surplus, unused federal land to Indians, the protestors claimed the infamous island. As Sioux activist Richard McKenzie declared, "Kneel-ins, Sit-ins, Sleep-ins, Eat-ins, Pray-ins like the Negroes do wouldn't help us, we would have to occupy government buildings."

That year Mel Thom and other NIYC members joined the "fish-in" protests of various tribes in Washington State—to be joined by such celebrities as Dick Gregory and Marlon Brando. At issue was the Medicine Creek Treaty of 1853, which Indians insisted assured their fishing rights. However, state officials argued that their treaty privileges were superseded by new fish and game laws. Before their dispute reached court, police clubs and Indian oars clashed along the Nisqually River.

Everywhere across the country Indians mocked Thanksgiving and Columbus Day holidays, harassed museums that they accused of desecrating their ancestral bones and exhibiting sacred regalia, closed public beaches and international bridges, demanded Indian Studies programs in schools and alcoholism clinics in cities, and picketed for nonstereotypical portrayal in books and movies. This unprecedented Indian militancy was documented by such best-selling books as Sioux author Vine Deloria, Jr.'s *Custer Died for Your Sins* (1969) and Stan Steiner's *The New Indians* (1968), and was reported in new Indian periodicals such as *The Warpath*, *Americans Before Columbus*, *The Indian Historian*, and *Akwesasne Notes*.

Born of the earlier Relocation era, urban Indian centers, often located in basements or community halls, offered a rallying spot for city activism. From makeshift headquarters Indians offered the support services that government failed to provide in counseling, apartment hunting, legal assistance, and opportunities for companionship. New urban leaders felt nostalgia for reservation life, and sometimes idealized the Indian past, but they were

When the New York State Power Authority planned a reservoir that would flood their reservation, Tuscarora Indians began a public and legal protest in 1958. Here, William Rickard (left) and Wallace "Mad Bear" Anderson (bottom right) warn officials to leave their land alone. The reservoir was eventually constructed.

also liberated from the reservation Indians' hesitation about offending the white man.

In the middle-western cities of Minneapolis, St. Paul, and Chicago, a brand-new group, the American Indian Movement (AIM) borrowed tactics from black militants. It monitored police who were harassing the Indian bars and skid rows of the Twin Cities area. Leaders like Dennis Banks, the Bellecourt brothers, and Russell Means outfitted "Indian Patrol" cars with two-way radios, cameras, tape recorders, and red jackets and reduced police brutality.

When the "Indians of All Tribes" took over Alcatraz Island for a second time in November 1969, AIM joined in. The following summer its "warriors" climbed Mount Rushmore, South Dakota, taking well-publicized custody of the gallery of presidential faces. AIM's intimidating effectiveness was demonstrated in August 1970 when Dennis Banks hefted a large cross onto a Lutheran Church conference podium to dramatize the plight of the Indian today. The churchmen quickly pledged them $250,000; AIM also won financial help from Catholics, Baptists, and Mormons.

In the fall of 1972, an automobile caravan composed of urban and reservation Indians calling themselves the "Trail of Broken Treaties" converged on Washington to present a twenty-point position paper to the Bureau of Indian Affairs. They wanted a radical return to Indian sovereignty—renegotiation of all treaties, restoration of a 110-million-acre land base, and exemption from all state laws. When BIA officials refused swift compliance, AIM members occupied and trashed the Bureau's headquarters. Next AIM turned to racial discrimination against South Dakota's Indians. After a white man was charged with manslaughter for killing a Sioux in Buffalo Gap, AIM led angry protesters to the courthouse of Custer, South Dakota, which was burnt to the ground.

It was in February 1973, however, that the decade's major protest captured the American imagination. At the request of Oglala Sioux traditionalists, AIM took sides in a local dispute between them and the regime of Pine Ridge Reservation chairman, Richard Wilson. They claimed that Wilson, backed by his authoritarian tribal police and local BIA officials, was denying the traditionalists their say in tribal government. Eventually armed AIM members stormed the hamlet of Wounded Knee—the same site where Sioux Indians were massacred by U.S. troops in 1890.

Occupying the community church and general store, AIM's riflemen posed with guns as national media exploited the spectacle of embattled Indians encircled by the most heavily armed force of white soldiers to confront Indians in this century. The veteran protester and essayist Vine Deloria, Jr., reminded the militants of the American public's short attention span, and urged them to use their moment in the limelight to publicize Indian problems on and off reservations.

Tracer bullets lit up the Pine Ridge sky; Indians returned fire from frozen bunkers; two AIM members were killed in crossfire. When negotiators finally arranged a cease-fire and evacuation, the ten-week news story was over. Chairman Wilson's administration was effectively crushed, but some Indians said that so was their chance to educate the public about wider issues confronting Indians everywhere. To AIM leader Dennis Banks, however, Wounded Knee was "the ultimate in a man's life, to see your own people moved to that type of action. Looking back, I really believed that the broken hoop was mended at Wounded Knee, and that the water was being given to the tree of life. Wounded Knee was an attempt to help an entire race survive. . . ."

Meanwhile, the FBI and other government agencies added Indians to the antiwar and civil rights militants they intimidated, infiltrated, and provoked into crimes they could then prosecute. Discontent at Pine Ridge simmered for another two years, with many AIM members dying under mysterious circumstances. It peaked with a gun battle between federal agents and Indians in which two FBI agents and one Indian were slain. The ensuing trial and conviction of AIM member Leonard Peltier provided a lightning rod for new Indian protest through the 1980s.

By 1978, as activists from various tribes joined "The Longest Walk" to Washington, D.C., demonstrating against a slew of "new termination" legislation, Indian fury was largely replaced by a new tone of self-reflection and quiet renewal. The following selections provide personal sidelights on the "Red Power" era. These fifteen explosive years exposed deep Indian concerns and cleared the air to address them.

1

THE NEW INDIAN WARS

In mid-October 1965 a group of Washington State Indians staged one of their "fish-ins" to protest state conservation prohibitions against traditional fishing. In jeopardy were rights which Northwest tribes like the Nisqually, Puyallup, and others enjoyed since the days of their treaties, signed in the 1850s, to fish and net salmon on the Nisqually and other rivers. According to the protesters, the white man's dams, pollution, and commercial fishing were depleting the salmon, not their smaller operations.

During the 1960s the fishing controversy caused numerous "battles" around Puget Sound, and on the Columbia River, between state officials and lawmen and Indians who refused to stop fishing. In the forefront was Janet McCloud, a Tulalip Indian mother of eight. Six Indians were arrested and temporarily jailed; their trial was held six years later. This "fish-in" and its consequences is recounted by Laura McCloud, one of her daughters.

ON OCTOBER 13, 1965, we held a "fish-in" on the Nisqually River to try and bring a focus on our fishing fight with the State of Washington. The "fish-in" started at 4:00 P.M. and was over at about 4:30 P.M. It ended with 6 Indians in jail and dazed Indian kids wondering "what happened?"

My parents, Don & Janet McCloud; Al and Maiselle Bridges; Suzan Satiacum and Don George Jr. were arrested that day. They were released after posting bail a few hours later. The charges against these six Indians was "obstructing the duty of a police officer." Now all we could do was wait till the trials started. There was a seventh Indian who was later arrested for the same charge, Nugent Kautz. And he had not been at Frank's Landing on that day.

The trial was to begin on January 15, 1969, at 9:30 A.M. We went into the courthouse that Wednesday certain that we would not receive justice as was proven to us in other trials. As we walked into the hallways there were many game wardens standing there, some dressed in their uniforms and some in plain clothes, but we recognized all of them.

Many of us were dressed in our traditional way with headbands, leggings and necklaces. As we walked the length of the corridor to the courtroom, the game wardens were looking us up and down, laughing at us. I said to my cousin, "Don't pay any attention to them, they don't know any better." . . .

The first witness for the State was a field marshal for the game department—Zimmerman. He stated that he was directing the game wardens at the Landing on Oct. 13. He was in charge of the reinforcements from all over the State that came down on us like a sea of green. At the time of the fish-in I thought that there were about a hundred game wardens.

The next State witness was the public relations man for the game department. He had 16 millimeter motion pictures to show. He had been posing as a newsman on the day of the fish-in. Our attorney objected to the pictures because they could have been cut and fixed to the State's advantage or taken for the State's advantage. But the State got their way and the motion pictures were shown. And to this moment I can not understand why they wanted these pictures shown because they sure looked better for our side than for theirs. . . .

The next morning the State started off with their last witness, State Fisheries Biologist, Lasseter. He talked about how we Indians are the ones who depleted the fish in the Puyallup River and if we weren't controlled we would do the same to the Nisqually River. The Puyallup River is filled with pollution more than it is with water. And why would we want to wipe out our livelihood? Our attorney made Lasseter state that it could have been the pollution not the Indians who depleted the fish in the Puyallup River.

Now, it was our turn! The first witness for our defense was Bob Johnson. At the time of the fish-in he was the editor of the "Auburn Citizen" newspaper. He told of the tactics the game wardens used on us. Mr. Johnson also had evidence with him, pictures of the game wardens, showing billie clubs and seven-celled flashlights. The Prosecuting attorney got real shook up about these. It seemed like he was saying "I object" every few minutes. . . .

The next defense witness was Janet McCloud, Tulalip Indian. She told the facts about why the Indians had had the fish-in demonstration on that day and what the mood the Indians had before the fish-in. This was important because the State thought we were after blood that day. And we were not expecting any violence because all my brothers and sisters were there and the youngest was 4 at that time. And if we had expected any violence none of the children would have been there. She told how she felt when she realized that the game wardens were going to ram our boat and how she felt when she realized these men meant business with their 7-celled flashlights, billie clubs, and brass knuckles. My two little brothers were in that boat when it was rammed, the youngest was 7 and could not swim. Besides, once you get tangled in nylon mesh it is very easy to drown. While she was telling this story, we could tell she was trying very hard to keep from crying, but this did not help because she started to. And every Indian in that courtroom that was there that horrible day started to remember the fear and anger that they had felt that day. . . .

The next witness was Don McCloud, Puyallup Indian. He was one of the Indian men in the boat that day. He told how the boat was rammed. (Oh, incidentally, the game wardens said that they did not ram the boat.) He also said how he had seen a game warden with a steel pipe and how a game

Janet McCloud

warden tried to knee him in the groin. And the other acts of violence that he had witnessed the game wardens doing. . . .

With all this testimony and evidence, it was plain to see that the game wardens had lied. We only hoped that the jury would believe our side of the fish-in story. We also learned the names of the game wardens whose pictures we had, especially the one who had been beating on Alison and Valerie Bridges.

Mr. Ziontz called one last witness—a hostile one—a game warden. This was the one who had been carrying a leather slapper which the Indians confiscated on 1/13/65 from his hip-pocket and had entered as evidence. His name was engraved on the slapper. He admitted that it was his and had been taken out his pocket but he said that he never used it.

The State called "Colonel Custer" Neubrech for their rebuttal witness. He said at the briefing he had given his men the night before the fish-in he had told them to have extreme patience with the Indians. Either they don't know the meaning of extreme patience or else they didn't understand him right. . . .

After the two lawyers gave their summations the jury went into session. This was at ten o'clock at night. They were out until midnight. The foreman came in first and said, "The rest are afraid to come in." I thought, here comes another guilty. When the foreman handed the judge the decision the room became very silent. Then the judge read, "The jury finds the defendant Nugent Kautz 'not guilty.' " He read the rest of the names with the same verdict. I didn't believe it. I turned to my cousin and said, "Did I hear right?" She nodded her head, yes. Everyone was happy, except for the State. The game wardens were very hostile after this.

Footnote: The game wardens, incensed at the adverse verdict, left the Tyee Motel where they had been celebrating, prematurely, their victory and went down in large numbers to Frank's Landing. A sympathetic soul overheard the wardens and called the Landing to warn the Indians. Nevertheless the wardens caught a car load of Indians at the railroad trestle and surrounded them in their state game cars—they proceeded to hit the Indians' car with their nightsticks, cussing them and trying to provoke Al Bridges and Hank Adams to fight. It was obvious to the Indians that they had been drinking. . . . So the war goes on—which goes to prove that the history books are wrong when they talk about "the last Indian wars." They have never stopped!

LAURA MCCLOUD, *Tulalip*

2

INVADING ALCATRAZ

*A*n early alert of the feisty Indian spirit of the 1960s was the symbolic occupation, for three hours in March 1964, of Alcatraz Island by four urban Sioux. The previous year the federal prison had been shut down; the militants invoked an 1868 treaty turning over to Indians abandoned federal properties. Next the militant coalition Indians of All Tribes staged a second symbolic takeover on November 9, 1969. Slipping ashore at night, fourteen Indians evaded "capture" for nineteen hours.

But these were rehearsals for the true Alcatraz occupation eleven days later. For nineteen months Indians camped on the island, demanding attention to Indian health, educational, and cultural needs and broadcasting over Radio Free Alcatraz.

Adam Fortunate Eagle joined the November 9 invasion, as he relates here. Born in 1929 on the Red Lake Chippewa Reservation in Minnesota, he spent ten years at Pipestone Indian Boarding School. For another five years he attended Haskell Indian Institute in Kansas, and today is a sculptor on the Stillwater Indian Reservation in Fallon, Nevada.

WE SET OUT from San Leandro, my family and I, with our tribal outfits packed, and with $24 in beads and colored cloth arranged in a wooden bowl for the symbolic purchase of Alcatraz Island from the government. With a feel of optimism we were soon on the Nimitz Freeway, driving for Fisherman's Wharf in San Francisco, and Pier 39.

The weather on Sunday morning, November 9, 1969, was beautiful and calm. This was a pretty strange thing we were doing. Indian people, twentieth-century urban Indians, gathering in tribal councils, student organizations, clubs, and families, and joined by concerned individuals from all over the Bay Area, with the intention of launching an attack on a bastion of the United States government. Instead of the horses and bows and arrows of another era, we were riding in Fords and Chevys, armed only with our Proclamation but determined to bring about a change in federal policy affecting our people.

We didn't drive so fast that we couldn't take in the beauty of this place where we'd chosen to live after boarding school, Treasure Island, and across the bay the Golden Gate Bridge. And there in the middle was the forlorn, abandoned little island of Alcatraz—our destination. If things backfired I couldn't see myself involved in Indian programs anymore for the community; an Indian would be banished if he brought embarrassment to his people. I also worried about that other half of my life, my business and family. What if there was violence? What if I went to jail?

At Fisherman's Wharf we parked and joined a growing group of Indian students. When I learned that our scheduled boat was nowhere around I suggested they stall while I looked for another. Richard Oakes went to the end of the pier to read our Proclamation, with Indians and television crews in tow, while I looked around. Then I noticed this beautiful three-masted barque that looked like it had come right out of the pages of maritime history. Its name was the *Monte Cristo*, and its owner, who, with tight pants and ruffled shirt looked like Errol Flynn, was Ronald Craig.

When I approached he said, "Hey, I'm curious—what's going on over there with all those Indians?" I explained the fix we were in, pointing out the media contingent that had come to cover the landing. "I'll take you," he said, "on condition we get permission from the Coast Guard and that we carry no more than fifty people. The boat rides deep because of the keel, and I can't land on the Alcatraz dock. We'll circle a couple of times, a sort of sight-seeing tour to get your message across, OK?"

After he counted to make sure we were only fifty, he fired off the little cannon on the bow. Here were Indians sailing on an old vessel to seek a new way of life for their people. I thought of the *Mayflower* and its crew of Pilgrims who landed on our shores. The history books say they were seeking new freedoms for themselves and their children which were denied in their homeland. Never mind that Plymouth Rock already belonged to somebody else. What concerned them was their own fate, their own hopes. Now, 350 years later, its original citizens, to focus national attention on their struggle to regain those same basic rights, were making landfall on another rock.

The *Monte Cristo* headed for the west side of the island, with its huge walls surrounding the former prisoners' recreation yard. We made out the catwalks and the coiled barbed wire atop the walls, the old guard towers, silent and empty now. The metal ramps and catwalks were corroded by salty air and were buckled into grotesque shapes. The empty machine shops and laundry facilities came into view as we rounded the northwest corner.

Suddenly Richard Oakes climbed on the vessel's rail and dove overboard. All he had stripped off was his shirt; he was still wearing his boots! A cheer went up. Another student followed into the frigid waters, then another, then another. Four Indians were swimming as hard as they could toward the island before the captain could react.

"What the hell are those guys doing, Adam?"

"They're swimming to Alcatraz," was all I said.

"What the hell for?"

"To take it for the Indian people."

"Jesus Christ, man," Captain Craig shouted, "don't you realize we're flying the Canadian flag? This could be considered an act of war. You've got to stop them."

To discourage more leaping into the water his helmsman swung wide, turned, and headed back to San Francisco. One swimmer, Joe Bill, an Eskimo, made it to the craggy shore. All of the other swimmers were brought back by friendly boats. With one swimmer's landing we achieved at least a token victory.

Back at the Indian Center that evening the building was jammed with excited people of all ages and tribes. We went over and over the day's events. Everybody was eager to go back and land in force. As it happened, my brother had skippered for some deep-sea sports-fishing parties, so I called some of his friends. Our luck held out. The *New Vera II* had just docked and her crew was washing the decks. The captain would take us for three dollars per person or fifty dollars minimum. Some called it scalping, white man's style, but beggars can't be choosers.

Our people gathered up their sleeping bags and blankets and once again headed for Fisherman's Wharf. This time there was no press, no curious bystanders, no tourists. We were secretive, Indians in little bunches walking past Castagnola's Restaurant, past boats under repair on their sides, past reeking fish containers, until we saw the *New Vera II* across from Scoma's Restaurant.

"Hurry up, you guys," the skipper yelled, "we've got to get going!" As we cleared the dock area, we clasped our jackets around us, others wrapped in blankets, Indian style, against the damp chill wind. The wet deck soaked through our moccasins. My family went below. The tide was going out, resisting the skipper as he sidled up to a water barge at the Alcatraz dock. A single light was no help. He revved the throttle to position his boat, but had to pull away. Then a watchdog began barking at us. The skipper swung sharply, heading straight for the barge, reversing the propeller at the last moment so we gently nudged the barge.

Indians spilled over the bow, one securing a line while the rest clambered overboard. Sleeping bags and blankets were passed after them. "What's going on?" the skipper asked. In an offhand way, I said, "We're taking over the island." His sudden realization that he might be charged with a crime, plus his worry about the rushing tides, made him throw the gears into reverse. The tie line snapped and one of our guys was knocked back into the boat.

As we accelerated for San Francisco, disappointed we hadn't made it off the boat too, we spotted fourteen Indians on the island's shore. One was Richard Oakes, three were women. Scrambling up the stairway, they disappeared quickly into the darkness. The occupation of Alcatraz was now a fact. In its heyday desperate men went to any extreme to escape the place; now Indians were just as desperate to get on it for their freedom.

The morning of November 10. The scene that greeted the Alcatraz Indians seemed right out of a Keystone Kop movie. Ships, motor boats, sailing yachts, launches, dinghies, cutters—all heading toward them. Banner newspaper headlines and TV and radio bulletins had spread the word through the Bay Area and beyond. One bold headline proclaimed: "INDIANS INVADE ALCATRAZ; U.S. PLANS COUNTER-ATTACK."

As the armada docked at Alcatraz, federal marshals, the representative of the General Services Administration, Coast Guardsmen, newspaper, radio, and TV crews searched for Indians to interview. At the landing area Richard Oakes read our Proclamation again to reporters. Thomas Hannon, the regional administrator of the GSA, with authority over the abandoned prison, had been brought by a Coast Guard cutter. He listened patiently, but his distress was apparent. Then he told the assembled reporters that if the Indians didn't leave peacefully, he would consult with the U.S. Attorney's office about filing trespassing charges. Finally, Richard and the rest agreed to leave the island, so negotiations could take place ashore in a calmer atmosphere. As the fourteen boarded his boat for the ride back to San Francisco, Richard Oakes's voice could be heard loud and clear: "This occupation has established Indian squatters' rights to Alcatraz Island. We'll be back."

ADAM FORTUNATE EAGLE, *Red Lake Chippewa*

3

DISCOVERY: THE BEEAH TRIBE

Shortly after college-educated Indians organized their National Indian Youth Council in 1960, they founded their own newspaper, ABC, which stood for "Americans Before Columbus." Its editorial perspective was often satirical, as exemplified by this anonymous column from ABC for April 1970. It should be no mystery which federal government agency is the butt of its attack.

R E C E N T L Y anthropologists, who are dedicated to keeping the Indian alive if for no other reason than they can make money studying them, discovered a new tribe.

This newly discovered group is known as the Beeah Tribe (pronounced BIA Tribe). A new book, A Man Called Horse S——, by Dr. He-Sells-Out, beloved Indian expert, has been released by the Association on Preserving the Cute Ways of Brown People.

The book describes the strange rites and rituals of this much persecuted tribe. Torn from their ancestral homes on Fifth Avenue in New York City to far flung agencies around the country, the Beeah Tribe is held together by its function of running the affairs of all other tribes.

Incantations such as "Let me refer you to this other office," and "I'll look into that," are invoked daily to magically free one's self from harassment by people asking questions as "I'm hungry, what can I do?"

The chief is appointed by the President of the United States and all members are ranked from GS-1 to GS-18. The lowest ranking members are usually those who belong to other tribes as well as to the Beeah Tribe.

The daily rituals of the tribe are graphically described. These include one hour coffee breaks, 100 dollars a day consulting fees, the feet-propped-up-on-desk-cigar-in-mouth-ritual, being photographed holding an Indian child, buck passing, and back slapping.

One of the most terrifying rituals described is the back stabbing ritual by which a member of a lower rank stabs a higher ranking member in the back so that he can take his place. This ritual is traced from primeval times when their ancestors were living in caves in Europe.

Dr. He-Sells-Out, in one of his more revelatory findings, has noted that the Beeah Tribe exists only at the expense of other Tribes. It cannot seem to live unless it has drained the other Tribes' human and natural resources and has sapped its leadership and initiative. In the language of the Beeah Tribe this is known as "community development" (pronounced rob-ber-ry).

Needless to say, the mind of the Beeah Tribe is mystifying to outsiders.

With a straight face a member of the Beeah Tribe will say that Indian religion and dances are bad and should be eradicated. But if you can find some white people to charge other white people to see you perform them, it is all right. Or, they will say that every Indian should be educated; but once educated he should not be given a job that his education merits.

This is a war-like tribe in constant conflict with other tribes. Occasionally, through incompetence the Beeah Tribe does something the other tribes like but these lapses are quickly corrected.

We thank Dr. He-Sells-Out for his valuable contribution to Knowledge we already know.

ANONYMOUS

4

BIRTH OF AIM

he Bellecourt brothers were city-smart Indians from Minneapolis. As Vernon Bellecourt remembers here, they helped found the American Indian Movement, or AIM, the most militant of the Indian protest groups of the 1960s. Some of its members were urban Indians and ex–prison inmates with little patience for nonviolence and carrying placards. As with more militant black and Hispanic rights organizations, AIM preferred armed self-defense and direct confrontation. As they protested police excess and other urban Indian problems, they also tried to support reservation Indians in their struggles. But their threatening, theatrical style could cause differences between them and the more conservative rural peoples they sought to serve.

I **HAD** seven sisters and four brothers. First I went to a public school, and it became a parochial school open to all the kids in the community. I went there until the eighth grade, to junior high school for one year and quit. Couldn't handle the racist attitudes, the abuse I got, so I dropped out in the ninth grade. . . .

I lived on the reservation until I was fifteen. I recognized despair was setting in, because I was caught up in poverty in a large family with never quite enough food on the table. Leaving the reservation and going into the city was the start of becoming Anglo-oriented. . . .

When I was about twenty years old, I was an armed robber, sort of a Robin Hood type. It was my way of getting back at the system for ripping us off. This was in Minnesota. I ended up in prison doing a forty-year sentence. They have what they call a youth program; if you don't commit any more crimes after they release you, they wipe your record clean. But I was bitter. When they let me out I did it again, and I got caught. Then I had forty years to do plus another five. I did three and a half years, finally won a discharge on the forty-year sentence and got paroled on the five. Then I knew I could never do that again—not especially because I thought it was wrong, but because I didn't want to go to jail anymore. In prison they taught me how to be a barber, and after I came out, I ended up owning a beauty salon. From that I went into the import business, gift items and such. . . .

My brother Clyde was doing a tremendous amount of time in Stillwater State Prison in Minnesota, and he just gave up in despair and wouldn't eat. He went on a hunger strike and was going to stay on it until he died. He met a young Ojibwa brother who was from a medicine family, a family of spiritual leaders, and this young man was also a spiritual leader.

This young medicine man, Eddie Benton, was sort of a trusty, and he'd come by my brother's cell and try to talk to him and ask him to eat. But Clyde wouldn't eat. Finally Eddie started throwing candy bars in there, but they just piled up, and my brother wouldn't touch them. Then one day he started quoting literature, telling about the Ojibwas and our proud heritage. And finally one day, I guess just out of boredom, my brother picked up a piece of this literature and started reading about us. And he finally recognized he wasn't the dirty Indian he'd been told he was by White students at school. . . .

So anyway, Clyde started reading this literature, and it brought him back to life and gave him renewed strength and dignity. He started eating and started to get involved. He and Eddie Benton started an Indian awareness program in the prison and were instrumental in keeping our young Indian men out of jail once they got out. . . .

Vernon Bellecourt

When Clyde got out of prison early in 1968, he went to work for a power company. He had one of the first organizational meetings, in mid-1968, with a group of people in Minneapolis, in the Indian ghetto community. Everything was deteriorating rather than getting better. There were police harassment and brutality, because of a complete breakdown of police-community relations.

At the first meeting Clyde attended, they voted him the national director. There were twenty-seven or twenty-eight other Indian organizations in the Minneapolis community. Most of them were related to various churches—missionary work in disguise. For the most part, the boards of these organizations were White dominated. White do-gooders as consultants and advisers controlled them.

So the first AIM was formed in Minneapolis, as a non-profit corporation with an all-Indian board and staff. They were going to call the organization The Concerned Indian Americans, CIA. They couldn't use that! So a couple of older, respected women said, "Well, you keep saying that you *aim* to do this, you *aim* to do that. Why don't you call it AIM, the American Indian Movement?" That's how we got our name. . . .

I watched what they were doing, and I could see the pride in these young men and women. A new dignity, a new awareness, a new power, a new strength. Then I looked at myself, I was making money and living in White suburbia. . . . So I went up to Minnesota, and for about a week I visited with my brother and other people in the movement—Russell Means, Dennis Banks and some of the founders. Finally I got so involved I started letting my hair grow long, and I stopped wearing a tie and started to sort of de-program myself, to become just a simple person, a simple man. More humble. I saw in that something I could identify with. . . .

When AIM was forming, one of the first things they zeroed in on was police-community relations. Young men and women in the community formed the AIM Patrol. They had red jackets with thunderbird emblems on the backs.

Sometimes they appointed somebody to the Patrol who had a bad drinking problem; one of the qualifications, of course, was being sober. So it was really an alcoholic rehabilitation program at the same time. . . .

They got a small grant from the Urban League of Minneapolis to put two-way radios in their cars and to get tape recorders and cameras. They would listen to the police calls, and when they heard there was going to be an arrest or that police were being dispatched to a certain community or bar, they'd show up with cameras and take pictures of the police using more than normal restraint on the people.

They got evidence of beatings and of ripping people around with handcuffs too tight, ripping their wrists. It was very vicious. This sometimes becomes a way of life for the police. They just fall into it. They think that's the way Indians have to be treated. So AIM would show up and have attorneys ready. Often they would beat the police back to the station. They would have a bondsman there, and they'd start filing law suits against the police department. . . .

Members recognized there was something missing from the movement. They heard about a medicine man in South Dakota, a holy man, a spirit leader. Now, the spirituality of Indian people has always been strong and has remained intact in some areas of South Dakota. They heard about Leonard Crow Dog, a medicine man who was maybe twenty-five. They were curious, and they went to visit him and his dad. . . . Well, they went there for advice, and one of the first questions they asked was, "What is an Indian?" They wanted to redefine what they were. And they were told that to be an Indian is to be spiritual. . . . We have the spirituality, yet we are warriors. We'll stand up and fight for our people. We haven't had that for many years. The warrior class of this century is bound by the bond of the drum. . . . That circle around the drum brings us together. We can have two or three hundred people around that drum, all from different tribes, all singing the same song. We put out a bumper sticker, "AIM for Sovereignty." Most of our people didn't even know what the word meant. Now they know.

VERNON BELLECOURT, *Chippewa*

5

CONFRONTATION OR NEGOTIATION

Not all Indians felt comfortable with the AIM approach. In 1972 the prolific Chippewa Indian novelist and poet Gerald Vizenor witnessed a meeting between the militants of the American Indian Movement and local Indian leadership at the Leech Lake Reservation, a Chippewa community in Minnesota. It inspired *the following biting blend of journalism, satire, and editorial, in which Vizenor weighs the pros and cons of physical threat as a catalyst for social change.*

EIGHT YEARS AGO Dennis Banks, dressed in a dark suit, white shirt and narrow necktie, strode into the office of the director of the American Indian Employment Center and told him to stop picketing the Bureau of Indian Affairs.

"Demonstrations are not the Indian way," Banks said then, wagging his finger. The director of the center had organized a peaceful demonstration in front of the Minneapolis area office of the Bureau of Indian Affairs, demanding equal services for urban tribal people.

Since then Banks and hundreds of young adventurers have trouped across the country, from Plymouth Rock to Alcatraz, dressed in century-old tribal vestments, demanding recognition of treaty rights, equal justice and sovereignty. The occupation of Wounded Knee may be the last symbolic act for the aging militant leaders.

The American Indian Movement is an urban revolutionary movement whose members have in recent years tried to return to the reservations as the warrior heroes of tribal people. . . .

In the late 1960s the American Indian Movement became a symbolic confrontation group. The confrontation idiom means punching out the symbolic adversary of racism and oppression at the front door, with the press present, and walking out the back door. Those who followed the ideologies of confrontation were in conflict with those who believed that confrontation should lead to negotiation and institutional changes. The negotiation idiom means punching out the adversary at the front door with the press present, but waiting around for an invitation to return and grind out some changes.

The problem in the differences of approach was not only political ideology, but the response of the press. Journalists seldom reported what happened beyond the symbolic punch-out at the front door. The press presented the heroes of confrontation, but not of negotiation. . . .

Behind the scenes, tribal people have been arguing about the use of violence as a means of change. Some say that violence has only polarized the dominant white society and strained interpersonal relationships. Other tribal people argue that violence has made the job of moderates working within the system much easier. White people listen better after violence. . . .

Consider these changes through education: Hundreds of tribal people have earned high-school equivalency certificates on three reservations in Minnesota in the past three years. Many have gone on to college and have found better-paying jobs. Six hundred tribal people are attending colleges in Minnesota compared with fewer than a hundred fifteen years ago.

Consider these changes through the law: There are legal-services programs on most reservations, and hundreds of tribal people are studying in law schools across the country. There have been several successful treaty-law arguments in federal and state courts, including the hunting and fishing suit won by the Leech Lake Reservation.

Consider these changes through economic development: The Red Lake Reservation has a home-construction business and a new vocational school. The Leech Lake Reservation has a food market and service station and a camping and recreation complex.

Now consider the changes through violence and radical ideologies: At Cass Lake the leaders of the American Indian Movement were critical of elected tribal officials for negotiating a legal agreement with the state over the hunting and fishing rights won through a federal court decision. The agreement, ratified by the state legislature, will bring millions of dollars a year to the reservation.

This was the scene:

Thirteen armed leaders of the American Indian Movement, including Russell Means and Dennis Banks, filed into the tribal Headstart classroom on the Leech Lake Reservation and took their seats on little-people chairs. They sat with their knees tucked under their chins, dressed in diverse combinations of Western cowboy clothes and traditional tribal vestments from the turn of the last century. . . .

Simon Howard, then president of the Minnesota Chippewa Tribe, entered the classroom, took his little seat, and twirled his thumbs beneath his heavy stomach while the leaders argued about their places in the chain of command—who would stand next to whom at the next television press conference. Howard wore a nylon bowling jacket and a floral print fishing hat in contrast to the renascence of traditional vestments worn by the militants. Howard was born on the reservation and had lived there all his life. He was at the meeting as an elected tribal official to keep peace between white people and the militants. The militants were there for an armed confrontation with white people on the opening day of fishing. . . .

"All right boys, quiet down now and take your seats again," Howard said.

The tribal leaders and militants had agreed to meet twice a day with each other and then with the press. "Now, I don't know everyone here, so let's go around the room and introduce ourselves," Howard said. "Let's start with you over there. Stand up and introduce yourself."

The man stood up, dragging his feet forward and swinging his rifle. "My name is Delano Western, and I am from Kansas," he said in a trembling voice. Western, leaning forward and looking down like a shy school child, was dressed in a wide-brimmed black hat with an imitation silver headband, dark green sunglasses with large round lenses, a sweatshirt with "Indian Power" printed on the front, two bandoliers of heavy ammunition, none of which matched the bore of his rifle, a black motorcycle jacket with military colonel's wings on the epaulets, "Red Power" and "Custer Had It Coming" patches, and a large military bayonet strapped to his body next to his revolver.

"We came here to die," Western said in a loud voice and sat down. He and about six hundred militant followers had come to Cass Lake on the Leech Lake Reservation to fight for the treaty rights to hunt and fish on the reservation, which had already been won by reservation tribal officials in federal court.

When white officials from Cass Lake had refused to pay the money demanded by the militants, who were camping on treaty land given over to a church group by the federal government for a summer camp, the leaders held a press conference on a rifle range to scare the public.

Means, smiling for television cameras, was plinking with his small-caliber "white people shooter," as he called his pistol. Banks . . . was preparing for fast-draw target practice. Dressed in a black velvet shirt with ribbon appliqué, he stood before a collection of empty food cans . . . dropped to one knee, and attempted to draw his small-gauge sawed-off shotgun. It stuck on the rope holder attached to his belt. He stood up and tried again, but it still stuck. This was the first time the Movement had taken up the use of firearms.

During the occupation of the offices of the Bureau of Indian Affairs in Washington, radical leaders demanded another investigation and reorganization of the paternalistic bureaucracy that has controlled the lives of tribal people on reservations for more than a century. The militants had a powerful position from which to negotiate their demands: It was an election year and scores of congressional liberals were sympathetic. But rather than negotiate the demands, the leaders of AIM accepted more than $60,000 to leave the building and the city. . . . The leaders were at Wounded Knee voicing the very same demands which they sold out in Washington. . . .

The American Indian Movement has raised good issues through the press, but it has seldom followed through to negotiate. At Custer the militants drew national attention to the wrongful death of Wesley Bad Heart Bull. They said the white man who stabbed Bad Heart Bull should be charged with murder. The fire in the courthouse was a violent stunt that detracted from the issue of legal injustices.

The militant leaders are dedicated men who have given many years of their lives to a cause, but it takes more than a rifle and the symbolic willingness to die to bring about institutional changes that will benefit tribal people.

GERALD VIZENOR, *White Earth Chippewa*

SO LONG AS THIS LAND EXISTS

The sacred Blue Lake, Taos Pueblo, New Mexico

I n the summer of 1968 a caravan of old cars and pickup trucks left an
Indian reserve near Hobbema, western Canada, searching for the promised land. Leading them was an elderly man with graying braids and
wearing deerskin moccasins, named Robert Smallboy. As chief of the
Ermineskin band of Plains Cree, for nearly a decade Smallboy had petitioned
Canadian authorities for open land that was *ka-na-tan*, or "clean." That
meant uncontaminated by overpopulation, alcohol or drug use, or white
man's towns. Getting no satisfaction from Ottawa, he struck out on his own.

Smallboy's pursuit of cultural renewal was reminiscent of previous Indian
efforts to restore old traditions in new surroundings. As early as the 1700s
the Kickapoo migrated south from the Great Lakes, ultimately establishing
their wigwam villages in the Coahuila desert of northern Mexico where
they live today. Cherokee traditionalists once sought sanctuary in the South
American nation of Colombia for similar reasons.

During the first winter Smallboy's followers camped in the Kootenay
Plains, but then pushed deeper into the mountains of Jasper National Park
to hunt and pray and live like their grandparents. The government branded
them squatters and threatened to evict them, but Canadian Indian organizations leapt to their defense. Through it all, recalled a visitor, "Smallboy
has just continued to smile and speak softly, 'I don't want to cause trouble.
But we will remain in the wilderness so long as this land exists.' "

Smallboy's stand represented a growing spiritual undercurrent of the militant Indian movement. His generation had been taught tribal ways during
World War I; many were now respected "elders" in their own right. "No
one had dreamed," observed Vine Deloria, Jr., "that the offshoot of activism
had been to revive the inherent strengths of basic tribal beliefs." All around
him, Deloria noticed Indians reexploring traditional philosophies, discussing
government by old-time council instead of elected officials and replacing
white laws with Indian customs, and reviving rituals.

Throughout the 1970s the stature of Indian "elders" like Smallboy was
enhanced within and without their immediate communities. Some gained
local reputations, such as war hero Edison Chiloquin, who turned down his
Klamath termination money and built a traditional retreat on Oregon's
Sprague River. Others became national celebrities, lecturing widely on In-
dian spirituality—men like Thomas Banyacya, a Hopi from Arizona; Mad
Bear Anderson, a Tuscarora from New York; and Rolling Thunder, a
Cherokee-Shoshone from Nevada.

Leaders of the American Indian Movement started to stress the more private, religious side to their program; their medicine men, such as Pete Catches and Leonard Crow Dog, opened the Sioux Sun Dance to other tribes. In 1970 the first North American Indian Ecumenical Movement invited "medicine" people representing diverse traditions to the Crow Indian Reservation in Montana. All affirmed the central role of Indian prophecy, the bond between Indians and "Mother Earth," the existence of sacred "powers" by which ritual specialists benefited their people. They agreed to restore spiritual practices, encourage native language use, and combat alcoholism and family disintegration.

This focus on cultural revitalization sharpened the old debate within Indian communities over how white to become, and resurrected the question "What is a tribe?" "Is it a traditionally organized band of Indians following customs with medicine men and chief dominating the policies?" as Deloria phrased the choice before many native groups, "or is it a modern corporate structure attempting to compromise with modern white culture?" Indians who had gained power and prestige within the tribal government system found themselves at odds with the new nativists. Sioux politician Ben Reifel insisted that "The Indian cannot go back to the buffalo economy, and they know it. Romanticists want to keep them the same as they were, but Indians have to accommodate to today. They want a modern standard of living the same as whites."

Through the Nixon years official policy reflected this vacillating emphasis between maintaining old ways and confronting economic realities. Among President Richard M. Nixon's first acts was the restoration to Taos Pueblo in New Mexico of forty-eight thousand acres in the Carson National Forest. This mountain stronghold held the tribe's sacred Blue Lake, heart of their culture and site of their secret August pilgrimage. Even the Collier regime was unable to return this holy place, which had been taken from Taos in 1906.

The Taos decision accorded with strong national sentiment in the early 1970s, especially among the youthful "counterculture," for everything Indian. Films and books on native religion, land rights, and historical injustices were the rage. When this trend declined in the 1980s, Indians saw it as another warning of the white man's contradictory feelings and short attention span: first they were adored for their beautiful, wise traditions; then they were deplored for not fitting into wider society.

Robert Smallboy at his mountain retreat, 1970

IN SUMMER 1970, as the Indian population was growing four times faster than the national average, President Nixon proposed his "Self-Determination policy." Although his predecessor, Lyndon Johnson, already had called for "programs of self-help, self-development, and self-determination," it was the Nixon administration that pushed through the Indian Self-Determination and Education Act of 1975.

The Nixon approach coupled a repeal of dreaded termination with intensified emphasis on reservation development "to strengthen the Indian's sense of autonomy without threatening his sense of community." Nixon also spoke of beefing up Indian health programs, assisting urban Indians, and protecting Indian land and water rights. As usual, some Indians suspected hidden motives. Was "self-determination" a ploy to pacify Indian militancy and make reservations solvent only to withdraw federal assistance and open up their natural resources? If more day schools, Indian teacher-aides, and culturally responsive educational materials produced higher student retention rates, would the programs then be considered successful and the money terminated? Had Nixon's Indian officials established the National Tribal Chairman's Association to empower "acceptable" native leaders who would offer less resistance when deals were struck involving land and water rights?

At the same time, the energy that had fueled well-publicized Indian protests over the late 1960s and early 1970s was channeled into quieter courtroom struggles where Indians and sympathetic attorneys—including a generation of sophisticated native lawyers who organized the Native American Rights Fund—were resurrecting old treaties and reexamining earlier estimates of tribal lands. They documented how the full extent of tribal territories were undervalued in the past and eighteenth-century trade agreements were violated. Their legal victories were often of more lasting value than colorful protests.

In the greatest claims case, the 3,000 members of the Penobscot and Passamaquoddy tribes in Maine recovered "aboriginal title" to practically two-thirds of the state. Based upon their reanalysis of the overlooked Non-Intercourse Act of 1790, Maine Indians negotiated an out-of-court settlement that yielded more than 300,000 acres—repurchased by Congress from lumber firms—together with a $27-million trust fund and additional money for new housing and launching their own light industries.

On the Pacific Coast, a federal judge who reexamined past treaties concluded that twenty-five tribes of coastal Washington State were entitled to fifty percent of Puget Sound's annual salmon catch. In Michigan reconsideration of a nineteenth-century treaty affirmed special privileges for Chippewa spear fishermen; the Quechan along the California-Arizona border were allowed to enlarge their reservation to boundaries assigned in their 1884 treaty.

After the Menominee tribe of Wisconsin signed their "termination" agreement in 1959 (top photo), the community fell upon hard times. Unable to support itself, the tribe watched its people rendered landless and impoverished. The struggle to restore the Menominee Reservation, led by tribal activist Ada Deer (bottom photo, third from left), resulted in the tribe's recovering its reservation—in this ceremony with Interior Secretary Rogers Morton (far left) in 1975.

Learning from third world countries, other Indian tribes consolidated control over natural resources on their treaty-protected lands. The Middle Eastern oil conglomerate was a model for CERT (Council of Energy Resource Tribes), which was established in 1975 by twenty-five Indian tribes, located throughout ten western and southwestern states. "CERT exists," explained its key organizer, Navajo tribal chairman Peter MacDonald, "because of a twist of geological fortune: a subsector of American society that has been overlooked for hundreds of years, which inhabits less than five percent of the land that was once theirs, today finds itself the owner of a potential energy resource whose wealth is so vast it has not yet been measured." Not only did CERT demand higher oil, coal, and uranium royalties, it envisaged training Indian professionals to become full-scale, independent producers who might someday satisfy the nation's energy needs on their own.

Enticing summer tourists to Indian country was another way for Indians to survive off their lands. Seeded by government grants and often in partnership with private non-Indian concerns, they built motels, dammed rivers for boating lakes, cleared slopes for ski lifts, and advertised the recreational attractions of rodeos, powwows, and outdoor sports in national magazines.

In all these struggles to stay Indian and stay alive there were wins and losses. Smallboy's mountain camp hung on but other "back to the land" efforts could not keep their young from public school, from looking for steady work, from the comforts of electricity, plumbing, and the supermarket. The Penobscot and Passamaquoddy turned their newfound wealth into successful blueberry farms and radio cassette assembly plants. For other tribes, the high hopes for on-reservation Indian-run businesses were dashed by poor management and uninspiring assembly-line work with its relentless production quotas. CERT found that the energy industry was not thrilled at the prospect of Indians joining their ranks. Some Indian tourist operations did admirably, such as Arizona's Mescalero Apache ski lodge, the Hopi Cultural Center and Cherokee outdoor dramas and "traditional village" displays in Oklahoma and North Carolina. Others languished because of overambitious consultants, insufficient financing, or incompatabilities between the expectations of non-Indian visitors and their hosts' cultural style.

In this chapter Indians perceive more keenly than ever that their land base, its natural resources, and their cultural ways are the only leverage they have in the white man's world, but that increasingly they are forced to make choices between economic or cultural survival.

1

GOING BACK

*I*n the late 1970s the spirit of Indian militancy turned inward. Instead of well-publicized protests, younger Native Americans, in particular, began searching for their own roots. Urban and rural Indians withdrew into spiritual activities; college students returned to their home reservations to see how they might fit into the fabric of everyday life. But this quest was not always easy for those who had made it in the outside world. Their difficulties at reentering the tribal community are evoked by a native writer named Little Star.

THESE PAST FEW YEARS, it's been a very "in" thing to talk about how you're going back to the reservation when you finish school. Many will go, but few will stay. They'll return to the city in two or three years, disillusioned. It is easy to talk about Indian unity, Indian power, the strength of the land, Indian input, but it's hard to put these ideas to work on a reservation where the main thing people want is something to eat.

The first thing that hits you when you go home—after you realize that you *live* there now, and you're not leaving in a few weeks—is that your college degrees don't give you the prestige on the reservation that you assumed they would. BIA people and some councilmen may be impressed, your own family may be proud, but people couldn't care less. You've been away for a long time and they study you for a while.

Some try to prove themselves one of the people by drinking around a lot, saying see I'm still one of you but the people trying to make up their mind about you wonder because we don't need more drunken Indians on the reservation, we have enough. Some miss their group at school, heads especially try to set up a copy of this little group on the reservation. They find they have to include whites, young VISTAs or public health people, there not being enough heads around the reservation that are past high school age. And the people hear rumors. Some go into a frenzy of activity to prove themselves, they get involved in everything, but still miss the point because they don't really care about the people—they care American style about getting the job done.

Traditionally educated Indians have had a difficult time working on their own reservations. When you get out of school you know so much and have so many solutions to reservation problems that you want to get things done and methods changed.

But you've been away a long time, and some things have already changed. So you start with the problems where they are now, not when you left. You spend a long time finding this out, maybe even talking to council members you joked about for years. You respect them for they know more about the situation than you. And you thought you knew everything.

If you want to get something done you either have to work thru the system or change that system. You talked about tribal government and structure, but when you're there you see that what actually gets done and the way it gets done has little to do with your Tribal Constitution and by-laws. A master's degree has nothing to do with leadership on the reservation, and you want to be a leader. You've forgotten how to work with your own people.

You miss the exciting discussions about what it means to be an Indian, Pan-Tribalism and Unity thru the Indian religion. The people on the reservation accept being Indian and they see no reason to wonder about what that means—they know what it means. They know people from other tribes and have centuries-old prejudices against some tribes, and you discover that the road to Pan-Tribalism is a quiet, soft, steady one, not one filled with a loud, third-world type rhetoric. Religion is not something to talk about lightly on the reservation, some things you do not even talk about in daylight, and you can't just go up to a medicine man and expect him to tell you things because you are sincerely interested in "the Indian religion."

You find yourself being as paternal as the BIA superintendent and maybe more patronizing. It's hard to realize that these people are the ones you've spoken of for so long as "my people." When you finally realize that they don't belong to you, but that you belong to your tribe then you're really on your way back. Then you can find what your spot is in the circle of your tribal world. And just maybe you'll be an Indian again.

LITTLE STAR, *tribe unknown*

2

HOPIS AND THE LOVE GENERATION

When the "hippie invasion," as some Hopis called it, drew white youth to Indian country in the late 1960s, their behavior confused local people. With their long hair and bead necklaces, the "flower children" claimed a special affinity for native ways. But the Indians were sometimes bothered by their exhibitionism; their hair and clothing were unwashed, they did not move around quietly, and they sometimes meddled in community disputes.

In the first selection Peter Nuvamsa, Sr., compares Hopi and hippie attitudes. In the second, Fred Coyote, a Wailaki from California and friend to the Hopi, tells another story that highlights differences between Hopi and white values.

YOU CAN STOP people from bringing cameras into the village to take pictures of the ceremonies, but you can't stop the missionaries. So when they come to me I am hospitable, the way Hopis are supposed to be. I listen, but I don't say anything. One time, though, I gave a long talk to one of those missionaries and told him why I thought he ought to give up being a Mormon and become a Hopi. I never saw him again after that.

There was that time when the hippies came over here and sort of took over the village, as if they owned it. They just camped in the plaza and went around, going into people's houses and things like that. We didn't want them but they refused to go. Shongopovi people had to avoid them by going inside and closing their doors. Those hippies offended our way of life. They hugged each other and kissed in public as if they didn't have anything else to do and nowhere else to go. I went out there and spoke to some of them. I said, "Why are you here? Why do you behave this way, doing anything that comes into your head? We do not like the way you are behaving. It's not our way. It's improper."

They said, "What's wrong with what we are doing? We are here because we're on your side. You have been put down by the establishment, and we are against the establishment." I told them, "No, you are not on our side. You don't behave well. Whatever you want, you take it. Whatever you want to do, you do it. There are rules in the world. You can't be just anything you want." They said, "The rules are wrong." I said, "Don't you believe there is a Great Spirit somewhere that created us and is watching us?" They

Tourist Season, *painting by Navajo artist Quincy Tahoma*

said, "No, we don't believe it." I said, "Well, then, who created you? Do you think you created yourself?" They didn't say anything. Finally the Hopi police came and made them get out.

Those hippies set a pretty bad example for our own young people. We don't seem to be able to guide the young people the way we used to. We try, but they say, "You are going by the old ways; it isn't that way anymore." It's pretty hard for us because the young people are being sent away to schools, and you can't guide them when they aren't in the village. Quite a number of young girls come home pregnant. I don't say that sort of thing didn't happen in the old days. But when we had our children growing up in the village and being initiated into the kiva fraternities we had a better chance to teach them the right way of living. The women could teach the girls and show by their own behavior what was right. Boys would get teaching from their fathers and their [ritual and clan] uncles who sponsored them and guided them. Of course, the ones who go away to school are getting an education they can't get here. Maybe that will help them in days to come. I hope so, because there's no doubt the world is changing. But I hate to see them lose the old life.

PETER NUVAMSA, SR., *Hopi*

FIRST OF ALL, I want to share with you a story that was given to me by one of the Elders of the Hopi people, who was one of my teachers for a while. I have had the privilege to travel and study among many of the great Indian teachers. This story is about an anthropologist who came to visit an old man one time and wanted to record some music, Hopi music. So the old man took him out on the edge of the Mesa and he sang a song. The "anthro" was recording and making notes and he said, "What is that song about?"

The old man said, "Well, that's about when the *kachinas* came down into the mountains and then the thunderheads build up around the San Francisco peaks and then we sing and those clouds come out across the desert and it rains on the gardens and we have food for our children."

And the old man sang him another song. And the "anthro" said, "What was that song about?"

The old man answered, "That song was about when my wife goes down to the sacred spring to get water to prepare foods for us and to prepare the medicines because without that sacred spring we wouldn't live very long."

And so it went all afternoon. And every time the old man would sing a song, the "anthro" would say, "What's that about?" And the old man would explain it. It's about something or other—a river, rain, water.

And this anthropologist was getting a little short tempered. He said, "Is water all you people sing about down here?"

And this old man said, "Yes." He said, "For thousands of years in this country we've learned to live here. Because our need for this water is so great to our families and to our people, to our nations most of our songs are about our greatest need." And he said, "I listen to a lot of American music. Seems like most American music is about love." He said, "Is that why? Is that because you don't have very much?"

FRED COYOTE, *Wailaki*

3

ESKIMOS AND "THE ACT"

This selection is actually a collaboration between an Alaskan Eskimo, Fred Bigjim, and a former Peace Corps volunteer, James Ito-Adler. In the early 1970s they coauthored some letters to a native newspaper, the Tundra Times, commenting on the dramatic changes affecting Alaskan natives due to the largest land settlement in American history. Their invention of a fictitious Eskimo writer, Naugga Ciunerput, and his white friend Wally Morton, a VISTA community volunteer worker, freed them to critique the Alaska Native Claims Settlement Act.

Between 1946 and 1978, the Indian Claims Commission was delegated to compensate deserving Indian communities for lost lands. In 1971 the Alaska natives recovered more than forty million acres, $462.5 million, and up to an even larger amount in mineral royalties. Coupled with "The Act," however, was reorganization of Eskimo society into "corporations," with every Eskimo now a "shareholder." The social effects of this transformation, of the recently built Alaska pipeline, and concern for the Eskimo future are covered in these three "Letters to Howard," (along with an eerie forecast of the Exxon oil spill of March 1989).

Land's End Village
State of Alaska
July 30, 1973

Dear Howard:

There were some people here in the village who heard about the last letter I wrote to the *Tundra Times*. They were upset because I had written that AN ACT was like a disease that would leave no living Natives in 20 years. Some people got mad because they think that the money we are to get will be helpful to our people. Other people just didn't understand what was troubling me so much. Now I can see that many things that I had written about in earlier letters were adding up for me to say that in the last letter.

My youngest daughter had a baby girl last week, and we all realized that, unlike her older brother, who is three years old, she will never be enrolled as a Native in Alaska. By the time she grows up and has her own family, anybody will be able to buy and sell Native land, anybody will be a stockholder in the Native Corporations, and brother will be set against brother according to which was enrolled. Wally pointed out that I had always said that I was a Native whether I was enrolled or not—and that is true. But I realized that, while 20 years may be a long time in the life of one person, it is nothing in the life of a people. I thought about my children and my grandchildren and their children. What does 20 years mean to them before they are born, before they can know the land and way of life of their parents?

To be honest, I don't know what our life will be like when we have corporations in every village and our land taxed and sold. But I am afraid we will lose whatever control over our lives that we ever had. Will our children have to go to the city to make money so that they can eventually come back to their grandparents' land some day like rich tourists? Will they too complain of the crowded cities and cry when they have to return?

These questions bother me because every time a child is stolen from us to be educated, we are made to feel as nothing. Our children are treated as orphans because their parents' way of life is being destroyed. Why should this be so? I am an old man, Howard, but my vision is set on the future as well as the past. Sometimes I wonder what will become of our people if they want dollars more than their own land and they forget their children.

Your friend,

Naugga Ciunerput

September 7, 1973

Dear Howard:

Last week we had a visitor here in the village from a University in California. He was a pleasant fellow named Seth McGraffee, who said that he was an anthropologist. He was real interested in Native culture and customs and wanted to talk to some of the older people in the village. Well, I told him a couple of old stories and a few tall tales and darned if he didn't write them all down in a notebook. At first he said that he was doing a little summer research, but by the second day he said that it was going to be a thesis. By the third day, he was going to write a book about our village and by the time he was ready to leave it was going to be a movie film too. These young people sure do have a lot of big ideas when they first set foot here in these "primitive" villages.

He seemed a bit disappointed that we had snow machines, outboard motors, and rifles, but it was certainly nice that he was interested in the way we Native people used to live our lives. We did have some serious conversations about the problem of passing on our Native heritage to the younger generation, but he didn't really seem to understand all of the pressures on our younger people. They see an entire world beyond their grasp, while this young fellow Seth has the resources to travel freely between these worlds. This means that he can be interested in Native culture this week and be back in California next week. Maybe if our young people had this freedom they would see how empty that world is if what Seth told us was true.

I asked Seth if he had read AN ACT yet, and was surprised when he said no he hadn't. The three of us, Wally, Seth, and me got to talking about AN ACT and how it was going to affect Native life in Alaska. We asked him how the research he was doing was going to help Native people deal with these problems. At first, he said that it would be necessary to preserve as much of Native culture as possible before it disappears. While this is a noble goal, it still misses the main problem. We are the Native people. What we do is the Native culture. How are we going to react to these changes? We can't always go back to the past, but we can and must have a voice in our future.

I asked Seth if anthropologists knew what the difference was between a village, a corporation, and a village corporation? Could he tell us what the difference would be in our lives if we had a profit or a non-profit village corporation? What would be the best set of by-laws to maintain, not preserve, Native values? We don't want a dead culture in a museum, we want a live culture here in Alaska. Maybe he should go and talk to some of the older men in Washington to find out what they had in mind when they wrote AN ACT. That is the kind of research we Natives really need.

Your friend,

Naugga Ciunerput

November 26, 1973

Dear Howard:

A friend of mine left off some old copies of the *Anchorage Daily Times*, which told about the Secretary of Interior, Rogers C.B. Morton, and his fantastic Six Day/3,000 mile "Visit to Alaska" this past summer. It is certainly interesting to read old newspapers when you know what has really happened since then. One of the things that caught my eye was the following paragraph in an article about the Secretary's visit to Valdez:

The secretary said the building of the pipeline was analogous to the construction of the pyramids of Egypt in that it is the most expensive and extensive man-made venture to date in history.—*Anchorage Daily Times*, August 20, 1973 (page 2)

Well, I asked my friend Wally about the Egyptian pyramids—who built them and why? He said that they were built by Egyptian Kings with slave labor for religious purposes like preserving the royal bodies as mummies. Maybe the Pipeline is being built by the Government for the religious purpose of preserving the American Economy, but now they won't need slaves since there are so many unemployed people.

When I read that passage to Wally, he just laughed and asked me if the Pipeline would be visible from the Moon. He said that the Brazilian Government is building a 3,000 mile highway through the Amazon jungle which they claim will be one of the only man-made objects visible from the Moon. Wally also pointed out that the astronauts in the space satellite could see a big cloud of pollution from the Black Mesa power plant at Four Corners in the American Southwest.

Wally said that the Brazilians claim they are opening the last frontier and integrating the Natives into the national society (and killing the rest). The *Anchorage Daily Times* said that Secretary Morton is visiting the last frontier and we can all see how Natives have been integrated into the American Way of Life. First they take our land, water, game, and fish—then our children—and if there is anything left they will build a museum or make a movie to preserve it. Well Howard, I guess we will have our monument if they have a nice big oil spill. Maybe they will be able to see it all the way from the Moon or if there is enough oil maybe even from the top of one of the new office buildings in Anchorage.

Your Native friend,
Naugga Ciunerput

FRED BIGJIM, *Eskimo;* and JAMES ITO-ADLER

4

DARK SKY OVER BLACK MESA

To survive off their natural resources, some western tribes, such as the northern Cheyenne of Montana and the Navajo and Hopi of Arizona, negotiated with big energy firms to strip-mine their coal and cool huge power plants with their water. Electricity generated by these plants would pass through large cables to Los Angeles, Las Vegas, Phoenix, and Tucson, much as the Alaskan oil moved from Eskimo country to the more heavily populated "lower forty-eight."

Selling these resources divided local Indians. The resistance of Navajo and Hopi traditionalists to the Peabody Coal Company's open-pit mining on top of Black Mesa was especially well organized. They objected to the sacred mesa being cut open and to their water being used to transport the smashed coal to the Mohave electrical plant 273 miles away.

During hearings on Black Mesa in Washington in spring 1971, an old Navajo woman who was born there gave her reasons against the mine.

I N E N G L I S H they call me "Kee Shelton's Mother." In Navajo my name is Asa Bazhonoodah, "woman who had squaw dance." I am 83 years old.

I am originally from Black Mesa. I was born and raised there. My parents and grand parents were all from that same area.

At present I live east and not far from the mining site. I was born in a hogan which was still standing the last time I saw it. But now I don't know, maybe they have torn it down.

They tell me my parents used to live right down at the mining site at the time my mother was pregnant with me. Then when she was going to give birth to me they moved eastward to the place where I was born. This is not too far from the place they grind the coal. There is where I was raised and after I got married my husband and I lived at the same place. During that time my husband cleared land and built a fence for a cornfield near where we lived. We used to move to the cornfield to plant and harvest the corn.

My mother died and was buried right there at our permanent home. Following that my husband died during the time people were killed by some kind of disease and he also is buried there. After this happened I moved to the cornfield which my husband had established. The cornfield is still there and I plant a little bit of corn every spring. I haven't planted yet this year but I will soon.

I strongly object to the strip mining for many reasons. The mine workers do a lot of drinking and they take youngsters with them and give them liquor and wine. These are the children of my husband's grandchildren with whom we used to live.

The particles of coal dust that contaminate the water kill our animals. I know this for a fact because many of the sheep belonging to my children were killed. I have some cows and they started dying off. And now it has become too frequent, almost every day. We were asked to report every dead sheep or animal but it is impossible to do that because of the lack of communication. We don't have a trading post or a police station on Black Mesa where we could report these happenings.

Because of this we think the effects of the mining are dangerous to the animals and to ourselves.

We don't not like the explosions at the mine because it scares our horses. Many of us herd sheep on horseback and every time an explosion goes off it scares the animals and they are afraid and try to run away.

We, the residents of Black Mesa, were never consulted or told about the area to be mined, otherwise we could have opposed it. The land or area being strip-mined now was given away by people that don't even live within the area. In fact, this Lee Bradley from Kayenta persuaded three men by promising them jobs. One of the men is deceased and the other two are still living. It was these three who were primarily responsible for bringing in the mining on Black Mesa. The rest of the people were not consulted. One of the three that made the original agreement is not from the immediate coal mine area. Two of the same group were not too far from the mining area. One of the men was my very husband's brother.

A long time ago the earth was placed here for us, the people, the Navajo, it gives us corn and we consider her our mother.

When Mother Earth needs rain we give pollen and use the prayers that was given us when we came from the earth. That brings rain. Black Mesa area is used to ask for rain. And afterward (after the mining) we don't know what it will be like. We make prayers for all blessings for Mother Earth, asking that we may use her legs, her body and her spirit to make ourselves more powerful and durable. After this the pollen is thrown into the water.

Air is one of the Holy Elements, it is important in prayer. Wooded areas are being cut down. Now the air is becoming bad; not working. The herbs that are taken from Mother Earth and given to a woman during childbirth no longer grow in the cut area. The land looks burned.

The Earth is our mother. The white man is ruining our mother. I don't know the white man's ways, but to us the Mesa, the air, the water, are Holy Elements. We pray to these Holy Elements in order for our people to flourish and perpetuate the well-being of each generation.

Even when we were small, our cradle is made from the things given to us from Mother Earth. We use these elements all of our lives and when we die we go back to Mother Earth.

When we were first put on Earth, the herbs and medicine were also put here for us to use. These have become part of our prayers to Mother Earth. We should realize it for if we forget these things we will vanish as the people. That is why I don't like the coal mine.

How much would you ask for if your Mother had been harmed? There is no way that we can be repaid for the damages to our Mother. No amount of money can repay, money cannot give birth to anything.

Black Mesa is to the Navajo like money is to the Whites. Our Mother gives birth to the animals, plants, and these could be traded for money. Black Mesa is my billfold. Black Mesa gives life to animals and these animals give us money. The staff that I prod my donkey with is like the pencil the whites use.

This is why I don't like it. The whites have neglected and misused the Earth. Soon the Navajo will resemble the Anasazi ruins. The wind took them away because they misused the Earth.

The white men wish that nothing will be left of us after this is over. They want us like the Anasazi.

Who likes it, nobody likes it, everybody has something to do with it. Our Mother is being scarred.

This is what I am saying, how much would you ask if your Mother was harmed.

Mother Earth is like a horse. We put out hay and grain to bring in the horse. So it is when we put out pollen to bring life from Mother Earth.

We pray to Mother Earth to ask blessings from the water, the sun, and the moon. Why are they going up there? (to the Moon) I'm also against this. This fooling around with the sacred elements.

This pollution is what I'm especially against. When I first realized I had eyes, I saw that it was clear. Now it is getting hazy and gray outside. The coal mine is causing it. Because of the bad air, animals are not well, they don't feel well. They know what is happening and are dying. Animals are worrying, that is why they are dying.

The reason why is that the things that we ask blessings for are being tampered with. The holy elements have been tampered with. The plants no longer grow because the elements have been tampered with. That's why our values of things are no good anymore. I want our children to have future generations not like Anasazi ruins.

I don't think they (Peabody Coal Company) can replant. There is nothing but rocks, no soil. I don't see how they could replant. The soil is underneath. It won't be replanted, no possible way. They advocate that the place will be beautiful when they finish. I don't believe that this place will be beautiful when they finish. If they replant, they will not replant our herbs. Even now our herbs are vanishing.

I have gone three times looking for herbs. I couldn't recognize the place where we find them. Finally I found some plants but they were scorched. I couldn't find my way around the mountain because it was so distorted. The mining operation is near by.

We have herbs that cure diseases that white medicine doesn't cure. Sometime the people come here to find medicine when the Public Health Service doesn't cure them. They pray and give Mother Earth something for curing them. This the white people do not know about.

Our prayers and healing have been tampered with and they don't work as good anymore.

How can we give something of value to Mother Earth to repay the damages that the mining had done to her. We still ask for her blessings and healing, even when she is hurt.

They are taking water and other Holy Elements from her veins.

I don't want highways built because stock will be runned over and the children might get hurt.

I see the cedar trees next to the ponds they built have turned red. The grasses are dying.

I want to see them stop taking water from inside the Mesa. The water underground works with the water that falls to the surface of Mother Earth, will wash away.

I want to see the burial grounds left alone. All of my relatives' graves are being disturbed.

I want to see the mining stopped.

ASA BAZHONOODAH, *Navajo*

Conflicting forms of life: a young Navajo shepherd herds his sheep in the shadow of the coal-burning Four Corners Power Plant at Fruitland, New Mexico, 1979.

5

INDIAN CHILDREN IN CRISIS

During the late 1960s and early 1970s the psychiatrist Robert Coles tried to understand how young Indians and Eskimos thought about Indian and white relations. The youngsters spoke with remarkable eloquence. He heard this from a Hopi girl of thirteen on the downfall of the Nixon presidency: *''The news of Watergate is a dark cloud. The sky was clear, and the hunters ran wild; then dark clouds gathered and rain fell, and the hunters stopped for a while. Will we*

*soon get more hunters, just as greedy? Or will we learn to control greed, so that
we don't just pray and pray for bad weather to stop the hunters in their tracks?''*

*In these pieces of testimony collected by Coles, an Oklahoma Indian boy and a
Hopi girl tell of coping with the white man's overweening power.*

AT SCHOOL they show us their guns and submarines and tanks; we
know of them, anyway. Aren't we here, on a reservation? We didn't just
walk here, whistling and saying it's a sunny day, and let's live where we
won't bother anyone, and let them tell us everything to do, because we're
glad to wait on them.

I look out the window a lot when I'm in school. I take walks, only the
teacher thinks I'm sitting at my desk, taking in all her words. (Why is it,
all teachers sound alike? They have sirens in their voices, and whistles, and
they wave their hands as if they're holding a rifle, and don't know who to
aim it at, and when to fire.)

I have our dog with me on the walk I imagine I'm taking. He is a wise
dog. He teaches me. I climb trees; I don't want to go higher—no airplanes
for me.

My grandfather says the land vomited its oil for the white man, and soon
the white man will leave the land alone, and at least we will have quiet
here. But my grandmother says no; the white man will never leave. He is
a tornado, and we have tornados every year in Oklahoma.

When the white man landed on the moon, my father cried. He said the
day had to come, he knew; but still, he cried. I told him there weren't any
Indians on the moon, so stop crying. He said nothing for a long time. Then
he said our spirits were there, too—and he was sure Indians were crying
up there, and trying to hide, and hoping that soon they'd go back to their
Earth, the white men, where they make so many people unhappy, and
where they don't know what to do next.

But my aunt told me, 'the moon is yours to look at and talk to, so don't
worry.' And I don't. One day, you know, everything will settle down; there
won't be the Federal Government and their troops, or the army and navy
and air force—only some people growing their food and saying hello and
smiling when they speak and not worrying about landing on the moon.

Well, I hope that day will come. When I take my walk away from school,
while I'm sitting there at my desk, that's what I say to myself: the day will
come, the good day. And then we'll all be friends.

ANONYMOUS, *Oklahoma Indian*

WE ARE NOTHING to the white people; we are a few Hopis, but they are Americans, millions of them. My father told me that their leader, whoever he is, ends his speech by saying that God is on their side; and then he shakes his fist and says to all the other nations: you had better pay attention, because we are big, and we will shoot to kill, if you don't watch out.

My mother says all the big countries are like that, but I only know this one. We belong to it, that is what the government of the United States says. They come here, the BIA [Bureau of Indian Affairs] people and they give us their orders. This law says . . . another law says . . . , and soon there will be a new law.

In case we have any objections, they have soldiers, they have planes. We see the jets diving high in the sky. The clouds try to get out of the way, but they don't move fast enough. The water tries to escape to the ocean, but can only go at its own speed.

Everything, everyone, is the white man's; all he has to do is stake his claim. They claimed us. They claimed our land, our water; now they have turned to other places, and my uncle, who knows the history of our people, and of the United States, says it is a sad time for others; but when my brother began to worry about the others, our uncle sighed, and said: "At least our turn is over, and don't be afraid to be glad for that."

They are not really through with us, though. They come here—the American police, the red light going around and around on their cars: visitors to our reservation from the great United States of America. "There they are," my father always says. He tells us to lower our eyes. I have stared at them and their cars, but I will never say anything, I know that.

If their President came here, I would stay home or come to look at him, but not cheer. I have seen on television people cheering the President. In school they show us pictures of white men we should cheer. I never want to. I don't think the teachers expect us to, *want* us to; just to pretend. So, we do.

ANONYMOUS, *Hopi*

IT'S HARD
TO BE INDIAN

For some Indians, national holidays involving historical Indian-white interactions, such as Columbus Day and Thanksgiving, are no cause for celebration. In November 1982, Dennis Banks conducted an "unthanksgiving ceremony" at abandoned Alcatraz Island, site of two famous Indian militant takeovers in the 1960s. Ten years later, Indians would similarly protest the five hundredth anniversary of Columbus's arrival to what the white man termed the "New World," where Indians had already been living for more than ten thousand years.

Before Ronald Reagan moved into the White House, Indians got a hint of his thoughts about them. As a presidential candidate he was asked what famous lives he wished he had lived. Reagan confessed to being "fascinated by those who saw this new world—Cortes, Lewis and Clark, Father Serra—when it was virtually untouched by man." Indians had to wait until Reagan was leaving office to hear him speak from the heart again. In spring 1988, a student in Moscow asked how the United States could justify its Indian policy. "Maybe we made a mistake," Reagan answered, "in trying to maintain Indian cultures. Maybe we should not have humored them in wanting to stay in that kind of primitive life-style. Maybe we should have said, 'No, come join us. Be citizens along with the rest of us.' "

Back home native leaders were beside themselves; Reagan was reviving Colonel Henry Pratt's old dictum "Kill the Indian; save the man." "I was appalled by the President's performance, but not surprised," said Suzan Harjo, executive director of the National Congress of American Indians. "President Reagan," snapped Salish-Kootenai tribal chairman Michael Pablo, "needs a crash course in the history of the American Indian." To native activist Antonio Gonzales, Reagan "declared war on Indian people with that racist statement." Other Indians demanded to know whether it was "humoring" Indians when the government observed its legal, legislative, or treaty obligations? Were Indians not following the American way when they remained loyal to community and family? Indian journalists asked how this student of history could be unaware that most Indians were citizens by law in 1924, even if southwestern tribes could not vote until 1948.

So outrageous was Reagan's performance that it called for hasty damage control: the President was merely explaining that the United States did not impose assimilation; Indians needn't worry, administration spokespeople added, the 1950s Termination days were repudiated, the Nixon-era Self-Determination policy remained intact; the government-to-government relationship still obtained between Washington and Indian communities—what Reagan misspoke as "preservations" in Russia. Unconvinced, Susan Harjo retorted that "He [Reagan] has headed the worst administration for Indians since the days of outright warfare and termination."

Some were relieved that the President's true opinions were out in the open; they clarified why Indians felt ignored during the previous eight years. When Reagan took office in 1980, the U.S. Census revealed that about a third of the 1,750,000 Indians, Eskimos, and Aleuts in the United States were living on 278 reservations and nearly two hundred Alaskan villages. Of the 225,000 Indians found in California, the majority hailed from out-of-state tribes. On one hand, Indians seemed as mobile and suburb-bound as other Americans; on the other, the census disclosed that some twenty-eight percent still existed below the poverty line and suffered disproportionately from health and social problems. What the census did not reflect was what those reservation lands meant emotionally and economically to Indians—their special inheritance of culture, political sovereignty, and natural resources.

Reaganism hurt Native Americans as it did poor Americans everywhere. "In 1983 alone," summarized sociologist Stephen Cornell, "[Indian] aid was slashed by more than a third, from $3.5 billion to $2 billion, affecting programs on every reservation. Cancellation of the CETA program cost the Poncas [in Oklahoma] two hundred jobs overnight. The intertribal Alcoholism Treatment Center in Montana lost half its counselers and most of its beds. In 1982 the Navajo tribe reported that yearly per capita income had declined 25 percent." In the words of one tribal planner, "Trickle-down economics feels a lot like being pissed on."

Ross O. Swimmer, a Cherokee businessman from Tahlequah, Oklahoma, was Reagan's point man for Indian affairs. As tribal chairman back in Oklahoma, Swimmer tripled income from tribal-owned businesses between 1975 and 1986. Instead of praising welfare workers for their number of clients, he rewarded them when they found alternative support for the impoverished or impaired—lowering the Cherokee caseload by a third. Retaining culture and language might be desirable, Swimmer believed, but not at the cost of keeping Indians poor, dependent, or unproductive.

The Reagan-Swimmer watchword was "economic development" founded upon tribal initiative, private ownership, and the profit motive. When legislation calling for cash settlements to tribes arrived on the President's desk—such as a $112-million offer to resolve debts to the Papagoes of Arizona or a $900,000 offer to the Pequod Indians of Connecticut due them for land claims, Reagan generally vetoed the bills.

To a lot of Indians, the early 1980s felt like Termination in a new guise as tribes were forced to squeeze local resources in order to become the entrepreneurs Washington envisioned. By 1982 forty-five tribes from twelve states were involved in oil production, and fifty-two were receiving in-

(handwritten in left margin: Negative effects of Reaganism)

come from mining. But while it was estimated in 1979 that the coal deposits underneath Indian lands were worth $1 trillion, such natural resources were distributed unequally among the reservations; by 1985 a government task force reported that only fourteen percent of American Indians lived on reservations that received oil or coal revenues equal to $500 or more per reservation resident. This was not turning out to be the American Middle East that Indian energy proponents had dreamt about a decade before.

Tribes made out the best they could; some showed initiative and staying power against considerable odds. The Choctaw diversified into manufacturing electrical appliances and auto parts and printing greeting cards; by 1990 they were Mississippi's fifteenth-largest employer. A few eastern tribes turned their land-claims dollars into educational and welfare programs; after satisfying their people's basic needs, the Passamaquoddy of Maine took out a patent on making fertilizer and distilling water from coal smoke and won a Department of Energy $4.8-million financing grant. In 1986 the Klamath of Oregon won reversal of their terminated status, and acquired new timber and funding to restore their tribal government.

At the same time Indians stunned everyone by imaginatively exploiting the white man's get-rich-quick ethic and their own freedom from state taxation, as firmly established by a string of court decisions. They initiated Indian gambling. In 1979 the Seminole of south Florida opened the first bingo hall. When state officials padlocked the building, the courts ordered it legal and open. Buildings as big as airplane hangars and jammed parking lots began appearing on Indian reservations. By 1987 almost fifty tribes were running bingo parlors, bringing in more than $250 million annually; that year the U.S. Supreme Court told the states to keep their hands off Indian bingo for good.

Some Indians worried that bingo was only a "quick fix" to the desperate need for a reliable income base. Gambling was certainly not what the administration had in mind by "economic enterprise," but Republicans had to admire such financial spirit. Even if gambling went bust in another decade, said one southwestern tribal leader, "you'll see that what Indian bingo really is is a crash course in business management for Indians."

The courts smiled on Indian capitalism but not on Indian spirituality. President Jimmy Carter's American Indian Freedom of Religion Act of 1978 vowed to protect Indian use of protected wild animals whose feathers or skins were featured in rituals, for ceremonial use of peyote, and for

Indian sacred lands that were used for religious pilgrimages, burials, or vision questing. But Carter's edict had no teeth. In legal challenges that reached higher courts the Navajo and Hopi could not prevent an Arizona ski firm from developing their sacred San Francisco Peaks, the Cherokee failed to halt the damming of Tennessee's Tellico River and drowning their ancestral townsites, the Sioux lost exclusive rights to the Black Hills fasting sites, and the Yurok of northern California watched the Supreme Court allow the U.S. Forest Service to run a road through their holy "high country" in the Siskiyou Mountains. "Even if we assume [the road] will virtually destroy the Indians' ability to practice their religion," wrote Supreme Court Justice Sandra Day O'Connor in 1988, "the Constitution simply does not provide a principle that could justify upholding [the Indians'] legal claims." To dissenting Justice William J. Brennan, this reduced the Indians' religious freedom to "nothing more than the right to believe that their religion will be destroyed."

But the white man's conscience could be tugged both ways. No sooner were Indians dismayed by the California verdict than they achieved national success in pressuring museums to return Indian skeletons for reburial and sacred artifacts to their original tribes. When physical anthropologists protested that Indian bones constituted a unique chronicle of human evolution and experience that might be "read" someday by techniques yet uninvented, Indians retorted, "read your own grandparents' books."

With special Senate hearings on Indian affairs in 1988 and 1989, it seemed as if, as Vine Deloria, Jr., observed, "Indian Affairs is comparable to a Grade B movie. You can go to sleep and miss a long sequence of the action, but every time you look at the screen it's the same group of guys chasing the other guys around the same rock." After a stream of more than 2,000 witnesses, 172 public hearings, and visits to 70 different tribes, the committee called for a "New Federalism." It sounded fine enough: Indians should be empowered, and financed, to run their own lives. But this well-reasoned call for a new New Deal was undercut by reservation realities exposed by the hearings. Housing programs were infiltrated by firms that pretended to be Indian-owned but were run by white profiteers. At reservation schools the Bureau of Indian Affairs dragged its feet in dealing with child abuse. Sixteen percent of the nation's Indian houses still lacked electricity, twenty-one percent were without plumbing.

Unfortunately, perhaps, much of the committee's energy and publicity was soon diverted to the Navajo reservation, where the corruption of tribal chairman Peter MacDonald, once the epitome of the modernizing Indian leader, came to light. Waste, incompetence, and outright illegality during his fifteen-year regime had harmed the forty percent of Navajos who were still unemployed. MacDonald himself was accused of favoritism, bribery, and major fraud, charges for which he was convicted in 1990. Indians were worried that, rather than helping them, the Senate hearings wound up "making all of us look corrupt." At the same time, Congress appropriated nearly $70 million for a new National Museum of the American Indian, the last great exhibition hall on Washington, D.C.'s central mall, to be built by the year 2000. It would stand as a major testimonial to the art and heritage of all America's Indians.

To many Native Americans the spread of AIDS in the 1980s—described in the Eskimo language as "the sickness forever"—resurrected memories

After an old Indian cemetery was desecrated by grave robbers in Kentucky in 1987, the disturbed remains were reburied on Memorial Day a year later. Here, a Shawnee-Delaware from Oklahoma offers tobacco to the spirits at the reburial site overlooking the Ohio River.

of other non-Indian scourges: smallpox, TB, trachoma, influenza—which had killed more Indians since 1492 than warfare or old age. "If AIDS started," feared Hupa Indian doctor Emmett Chase in 1987, "it could make some smaller tribes extinct."

That year there were only thirty-eight cases of Indians known to be infected with the AIDS virus. Yet there was cause for concern: The year-round visiting between urban centers and reservation homes could easily transmit viruses into rural areas. Despite the idealism with which cosmopolitan Indians imagined sexual tolerance in traditional days, Indian homosexuals were as terrified of social ostracism as non-Indians. "We say, 'AIDS only happens in cities to those queers,' " declared a Paiute-Creek-Seminole leader of the American Indian AIDS Institute. "Well, those 'queers' are your brothers, sisters, and uncles." On some western reservations, Sun Dance priests who pierced the dancers' chests during rituals began using disposable blades and rubber gloves while tribal newspapers disseminated AIDS hotline phone numbers.

As the official U.S. Census for 1990 revealed that the population of American Indians (including Eskimos and Aleuts) had nearly reached two million, the oldest questions about Indian cultural survival seemed as timely as ever. Was this modern world, run by non-Indians, forcing them to choose between cultural and physical survival, between, as *The New York Times* put it, "tribal loyalty and the need to assimilate"? Was there any hope for equitable Indian and white relations, where the different cultures could be anything but trains passing in the night? What could Indians offer a planet threatened by pollution of the environment and extinction of animals and plants? Or did the white man secretly possess, as one Oklahoma Indian put it, "a termination mentality, the idea that sometime Indians will finally disappear?"—and the man added, "They act as if we are not part of the future."

The Karuk Indian author and researcher Julian Lang has often said, "It's hard to be an Indian." He means the struggles to maintain traditional knowledge and mythological values in a modern era. But he is also referring to the sheer grit it takes to fight for personal and tribal identity in the face of surrounding disinterest, prejudice, misrepresentation, or bureaucracy. He is talking about the uphill battles described in this chapter.

1

WHAT AM I

Q uestions of identity often trouble modern Indian youth, especially those of mixed Indian and white ancestry. Is being Indian a matter of adopted lifestyle and point of view, they wonder, or of physical appearance and the amount of genetic Indianness, which is traced by reconstructing a family tree?

During congressional hearings into Indian education in 1969, a Ponca Indian witness was asked by an Oklahoma senator, "When you talk about Indians, whom are you talking about?" The man replied, "Somebody who wants to be an Indian, and somebody who knows he has to be an Indian." Unfortunately, a mixed-blood's self-assurance is not usually achieved that easily. In this essay a student at the Institute of American Indian Arts in Santa Fe, New Mexico, tells what it feels like to negotiate between identities and stereotypes. Opening in 1961, the Institute was a pioneering effort in education that did not turn natives from their own culture. Today there are twenty-seven tribally controlled Indian colleges, mostly located on reservations, which teach math, science, and business administration alongside classes in Indian history, literature, and languages. It has been estimated that a native student who attends such an institution for only a year is forty times more likely to succeed at a non-Indian institution than one who enrolls directly.

ONE THING I can't get over is the way many Indians talk about Whites. I am particularly sensitive to it because I am part White. I realize that some Indians, having had discriminatory experiences with Whites, may have reason to feel anger; still this does not justify reverse discrimination. But the real hypocrisy is with those who are partially White themselves (most Indians, even those on the reservations have some White blood, as their French, Spanish, and German names may indicate).

Recently I heard a guy who is half Indian sneer at "White ways." Today the dominant society has great influence upon Indians. Many Indians, even those who are pure bloods, have adopted White ways. They drive cars, work at factories, worship at White churches, adhere to White morals, and dress as Whites. Most Indian customs are just remnants. The true Indian (one who knows his religion, customs and their meanings, practices Indian crafts and can survive in the wilderness) is rare.

What is Indian? I don't know. Perhaps that is because I have been raised in White society. My mother was raised on the reservation so perhaps I should know what Indian is. People say, "It doesn't matter how much Indian you are if you feel Indian." I don't "feel" Indian. I accept my mother as I do myself without pinpointing what is Indian. Perhaps this feeling of Indian is feeling kinship for people with Indian blood.

I am defensive because I do not feel truly Indian. People talk about White ways and I fear being called an Apple [red outside, white within] I wonder how many other people feel the same way and thus knock Whites.

I search for something to validate myself as an Indian. I can make general statements about Indians such as: they are sharing and giving people, they lack materialism and live close to nature. But these apply only to Indians of the past who have lived close to the old culture. The true Indians are all but gone.

Within myself I feel rejected or feel the threat of rejection. My mother married a White man. Her family wanted her to marry an Indian. My aunt excludes my father from the address on her letters. As the offspring of such a marriage I am in a precocious position. I feel like an outsider.

When I was growing up I feared being rejected for my dark skin. I saw drunkenness and poverty when I visited the reservation during the summer. I wanted to be accepted in White society with Donna Reed mothers and modern homes. I was ashamed of being Indian. My White relatives talked about "Dagoes" in reference to Latin Americans and Italians. They are dark and so again I felt defensive about my skin color. As a halfbreed, I was not fully accepted by either set of relatives.

In the TV commercial society, where Whites reign, any deviate color was inferior. I set out to prove that I was White. I believed in good grades, popularity, etc. Now I am tired of that, although these expectations still haunt me. Unfortunately many traditionalists are turning to these same shallow values. Many Whites are turning to Indians for an alternative to these values. Where are the Indians who still have an answer and are willing to share their wisdom with those who listen sincerely?

Probably most Indians will adopt materialistic values. But an alternative should be available for those who want it.

ANONYMOUS

2
ALONE AND VERY SCARED

This testament of pain is from the handwritten diary of a seventeen-year-old Chipewyan Indian named Richard S. Cardinal, which he titled "I Was a Victim of Child Neglect." The document was found after the teenager nailed a piece of wood between two trees and hanged himself on June 26, 1984. At age three Richard had become a ward of the Canadian province of Alberta. Over the next fourteen years his residence changed twenty-eight times; he roomed with sixteen different sets of foster parents. Richard tried twice to take his life before succeeding.

Teenage suicide is the most unambiguous sign of community disintegration and personal despair. In Alaska, Native American suicide is four times the national rate; in the past twenty years suicide attempts by American Indians between twenty and thirty years of age increased 200 to 300 percent over that of whites in that age range.

Sometimes government practices, such as Canada's Indian child welfare practices, exacerbated these trends. But pervasive loss of self-esteem, poverty, alcoholism, and alienation created a frightening future for many Indian youth in the 1980s.

I WAS BORN in Ft. Chipewyan that much I know for certain, because it's on my birth-certificate.

I have no memories or certain knowledge of what transpired over the next few years. I was once told by a Social Worker that my parents were alcoholic's and that all us kids were removed for this reason. I was separated from the rest of my family and placed in a foster home some-were in fort MacMurry.

My earlyiest memories are from when I was liveing with a family in Wandering-River. I have little memory of this home but I do remember that I was playing with some wooden matches and I guess when I left one was still going and the outcome was desastrous, the shed in which I had been playing had caught on fire, which spread and caught onto the hay stack. When they had finally put the fire out and managed to save ¼ of the stack I was given the wipping of my life. . . . I was also reunited with my brother at this home so I did not feel so alone any more. We were moved after about a year.

Our next home was in the same town just a few miles away. This home was good in one way but bad in alot of ways. It seemed that for every good happenings there were two bad ones . . . about three months later my sister Linda (who is the oldest of the girls in our family) was moved into our foster home. Charlie and linda were always playing together and seeing as I was still pretty small I was always left-out so I began to spend alot of time alone . . .

Our next move was a few month's later, we were moved to live—we lived with a elderly couple my the name of ———. I enjoyed this home for the first two days then everything went wrong when we had to go back to school. The first day I was sent to the office three time's in the same day for fighting. . . . I began to get into a lot of trouble for neglecting my chores and was hit several time's with a stick and sent to bed. I could hear Mr. & Mrs. ——— arguing late into the night, About them hitting me. In school it was worse than ever I was constantly in trouble with the principle for fighting and not doing my work in class. . . . When fall returns it was back to school for us kids I can remember—trying to get us ready before the bus arrived but we were so excited that we were hopping around like grasshoppers on a hot summerday. I would be returning to grade two this year. I was not considered an outcast this year and got my first tast of puppy love with a girl named Heather. I was halfway through the school-year when a Social Worker came to our home and I was to be moved and asked me how soon I would be ready to move and I answered, 1 week, I should have answered never. When I would move alone Charlie and linda would stay.

I had 4 hours before I would leave my family and friends behind and since linda and charlie were at school, I went into the bedroom and dug-out my old harmonica and went down to the barn yard and sat on the fence and began to lay to the cows. I didn't know how to play at all but I played real slow and sad like for the occation, but before halfway through the song my lower lip began to quiver and I knew I was going to cry and I was glad so I didn't even try to stop myself. I guess that ——— heard me and must have come down to comfort me, when she put her arm around me and I pulled away and ran up the road aways. I did'nt want no one's love any more I had been hurt to many times so I began to learn the art of blocking out all emotions and I shut out the rest of the world out and the door would open to no one.

The Social Worker arvied to take me away to my new home. On the way their he tryed to talk to me but I was'nt hearing or trying to hear. When we arrived the Social Worker wanted to talk to the parents alone so I remained in the car. . . . I was taken into their house and —————— showed me were I would sleep. The room was in the basement of the house. When I walked into the room I could not believe my eye's. The floor was covered with water (about an inch and half) and there were boards on the floor to keep your feet from getting wet. The walls had been painted red but had long before began to peel off, the window which was no bigger than a atlas had a gape between the foundation and the bottom which let in the cold winter wind and the beds were no wider than two feet across and about a foot off the floor. there was a 40 watt light that was in the ceiling (which was not completely finished) and you had to pull a string to turn it on. It looked like something that you would see in a horror movie! "You'll be sharing this room with another boy" he said and with that returned upstairs. The night was a night mare in it self, The wind constantly blew through the crack in between the window and the wall and it was like sleeping in a cool room I had a spider crawl acros my face twice before I fanally killed the dumb thing and I was constantly cold. In the morning I as assigned chores to do and I would be fed after they were done. When I was finished I was returing to the house to eat and found a lunch bag in the door way, this was my breakfast. I was not allowed to eat with the family in the house, and the same with lunch and supper. The next few days were like living in a jail, I was set boundries in which to stay in and I was to come running "when I was called." I kept telling myself that this was all a bad dream and that I would wake up soon with charlie and linda and the rest of the family in our home back in Ft. Chipewyan, but in reality I knew that I would'nt wake up and that this was real, and not just some bad dream. The first month's rolled by slowly and then bang! it was my birthday, I was now nine however it seemed that everybody could careless. I remaind "looked in my own little world and would and would not let anything in or out" I was enrolled into Westlock Elementy School, I was better hear I was away from the farm and the family that lived their.

Here I began to fall into bad company and got into alot of trouble. We were let out of school for two weeks for Christmas holadays. I figure things would eased-up abit between The Family and I during this period however I was wrong Things got worse. I was beginning to feel rejected and unwanted. Christmas morning I was sent outside and not allowed back in till dinner and even then I had to eat in the basement, This was it I could'nt take anymore of this I had to leave, go somewere were nobody would find me. I pack my belongings into my back-pack and I had stoled a bottle of rye so I packed that to the garage and rolled up the old tent and secured this onto my pack I was almost ready.

I went back into the house and got a box of wooden matches and stuffed it into my pocket's as I was comeing back-up the stairs and noticed for the first time the guns hung on the wall ther was a box below the gun rack and I opened It up. "Beautiful I told myself, the box had pagages of shells for the guns. Each pack contained 3 boxes of fifty shells. I took two packs and stuffed them into my jacket. When I had got the gun out of the house to the garage. I slipped on my pack picked up the gun and head away from the house. I had been gone 4 days before I was caught and brought back to the farm however I felt as though I had done darned good since I was only 9 years old.

I spent the rest of the winter here feeling lonly and very depressed, And I began to seriously think about suicide. The first time I attempted it I used a rasor blade to cut my arms but it hurt to much so I didn't try that again. When school started up once more I began to skip classes and the ——— were informed. When I return to the farm that evening ——— was waiting for me and he began to yell and scream at me. I was'nt listening and did not care. finaly he blew his stack and hit me. It was the first time I was hit by him and I guess he exspeted me to start in bawling but I didn't I just stood there and stared blankly at him. This must have scared him because he backhanded me. My lip began to bleed quite badly. When I tasted the blood I spit it beside his shoe's and told him to "GO TO HELL," and with that I walked away while I left him standing there looking rather stupid.

After school I would do my chores and sit in the barn and think and one day I was in there thinking, and it struck me I could kill myself now and no one would know until it was to late, and it just so happenes that the bail I was sitting on still had a bailer twine on it so I slipped it off and climbed up into the rafters. After I had secured the rope I climbed down and placed some straw underneath the rope I climed on and stood up determined to go through with it. I said a short Prayer for god to take care of my family. I placed the rope around my neck and kicked my lungs felt like they were melting right off my head. Finaly I blacked out and was engulfed in a blanket of black.

Unfortunately I woke up. I could see alot of people above me, all of a sudden thay all began to talk to me at the same time. I could not make out what they were saying all the words were echoing in my head and my eye's would not focus in on the people above me then I was swept back into a sea of blackness.

I was released from the hospital after about a week. I was returned to the ——— family my social worker was there. We sat and talked for about two hours about how things were going. I exsplained to him that I wanted to return to ——— and I wanted to be with Charlie and Linda, however he tryed to exsplaine to me how that was impossible for me to go back because

[The original of Richard's journal ends here. But the copy of the original made by the police soon after Richard's death carries on for two more pages. These pages have since been lost.]

she was getting too old for so many young kids to take care of an eventually the ——— would get another boy my age and just before he left I was informed that I would be seeing a phychologist every three days, then he let.

On the first day that I went to see this phychologist, we just sat there and talked about each other, generally just getting to know each other. He kept caling me "my friend" I did not consider him my friend I thought of him as an enemy. He was trying to make me remember, I didn't want to, I just sat and stared at him blankly. . . .

I want to say to the people involved in my life, don't take this personal it's not your fault. . . .

> Love can be gentle as a lamb or
> ferocise as a lion.
> it is something to be welcomed yet it is
> something to be afraid of.
> it is good and bad. yet people live
> fight, and die for this.
> somehow people can cope with it I don'
> now, I think
> I would not be happy with it yet I am
> depresed and sad without
> it. love is very strong.

RICHARD S. CARDINAL, *Chipewyan*

3
NOTES FROM INDIAN COUNTRY

Among the forces that enliven Indian reservation communities are native me-dia, especially local radio and newspapers. Families enjoy powwow music and Indian-language talk shows over reservation airwaves, and Indian journalism has proliferated—from 18 reservation newspapers in 1963 to over 220 by 1978.

Tim Giago is a popular Oglala Sioux columnist for the Lakota Times, located in Rapid City, South Dakota. His work is widely syndicated; his columns cover politics, religion, culture, and land issues. His native Lakota name, Nanwica Kciji, means ''Defender''; in this 1987 piece Giago stands up for ''the good old days'' of the 1930s when reservation Indians enjoyed greater power to adjust on their own terms.

FLANDREAU, S.D.—My mom used to place our radio next to a window so the wire running to the car battery outside of the house would not have so far to travel.

My father had rigged up the radio and topped it off by running another wire to an iron rod stuck in the ground. He called this the ground wire.

While my brother, sisters and I were busy playing games like "Annie, Annie, over," "Red rover, red rover," and "Red light, green light," we could hear the popular songs of the day drifting from the window.

On Friday nights everything had to be perfectly quiet while my father prepared to listen to Don Dunphy and the Friday Night Fights.

Back in the late 1930s, popular songs seemed to stay on the airwaves forever. We enjoyed songs like "Tumbling Tumbleweed," "The Blue Ridge Mountains of Virginia" and "Somewhere Over the Rainbow," and never worried about whether they were rated highly on the Top 40 charts because back then there was no Top 40 chart.

Indian reservations were much different in those days. The people of the tribe lived and worked on their own land.

This was long before the U.S. government decided that it would be ex-tremely economical to build houses in clusters in town in an effort to save on plumbing, sewage and electrical costs. This was the beginning of in-stant ghettos on many Indian reservations.

Tribal members were told that life would be much easier for them if they would move from their land and settle into the brand-new cluster housing projects.

Indian people abandoned homes on their own land in droves. They sold their cattle, horses, and in the case of many Navajo families, their sheep, and moved to the cluster houses.

Although they had scratched out a meager living on their own land, at least many tribal people had maintained a sense of pride.

Since there are few job opportunities on most reservations, by abandoning their land, and hence their livelihood, many tribal members gave up what little independence they had for nearly total dependence.

The stroke of the pen in Washington, D.C., that created cluster housing on Indian reservations also created hundreds of miniature welfare states.

The land on the reservation either became dormant or was leased out to white ranchers and farmers.

Why did so many Indian people abandon their homes and independence and move into the cluster homes?

When a person has nothing, or very little, and is told by a trusted source, the U.S. government, that life will be better for them if they move into town, into the new homes, what are they to believe?

My mother and father moved to the town of Kyle on the Pine Ridge Reservation from their home at Three-Mile-Creek long before the advent of cluster housing. They moved because my dad got a job at one of the stores in Kyle.

As I drove through the reservation last week and saw the house I lived in as a boy, the thoughts of those days gone by came back in a flood of memories.

Maybe people have a tendency to put too much stock in "the good old days," but I am convinced that those days of peace, tranquility and friendship were, indeed, the good old days.

Oglala Chief Andrew Fools Crow never left the land. He refused to move into the cluster houses.

Now in his 90s, Fools Crow stood in his back yard at Three-Mile-Creek a couple of summers ago and pointed at the rolling green hills surrounding Kyle. "Your father and I used to ride our horses through those canyons and hills," he said.

He quickly turned his face from me, but I'm sure I saw a tear run down his weathered cheek.

A car roared by on the blacktop road running past Fools Crow's house as its radio blasted out one of the tunes from the Top 40.

TIM GIAGO, *Sioux*

4

BEFORE AND AFTER GAMBLING

*A*n Ojibwe or Anishinaabeg ("Shinnob") Indian, Vietnam veteran, and newspaper columnist, the writer Jim Northrup regularly produces marvelous blends of humor and social insight for a number of native periodicals. In this meditation on the pluses and minuses of Indian gambling, he reminds his readers of how it has not improved persisting problems in Indian-white relations.

WHAT WAS LIFE LIKE on the Reservations before gambling? Let's go back and take a look.

In 1980, Shinnobs were facing discrimination and prejudice on a daily basis. Bigots were everywhere. The towns around the Reservation were the worst for racism. I called it a "hate circle" around the Rez.

Most Americans were not aware of the problems we faced every day. Their view of us was a mix of twentieth-century Hollywood and nineteenth-century idealism. Some people were surprised that we were still here. We learned how to survive and even flourish in spite of the racism. We continued to teach our children how to live in a racist society.

The system's tentacles reached deeper into our lives than those of any other population group. Once a Shinnob got wrapped up, it was difficult to escape. We were not people, we were clients, patients, or inmates. Sometimes we were lumped together and called a caseload.

The probation officer talked to the judge who talked to the police who talked to the lawyer who talked to the social worker who talked to the counselor who talked to the child protection worker who talked to the probation officer. Shinnobs enmeshed in the system rarely got away without losing their dignity, their freedom, or their children.

Jails always held more than their share of Shinnobs. The sentences seemed to be longer and the punishments more severe. A jury of their peers was a joke. I couldn't name one Shinnob who ever served on a jury even if you held a bayonet against my throat. The only Shinnobs in the courtroom either wore connected steel bracelets or were called defendants. Going to jail was considered normal and not an aberration. There were many family reunions held in the cell blocks. Shinnobs were 1 percent of the population of Minnesota but made up 25 percent of the jail and prison populations. It was tough being a free Indian in those days.

Schools added to the problem by labeling most Shinnobs as learning disabled. Once a label was applied, it was difficult to remove. In school, the students learned that they were "discovered" and were a "conquered people." They also learned about the wisdom of the white man with no mention of their own contributions.

White students were especially cruel to the Shinnobs. My son, Joseph, told me it doesn't feel good to be called a dirty Indian in class. Some schools used Indians as mascots, something less than human. It was a challenging test to be an Indian in the schools then. It is no surprise that most students quit school before graduation.

Foster homes and adoption agencies did a brisk business in Indian children. The Shinnobs were taken from their families at an alarming rate. We also learned a new word: dysfunctional. The word meant someone else was going to raise your children. It was sad to watch these born-Shinnob-raised-white people returning to the Reservation. We helped them find their identity that was taken by the system. It was hard to even remain Indian back in the '80s.

Shinnobs exercising their treaty rights were arrested by game wardens and harassed by white people. Wild rice, deer meat, ducks, and fish were confiscated by the game wardens. Canoes, nets, and guns were also taken away. Each arrest and confiscation was a reminder of how the United States kept its word in the treaties. People still continued to exercise their rights in spite of threats, gunfire, and bombs. They were the only ones who believed in the words of the treaties. It was hard to be a treaty believing Indian in the 1980s.

Back in the bad old days, tribal governments were trying to qualify for federal and private grants. Job training programs blossomed and then withered. A lot of us learned a little about a lot of different occupations. On my Rez, we had welders, carpenters, heavy equipment operators, natural resources technicians, and electronic workers. We followed the Golden Rule in those days—those with the gold make the rules. Washington and foundation dollars ruled the reservations with their policies.

Tribal governments were just learning to flex their economic muscles.

Here it is the '90s and little has changed except the calendar. We are still facing racism, personal and institutional, every day. But there is one difference, the tribal governments have control of the gambling gold.

JIM NORTHRUP, *Ojibwe*

5

SOVEREIGNTY REVITALIZED

Throughout the 1980s "tribal sovereignty" was an oft-heard Indian rallying cry. To most native commentators it encompassed their treaty-protected rights to determine their own tribal cultural, economic, educational, and religious destinies. To President Reagan's Indian officials it was a cover term for getting Indian reservations to use their own resources to fend for themselves and cut back on federal aid.

For many Indian communities the greater challenge was to develop an economic and political foundation for self-sufficiency in today's business world and yet to remain traditional in their interpersonal lives. According to Indian historian Donald L. Fixico, this delicate balance is what his people have sought in eastern Oklahoma.

SO WHAT IS an Indian sovereignty in its natural state? Allow me to attempt to furnish a contemporary example. There is a small Creek town in Oklahoma which lies within the Creek Nation. The name of this town is Thlopthlocco. Thlopthlocco is a small independent community which operates almost independently. They are not very much dependent on the federal government, nor are they dependent on the Creek Nation. So they're kind of a renegade group. Among the Indians of the Southeast, the Creek Nation was a very large confederacy consisting of Muskogean-speaking people; and as they went to war, the Red Stick faction did most of the fighting. They conquered other peoples and brought them into the confederacy. Well that same type of system, pretty much, is in effect today in the state of Oklahoma. But this renegade group is on the outskirts, the Thlopthlocco people. . . .

The Creek Nation itself, the larger entity, is becoming a powerful bureaucracy. When you go to their business office and try to talk to the chief, for example, usually one of a battery of tribal attorneys is nearby. Then he also has this very large executive desk, sitting there with his white shirt on. (Now remember this is Oklahoma, so he usually has a bolo tie on.) And so he's sitting there and then the chief listens to you very quietly and he's quickly thinking at the same time because he is a very sophisticated tribal leader. He has to be, because not only does he run this bureaucracy, but he runs a very large tribal complex and its complex entities.

One of these entities is the business venture in the operation of Big Bingo. I think we better call it Big Bingo these days because it's just not little bingo. It's in the thousands and millions of dollars. In the state of Oklahoma, in nine operations alone (and there's something like 23 operations of bingo) it was estimated that they pull in something like seventeen million dollars into the bank. Thlopthlocco has also developed a bingo operation. They're more traditional and not as progressive (if you use the terminology of progressive as meaning to assimilate and to acculturate like the white man). The situation is that their bingo operation is interfering with the Creek Nation's bingo operation. When the bingo operations are set up, what they usually do is to draw a focal point for a site and then draw kind of a circumference area of where they are going to draw the clients.

The people who play bingo are typically 45–55, usually people who are retired, people who have a lot of money, people who can afford to go there and play all the time. It's amazing. And they play for many many reasons, some people even have dinner there at the Creek Nation bingo complex in Tulsa. The Creek Nation bingo complex has three facilities, the largest one in the city of Tulsa, which has the capacity of something like 1200 players. That's large! The second one is in Bristol and the third one is in Okmulgee, the site of the capital complex. But it is in the circumference area of Okmulgee where the Thlopthlocco people are; their circumference area overlaps. And so now it becomes kind of an economic war between the two groups for the same bingo clients.

Here is my point: to what degree does the Creek Nation have sovereignty and to what degree does the Thlopthlocco town have sovereignty? One, perhaps in the terminology of today's society, is more primitive, more secretive. . . . Yet they practice their customs. If you talk to the Thlopthlocco people, they will address you in their native tongue so there's a language barrier immediately and they maintain it. Yet they're going into this area of business venture and becoming entrepreneurs, and they're becoming very good at it. Perhaps that's more of a pure sovereignty than I mentioned earlier. The Creek Nation, however, is more progressive in today's societal definition: having new values, but at the same time their basic values are old.

The Creeks have . . . established a capital in Okmulgee. Okmulgee was a traditional town of the Southeast. Yet at the same time, they had communities (remember when I was talking about the confederacy in the Southeast), and in these different towns they had a confederacy. Well, they also have those same towns in eastern Oklahoma which also might be referred to as communities. Dances, not so traditional as they once were, are also held in these communities. And yet these towns and these communities are served by the capital complex in Okmulgee. There's just one site where everyone has to go to for services. Economic ventures have been initiated by the Creek Nation, and so it helps to develop the communities. One community might be working on an agribusiness for example, one might be doing a bingo operation and so they're helping the communities, their own communities, in that regard. This pattern is perhaps like the old confederacy did hundreds of years ago.

Have you seen the film called "The New Capitalists"? . . . If you want to impress students, it's appropriate to any group. It describes some of the tribal nations who are involved in economic areas which you won't believe. One of the tribes in Arizona has a drag race track. So they have that kind of revenue coming in. They're into all kinds of business areas. . . .

. . . This is the same situation with other tribal bingo operations. They're not just taking the money and expanding into other bingo complexes. They're taking the bingo money and, for example in the Creek Nation, putting it into their own hospital; . . . they have a staff with Indian nurses and Indian doctors. They're taking that money and putting it into scholarship money for college aid. So whatever the BIA only gives you up to a certain scholarship amount, then the tribe will help to fund that as well. They've reinvested that money back into the tribe, into various programs, not business programs but types of social services to help their own people: a tribal elderly program, a feeding program, a nursing program, and all kinds of things like that, in addition to putting much of the money into kind of war chests. Because . . . the Bingo operations of the tribes of Oklahoma have banded together into a coalition and the state government attorneys are restudying tribal sovereignty to tax bingo tribes. It's going to be a war of economics.

DONALD L. FIXICO, *Creek-Seminole-Shawnee-Sac and Fox*

Throughout the 1980s, large bingo halls, exempt from state taxes, increased tribal incomes across the country. This Lake County hall is run by California's Pomo Indians.

6

RESTORING LIFE TO THE DEAD

In the 1980s, the concept of "repatriation"—returning to Indians sacred land rights, religious artifacts, and ancestral skeletons—became a hot issue. Indians felt that Native American bones—whether desecrated by grave robbers grubbing for artifacts or meticulously excavated by archeologists trying to reconstruct America's prehistory—should be blessed and reburied.

Non-Indian scholars fiercely debated the topic. Physical anthropologists, who chemically analyze bones to discover ancient diseases and evolutionary linkages, stood with many archeologists who resisted returning "cultural materials." Cultural anthropologists, on the other hand, who studied living Indians, were more responsive to Indian feelings. Said one anthropologist who had worked on a seventeenth-century Narraganset Indian cemetery in Rhode Island in the late 1960s, "I realized I had not done a good thing. . . . I would not have liked it if someone excavated my seventeenth-century ancestors, and I had second *thoughts. . . .'' Skeletons from this Narraganset excavation were among the first in the country to be reburied by an Indian tribe.*

In this reminiscence, California Indian Rosemary Cambra reaches into her own past for the personal spark that led to the much-publicized reburial of Indian bones turned over by Stanford University. According to Indian lawyer Walter Echo Hawk, well over 500,000 Indian bodies have been dug up and carried away, making this ''the paramount human rights problem for American Indians today.''

ABOUT THE STANFORD REBURIAL, let me begin by telling about the death of my mother's mother a long time ago. Then maybe you can understand.

My mother was left without parents at eight. Her mother, my grandmother Ramona Marine Sanchez, died in childbirth. My mother and her older brother Enos assisted in delivering her last child, my aunt Margaret. At this time when my grandmother was hemorrhaging, my mother and her brother nursed her. My mother remembers them going to the creek to get the water, then coming back and bathing my grandmother, changing and washing her sheets.

Both my grandmother and grandfather were Costanoan/Ohlone Indians, from what we now call the Muwekma tribe. My grandmother came from the Alisal Rancheria where the last Indian family was forced out by fire in 1913. By the early 1920s my family was living on the Geary Ranch in Sunol. With my grandfather away from home as a cattleman, a lot of responsibility was left to my mother and her brother.

My mother remembers when she and her brother put those wash basins on their heads and carried them down to the creek. My uncle said, "Look at the woman floating in the water." So my mother put her basin down and saw "La Llorona" flowing with the water. "La Llorona" flows with the water and cries for her lost children. A week or two later my grandmother died.

My grandfather took the new baby to her godparents, sent his sons to a Catholic orphanage in Utah, and took my mother and her sister to Saint Mary of the Palms orphanage at Mission San Jose. This little girl was one of the last of her tribe. The 1905 Kelsey census lists only 350 Costanoan people left out of 10,000 Costanoans living here before the non-Indian invasion.

My mother was eight when she was sent to the mission orphanage and she stayed there until she was seventeen. It gives me chills when I think about it, because my mom was separated from her brothers for nine years. But when she was seventeen they came looking for their sisters at that orphanage. From that day on, they never separated.

My mother did not tell me this story until I was facing my own death in childbirth. The last of my three children, Janice, was born in 1979. I was rushed into surgery and was told I had cervical cancer. I stayed at home in treatment for two years, depressed, and my mother stayed with me. She said, "Take a good look at what happened to my mother. Try to understand me." She was reassuring me that I had medical technology to help me, which my grandmother did not have. And she was reassuring herself by telling me of her struggle and pain. It was then, because of our crises, that we encouraged each other to link our lives to those who went before.

We went to my mother's aunt Trini Rauno, my grandmother's youngest sister and our family historian. We wanted her blessing on our archival research, and she gave it. But she warned me, "Once you lie to yourselves and the families, the blessing will be taken away from you." I went on to accumulate all our research information and to help family members who needed assistance. Our plan was somehow to publish our family's history.

In 1980 I went to De Anza College, to the college anthropologist, Nancy Olsen. I turned over to her what family information I had. I introduced her to family members and Elders for their approval. After two years of letter writing, Father Bill Abaloe let me research at Mission San Jose. I met anthropologists and archeologists from other universities in the Costanoan area and asked about Indian burials. I was told that archeologists were the authorities on Ohlone/Costanoan people, but when I read their reports I realized how little they knew.

So for four years I went to City Council meetings, to educate politicians about how little archeologists knew about our culture. Archeologists in turn did not want to inform my family of any excavations that might affect our heritage. In 1984 our family's legal adviser suggested we set up a business to address the burial issue and assist Indian families.

As I approached different City Councils the response was usually, "What is she talking about? What does she want?" To me the burial issue was extremely sensitive, and a violation of my religious and human rights. Their coldness, I believe, was due to their unawareness that any Costanoan/Ohlone Indians still existed. They asked us, "Where are your men?" I said, "They were working to support their families." They did not take us seriously and tabled our issues. Meeting after meeting passed and my words on the burial issue fell on deaf ears. A turning point came when an archeologist provoked me and I hit him with a shovel, creating a lot of publicity.

After that incident there was a growing understanding within our Indian community that our religious rights should not be overlooked. Small milestones followed. In 1987 the County of Santa Clara adopted the Native American Ordinance Monitor Observer Program to address the burial issue. The state law on Indian monitors was enforced in Santa Clara County. In October of 1988, Stanford University invited me to see the extensive Indian basket collection housed in their basement. But I was overwhelmed to find boxes and drawers of human skulls and bones sitting on shelves. Even more so when I found out that most of the collections were from my ancestral land in the East Bay.

After that I met with the Elders in my family and it was decided to write to the Chairman of Anthropology. That led to meeting after meeting until June 5, 1989, when Elders of our tribe received a letter from Stanford's vice president stating that the remains would be returned for reburial. It took a year for that to happen.

The reburial occurred on June 3, 1990. We arrived at Coyote Hills at 8 A.M. along with about fifteen descendants we called to assist us. That day they were not talking about their work or federal acknowledgment or writing a book or becoming a chief naturalist for some district. We were just laying these 360 old people out to rest, just helping each other.

Stanford had sent an initial truck with the burials to Coyote Hills Park. We removed all the remains from baggies, small boxes, plastic containers, glass bottles, some shoe boxes, some were in cigarette boxes, match boxes, all kinds. We put the remains in our trucks and drove to the actual site. We laid them out individually in three separate areas, because there were so many. They were laid out as individuals. There were rows of skulls, rows. We laid them over wormwood we'd put down to bless those areas. We'd handpicked the wormwood, pulled it out by the roots, bags and bags of it.

Everybody was very quiet and respectful, almost like we were all praying as we went working. My mother said the Lord's Prayer. Logan sang in his own language, Cherokee. He made sure that we were all smudged and cleansed. Then he had everybody say something, to release whatever they wanted to say. Almost everybody spoke—thanks for allowing them to participate, for being part of that whole ritual. Some prayed, some just a few words.

We wheelbarrowed three feet of dirt over the remains and then put another five feet of dirt over them with a back hoe. They were returned to their original trenches which had been left open by the archeologists all those years. One thing fascinated me about this whole Stanford situation. That was that it took a descendant from the East Bay to see that the remains from East Bay were returned to the original trenches they were taken from, protected by a fence as part of Coyote Hills Park. It took two women to put the reburial idea into the minds of the Stanford people. No threats, no arguments. It didn't take a whole band or a whole tribe of 200,000 Indians to rebury these people. It was just laying down a truthful foundation.

We were helped by the Great Spirit, through the prayers of women and men who have a healthy relationship with each other. My grandmother gave life to my mother, and she died and my mother lived. My mother said to Stanford, "If it wasn't for these people, we wouldn't have life today." Our old ones gave life to us. Now we gave a final life to them by putting them to rest back where they belonged.

ROSEMARY CAMBRA, *Muwekma*

7

FIRST AND LAST ESKIMOS

*I*n this selection two Eskimos reflect upon their swiftly changing identities in modern times. This grandmother and granddaughter were interviewed by child psychiatrist Robert Coles after he began, in 1973, visiting Alaska with photographer Alex Harris. Coles soon realized that his native witnesses could not get over a central theme in their lives: "the accelerating change from a somewhat self-sufficient, if precarious, culture of hunting and fishing, to the world of welfare checks, food stamps, snowmobiles, motorboats, and oil pipelines. . . ."

While holed up during a blizzard, Coles first talked with the ten-year-old girl (part two); then a year later he spoke with her grandmother (part one). Their comments underscore the differences in generational experiences that many Indian elders fear will block the transmission of traditional ways. Those changes also challenge their children and grandchildren to redefine what it means to be Native American.

I AM STILL SURPRISED when I hear my grandchildren say that they are counting the days until summer. Why count? Each year they talk like that. Each year I smile! I want to tell them to become more like their Eskimo ancestors, but I feel my father's squeeze on my shoulder; he always said that an Eskimo will never stop being an Eskimo, even if he goes to the lower forty-eight, and comes back here dressed up like a white man from Fairbanks. An Eskimo is born to be an Eskimo, and he may talk like the white man (my grandchildren do, more and more), but he will never stop being part of our people.

Native peoples across North America use state-of-the-art technology to "take tradition to tomorrow," as the American Indian Science and Engineering Society slogan puts it. Here, an Eskimo linguist uses a special word processor keyboard to translate English-language copy into the Eskimo language for the Nunatsiaq News, *a weekly newspaper in northern Canada.*

Last winter—at the end, near melting time—I saw a man from the oil company. He came here and promised our children everything. I expected him to take the sun or the moon out of his pocket and put it on the table. I expected him to wave his pencil and turn our village into an oil well. The day may come! One of my grandchildren talks of Fairbanks; that is all I hear from her—the future she will have in the city. I feel my knees getting weak after I have listened to her. I can see her, while I sit in my chair, walking all over a big city, trying to find a home. . . .

I remember one time a missionary was visiting us. I was a girl, but I was almost a woman. He kept telling me I should be "good." I didn't know what he meant. Out of the corner of my eye I saw the dogs, pointing their noses. Their heads were very high. They weren't moving, just standing there. Then, they started to go around and around in a circle. I wanted to go get my father. He was in the village. Did he know a storm was coming? I told the missionary, finally, that we were in danger, and we'd better go get my mother, who was with my aunt, and my father. The missionary looked up at the sky. It was clear. He said that there was no storm coming. I said there was, I knew there was. He wanted to know how I knew. I told him: the dogs. He asked me to explain. I did. He laughed. He told me I was superstitious. It was the first time I heard the word, and I didn't know what he was talking about. How often I would hear that word over the years. The Eskimos were always hearing, then, that they were superstitious. But I knew what I knew! I told the missionary that I had to leave, right away. He said I wasn't being a good Eskimo; I was leaving *him!* I asked him to come along with me. He did. We reached my mother, and she joined us, and we found my father, and we went home. I remember seeing some clouds in the sky, as we came home. The dogs were beginning to howl. They were hungry, but not howling hungry. They were upset with us. Why weren't we doing something faster to protect ourselves from the storm? A dog keeps a close eye on his neighbors— people.

Before we could do anything, the missionary had to leave; otherwise, to be polite, we would have to stand there talking with him. My father called me away to the back of our house, and said I should pretend to get sick. He told me to hold my stomach and come to him and say it hurts. I waited for him to go back to the minister, and then I came over and did what my father wanted me to do. The minister excused himself and left—after my father excused himself because he wanted to take me in the house and look after me. My mother could tell that my father and I had figured out a way to send the minister off. We watched him leaving, and suddenly the storm came upon us—like lightning in the summer. The wind pushed at us; it wanted to sweep us away. My father realized that the minister might not make it back to his church. I went with my father on the sled, to get the minister. We caught up with him, but he wanted to keep moving. He said we shouldn't worry. God would look after him. I was only a child, and I had no right to say anything. But I did. I said that the wind is God's breath, and we have to be careful, because when he blows that hard, he means for us to go inside and wait until he's decided to stop. The minister told me I was superstitious, again! Then he went on, and we went back home.

We stayed inside for a long, long time—over a week, my grandchildren would say. It was a bad storm, but we had a good time. I helped my mother sew. We had enough food. The baby cried, but the wind was noisier than the baby. It was very hard to clear a path from the house to the shed. Later, we heard that the minister had died on his way back to the church. The storm had taken his spirit. My mother believed that the storm lasted such a long time because the minister was trying to break away from the storm; the longer his spirit fought with the wind, the worse the wind became. When the wind left us, it went to the mountains, far inland. That is where the minister's spirit is. Our ancestors are there, and I'm sure they are looking after the minister.

I hope he doesn't wave his finger at them the way he did at me when I was a girl. I can see him now, pointing at me and telling me I should listen carefully to everything he said. My grandmother told me that the white man never listens to anyone, but he expects everyone to listen to him. So, we listen! The wind isn't a good listener! The wind wants to speak, and we know how to listen. My father always told me that an Eskimo is a listener. We have survived here because we know how to listen. The white people in the lower forty-eight talk. They are like the wind; they sweep over everything. I used to think we would survive them, too. But I'm not so sure. When I look at my grandchildren, I am not sure at all!

ANONYMOUS, *Eskimo*

WE'RE NOT just Eskimos anymore. That's what my grandmother told me. At first I didn't know what she meant, but now I do. She meant what she said! She said that in this family we have Alaska's last and its first Eskimos. She was lying down, and I thought she was going to fall asleep after she told me that, but she didn't. She sat up, all of a sudden. She said that she was one of "the last." She said I'm one of "the first." She said I'd be lucky if I even remember when I'm older what it used to be like in our village. She said she's the child and I'm the grown-up, only she won't live long enough for me to teach her what I know.

I thought she was talking in her sleep. I didn't understand her at all! But she helped me out. She put her head down on the bed again. She stared at the ceiling, and started describing what she did when she was my age. Then she told me what my mother did at my age—the same thing her mother did.

But it's different for me, I know. I learned in school from the teachers how planes fly. They told us! I told my grandmother, and my mother. They laughed. They said that's for me to know. I've never seen a whale. I don't like fish. My mother says I'm the first Eskimo she's met who doesn't like fish. I told her she may be the last one in our family to like it so much!

ANONYMOUS, *Eskimo*

8

RESISTANCE AT OKA

In 1990, along both banks of the St. Lawrence River, the troubled history of Iroquois land rights was a backdrop for revived tensions. The western New York town of Salamanca was panicked over the expiration of its ninety-nine-year lease with the Seneca tribe. The Indians were demanding honest dollar for the town's landbase. Was eviction of an entire municipality a possibility? After national media made hay of the story, the town reluctantly agreed to a new, forty/forty-year lease, a deadline for signing updated lease agreements with private residents, and a $700,000+ rent each year, with a $60 million settlement from the U.S.A. and New York State for past inequities.

On New York's St. Regis reservation, debate over casino gambling opened a deadly rift within the resident Mohawk population. The militant "Warrior Society," promoters of multimillion-dollar gambling and tax-free gas and cigarette smuggling businesses, were pitted against "traditional" tribesmen who decried these corrupting forms of commerce. Before passions dissipated, two Indians were shot dead and thousands had fled their homes in a terrifying atmosphere of daily gunfire and vigilantism.

Then trouble arose among the Canadian Mohawk, as Peter Blue Cloud, himself a tribal member, relates here. At apparent issue were fifty-five acres of threatened pine forest; but underneath, unresolved resentments over lost lands and official neglect of Indian claims simmered. In the heat of confrontation, however, underlying issues were eclipsed by breaking events. Blue Cloud, author of a book on the Alca-

traz Island invasion of the 1960s, here bears witness to the violent seventieth day of his people's stand, writing "from my own observations and thoughts. I speak for no one else." On September 26 the barricades finally came down, leaving a shaken nation to reassess its Indian policies.

THE ST. LAWRENCE RIVER VALLEY area around Montreal, Quebec, is but a fraction of what is still rightfully the territories of the Mohawk Nation. Larger still are the territories of the Iroquois Six Nations Confederacy of which the Mohawk Nation is a part. These territories are mostly in what is now called the United States of America, but were ours long before the coming of the Europeans.

Kanesatake, on the north shore of Lake St. Louis, some fifteen miles from Montreal, was permanently settled in the early 1700s by natives, including many Mohawks from Kahnawake, on the south shore. The Sulpicians, a Catholic order, were given Kanesatake lands to hold in trusteeship for the natives, to remain their property until natives left them or died out. But the Sulpicians sold and leased out large tracts of these lands, including the town of Oka, which borders Kanesatake. That started the trouble, since the Mohawks never left Kanesatake, and so those sales and leases were illegal.

Recently, the town of Oka wanted to expand its nine-hole golf course to eighteen holes. The expansion was to take place in the Pines, a forest planted by natives almost two hundred years before. The area includes a cemetery of the Mohawk people and holds the remains of their parents and grandparents.

The Mohawks tried to fight the expansion by legal means, but they lost and the lands were declared no longer theirs. There was no other recourse but to declare it Indian Land.

On March 11, 1990, the Mohawks set up a barricade to prevent any development of the Pines. They were armed and ready to defend their land.

On June 30, 1990, the Oka town council won a court order to have the roadblock removed. The Mohawks began reinforcing their barricades.

On July 11, 1990, Quebec's Provincial Police, the Súrete du Québec, began arriving in great numbers just before dawn. The first assault against the Mohawk people began. As this news reached Kahnawake, our traditional clan mothers ordered our Warriors to blockade the highways going through our lands, to support our relatives at Kanesatake.

During the long standoff we witnessed our Warriors burned in effigy at our borders, saw rioting non-natives attacking their own police with rocks and Molotov cocktails, watched as a caravan of our children, elders, and women, fearing invasion and trying to leave, were stoned by a mob while police stood by.

We were subjected to rationing as police hindered the delivery of food, fuel, and other necessities. When we used boats to get food and supplies from nearby towns, we faced mobs and were confronted by a Canadian gunboat. Even our non-native doctors and nurses, working with dwindling supplies, were harassed by mobs.

We watched the Canadian Army replacing the police with tanks, armored personnel carriers, helicopters, and hundreds of fully armed soldiers. And then they invaded our territory, and most of us stayed because it was our home.

Day 70. 18 September 1990.

A light ground frost shimmers the grass. Bright stars poke in and out of white clouds. I sit in darkness, sipping coffee and thinking of the coming winter. It is time to pick the remaining foods in the garden. As on other mornings in the past few weeks, I try to think of things unrelated to the presence of the Canadian Army surrounding our lands. I am very tired of being a hostage to Canada. I want it to end soon. Why doesn't the government negotiate as they promised?

I am sitting on my porch above the very beach where I learned to swim and to fish as a child, remembering when violence and death were dreamlike happenings in a World War far away—the only visible evidence, back then, in the many uniformed men walking our roads to visit relatives for that final good-bye.

This image of yesteryear ended abruptly with the sudden whacking, roaring sounds of a huge helicopter directly over my house. I was thinking in terms of a rescue mission, or some other such act of humanity, as it crossed the small stretch of water, to hover close to ground and disgorge a fully armed assault team.

Quickly, other choppers appeared and spewed out their loads of troops. At a crouching run, the troops headed for the small bridge which connects the island to the mainland. Other choppers dropped rolls of razor concertina wire, and other equipment to accompany whatever demonic drama was unfolding before my eyes.

The reality of this bizarre scene became evident with the immediate arrival of honking cars from all over town. Mohawks—men, women, and young people—poured onto the bridge, in outrage and anger that our sacred territory was being invaded by an armed force of the military.

The people of Kahnawake, unarmed, crossed the bridge and confronted automatic-weapons-carrying troops. There was no fear on the faces of our Mohawk people, only anger. The Army quickly grouped, weapons at the ready, and ready, too, to say, "We were only following orders."

"Get off our land!" was the main cry of the people, nose to nose with those apprehensive-looking soldiers. As the crowd grew and pushed into the line of soldiers, the first barrage of tear gas and concussion grenades was hurled. Little panic ensued as the people returned the cannisters of gas, accompanied by stones and fists.

Another barrage of tear gas, and the people were forced to retreat. The Army moved quickly to cross and take the bridgehead. They didn't make it, the people regrouped, and by sheer force of bodies pushed the soldiers back to the other side. This began a long, drawn-out retreat by the Canadian Army.

I stood at the center of the bridge when the third barrage of tear gas fell. I stood at the center of myself and my people. When I heard the unbelievable chatter of automatic fire I wondered, can it be that they would kill?

Tear gas fell. Screams of outrage echoed across the waters. Rifle butts smashed into bodies to be answered by fists and feet. At least eight helicopters circled and roared overhead, unheard by those creating their own fury of sound. People jumped to water to relieve the burning tear gas. I saw soldiers thrown to ground. There were injured people on the rocks beneath the bridge. I heard fists striking flesh.

The single roll of razor wire the Army managed to unroll was tossed to the side of the bridge. The crowd never let up pressing the Army into retreat, taking their rolls of razor wire with them. The soldiers formed a right-angle wedge, with soldiers behind them. Then, at a command, they stepped back four paces. Then again and again. And again. This went on for a very long time—they were retreating!

We formed our own line thirty feet from the Army. Soldiers in small groups left the wedge and ran to waiting helicopters for evacuation. As it grew dark, we built fires. Spotlights from choppers made the scene glaringly real.

When the last of the soldiers finally left in darkness, a great cheer went up from the crowd. Later, Army Lieutenant Colonel Greg Mitchell, in charge of the invasion of Kahnawake, said, "The strong resistance surprised us. It was amazing the way they reacted, especially since we weren't at the Longhouse or a sacred place."

Dear Mr. Mitchell and Dear Canadians: Will you ever begin to understand the meaning of the soil beneath your very feet? From a grain of sand to a great mountain, all is sacred. Yesterday and tomorrow exist eternally upon this continent. We natives are the guardians of this sacred place.

PETER BLUE CLOUD, *Mohawk*

9

CONFRONTING COLUMBUS AGAIN

With the approach of A.D. 1992, Indians across the United States braced *themselves for international hoopla over the five-hundredth anniversary of the arrival of Christopher Columbus to the western hemisphere. "It's ridiculous," maintained Rayna Green, director of Indian Programs for the Smithsonian Institution. "It's being extrapolated as an Italo-Hispanic event, and I don't think there's anything to celebrate at all." Nonetheless, she felt, the commemoration presented an "extraordinary opportunity" for Indians to define the event to their own advantage. Throughout the United States, Indians huddled to do just that. Journalist Tim Giago called for October 12 to be renamed National Native American Day; as Columbus Day, he maintained, it was only "a day of mourning." Press statements surrounding Spain's forthcoming Olympics and World's Fair were deplored for extolling only the Iberian "invasion" of Indian America. Indian novelists Louise Erdrich and Michael Dorris won a $1.5-million advance for a novel about an Indian scholar, a woman, who uncovers a long-lost diary of Columbus. In Indian reservations and neighborhoods people debated over support for a multitribal caravan of Indians targeted to reach the nation's capital on that signal date, October 12, 1992.*

To Pulitzer Prize–winning novelist N. Scott Momaday, the Quincentenary recalled the bearing of "the whole history of Europe" to a land whose peoples "couldn't imagine what was coming upon their shore." His search for common ground with non-Indians around the event is expressed in this selection. The son of

a Kiowa father and part-Cherokee mother, Momaday was born in 1934 and stud-
ied literature at Stanford University. A poet, novelist, and essayist, he won the
Pulitzer in 1968 for his second book, the novel House Made of Dawn, *which tells*
of a World War II veteran's struggle to recover his spirit in the white man's world.

I'VE DONE some thinking on Columbus. I'm very much interested
in the significance of the occasion. I think that it's a wonderfully important time to reflect over the meaning of Columbus's voyages to America,
and the following establishment of colonial settlements in the world. The
whole history of Indian/white relations from 1492 to the present is a large
subject to get at, but is eminently worth thinking about. I would hope that
the question would produce greater awareness of Native cultures, the importance of those cultures, and indeed the indispensable importance of
them in the light of the twenty-first century.

I think we're on the brink of disaster on many fronts. I believe that the
Native people can help us out of that, help push us back away from that
brink. At one time I was more optimistic than I am now, but I think that
we have to operate on hope, that it is possible to reverse this march toward annihilation that we have begun on the nuclear front and on the
ecological front. I think that the Native American broad experience of the
environment in the Americas is an important research resource for us.

I just returned from Europe, and I talked to a good many people there
who seem to be more keenly aware of ecological problems than we are
here. We're very comfortable. We have committed ourselves to a techno-
logical society in such a way that it is hard for us to see anything outside
that context. So it's very hard for us to understand that we are polluting
the atmosphere. We know we are, but we have the tendency to think that
we are so intelligent as a people and we have achieved such a high degree
of civilization that the solutions will come about in the course of time.
That's a dangerous attitude.

I think Native people are receiving information about this just as the
rest of us are. Native people seem to live harmoniously with the physical
world as it is, and so I think that the dangers of pollution are more keenly
felt outside the Native American world than in it. Native Americans need
to be as informed as the rest of us, because they probably have more solutions.

I think we're at a crucial point with youth not learning traditions. In the
60s and 70s, for example, there was a great concern among Native Amer-

icans to preserve cultural values and young people were anxious to learn the traditional ways. I'm no longer so sure that those values are being maintained. I hope they are, but I can't feel as confident about it as I was, say ten years ago. I would like to be in a position where I observe more closely what is going on with Indian people.

I have done three large paintings, acrylic on canvas, of what I call the Columbian triad. Each of these is a portrait of Columbus. One is a skeletal, skull-like portrait with a mermaid above it, titled "Admiral of the Ocean," and then there is one of a dark full-face portrait called "Palos," which is the port from which Columbus set sail. The third one is "San Salvador," a depiction of Columbus in a full figure adjacent to an Indian child. Columbus is an emaciated, death-like figure, and the child is pure, innocent, small and naked. It's a confrontation of the old world and the new world.

I was thinking about what his discovery meant finally, in the long run. Of course it is hard to say, but certainly one valid aspect is the complete revolution in the Americas. When Columbus came to the Americas, apparently he was very benevolent to the Indians, as they were to him, but there followed a clash of cultures which worked against the Indians and destroyed their culture. I wanted to represent Columbus as an unwitting threat to the culture, and that was reenacted many, many times in many places. And that's what I point to in the irony of the confrontation. Columbus had no idea where he was. He died believing he had been to China.

I have mixed feelings about celebrating this event which was certainly, from some perspectives, tragic. I had a hard time giving my support to the task force because my colleague Vine Deloria was not willing to serve on it. He felt it was a betrayal of so many of the Indian people. I had similar feelings in 1976 at the Bicentennial of the Constitution. I had a hard time with that, as a Native American, knowing that there was no reason whatsoever to celebrate the 200th anniversary but, on the other hand, I felt that was a fairly narrow attitude. Indians just as much as anyone else have the right to celebrate the occasion. I think if Indians exclude themselves from it, that's a negative thing. If they can find a way to celebrate it on a real basis, that's positive. They have come to an interesting and crucial point in their history. They stand to teach the rest of the world that there's something good about celebration.

It's very hard to be specific about how to change the future. The major issues we face now are survival—how to live in the modern world. Part of that is how to remain Indian, how to assimilate without ceasing to be an Indian. I think some important strides have been made. Indians remain Indian, and against pretty good odds. They remain Indian and, in some situations, by a thread. Their languages are being lost at a tremendous rate, poverty is rampant, as is alcoholism. But still there are Indians, and the traditional world is still intact.

It's a matter of identity. It's thinking about who I am. I grew up on Indian reservations, and then I went away from the Indian world and entered a different context. But I continue to think of myself as Indian, I write out of that conviction. I think this is what most Indian people are doing today. They go off the reservations, but they keep an idea of themselves as Indians. That's the trick.

I have been asked, how do you define an Indian, is it a matter of blood content? I say no, an Indian is someone who thinks of themselves as an Indian. But that's not so easy to do and one has to earn the entitlement somehow. You have to have a certain experience of the world in order to formulate this idea. I know how my father saw the world, and his father before him. That's how I see the world.

N. SCOTT MOMADAY, *Kiowa*

TOWARDS A NATIVE MILLENNIUM

s they faced the challenges of surviving as distinctive peoples past the watershed year of 2000 A.D., the nation's officially designated 554 American Indian tribal groups often found their struggles for political sovereignty and cultural identity ignored in favor of dry statistics that lumped them all together and made that future look unpromising. Forecasts of an Indian population of nearly three million for the year 2080 were coupled with the prediction that fewer than 8 percent of those folks would have one-half or more Indian blood, and three-fourths of all Indians would be living in cities or suburbs. By the late 1990s, a number of western Indian reservations were suffering from murder rates two or three times those of the urban landscapes of Chicago or New Orleans. Of the 175 American Indian languages with any native speakers still around (out of an original 300 languages spoken in 1500 A.D.), by the end of the twentieth century barely 20 of them were used by mothers to their children around the house.

But the most commonly-publicized statistic, one that made a number of non-Indians frightened or jealous of a native future, was the revelation that by 1999 Indian gambling operations had blossomed into a $6 billion (and still growing) industry—netting over 10 percent of the nation's gambling revenue. Indians were shocked to discover that not everyone applauded their ingenuity at succeeding economically on their own—as the white man had badgered them to do for over a century. These "new buffalo" pouring from hundreds of thousands of ringing slot machines seemed to threaten white financiers, politicians, and moralists alike.

American Indian gold, silver, timber, and fur may have underwritten the European Renaissance, bankrolled Europe's educational and commercial systems, and built the vessels that carried colonialism around the earth, but how dare American Indians make a financial killing off the same greed that had seen them dispossessed of their lands and natural resources in the first place? As Lakota journalist Tim Giago bitterly observed, "Nobody loves a wealthy Indian," nor were Indians supposed to wield political clout.

In the view of state governors like Tommy Thompson of Wisconsin and

Pete Wilson of California, the federal government created a monster when it passed the Indian Gaming Regulatory Act (IGRA) in 1988. That bill recognized the Indian right to run their own gaming operations and ordered states to keep their hands off these operations, so long as casinos were also allowed off the reservations. Soon the Indian gambling halls were being accused of attracting organized crime, of enriching a handful of influential Indians, of draining tax revenues, and of discouraging Indians from more constructive ways of making a living.

Apart from the insulting paternalism behind such accusations, they were usually wrong. Indian gambling was no uniform phenomenon; it demanded assessment on a reservation-by-reservation, community-by-community, basis. Of course some tribal big shots got caught skimming proceeds, but for the most part the native operations were freer from graft and corruption than, say, those in Las Vegas, Reno, or Atlantic City. By the IGRA law, Indians were mandated to divert gambling revenues into new housing, schools, roads, sewer and water systems, health care, and other forms of community development. After hundreds of years of being shunted onto isolated, arid, unwanted reservation lands, and more recently buffeted by government policies to relocate in faraway cities, gambling offered steady work near home at living wages for Indians across the country, while dropping millions into local economies *and* state treasuries. Furthermore, the American public seemed to look favorably on Indian gaming, apparently feeling that Indians deserved a fair shake at governing their own reservations and enjoying whatever economic rewards their all-American sense of capitalist initiative had earned them.

Big money did bring new problems, as the twenty-five or so tribes with thriving casinos sought lobbying leverage with state politicians. During the 1996 campaign year Indians paid $2.3 million to power brokers and $1.7 million to political parties, largely the Democrats. High stakes politics could get you in hot water, as Indians learned when a Senate Investigation Committee charged Interior Secretary Bruce Babbit with favoring one group of Wisconsin Indian donors over another in a case of competing gambling interests, tarring tribal reputations with the same brush.

The Indian gambling furor also raised the ante on the oldest conundrum in Indian and white relations. How can ethnically-singular "semi-sovereign" nations co-exist within the American Republic? Were Indians now "statelets," as one critic of Indian autonomy asked? A number of congressmen used the Indians' newfound economic power to ask why, if

Indians were able to look after themselves, did they need any more special federal protections? Leading the same sort of anti-Indian backlash that had arisen in the 1950s and 1970s, Senator Slade Gordon of Washington state tried unsuccessfully to slip two riders into a congressional bill which would deny Indians protection of "sovereign immunity" from civil law suits and force tribes enjoying a certain level of gambling revenues to redistribute them to less fortunate tribes.

The prospect of newly-rich Indians able to buy up non-Indian business and residential properties and stall non-Indian projects they didn't like alarmed their non-Indian competitors. Expressing a growing resentment, one Wisconsin woman wrote her state governor, "By giving them Native American sovereignty, we have given them the right to promote racism." But the Oneida tribal chairperson, Deborah Doxtator, responded, "They look at us as a racial minority, but we have a different relationship with the United States than blacks, Hispanics, or Asians, and people just don't see it. I'm beginning to believe they **refuse** to see it."

America's northern neighbor, Canada, adopted a more united and unequivocal response to the intensified sovereignty claims of her 1.3 million Indians. First, in 1998 Ottawa offered a "statement of reconciliation" which admitted to 150 years of destructive government policies, singling out its racist residential school system. "To those of you who suffered this tragedy at residential schools"—where children were torn from parents, forbidden from speaking native languages, and forced into Christianity— the official statement said, "we are deeply sorry." Following up the apology a month later, Canada offered near-total sovereignty to the 5,500-member Nisga'a tribe, a British Columbia nation that had fought for over a century to regain ancestral lands. Now this fishing and lumbering people would have the powers to collect taxes, provide jobs and public services, and manage timber, mining, and fishing resources within an area half the size of Rhode Island.

The furor over Indian gambling, and the American media's desperation to find sensational hooks (such as Donald Trump versus the Indians, dire population predictions, or reservation homicide rates) for putting Indians into national news, obscured the quieter complexities of Indian cultural survival. The late Cherokee anthropologist Robert K. Thomas once wrote that "persistent peoples" like Indians needed four basic elements to survive: 1) a sacred language, or some sort of mother tongue they could call their own; 2) a unique religion, which could also blend old and new beliefs, such as the dozens of American Indian Christian denominations across the country; 3) a sacred homeland, or stories that linked them to a special piece of ground; and 4) a sacred history, providing some sort of charter for that society's special heritage and destined right to exist. It was these deeply spiritual and communal elements, more than sheer political authority, which Vine Deloria, Jr. believes lend substance to any notion of tribal sovereignty: this is not power for its own sake, but for the perpetuation of unique cultural worlds. So how were Indians doing in terms of their cultural vision of themselves at the onset of the twenty-first century?

In the face of dire predictions that half of the world's 6,000 languages would disappear by 2090, American Indian communities began setting up emergency procedures to preserve their spoken tongues. In local high schools and Indian community colleges special courses offer Blackfeet, Crow, Hupa, and a few dozen other spoken dialects. Radio stations run by the Hopi and other tribes offer native language-only programming, and interactive CD-ROM technology now offers students a chance to double-check their own proper pronunciation of Twana, Cree, and Hopi-Tewa words. But even on Indian reservations such language recovery campaigns must wage an uphill battle against what one linguist calls "the cultural nerve gas of television."

In the reservation by-ways, hamlets, and off-road powwow grounds which are immediately recognized as "Indian Country" no matter the geographical region, it is often hard to cleanly distinguish a social from a religious gathering. And never have inter-tribal gatherings been so popular, with today's summer powwow circuit pumping Indian dollars into the nation's economy while affirming an encompassing "pan-Indian" commonality without sacrificing the myriad of regional, tribal identities. At the same time, "traditional" Indian rituals, many pre-Columbian in origin and often barred to outsiders, remain alive and well: the kachina dance cycles within the Hopi, Zuni, and Acoma pueblos, Green Corn observances among the Oklahoma Creek and Yuchi, potlatching among Northwest Coast peoples, World Renewal ceremonies in northern California, and funerary "cry" rites among the Colorado River tribes, to name only a few.

Furthermore, many tribes are reviving older traditions, such as the tremendous upswing in Sun Dancing across the plains, the enduring appeal of the peyote-using Native American Church, and the restoration of long-forgotten festivals such as the Mohegan Green Corn gathering in New England. To Richard Fournier, a Micmac Indian from New Hampshire, these gatherings of renewal "have provided at least a beginning to educate people about the culture—and the ones who need the education most are the Native Americans."

Some Indians were also willing to educate the general public. In the nation's capital, the last open space on Washington's central mall recently witnessed ground-breaking for the Smithsonian Institution's new National Museum of the American Indian. Conceptualized, designed, and administered largely by Indians, it will exhibit native arts and crafts, lifestyles, and histories. Indian communities are also dramatizing their local narratives with tribal museums and native-run tours, but none so elaborately as the Mashantucket Pequot Tribal Nation's $200 million Museum and Research Center. Located in southeastern Connecticut, it features full-scale dioramas of a caribou hunt, a sixteenth-century Pequot village alongside a rushing stream (complete with full-size human figures), and a yellow trailer home with an outdoor shower indicating their lifestyle in the 1970s before the tiny tribe obtained federal status in 1983, constructed Indian Country's mother of all casinos, and turned their fortunes around.

The enduring importance of sacred geography to American Indian traditions was given prominence in the court battles that followed the passage of the 1978 American Indian Religious Freedom Act. Indians lost the string of highly-publicized court cases in western Tennessee, northern Arizona, South Dakota, and northern California. Despite these painful defeats, Indian traditionalists continue to fight for historical sites, religious places, or burial grounds from which they draw strength and pride and fulfill responsibilities to their ancestors. Mount Shasta in north-central California, Mount Graham in Arizona, and Devil's Tower in northern Wyoming remain hot spots in the ongoing struggles between old Indian cultural interests and pressure from mineral extractors, recreational tourists, and New-Age seekers.

Preoccupations with their diverse pasts remained critical for America's tribes because their cultural and political claims enjoy the authority of such considerable time depth. Even this antiquity has been undergoing constant revision; in northern Louisiana archeologists recently dated one ceremonial cluster of mounds in northern Louisiana at two thousand years earlier than any previous Indian earthen constructions—around 5,300 B.P. (before present).

In 1990 native control over this past found legal expression in the Native American Graves and Repatriation Act (NAGPRA), which forced any museums receiving federal funds to inventory their old Indian bone collections along with any sacred or burial objects. The goal was for Indians to review items that might originate from their ancestors, respectfully rebury the bones, and even rejuvenate ceremonies with lost ceremonial items—as happened when Nebraska's Omaha Tribe recovered their "sacred pole" from Boston's Peabody Museum.

Yet Indians remain fiercely unwilling to let their own cultures fade into oblivion. "Lost" artisan traditions like southeastern Indian basketry, pottery, and beadwork have been revived and modified with modern materials and designs. In Minnesota the Mille Lacs Chippewas used gambling revenues to erect two old-style ceremonial roundhouses which have become magnets for food blessings, marriages, namings, and other community ceremonies. Resuscitating ancient ways could pit Indians against old friends. When the Makah Indians along the Washington state coast used their 1855 Treaty as the basis of a petition to the International Whaling Commission to revive their old-time whale hunts, using dugout canoes and hand-flung harpoons along with gasoline engines and firearms, many of the same environmentalists who had supported Indian cultural renewal were outraged.

Constantly shifting for many people are notions of just "who is an Indian." If a small group such as the forgotten Pequot tribe could "rediscover" their Indian roots, successfully press a case for tribal recognition, and emerge as the most financially powerful Indian tribe in the nation in less than a decade, nothing seemed impossible. Indians everywhere were insisting that they had every right to be doctors, lawyers and, Indian chiefs—and mixed-bloods as well. In the 1990s "identity" became the decade's watchword, as many were stumbling upon Indian roots which had been buried under other racial identities. As Eastern Cherokee poet Ron Welburn writes of his own past in the poem, "For A 'Home' Girl,'": "the benefit of tribes escaped so many of us . . . 'Colored' became best for the Drapers, the Bowers, Cooks and Swans, the Grays and Tyres and the Walses and the Welburns."

Sadly, the numbers game continued to govern the white man's notions of American Indian identity. After Indians noisily protested that President Clinton failed to appoint an Indian to his racial advisory board, the nation's leader made the point—hilarious to Indians who hear this particular boast all the time, as if it makes someone more authentically "American"—of announcing that he was one-sixteenth Cherokee. But the Oglala Lakota commentator Richard Williams reminded Clinton that "Belonging to a tribe, however, is about much more than a fraction of blood [a U.S. government-imposed standard]. It is about keeping traditions alive and being responsible for our people. The needs are so great that members cannot be 'part Indian.' " Williams likened the presidential comment to his telling his own children that he was a one-sixteenth father. As the selections in this final chapter suggest, for many Indians approaching the year 2000, the emotional, human side of having a "blended" or "mixed-blood" identity became an increasingly important theme.

Every decade or so, for at least two hundred years or more, white people have lectured Native Americans that their future is at a crossroads, that they are on the verge of extinction, that their days are numbered, that they had better give up being Indians and join the world. Indian people often quietly reply that they are the world, many different worlds, and remind white people that they are still here. For their part, Indian spiritual leaders and creation narratives also worry about the state of the world and the future of human beings as well.

"If the United States continues on its present course," warns Oren Lyons, an Onondaga "faith keeper" from upper New York State, "it will destroy both Indian and non-Indian people. If we destroy ourselves by our own folly, it is the working of natural law. When there are too many rabbits, they disappear. When lemmings overpopulate, they run into the sea. Human beings also may disappear. And it will mean nothing to the natural world, which is used to cries of anguish and pain. It is part of life."

To the sixteenth-century tribal ancestor of Oren Lyons, however, the prophet named Deganawidah, relations between Indians and whites were envisioned as a death struggle between red and white serpents, from which the Indian would emerge victorious.

According to the Gros Ventre Indians of Fort Belknap, the Creator left the fate of the earth up to human beings. "If you make this world ugly," he told his people, "then I will destroy this world also. Its up to you."

The Mandan of North Dakota were alerted by their culture hero, Lone Man, that the present epoch was finished when the Missouri River reversed its course and trees grew upside down. One can imagine how tribes people felt in the 1950s when the Garrison Dam project flooded their old village sites, and giant cottonwoods, bulldozed by the U.S. Army Corps of Engineers, floated with their roots in the air.

The Pueblo Indians have long been concerned about the future well-being of the world. The psychologist Carl Jung was told by Mountain Lake, a Taos Pueblo elder, "We are the people who live on the roof of the world, we are the sons of the Sun who is their father. We help him daily to rise and to cross the sky. We do this not only for ourselves, but for the Americans also. Therefore they should not interfere with our religion."

The selections in this final chapter deal with Indian efforts to survive in the immediate future, as individuals continue to rediscover and defend their personal identities as Indians, and as native communities fight to carry their political rights and spiritual heritages into a new day.

1

THORNS IN THE SIDE

*T**he centuries of gross misrepresentation of American Indians in non-native art and literature continue to the present day. Although more subtley and sympathetically depicted in contemporary films, Indians still complain about their portrayals in* Dances with Wolves *(which, they point out, required a white hero to engage its audiences) or* Pocahontas, *which Indian educator Cornel Pewewardy condemned as historically incorrect, sexist, and ethnographically suspect. But the greatest outcry from Indians has been directed at the persistent practice of Indian stereotypes, no matter how supposedly positive, lending attitudes of ferocity or courage to sports teams. Like the native author of this editorial, Leslie Logan, they wish white atheletes would just drop their "tomahawk chops" and war-bonneted logos so Indian social activists could move on to more important issues.*

IT WASN'T ALL that long ago when I did not want to be bothered by that damn, old, nagging Indian mascot issue. This is one of those issues that draws a mostly negative, yet tepid response. We know the issue, it

has been talked about and written about. We can't escape the image
of Chief Wahoo, the Redskins, or the tomahawk chop so sacred to Ted
Turner's Atlanta Braves baseball team. Ironically it is Turner who has the
ability to silence the chants. A megamillionaire, international philan-
thropist, and sometimes friend to the celluloid Indian—he has the power
to make change—but he does not and we don't press him about it much.
As I see it, the mascot issue is not really about whether you agree or disagree. The question for us real, live Indians is: Do you care or not?

I look around the reservation and invariably see at least one or two kids
sporting a baseball cap or jersey with some offending character on them.
We're not so offended that we refuse to buy our kids the merchandise or
prohibit them from wearing it. Call it native pride, call it indifference, call
it whatever you want. I call it surrender.

Before I went to the University of Illinois for a job interview, I never cared
enough about the mascot issue to register a public opinion on it. Then I began to seriously consider what reality would be like as the only native administrator on a campus that was more concerned about preserving a fake
Indian than being responsive to the living ones. Despite the prospect of
open hostilities, verbal attacks, and the likelihood of death threats from
Chief Illiniwek fans, I resolved to act as a change agent and create possibilities out of the mascot problem. Instead, in a bizarre turn of events, the
university withdrew the position. No offer, no opportunity, no real live Indian administrator on campus. Only Chief Illiniwek, a buckskinned, face-
painted, war-bonneted white boy who does cartwheels for the university.

To my own surprise I am happily relieved. I am off the hook. I do not
have to be confronted by or compromised by the daily dilemmas and post-
game conflicts of fighting an animated Indian. I can, like the rest of Indian
Country, go back about my business. The battle has been called off at the
University of Illinois. The real Indians have been told to stay at home. And
we concede . . . by staying at home.

I've come to view the mascot issue like a smoker with a nagging
smoker's cough. We are party to this affliction and though we are aware
of the potential for some later more debilitating fate, we don't cast the cigarette aside. We think that our tolerance is some form of strength, that
this affliction will not overtake us or kill us. We are party to this, we surrender to it. We aid and abet it. We care, but not enough to stop the cancer from growing.

LESLIE LOGAN

‖‖‖‖‖‖‖‖‖‖‖‖‖‖‖‖‖‖‖‖‖‖‖‖‖‖‖‖‖‖‖‖‖ 2 ‖‖‖‖‖‖‖‖‖‖‖‖‖‖‖‖‖‖‖‖‖‖‖‖‖‖‖‖‖‖‖‖‖

HISTORY REPEATING ITSELF

F or many mixed-blood children and parents, their native identity becomes a struggle between pride and anxiety. Jenine Dumont is the great-great-niece of Gabriel Dumont, a leader of Canada's famous Northwest Rebellion, in which Métis and other tribesmen fought for Indian freedom across the Plains of Alberta. Here she describes her own mixed emotions at acknowledging her own native identity, and her fears about the discrimination her own children were to suffer.

I BEGAN GRADE ONE when I was six and a half years old because of my December birthday. I loved school and knew a lot before I started. My youngest brother, who was in grade six, and I were the only family members attending the school. The school was a one-room school with grades one to nine. The two or three pupils in grade nine took correspondence courses and were supervised by the teacher. My first year passed without incident.

For my second year of school, we had the same teacher, and everyone was pleased because she was superb. My brother was in grade seven, and they happened to be studying social studies one day when Duck Lake and the Rebellion was discussed. The teacher, who knew our family, asked my brother if that was where our father was from, His reply was, "Yes, they're all a bunch of Indians there."

Nothing more was said, but a few days later or perhaps the next day the kids started teasing us, calling us Indians and half-breeds! This went on for some time. I couldn't understand why the teacher did not stop them, although the teasing occurred at lunch time and recess. One lunch hour, all the kids stayed inside the school while my brother and I were outside alone. Then one day, because we were Catholic, my brother and I were let out of school half an hour early when the Anglican missionaries came to the school to give a service. We walked and ran the two miles home as fast as we could to get home before the other kids. Our parents were surprised to see us home in thirty minutes. I had a sore throat that night, was in bed with a chest cold the next day, and missed school for two weeks. We must have told our parents about the teasing then. When I went back to school, the teasing had stopped. I assume my parents had intervened. My brother skipped school a lot that year and eventually dropped out. He was fourteen years old.

That was when I realized I was part Indian. I believe that was also the first time my father talked to me about being proud of my heritage. Over the years, he would often say, "Hold your head up high and be proud; it doesn't matter what they say."

I was particularly close to my father and believed him, so I did as I was told.

I walked that way so much that in high school people thought I was a snob; I really was shy and afraid of being hurt. I had some difficulty being proud of my Indian ancestry, as there were constant reminders that Indians were inferior. My own mother referred to Indians as "les sauvages" (the savages), as if they were inferior. I remember thinking, "Why are you saying that, we're part Indian too?"

I got a lot of mixed messages. We had a group of Métis friends with whom we spent holidays. All the women were the same, trying to be white and rather intolerant of Indians or the mixed bloods who had more Indian ancestry than we did. I remember my father as being very tolerant and being friendly to Indians. I never heard any of the other men make any racial statements.

Other memories stay with me. Once, when we lived in Birch River, I went to the butcher shop for my mother. The owner was always very nice to us. He used to give us wieners when we came into the store. This particular day I went in while a salesman was there, and the butcher gave me a wiener as usual. As I took it and turned to leave, the salesman, addressing the butcher, said with a laugh, "One of your little Native friends?"

I remember seeing that the butcher was somewhat embarrassed. Little things like that would keep reminding me that I was not white.

I spent a lot of years trying to be white. We used to always say that we were French. Shortly after I met my husband, I asked him if he was prejudiced. I think he must have replied negatively. It never seemed important to tell him I was part Indian. I think he figured it out himself. He's of Icelandic ancestry, and they seem to be a rather non-judgemental people.

After we were married, we lived in northern Manitoba for a year in a town that had a large native population. I remember denying my ancestry once while I was there. That bothered me for a long time. It took me until I was thirty years old to really come to terms with being part Indian. I had two children of my own by then, and you can be sure I told them they were part Indian. When my daughter was in grade two she told a friend about her Indian ancestry and this girl started to tease her and call her Indian. I went to the child's mother who stopped the teasing. I certainly didn't want history repeating itself.

When I was thirty-five and my last child was a precocious two year old, we stopped in a small northern Alberta town to buy something at a drugstore. My son was touching things, etc. When I went to the counter to pay for my purchase, the clerk looked through me with disdain and I got this terribly chilled feeling. It's a feeling that I cannot describe. It comes when you know that someone dislikes you because of your race. I thought I had come to terms with my native blood. Maybe I have, but other people have not.

I think the prejudice I was exposed to as a child affects the way I interact with people as I am not an open person and do not make friends easily. When I compare myself to my sisters, who did not suffer the same prejudices I did, I find them to be much more open and congenial. I would like to think there is less prejudice in the world, but is there? I have a ten-year-old son writing a story about an Indian Chief who killed a white-man's wife and then this white man relentlessly hunts down the Indian. The story is supposed to take place one hundred years ago. I guess the stereotypes are still there. Where else would this ten year old get his ideas?

JENINE DUMONT, *Metis*

3

OLD NAMES IN CHARGE

For many Native American cultures, an inheritance of psychological reassurance, spiritual sustinence, and individual destiny are to be found in their personal names. Some people might possess more than one name, with an Indian name, usually in the native tongue, to be used only during social or ceremonial occasions. In the following selections, two American Indian leaders who gained national prominence describe their growing appreciation of these powers. First, Wilma Mankiller, the child of a Cherokee named Charley Mankiller and a Dutch-

Irish mother named Clara Sitton who grew up to become the first woman Principal Chief of the Western Cherokee, offers background on her famous name. Then Colorado Senator Ben Nighthorse Campbell, a Cheyenne, recalls how he embraced his Indian ancestry and his new name.

ASGAYA-DIHI. MANKILLER. My Cherokee name in English is Mankiller.

Mankiller has survived in my own family as a surname for four generations before my own. It is an old Cherokee name, although it was originally not a name at all, but a rank or title used only after one had earned the right to it. To call someone Mankiller would have been like calling another person Major or Captain.

There were many titles in the early days of the Cherokees. Each Cherokee town, for example, had its own Water-goer (Ama-edohi) and its own Raven (Golana), and each town had its Asgaya-dihi.

My own people came from near Tellico, from the land now known as eastern Tennessee. My great-great-great-grandfather's name was written down as Ah-nee-ska-yah-di-hi. That translates literally into English as "Menkiller." No record exists of the names of his parents, and the only name recorded for his wife is Sally. The son of Ah-nee-ska-yah-di-hi and Sally was listed as Ka-skun-nee Mankiller. The first name, Ka-skun-nee, cannot be translated, but it is with this man, my great-great-grandfather, that the name Mankiller was established in the family line as a surname.

By the time I was born in November of 1945, my mother, Irene, had come to learn the culture of the Cherokees. The name Mankiller, which sounds strange to most white people, was not foreign to her because she had lived in Cherokee country all her life and had attended school with many Cherokee people. And even years later, when I grew up, the Cherokee last names were not at all odd sounding to a girl in rural Oklahoma. In fact, Cherokee names in my family were familiar and, quite often, revered. I know family and friends whose surnames are Thirsty, Hummingbird, Wolf, Beaver, Squirrel, Soap, Canoe, Fourkiller, Sixkiller, Walkingstick, and Gourd. Names such as those just are not unusual.

As I matured, I learned that *Mankiller* could be spelled different ways and was a coveted war name. One version is the literal *Asgaya*, meaning "man," combined with the personal name suffix *dibi*, or "killer." Another is *Outacity*—an honorary title that also means "Man-killer." Our Cherokee historians and genealogists have always told us that Mankiller was a military title, but we also heard that there was another kind of Mankiller in our past. We know that in the Cherokee medicinal and conjuring style, Mankillers were known to attack other people to avenge wrongs that had been perpetrated against themselves or others they served. This Mankiller could change things, often for the worse. This Mankiller was capable of changing minds to a different condition. This kind of Mankiller could make an illness more serious, and even shoot an invisible arrow into the body of an enemy.

Most of what I know about my family's heritage I did not learn until I was a young woman. That is when I discovered that many distinguished leaders from the past held the title of Mankiller throughout the various tribal towns. In the eighteenth century, for example, there was the Mankiller of Tellico, the Mankiller of Estatoe, and the Mankiller of Keowee. One prominent warrior and tribal leader, Outacity or "Man-killer," apparently joined a delegation of Cherokees visiting London in 1762, during the troubled reign of King George III, fourteen years before the Revolutionary War broke out.

Even though our family name has been honored for many centuries, during the years, I have had to endure occasional derision because of my surname. Some people are startled when I am introduced to them as Wilma Mankiller. They think it's a fierce-sounding name. Many find it amusing and make nervous jokes, and there are still those times when people display their ignorance. For example, I was invited in December of 1992 to attend President-elect Bill Clinton's historic economic summit meeting in Little Rock, Arkansas, just about a month prior to his inauguration. *The Wall Street Journal,* one of America's most respected newspapers, made a rather unfortunate remark about my surname that is best described as a cheap shot.

"Our favorite name on the summit list," stated the *Journal* editorial, "we have to admit, is Chief Wilma Mankiller, representing the Cherokee Nation, though we hope not a feminist economic priority."

Tim Giago, publisher of *Indian County Today,* a Native American newspaper, quickly fired back at the *Journal.* "The fact that this powerful lady has been featured in several major magazines . . . has appeared on countless television shows, and has been given tons of coverage in major, national newspapers, appears to have escaped the closed minds at the *Journal.* One has to ask if they ever get out into the real world."

Fortunately, most people I come across in my travels, especially members of the media, are more sensitive and generally more aware than that editorial writer. When someone unknowingly or out of ignorance makes a snide comment about my name, I often resort to humor. I look the person in the eye and say with a straight face that Mankiller is actually a well-earned nickname. That usually shuts the person up.

There were times in my childhood when I put up with a lot of teasing about my name. I would want to disappear when roll call was taken in school and everyone would laugh when they heard my name. But my parents told me to be proud of my family name. Most people these days generally like my name, many of them saying that it is only appropriate and perhaps a bit ironic that a woman chief should be named Mankiller. The name Mankiller carries with it a lot of history. It is a strong name. I am proud of my name—very proud. And I am proud of the long line of men and women who have also been called Mankiller. I hope to honor my ancestors by keeping the name alive.

WILMA MANKILLER, *Cherokee*

WHEN I DECIDED to run for the U.S. Senate, people said they'd never seen such fire in Ben Nighthorse Campbell's eyes. But winning wasn't what it was all about. It was important to live up to people's needs and expectations and to honor the Cheyenne name "Nighthorse" by doing the best job I could.

I'd experienced many things that helped develop my sense of competition and determination. My childhood in California wasn't easy. My mother was chronically ill with tuberculosis, and I spent much time in foster homes. Judo became an outlet for me and helped hone my competitive skills. It took me to the Olympics.

After winning the primary, the campaign machinery was ready to roll in my bid for senator of Colorado in 1992. It wasn't much to envy. We were sorely underfunded, and the significant lead I'd held coming out of the primary faded as I faced my opponent, Dick Lamm. My wife, Linda, found she had a congenital heart defect that required immediate open-heart surgery. That provided anxious moments until we knew she would be fine. The campaign lurched ahead.

The most difficult challenge was the TV debates. My opponent was well coached and a good debater. The most people said about me was that I was a natural, a diamond in the rough. Two weeks before the election, the *Denver Post* poll showed the race dead even with 44 percent each.

Looking back, I'd have to say I was depressed, tired, and discouraged. Those close to me said the change was apparent. It was at this time that various warriors and religious societies of the Cheyenne began praying and holding sweats for me.

A Vietnam vet by the name of Johnny Russell, schooled in the traditional way of the Cheyenne and active in the Chief's Society, felt special steps needed to be taken. He told me to carry a tuft of an eagle father with me and to apply special red paint to certain parts of my body. He even faxed me a sketch showing me where to put the paint on my body—dots on the hand, top of the head, and over my heart. When I realized I didn't have the proper paint, Johnny sent a container of the paint by Express Mail.

I talked all this over with Linda. It was a new experience for me. But we both felt there was nothing to lose and everything to win. This was my heritage and was to be embraced.

I know most people will find this hard to believe, but immediately, things began to get better. Money came in, I felt both physical and emotional strength flooding me, and my standing in the polls began to climb.

By election night, there had been a total reversal. I won by a 9.6-point margin, a landslide by Colorado standards. The northern Cheyenne felt great pride. They felt the ritual had served as a shield, given me courage and a new beginning. I couldn't argue with that.

My Indian name of Nighthorse was given to me in a 1966 Cheyenne name-giving ceremony in Lame Deer, Montana, bestowed by Alec Blackhorse, my grandmother's half-brother. It has always been important to me that my actions bring honor to that name.

It says to the world that I am a northern Cheyenne and that these are my people.

BEN NIGHTHORSE CAMPBELL, *Cheyenne*

4

DIFFERENT PROGRAMS

Entering *a major non-Indian academic institution can throw the brightest, most able, and promising Indian students off balance. The bureaucracy is* *often labyrinthian and impersonal, the social system can be alien and elitist, a soft-spoken individual can easily get lost in the crowd. Within their remarkable collection of testimonials by Indian college graduates—First Person, First Peoples: Native American College Graduates Tell Their Life Stories, Dartmouth College editors Andrew Garrod and Colleen Larimore include the following experience by Bill Bray.*

His native Muskokean name, however, is Fus Hutke Chupco, which means "Great White Bird." A poet and 1989 graduate of Dartmouth, Bray was able to transcend the difficulties he describes so well and go on to earn a master's degree in education from Oklahoma City University.

A KIOWA ELDER ONCE told me that the victories to be won today are educational. Most of the time now, we fight with words. Dartmouth College taught me to use words as arrows, a skill which led me to Stanford. But I was not comfortable or happy in this academic environment, and it took me a while to figure out why.

For myself as an Indian academic, the problem of locating "home" within the academic structure was serious. More than any people in North America, Indians can point to a piece of the world where home lies, and they can often even trace it back to specific rocks, trees, and bodies of water. The university is not where we point. We cannot adopt academia in the way Euro-Americans can. Having no concept of links that cannot be broken, Euro-Americans can pull themselves up by the bootstraps and plant themselves firmly in the academic community, a community historically conceived to take care of them. Aside from a few minor scrapes and disharmonies, they fit academia like a hand sliding into a glove. What, however, can an Indian do? What can Indians do when the glove is tailored to the white hand, and the white hand is already happily inside it?

One of the things that an Indian can do is leave, and we do so in droves. Indians have the highest university dropout rate of any group in the United States, on the undergraduate, graduate, and faculty levels. This is not surprising to either the academic world or the Indian world. I'll attempt to explain why this is so.

As a constant and enthusiastic user of computers, I have occasionally come across programs that have serious bugs. These are programs in which you attempt to do something that the program is purportedly capable of doing, yet actually is not. The commands are there, and the computer should be able to perform the task. In fact, the computer will insist that it is able. On the Macintosh, this results in a system error. The system error is the bane of the Mac user's existence, because it offers only one solution: turn off your computer, lose everything you have recently put into it, and start again from the beginning.

This is the situation of the Indian who stays within academia: the academic structure insists that it can accommodate you, and even gives explicit instructions on how this can be accomplished. You enter the system, begin to give input, and then out of the blue, you get a system error, incapable of correcting itself. As the user, you learn merely to avoid using that particular function. Unfortunately, the only way to discover a system error is to stumble across it and be sent back to the beginning.

Indians come from a place where the primary program is different and has been running for an incredibly long time. Most of the bugs are worked out. Indians enter academia expecting a fundamentally functional program. They press keys labeled "voice," "expression," "meaning," "creativity," and "use," and expect to find that something extraordinary happens. Instead, the machine stops. So Indians go home, a place that Euro-American academics have often forgotten exists, or they stay in a world they never made and don't fully understand.

After leaving Stanford partway through my Ph.D. program in education, I was hired as executive director of The Native American Preparatory School (NAPS). I took the job in order to protect our children from the type of Western education my family and I have endured. I refuse to believe that education must be painful and cruel.

The Native American Prep School took me many places, and my "education" continued. I flew across the country from New York to L.A., had meetings at private clubs and on yachts where no one looked like me, and asked people to donate money to Indian education, because Indians are the people of the future. And then I would go home and cleanse myself and vomit, because that is what you do if you are Creek and believe in our traditional ways and find yourself living in a world that is increasingly strange. Then I would return to work and laugh myself through another day, clinging to thirty-five thousand years of dances and stories and philosophy and thought and the comfort, joy, pain, and work that its survival implies.

The chairman of the NAPS board, like many wealthy older people in Santa Fe, lives in a security-controlled condo. As executive director of the school, I often went to visit him. In the beginning, I was consistently stopped at the gate by a series of white men, and each time I told them my business. When I told them that their tenant and I worked together, they would ask exactly what I did. They would ask where I lived. They would ask how long I expected to be there. I told the same people the same things for two months. I got to know them well by sight, and I would have thought that as I came and went twice a day, they would have gotten to know me, but such was not the case. Each time, they said, "We'll have to call and get confirmation."

One day, about two months into this process, I arrived late for my appointment, and as is so often the case, desperation became the mother of invention. I was stopped and they asked who I was. Out of irritation, I sarcastically responded, "I'm the gardener. Who do you think?" This changed our relationship in a way that I could not have anticipated. The guard at the gate thrust a pass at me. "Here," he said, "remember to bring this with you." He stepped back into the guardhouse before I could explain that I had been joking. But I now had a pass that would allow me to go anywhere in the complex. Sometimes, with all the education and degrees in the world, you're still just the gardener. A gardener is a respectable thing to be. My grandfather was a gardener. He raised potatoes, and I raise money. So maybe the guards had me pegged after all.

I once read a story in which one of the characters refused to let reality take shape. Through the sheer power of his denial, things would begin to realign themselves and reality would reshuffle itself. He was not an Indian, but he might have been. I should not be here. We should not be here. I read that we were all supposed to be gone by 1910 or 1940 or 1970. It seems that for people who have outlived the end of several worlds, it is only denial and laughter that keeps us going.

I have been told that there are ceremonies going on in Native America to call people home. There is an in-gathering and those who walked, crawled, or were carried away will be brought back. I had to go away to know that my education was my grandfather and grandmother and aunts and uncles and cousins, and that the land and the turtles who live on it were my education, too. I was schooled in the cold mountains of New Hampshire, and in California, but I was educated in a warm green forest in the rolling hills of Oklahoma. Simply put, I am a rare bird trying to combine a traditional Muscogee life with an Ivy League education.

BILL BRAY, *Creek*

5

REUNITING
WITH BEAUTY

*A*s a fourteen-year-old girl, Helen Morgan Tsosie-Ben, a Navajo from north-ern Arizona, gave birth to twin girls in 1950. They each weighed only one and a half pounds, and the hospital kept them under supervision while the mother waited. But without her knowledge they were given for adoption to a Mormon fam-ily in northern Utah. One of the girls, Rose Johnson/Tsosie, grew up to become a storyteller, business consultant, and was cited in the International Who's Who of Professional and Business Women for 1993. Here she recalls a dramatic mo-ment in her long return to "the Navajo way."

FOR MYSELF, there have been so many "ifs" in my life. For in-stance, the man who was most responsible for me meeting my natural mother—the man who knew my family and where they lived—was killed in an automobile accident after I met her. My mom had faith for thirty-three years. I know she had a lot of "ifs" in her life too.

When I returned to the Navajo reservation, I had no idea I would *ever* find my real mother. I got information about her, and then got permission to visit from my mission president. When I went up to the door of my mother's hogan, I didn't know if she would accept me or not.

When I knocked, a young woman, about twenty-two years old an-swered. I asked if Helen Morgan lived there. She said, "No." There was an awkward moment. I thought, "Oh, no, I have come all this way."

As I looked around inside the hogan I saw a picture. It was one of my sisters—and she looked exactly like me when I was younger! Then the young woman said her parents were gone and would not be back for a long time. But ten minutes later we heard a pickup drive into the yard and the girl said, "Oh, they're back already."

I went outside and saw a man in the front seat and a woman on the passenger side. The woman was just sitting there. I went around to that side of the pickup. She rolled the window down about two inches and stared at me. My Navajo interpreter asked if she was Helen Morgan Tsosie-Ben.

She nodded her head. My interpreter started talking. After several minutes of talk, I asked him to ask her if she gave birth to twins in the Keams Canyon Hospital in 1950. She cried and rolled down the window. She pulled me to her and we hugged. I couldn't cry, all I could do was think, "This is really happening!"

Mother got out of the pickup. She took me by the hand and led me into the house. She told the girl that I met at the door, "This is your sister, who has been lost. She's come home." We hugged each other. She cried.

Soon my brothers and sisters were coming from every door and from every direction. I discovered that I had fourteen brothers and sisters. Many of them were crying, too. Later we went into another hogan, where an older woman was weaving a rug. She smiled at me when I entered the room. She knew me. Beyond the shadow of a doubt, that *Saani* knew me—and yet we'd never been introduced. It must have been because I look like her grandmother.

My mother searched for thirty-three years. She had *faith* for thirty-three years that she would find her lost babies. I learned that when she and her husband left the house that day, he said, "One more day. This is the last time we will search for your babies. If you can't find any evidence today, don't ask me to help you search again."

They were twenty miles from home. They didn't know where they were going, but it was the last day and Mom wanted to find some evidence. Then she just said, "Turn around. Turn around and go back." I was getting ready to leave the hogan when they drove up. That's how close I was to missing my natural mother. That is the power of the faith that Mom had that one day she would find her babies.

Helen asked about "the other one," if she was still alive. I said yes and gave her a picture of my twin sister, Mary Annette. Later, I had Mary Annette call Mom and say, *"Yate'e'h shima nazonee"* ("Hello, beautiful Mother") in Navajo. This was just so she could hear Annette's voice.

When the time came, it was not hard for me to leave. It was not hard because I know that at any time I can go home. I know now that I am accepted. It did not hurt when I left because I am always welcome. I am a part of their family.

There is a lot of inner beauty in my people. It's not just the tradition itself, it's the whole life. It does not mean just from twelve to three o'clock, it means from childhood until you pass away. I know I've not been able to comprehend a lot of it because I was not raised in tradition, but I respect it.

When you live on the Navajo reservation, it is what you become. You are a living part of it. Your life is from the beginning. Your mother and father tell you different stories, they teach you certain words I can never learn how to say because they are part of the Navajo way.

I missed out on traditional ways because I was adopted. And yet I know. I have experienced some of it with the old people and I have felt it with the young when I taught on the reservation. You can't experience this feeling until you're down there. The families had so much to give, and yet they had so little compared to what we have here. The Navajo way is a very simple life, a beautiful and peaceful way of life.

Each time they give a dinner, they offer a part of themselves. When a baby is born and when it first laughs—there is so much meaning there. Whoever makes the baby laugh the first time has to give it a party. That is something we may be missing.

One thing that I feel sad about in non-Indian society is that when I tell people I love and cherish them, they think it is an act of physical possession. But to me it's something that goes beyond, it is eternal friendship. That's one thing about the Indian people—they give from within their hearts.

Many white people have been given so much—possessions, land, money—that they have forgotten what the real world is.

ROSE JOHNSON/TSOSIE, *Navajo*

6

SPEEDBOAT OR CANOE?

Indian people are often ambivalent about the use of humor in their communications. For while they complain that whites commonly depict them as grim, unsmiling, and monosyllabic, the constant joking and humorous storytelling that is essential to native community discourse is often used as a private, survival strategy. In this commentary, written in old-time Indian-English by an anonymous native commentator in the University of Arizona's American Indian Studies periodical, Red Ink, *a "Cherokee" wise man with the antiquated pen-name of Watt*

Scraper offers an acute metaphor for the different pace of white and "indin" worlds.

NOW LISTEN. When I look around nowadays I get the feelin' that the government is a-tryin' to do us in again. Or maybe it's just the white mens' way of talkin' outin' both sides of they mouths at once'd. I'll show what I mean.

I got a Granddaughter goes to school with the white boys and girls in a city. Every once'd and awhile she comes to visit me and tell me about her schoolin'. She says that all the white peoples tell her that she needs to get educated so's she can get a job in the big city. Now she don't like that much, but she knows that she can't get no job around here, except maybe for pluckin' chickens in Arkansas. Now pluckin' chickens in Arkansas might be good for some peoples, and I don't want to tear them down for somethin' they like to do. But I'd just as soon not have my Granddaughter, who's real smart, going into Arkansas to ring a chicken's neck.

Sometimes it gets hard knowin' what to do. I guess it's real hard for some of the young Indin boys and girls. They want to know about who they is. They want to know who they come from. They want to know about traditions and the stories and the ceremonies that keep us in with the spirits. We want them to know about all them things and still not have to go off to Arkansas. They're good Grandchildrens. On the other hand, they gotta go out and make a buck. Can't just live like we used to, 'cause they got laws about huntin', and fishin', and the like.

Now I think that the white mens got us boxed in. The young Indins is a-feelin' bad. Us old folks can't come up with answers for 'em, but alot of 'em look up to us anyways. We got a duty as old peoples to tell 'em straight out how the bird gets plucked.

Now it appears to me that our young peoples are a-goin' upstream with one foot in a Indin canoe and the other in a speedboat. Ones a-goin' real fast and the other is a-goin' pretty slow. Now what that does is make you go 'round in a circle without gettin' up stream. The Old Peoples used to say that everythin' goes in a circle and that's good. You always know where your're a-going. There's power in a circle. You see the strength. It's even. It's balanced. It's kind of like everythin's been put into one complete whole thing.

But I think white mens like us circlin' around in mid-stream. They say, "It's good that you peoples is gettin' in the speedboat, 'cause that means you're a-makin' progress." At the same time, they's sayin' that, "It's a good you peoples is stayin' in the canoe, 'cause you're keepin' your traditions alive." But I think they're just happy we ain't gettin' upstream.

I guess we got to decide if we want to get upstream or not. I think gettin' upstream means freedom. We once'd had that. Had our land, our ways, our own schools, our own ceremonies. Made our own way in the world. Had our own laws, which was good laws. We could do things on our own that we thought was best for us. It appears to me that if we get upstream we'd be on even ground with the white peoples again. 'Cause I don't think we can make 'em go back to where ever they come from no more, maybe we could get 'em to make deals with us again. The only way to do that is to be equal with 'em.

Now that might sound like I'm sayin' we should all jump into the speedboat. We could sure get upstream quicker. I reckon that's what a lot of the Indins is doin' with the gamblin' halls. Now I don't mind gamblin' and I sure don't mind takin' the white mens' money, but travelin' that fast in a gas-powered boat might not be too good either. We'd miss the beauty of the shore and the forest beyond that. We wouldn't be able to see the things that live in the river. The speedboat would foul up the water to boot. We couldn't even dip our hand in the stream to cool ourselves for fear it might be took off. Besides that, without usin' our muscles to paddle upstream how we gonna make ourselves stronger?

Toward the other side, if we all pile into the canoe it might just tip over. It's slow-goin' and everybody has to use the same muscle a-paddlin', just to keep us goin' straight. But if we was in the canoe, we wouldn't foul the water and we could look at the beauty around us. Not only that but usin' our muscles to paddle against a hard current is goin' to make them muscles grow and get real strong. When we finally get upstream to even ground we'd be much stronger than if we took the speedboat to get there.

I guess maybe I'll stick with the canoe.

Now listen, I am the *Unegadihi*, and I have spoken the truth.

WATT SCRAPER, *"Cherokee"*

7

AN EAGLE NATION

C arter Revard is a poet, essayist, Rhodes Scholar, medievalist, and university professor. But he is also a mixed-blood Osage whose early years were steeped in the rich cultural life of the Buck Creek Valley west of Pawhuska, on northern Oklahoma's Osage Reservation. Here he shares a triumphant memory that illustrates the unique ability of Indian traditions to communicate across human and animal species, to blend Indian and white worldviews, and to bridge the past and the present so as to survive into the future.

An Eagle Nation

For the Camp/Jump brigades

You see, I remember this little Ponca woman
who turned her back to the wall and placed her palms
up over her shoulders flat on the wall
and bent over backwards and walked her hands down the wall
and placed them flat on the floor behind her back—that's
how limber she was, Aunt Jewell,
when I was a boy.
And FAST! you wouldn't BELIEVE how she could sprint:
when an Osage couple married, they would ask Aunt Jewell
to run for the horses for them.
Now she's the eldest in her clan, but still the fastest
to bring the right word, Ponca or English, sacred or
profane, whatever's needed to survive she brings it, sometimes in
a wheelchair, since her heart
alarms the doctors now and then.
So one bright day we loaded
the wheelchair, and ourselves, and lots of chicken
barbecued and picnic stuff
into our cars and zoomed away
from Ponca City and White Eagle, *Southward Ho!*
To the Zoo, we said, the Oke City Zoo—we'd picnic there!

Grandchildren, see, they love the zoo,
and has she got GRANDchildren! well, maybe
one of her children knows how many, the rest of us
stopped counting years ago, so there were quite a few
with serious thoughts of chicken barbecue and we all rolled in
to the Zoo and parked, and we walked, and scrambled, and rolled,
we scuttled and sprinted, we used up all the verbs
in English, she'd have to get those Ponca words
to tell you how we made our way,
but somehow we ALL of us got in, and found
the picnic tables, and we feasted there and laughed
until it was time to inspect the premises, to see just what
the children of Columbus had prepared for us.
Snow leopards and black jaguars, seals and dolphins, monkeys and
baboons, the elephants and tigers looked away
thinking of Africa, of Rome, oceans, dinnertime, whatever—
and as for us, we went in all directions,
grandchildren rolled and bounced like marbles up and down
the curving asphalt ways, played hide and seek, called me to look
at camels maybe. And then we were all
getting tired and trying to reassemble, when Casey
came striding back to where we were wheeling Aunt Jewell
and said "Mom,
there's this eagle over here you should see,"
and we could tell it mattered. So we wheeled along
to this cage set off to itself with a bald eagle sitting,
eyes closed and statue-still,
on the higher perch inside, and there was a couple
standing up next to the cage and trying
to get its attention.
A nice white couple, youngish, the man
neatly mustached and balding, the woman
white-bloused and blondish: the man clapped hands
and clicked his tongue and squeaked, and whistled. The eagle
was motionless. Casey wheeled Aunt Jewell
a little to the side. The man stopped making noises.
He and the woman looked at each other, then at us, and
looked away.

There was a placard on the cage's side that said:
This bald eagle was found wounded, and
although its life was saved, it will never fly again,
so it is given this cage to itself.
Please do not feed him.
Aunt Jewell, from her wheelchair, spoke in Ponca to him,
so quietly that I could hardly hear
the sentences she spoke.
Since I know only
a few words of Ponca, I can't be sure
what she said or asked, but I caught the word
Kahgay:
Brother, she said.
The eagle opened his eyes and turned his head.
She said something else. He partly opened his beak
and crouched and looked head-on toward her,
and made a low shrill sound.
The white couple were kind of dazed, and so was I.
I knew she was saying good things for us.
I knew he'd pass them on.
She talked a little more, apologizing
for all of us, I think.
She put one hand up to her eyes and closed them for a while
till Casey handed her a handkerchief,
and she wiped her eyes.
"I guess we're 'bout ready to go now," Aunt Jewell said,
so we wheeled along back to the car, and we gathered all
the class and climbed aboard
and drove from the Zoo downtown to where
the huge *Red Earth* powwow was going on, because
her grandson Wesley, Mikasi, was dancing there.
We hadn't thought Aunt Jewell's heart
was up to Zoo and Powwow in one day, but as usual she
knew better. They CHARGED ADMISSION, and that really
outraged my Ponca folks, for whom
a powwow should be free. Worse than that,
the contest DANCERS had to pay a fee.
"That's not our way," Aunt Jewell said.

But once inside we found our way,
wheelchair and all, up to the higher tiers,
where we and thousands of Indian people looked down
to the huge Arena floor where twelve drums
thundered and fourteen hundred dancers spun and eddied round,
and dancing in his wolfskin there
was Mikasi where Casey pointed, and we saw
his Grampa Paul Roughface gliding
with that eagle's calm he has,
and I saw how happy Casey and Mike were then
that their eldest son was dancing down there, and I felt
what the drum did for Aunt Jewell's heart and ours, and she told us
of seventy years ago when she was a little girl and her folks
would load the wagons up there in White Eagle and go
and ford the Arkansas into the Osage country and drive all day
and camp at night on the prairie and then drive on
to the Grayhorse Osage Dances, or those in Pawhuska even.
I remembered how Uncle Woody Camp had told me
of going to the Osage dances later and seeing her
for the first time and asking:
"Who IS that beautiful Ponca girl over there?"
and someone said,
"Oh that's McDonald's girl,"
and they met that way.
And he and Uncle Dwain would tell
of the covered wagon in which they rode,
my Irish and Scotch-Irish mother's folks, from Missouri out
to the Kansas wheat harvest, and then on down
to the Osage Reservation in Oklahoma, where mules were needed,
and our grandfather hauled the bricks to build
the oil-boom Agency town of Pawhuska, where the million-dollar
lease sales, and the Osage Dances, were held.
So I was thinking how the eagles soared,
in their long migration flights, over all these places,
how they looked down on the wagons moving
westward from Missouri, eastward from Ponca lands
to meet in Pawhuska, how all the circles
had brought us into this Oklahoma time and what
had passed between cage and wheelchair before

we mounted up to view on this huge alien floor the long-ago drum
in its swirling rainbow of feathers and
bells and moccasins lifting up here
the songs and prayers from long before cars or wagons,
and how it all has changed and the ways are strange but
the voices still
are singing, the drum-heart
still beating here, so whatever the placards on
their iron cages may have to say, we the people,
as Aunt Jewell and Sun Dancers say,
are an EAGLE NATION, now.

CARTER REVARD, *Osage*

8

THE END OF
THE WORLD

*I*n *many Native American traditions, oral prophecy is more than the counter-*
part of the white man's written record. An important reference for Indians
still today, prophecy reasserts the powers of Indian mythology and cosmology over
mere chronology. It conveys the reassurance that Native Americans knew all
along what the future would hold—no matter how ironic or awful that future
might be.

Almost certainly such prophecies were part of tribal oral tradition long before the
advent of whites. But it is just as likely that some of the stories were retroactively
composed to restore some sense of order to frightening change. Stories of apocalyptic
finales to the earth and its creatures abound, especially in Native American reli-
gious movements, and they constitute a significant genre of Indian narrative.

The following two examples of Indians looking ahead to the future has, first, the
Zuñi people of New Mexico describing a more ominous time ahead, and second, an
older Chiricahua Apache prophecy from Arizona that turns the tables on Indians
and whites alike.

MANY YEARS AGO when our grandparents foresaw what our future would be like, they spoke their prophecies among themselves and passed them on to the children before them.

"Cities will progress and then decay to the ways of the lowest beings. Drinkers of dark liquids will come upon the land, speaking nonsense and filth. Then the end shall be nearer.

"Population will increase until the land can hold no more. The tribes of men will mix. The dark liquids they drink will cause the people to fight among themselves. Families will break up: father against children and the children against one another.

"Maybe when the people have outdone themselves, then maybe, the stars will fall upon the land, or drops of hot water will rain upon the earth. Or the land will turn under. Or our father, the sun, will not rise to start the day. Then our possessions will turn into beasts and devour us whole.

"If not, there will be an odor from gases, which will fill the air we breathe, and the end for us shall come.

"But the people themselves will bring upon themselves what they receive. From what has resulted, time alone will tell what the future holds for us."

THE ZUÑI PEOPLE

THE OLD PEOPLE used to tell us that when the end of the earth is coming all the water will begin to dry up. For a long time there will be no rain.

There will be only a few places, about three places, where there will be springs. At those three places the water will be dammed up and all the people will come in to those places and start fighting over the water.

That's what old Nani used to tell us. Those old Indians found out somehow, I don't know how. And the way it looks, I believe it is the truth.

Many old Chiricahua used to tell the same story. They say that in this way most of the people will kill each other off. Maybe there will be a few good people left.

When the new world comes after that the white people will be Indians and the Indians will be white people.

ANONYMOUS, *Apache*

(Next page) *According to Hopi traditionalists, this petroglyph outside their ancient village of Oraibi in Arizona depicts the Great Spirit's prophecy for Indian-white relations. The Great Spirit gave the bow and arrow* (lower left) *to the original Hopi* (large figure to the left), *who points to the spiritual path. Uppermost is the white man's path, with three figures: two whites and one Hopi who adopted white ways. The vertical line* (left of first man and circle) *represents the first contact between whites and Hopis since their mythic emergence from the underworld. The lower horizontal path represents the Hopis' spiritual path. The first circle is World War I, the second is World War II, and the third is the "Great Purification," which Hopis believe to be imminent. After that event, corn and water will be bountiful, while on the upper path the white man's future fades away. The quartered circle stands for the Southwest and the sacred directions; to these Hopi it also represents the abiding spiritual center of North America.*

NOTES ON
SOURCES

||||||||||||||||||||||||||||||||||||||||||||||||||||||||||||||||||||||||||||||||||||||||||||||||||||||||||||||||||||||||||||||||

The American Indian historical anthology is a relatively recent genre, but a genre it seems to have become. Beginning with Charles Hamilton's *Cry of the Thunderbird: The Indian's Own Story* (New York: Macmillan, 1950), quite a few collections have been devoted to Native American perspectives on Indian and white relations. Among them are *I Am an Indian*, edited by Kent Gooderham (Toronto: J. M. Dent and Sons, 1969); *Chronicles of American Indian Protest*, by the Council on Interracial Books for Children (Greenwich, Conn.: Fawcett Publications, 1971); *Red Power: The American Indian's Fight for Freedom*, edited by Alvin M. Josephy, Jr. (New York: McGraw-Hill Book Co., 1971); *To Be an Indian, An Oral History*, edited by Joseph H. Cash and Herbert T. Hoover (New York: Holt, Rinehart and Winston, 1971); *I Have Spoken, American History Through the Voices of the Indians*, edited by Virginia I. Armstrong (Chicago: The Swallow Press, 1971); *Of Utmost Good Faith*, edited by Vine Deloria, Jr. (San Francisco: Straight Arrow Books, 1971); *The American Indian: The First Victim*, edited by Jay David (New York: William Morrow & Co., 1972); *The Way: An Anthology of American Indian Literature*, edited by Shirley Hill Witt and Stan Steiner (New York: Vintage Books, 1972); *Great Documents in American Indian History*, edited by Wayne Moquin and Charles Van Doren (New York: Praeger Publishers, 1973); *Contemporary Native American Address*, edited by John R. Maestas (Provo, Utah: Brigham Young University, 1976); *I Am the Fire of Time: The Voices of Native American Women*, edited by Jane B. Katz (New York: E. P. Dutton, 1977) and her *Let Me Be a Free Man: A Documentary History of Indian Resistance* (Minneapolis: Lerner Publishing Co., 1975); *Red & White: Indian Views of the White Man*, edited by Annette Rosenstiel (New York: Universe Books, 1983); *First People, First Voices*, edited by Penny Petrone (Toronto: University of Toronto Press, 1983); Colin G. Calloway's editions of *The World Turned Upside Down: Indian Voices from Early America* (Boston: Bedford Books, 1994) and *Our Hearts Fell to the Ground: Plains Indian Views of How the West was Lost* (Boston: Bedford Books, 1996); *Surviving in Two Worlds: Contemporary Native American Voices*, edited by Lois Crozien-Hagle and Darryl Babe Wilson (Austin: University

of Texas Press, 1997), and the superb anthology of Collier era–to–1985
Indian-and-white relations, featuring prominent Indians in and out of
government, *Indian Self-Rule: Firsthand Accounts of Indian-White Relations
from Roosevelt to Reagan*, edited by Kenneth R. Philp (Salt Lake City: Howe
Brothers, 1986).

This anthology may differ in its deliberate thematic and chronological
movement through the major phases of Indian and white relations from
1492 to the present, its preoccupation with recurrent role relationships
which the two peoples have shared, and its emphasis upon individual experiences. I hope this combination makes more personally believable the
historical development and persistent themes of their long and problem-
atic interaction.

The publication in 1825 of "A Memoir of Catherine Brown, A Christian
Indian of the Cherokee Nation" was an early example of an important
source for these anthologies: the Indian's own story. A few other Indian
writers published their life experiences at this time, such as the Pequots
William Apes (1829) and Paul Cuffe (1839), and Chippewa authors
George Copway (1847), William Whipple Warren (1852), and Peter Jones
(1860), but many of the nineteenth-century American Indian life histories
were put into print by journalists and offbeat historians. After the anthropologist Paul Radin published "Personal Reminiscences of a Winnebago
Indian" in *Journal of American Folklore* (1913), scholars began eliciting life
histories in order to study the interplay of personality and culture. At the
same time, Indian writers found their way into print through Indian-run
newspapers and other journals, while the popularity of reminiscences by
Charles A. Eastman, the Sioux Indian writer, began the modern phase of
Indian writers reaching a trade readership. The best chronology of Indian-
authored early literature is A. LaVonne Brown Ruoff's "Old Traditions
and New Forms" and "American Indian Literatures: A Guide to Anthologies, Texts, and Research" (in *Studies in American Indian Literature*, edited
by Paula Gunn Allen, New York: The Modern Language Association of
America, 1983), while Bernd C. Peyer has anthologized early Indian-
written short stories in *The Singing Spirit* (Tucson: University of Arizona
Press, 1990). Other anthologies resurrecting forgotten native authors include *Native Writings in Massachusett*, edited by Ives Goddard and Kathleen
Bragdon (Philadelphia: Memoir of the American Philosophical Society,
v. 185, 1988) and *Native American Writing in the Southeast: An Anthology*,

1875–1935, edited by Daniel F. Littlefield, Jr. and James W. Parins (Jackson, Miss.: University Press of Mississippi, 1995).

To document olden days anthologists often draw from eighteenth- and nineteenth-century Indian speeches, such as those compiled by such editors as Samuel G. Drake and Benjamin B. Thatcher in popular works on Indian history and biography from the 1830s onward. Frequently overheard during diplomatic parlays between chiefs and white officials, this "Indian oratory" reinforced romantic images of the noble red man as a sort of New World Roman senator (a concept that was as unrealistic as that which saw them as bloodthirsty savages). The sentences were often dressed up by transcribers or rewriters with flowery figures of speech and non-Indian oratorical devices; they bear questionable resemblance to what came out of Indian mouths. I have used them only when the underlying sentiments or ideas rang true.

Library collections of Indian oral materials are found in the Ayer Collection at the Newberry Library, Chicago; they are included in the still-neglected WPA materials collected for many western states during the 1930s, which Theda Perdue used for her excellent *Nations Remembered: An Oral History of the Five Civilized Tribes 1865–1907* (Westport, Conn.: Greenwood Press, 1980); and the six regional centers of the Doris Duke Indian Oral History Project. The latter, an ambitious, privately funded project, enabled scholars around the country to tape tribal elders from 1967 to 1972. The resulting transcriptions supplied material for at least two anthologies, *To Be an Indian* (cited above) and *The Zuñis: Self-Portrayals* (Albuquerque: University of New Mexico Press, 1972).

The utility of oral tradition to objective historiography has been debated since at least 1915 when anthropoligist Robert H. Lowie criticized John R. Swanton's article "Primitive American History" with the remark, "When we find, for instance, that in an Assiniboine creation myth, the trickster-hero makes the earth, regulates the seasons, and created men and horses in practically one breath . . . we may well be skeptical as to historical reconstructions from native accounts." What escaped Lowie was how such retellings, fanciful as they seemed, often embodied native attitudes and critiques about historical interactions. I am as interested in how Native Americans experienced, learned from, and retold historical events as in piecing together how they might have "actually" transpired. Among the scholars articulating historical or cross-cultural interpretations embedded in Indian oral history and folklore are Catharine McClellan ("Indian Stories About the First Whites in Northwestern America," in *Ethnohistory in Southwestern Alaska on the Southern Yukon*, edited by Margaret Lantis, Studies in Anthropology n. 7, Lexington: University Press of Kentucky); Madronna Holden ("Making All the Crooked Ways Straight: A Satirical Portrait of Whites in Coast Salish Folklore," *Journal of American Folklore*, vol. 89, 1976), Kenneth Morrison ("Towards A History of Intimate Encounters: Algonkian Folklore, Jesuit Missionaries, and Kiwakwe, the Cannibal Giant," *American Indian Culture and Research Journal*, vol. 3, 1979), and Keith Basso (*Portraits of "the Whiteman": Linguistic Play and Cultural Symbols Among the Western Apache*, New York: Cambridge University Press). Andrew Wiget's *Handbook of Native American Literature* (New York: Garland Publishing, Inc., 1996) is a magnificent guide to the most traditional Indian narrative genres that transmit historical information and commentary.

But most eighteenth- and nineteenth-century Indian-expressed accounts are unearthed from documents and scholarship. One has to dig into official transcripts of treaty councils and testimony before congressional committees and plow through state historical society publications, the works of frontier journalists, and the memoirs of old military officers. Then one must rediscover the writings of nineteenth-century Indian authors and revisit the monographs of anthropologists, linguists, and folklorists. Such research is haphazard prospecting, and sometimes turns up fool's gold; a blatant example was the 1972 publication of *Memoirs of Chief Red Fox*, the life of a "Sioux Chief" that continued to sell in the thousands even after the authenticity of the text was challenged.

Some good bibliographies exist to guide interested students to buried gems of Indian oral tradition. *The Indians and Eskimos of North America: A Bibliography of Books in Print Through 1972*, compiled by Jack W. Marken (Dakota Press, 1973); *American Indian and Eskimo Authors*, compiled by Arlene B. Hirschfelder (Association on American Indian Affairs, 1973); *Indian-Inuit Authors: An Annotated Bibliography* (National Library of Canada, 1974); and *Native American Folklore, 1879–1979: An Annotated Bibliography*, edited by William M. Clements and Frances M. Malpezzi (Athens, Ohio: Swallow Press, 1984), are four useful directories. Analyzing much of the Indian autobiographical literature are Louis R. Gottschalk et al.'s *The Use of Personal Documents in History, Anthropology and Sociology* (New York: Social Science Research Council, Bulletin 53, 1949); L. L. Langness's *The Life His-*

tory in Anthropological Science (New York: Holt, Rinehart & Winston, 1965); H. David Brumble III's *An Annotated Bibliography of American Indian and Eskimo Autobiographies* (Berkeley: University of California Press, 1988); Rayna Green's *Native American Women: A Contextual Bibliography* (Bloomington: Indiana University Press, 1983); Gretchen M. Bataille and Kathleen M. Sands's *American Indian Women: Telling Their Lives* (Lincoln: University of Nebraska Press, 1984); Arnold Krupat's *For Those Who Come After: A Study of Native American Autobiography* (Berkeley: University of California Press, 1985).

For useful background texts the recent *History of Indian-White Relations*, vol. 4, Handbook of North American Indians, edited by Wilcomb E. Washburn (Washington, D.C.: Smithsonian Institution Press, 1988) provides exhaustive, highly scholarly coverage from the non-Indian perspective. Among helpful overviews, from an anthropological perspective, is Alice B. Kehoe's *North American Indians: A Comprehensive Account* (Englewood Cliffs, N.J.: Prentice-Hall, 1981), while Arrell Morgan Gibson's *The American Indian: Prehistory to the Present* (Lexington, Mass.: D. C. Heath and Co., 1980) is a companion historical textbook; the northerly tribes are surveyed in *Skyscrapers Hide the Heavens: A History of Indian-White Relations in Canada* by J. R. Miller (Toronto: University of Toronto, 1989). In both *American Indian Leaders: Studies in Diversity*, edited by R. David Edmunds (Lincoln: University of Nebraska, 1980) and *Great North American Indians* by Frederick J. Dockstader (New York: Van Nostrand Reinhold Co., 1977), one finds valuable biographical sketches of famous and little-known native figures.

Since publication of Part One of this anthology in 1978 it is good to note that scholars have responded to Vine Deloria, Jr.'s 1974 call for more scholarship and writing on twentieth century Native American history. (Historian Peter Iverson heard Deloria's speech that year in Fort Collins, Colorado, and heeded it by editing *The Plains Indians of the Twentieth Century* [Norman: University of Oklahoma Press, 1985].)

For Part Two my guide through the early twentieth century was historian Hazel W. Hertzberg's ground-breaking work *The Search for an American Indian Identity* (Syracuse: Syracuse University Press, 1971). Since then Kenneth R. Philp has chronicled the 1930s in *John Collier's Crusade for Indian Reform, 1920–1954* (Tucson: University of Arizona Press, 1977). In *The Navajos and the New Deal* (New Haven and London: Yale University Press, 1976), Donald L. Parman covers the controversial Collier years in the Southwest, while Laurance M. Hauptman documents how Iroquois of upper New York state fared through this same period in *The Iroquois and the New Deal* (Syracuse: Syracuse University Press, 1981) which he followed up with *The Iroquois Struggle for Survival: World War II to Red Power* (Syracuse: Syracuse University Press, 1986).

A twentieth-century journalistic report, Stan Steiner's *The New Indians* (New York: Dell Publishing Co., 1968), together with Vine Deloria, Jr.'s biting essays, *Custer Died for Your Sins* (New York: Macmillan Publishing Co., 1969), detonated popular (and scholarly) awareness that Indians were still around. Among publications which appeared immediately thereafter on modern Indian issues were *Our Brother's Keeper: The Indian in White America*, edited by Edgar S. Cahn (New York: World Publishing Co., 1969); *The American Indian Today*, edited by Stuart Levine and Nancy O. Lurie (Baltimore: Penguin Books, 1970); *Indian Americans: Unity and Diversity* by Murray L. Wax (Englewood Cliffs, N.J.: Prentice-Hall, 1971); *The American Indian in Urban Society*, edited by Jack O. Waddell and O. Michael Watson (Boston: Little, Brown and Co., 1971); *Native Americans Today: Sociological Perspectives*, edited by Howard M. Bahr, Bruce A. Chadwick, and Robert C. Day (New York: Harper & Row, 1972).

For the inaugural overview of twentieth-century Indian history, James S. Olson and Raymond Wilson coauthored *Native Americans in the Twentieth Century* (Urbana: University of Illinois Press, 1984), while modern Indian political initiative from the 1960s onward is the topic of Stephen Cornell's *The Return of the Native* (New York: Oxford University Press, 1988). Indian testimony on cultural conflicts of the 1980s is in Anita Parlow's two advocacy anthologies *A Song From Sacred Mountain* (Pine Ridge, S.D.: Oglala Lakota Legal Rights Fund, 1983), regarding Sioux and Cheyenne efforts to recover sacred lands, and *Cry, Sacred Ground: Big Mountain U.S.A.* (Washington, D.C.: Christic Institute, 1988) on the Navajo/Hopi land partition dispute.

Histories of specific Indian communities, combining field and archival research from an Indian perspective, are still rare; setting high standards are Loretta Fowler's *Arapahoe Politics, 1851–1978: Symbols in Crises of Authority* (Lincoln: University of Nebraska Press, 1982) and *Shared Symbols, Contested Meanings: Gros Ventre Culture and History, 1778–1984* (Ithaca: Cornell University Press, 1987). Peter Whiteley's ethnohistory of Third Mesa Hopi, *Deliberate Acts: Changing Hopi Culture Through the Oraibi Split* (Tucson: University of Arizona Press, 1988) discloses an altogether new, native explanation for the intra-tribal upheaval of 1906. Douglas Cole and Ira Chaikin provide a case history of cultural suppression in *An Iron Hand Upon the People: The Law Against the Potlatch of the Northwest Coast* (Seattle: University of Washington Press, 1990); it is hoped that similar studies will soon appear on the Sun Dance, peyotism, and Pueblo ceremonies.

Actively fostering Indian history scholarship through its fellowship programs, annual symposia, and publishing programs is the D'Arcy McNickle Center for the History of the American Indian at Chicago's Newberry Library. Pertinent to my anthology are their *Indians in American History: An Introduction*, edited by Center director Frederick E. Hoxie (Arlington Heights, Ill.: Harlan Davidson, 1988); *Scholars and the Indian Experience*, edited by W. R. Swagerty, which contains Donald L. Fixico's useful essay and bibliography, "Twentieth Century Federal Indian Policy" (published for the D'Arcy McNickle Center by Indiana University Press, Bloomington, 1984); plus such Occasional Papers as *Native Views of Indian-White Historical Relations*, edited by Donald L. Fixico (no. 7, Chicago: Newberry Library, 1989) and *The Struggle for Political Autonomy*, edited by Frederick E. Hoxie (no. 11, Chicago: Newberry Library, 1989). A comprehensive bibliography on the controversy over Indian "cultural materials" is Rayna Green et al.'s "American Indian Sacred Objects, Skeletal Remains, Repatriation and Reburial" (Washington, D.C.: The American Indian Program of the Smithsonian's National Museum of American History, 1988).

Two genres of historical documentation have been produced by Indian peoples themselves. First are the tribally sanctioned historical and/or cultural publications. The Navajo Tribe, through its Community College Press and the editorship of Ruth Roessel among others, has produced historical summaries and oral history collections, as have the Ute, Washoe, and Akwesasne Iroquois among other tribal groups. Secondly, the upsurge in Native American journalism has produced running chronicles of modern Indian events with fascinating reportage and fresh oral history edited locally for regional consumption. A few editors have compiled books from their columns: Tim Giago's *Notes from Indian Country*, vol. 1 (Pierre: State Publishing Co., 1984) exemplifies the range of contemporary Indian concerns. Surveys of American Indian journalism, which opened with publication in 1828 of the *Cherokee Phoenix* in New Echota, Georgia, are in John A. Price's "US and Canadian Indian Periodicals" (*The Canadian Review of Sociology and Anthropology*, vol. 9, no. 2, May 1972) and James and Sharon Murphy's *Let My People Know* (Norman: University of Oklahoma Press, 1981).

I acknowledge the enthusiastic intelligence of my editor at T. Y. Crowell Publishing Co., Marilyn Kriney, throughout the early phase of this project in the 1970s and early '80s, and the subsequent encouragement of my new editor over the past year, Michael Millman, at Viking. Both Don Congdon, who initiated the project with Thomas Y. Crowell, and Susan Bergholz, who introduced me to Viking, also deserve my sincere gratitude. The often unacknowledged collaborators in such a project are the librarians and archivists who have helped to track down materials: Rosalie Willie of the Native American Studies Library, U.C. Berkeley; John Aubrey of Chicago's Newberry Library, Chicago; Leslie Navari of the Pacific Grove Library, Pacific Grove, California; and Paula Fleming of the National Anthropological Archives in Washington, D.C.

For selection material or photographs I am grateful to Craig Bates, Gerry Vizenor, Donald L. Fixico, Tim Giago, Terry Straus, Thomas Buckley, Robert Black, Joseph Medicine Crow, David Saindon, Robert Coles. For friendship, colleagueship, and encouragement during the preparation of this work I am thankful to Bernd C. Peyer, Roy Clausen, Vine Deloria, Jr., Dr. Raymond Fogelson, Patrocinia Murillo, Dr. Frederick Hoxie, Valerie Kack-Brice, Malcolm Margolin, Dr. Triloki Pandey, Dr. William S. Simmons, Dr. William Sturtevant, and Abbie Lou Williams.

PART ONE

FIRST ENCOUNTER TO DISPOSSESION

CHAPTER 1 ▶ PREMONITIONS AND PROPHECIES

1. "He Will Use Any Means to Get What He Wants" from *The Great Resistance: A Hopi Anthology*, edited by George Yamada. Privately printed, March 1957.

2. "White Rabbit Got Lotsa Everything" from "Out of the Past: A True Indian Story" told by Lucy Young to Edith V. A. Murphey. *California Historical Society Quarterly*, vol. 20, no. 4 (December 1941). By permission of California Historical Society.

3. "Visitors from Heaven" from *Legends of My People: The Great Ojibway* by Norval Morriseau, edited by Selwyn Dewdney. Toronto: Ryerson Press, 1965.

Reprinted by permission of McGraw-Hill Ryerson Limited, Toronto. Copyright © The Ryerson Press, 1965.

4. "Thunder's Dream Comes True" from *Life of Ma-Ka-Tai-Me-She-Kia-Kiak or Black Hawk*, dictated by himself. Cincinnati, 1833. Available as *Black Hawk: An Autobiography*, edited by Donald Jackson. Urbana: University of Illinois Press, 1964.

5. "Easy Life of the Gray-Eyed" from *Flaming Arrow's People* by James Paytiamo. New York: Duffield, Duffield and Green, 1932.

6. "The Spider's Web" from *Black Elk Speaks* by John G. Neihardt. Lincoln: University of Nebraska Press, 1961. Reprinted by permission of University of Nebraska Press. Copyright 1931, 1959, 1972 by John G. Neihardt. Copyright © 1961 by the John G. Neihardt Trust.

CHAPTER 2 ▶ FACE TO FACE

1. "Their Wondrous Works and Ways" from *Indian Boyhood* by Charles A. Eastman. New York: McClure, Philips and Co., 1902.

2. "Before They Got Thick" from "The White People Who Came in a Boat" by M. E. Opler. *Memoirs of the American Folklore Society*, vol. 26, 1940.

3. "Silmoodawa Gives a Complete Performance" from *Legends of the Micmacs* by Silas Tertius Rand. New York and London: Longmans, Green and Co., 1894.

4. "A Different Kind of Man" from *The Assiniboines: From the Accounts of the Old Ones Told to First Boy (James Larpenteur Long)*, edited and with an introduction by Michael Stephen Kennedy. Norman: University of Oklahoma Press, 1961. New edition copyright © 1961 by the University of Oklahoma Press.

5. "I Hid Myself and Watched": Part one (Pretty Shield) from *Red Mother* by Frank Bird Linderman. New York: John Day and Co., 1932. Part two (Jaime) from *The Navaho Door: An Introduction to Navaho Life* by Alexander Leighton and Dorothea Leighton. Cambridge: Harvard University Press, 1944. Reprinted by permission of the publisher.

CHAPTER 3 ▶ EXCHANGE BETWEEN WORLDS

1. "Thunder, Dizzying Liquid, and Cups That Do Not Grow" from *The Menominee Indians* by Walter James Hoffman. 14th Annual Report, Part one. Washington, D.C.: Smithsonian Institution Bureau of Ethnology, 1896 (1897).

2. "Keep Your Presents" from *Pawnee Hero Stories and Folk Tales* by George Bird Grinnell. New York, 1889.

3. "Give Us Good Goods" from *Isham's Observations and Notes 1743–49*. London: *Hudson's Bay Record Society*, vol. 12, 1949.

4. "You Rot the Guts of Our Young Men" from *North Carolina Colonial Records,* vol. 5. Chapel Hill: University of North Carolina.

5. "Some Strange Animal" from *Story of the Indian* by George Bird Grinnell. New York: Appleton Publishing Co., 1895.

6. "Buttocks Bags and Green Coffee Bread" from "Rations" by M. E. Opler. *Memoirs of the American Folklore Society,* vol. 31, 1938.

7. "The Bewitched Pale Man" from "Tales from the Dogribs" by June Helm and Vital Thomas. *The Beaver Magazine,* Hudson's Bay Co., Autumn 1966,

CHAPTER 4 ▶ BEARERS OF THE CROSS

1. "Burn the Temples, Break Up the Bells" from *Revolt of the Pueblo Indians of New Mexico and Otermin's Attempted Reconquest 1680–1682* by Charles Wilson Hackett. Albuquerque: University of New Mexico Press, 1942.

2. "A Good Indian's Dilemma" from *Being a Mesquakie Indian* by Lisa Redfield Peattie. Chicago: University of Chicago Press, 1950.

3. "We Never Quarrel About Religion" from *Indian Biography* by B. B. Thatcher. New York, 1845.

4. "Janitin Is Named *Jesús*" "Testimonio de Janitil" from *"Apuntes Historicos de la Baja California"* by Manuel C. Roja. Berkeley: Bancroft Library (Mss. #295).

5. "The Freedom to Work" from *Indian Life and Customs at Mission San Luis Rey* by Pablo Tac, edited and translated and with a historical introduction by Minna and Gordon Hewes. California: Old Mission San Luis Rey, 1958.

6. "A Shaman Obeys" from "The Language of the Salinan Indians" by J. Alden Mason. *Publications in American Archeology and Ethnology,* vol. 14, no. 1. Berkeley: University of California Publications, 1918.

7. "Always Give Blessings and Be Thankful" from *Jim Whitewolf: The Life of a Kiowa Apache Indian* with an introduction and epilogue by Charles S. Brant. New York: Dover Publications, Inc., 1969.

CHAPTER 5 ▶ LIVING BESIDE EACH OTHER

1. "Remove the Cause of Our Uneasiness" from *Biography and History of the Indians of North America* by Samuel G. Drake. Boston, 1841.

2. "Mary Jemison Becomes an Iroquois" from *A Narrative of the Life of Mrs. Mary Jemison* by James Everett Seaver. New York: J. D. Bemis and Co., 1824.

3. "Our Very Good Friend Kirk" from *Letter Book of the Indian Agency at Fort Wayne 1809–1815* edited by Gayle Thornbrough. Indianapolis: Indiana Historical Society, 1961. Copyright Indiana Historical Society, 1961.

4. "The Frenchman Dreams Himself Home" from *The Winnebago Tribe* by Paul Radin. Thirty-Seventh Annual Report. Smithsonian Institution Bureau of Ethnology, Washington, D.C.: Government Printing Office, 1923.

5. "Incident at Boyer Creek" from *The Omaha Language* by J. O. Dorsey. Contributions to North American Ethnology, Department of the Interior, United States Geographical and Geological Survey of the Rocky Mountain Region, vol. 6, Washington, 1890.

6. "Our Stock of Food and Clothes" from *Basis of American Indian Ownership of the Land* by Frank Gouldsmith Speck. Philadelphia, 1915. Extacted from University of Pennsylvania, University Lectures delivered by Members of Faculty in the Free Public Lecture Course, 1913/1914.

7. "If I Could See This Thing" from *Life of George Bent: Written From His Letters* by George Hyde, edited by Savoie Lottinville. Norman: University of Oklahoma Press, 1968. Copyright © 1968 by the University of Oklahoma Press.

CHAPTER 6 ▶ THE LONG RESISTANCE

1. "We Must Be United" from *Memoirs of a Captivity Among the Indians of North America* by John D. Hunter. London, 1924.

2. "Black Hawk Stands Alone" from "Black-Hawk War" by William Jones. *Journal of American Folklore*, 24:235–27, 1911.

3. "Blood Scattered Like Water" from "The Stone and Kelsey 'Massacre' on the Shores of Clear Lake in 1849, The Indian Viewpoint." *California Historical Society Quarterly*, vol. 11, no. 3, (September 1932).

4. "Young Men, Go Out and Fight Them" from *Wooden Leg: A Warrior Who Fought Custer*, interpreted by Thomas B. Marquis. Lincoln: University of Nebraska Press, 1962.

5. "Geronimo Puts Down the Gun" from *I Fought With Geronimo* by Jason Betzinez with Wilbur Sturtevant Nye. Harrisburg: Stackpole Company, 1959.

CHAPTER 7 ▶ THE TREATY TRAIL

1. "Let Us Examine the Facts" from *Tatham's Characters Among The North American Indians*. Annual of Biography and Obituary. London, 1820.

2. "Osceola Determined" from *The War in Florida: Being an Exposition of Its Causes* by Woodburne Potter. Baltimore: Lewis and Coleman, 1836.

3. "My Son, Stop Your Ears" from "An Indian's View of Indian Affairs." *North American Review* vol. 269 (April 1879).

4. "We Are Not Children" from U.S. National Archives, Office of Indian Affairs. Letters Sent: Otoe Agency (1856–1876).

5. "Plenty Coups Travels to Washington" from the unpublished manuscript "A Crow Miscellany" by William Wildschut. New York Museum of the American Indian, Heye Foundation.

CHAPTER 8 ▶ EXILES IN THEIR OWN LAND

1. "Plea from the Chickasaw" from *Journal of Chickasaw Council, October 16, 1826 to November 1, 1826*. American State Papers, Indian Affairs, vol. 2.

2. "Tushpa Crosses the Mississippi" from *The American Indian Magazine*, October-November-December 1928, and January 1929. Tulsa, Okla.

3. "Corralling the Navajo" from *The Navajo Indians* by Dane Coolidge and Mary R. Coolidge. Boston and New York: Houghton Mifflin Co., 1930.

4. "The Uprooted Winnebago" from U.S. Senate Report no. 156, 39th Cong., 2d sess., 1866–1867.

5. "Standing Bear's Odyssey" from *A Century of Dishonor* by Helen Hunt Jackson. Boston: Roberts Brothers, 1893.

CHAPTER 9 ▶ THE NATION'S HOOP IS BROKEN AND SCATTERED

1. "The Buffalo Go" from *American Indian Mythology* by Alice Marriott and Carol K. Rachlin. New York: Thomas Y. Crowell Company, 1968.

2. "Take Care of Me" from *Broken Peace Pipes* by Irwin M. Peithman, foreword by Loren Taylor. Springfield, Ill.: Charles C. Thomas, Publisher, 1964. By permission of Charles C. Thomas.

3. "I Am Alone" from "Reflections of an Interview with Cochise," by A. N. Ellis, Kansas State Historical Society, vol. 13 (1913–1914).

4. "I Have Spoken" from *Twenty Years Among Our Savage Indians* by J. Leo Humfreville. Hartford: Hartford Publishing Co., 1897.

5. "I Want to Look for My Children" from U.S. Congress, House Executive Document, 45th Cong., 2d sess., 1877–1878.

6. "No Dawn to the East" from *Red Man's Reservations* by Clark Wissler, with a new introduction by Ralph K. Andrist. New York: The Macmillan Co., 1971.

7. "Gone Forever" from *Waheenee: An Indian Girl's Story Told by Herself to Gilbert L. Wilson. North Dakota History: Journal of the Northern Plains*, vol. 38, no. 1 & 2 (Winter/Spring, 1971).

8. "This Awful Loneliness" from *Prairie Smoke* by Melvin R. Gilmore. New York: Columbia University Press, 1929.

9. "A Wish" from *Apauk: Caller of Buffalo* by James Willard Schultz. Boston and New York: Houghton Mifflin Co., 1915.

PART TWO
RESERVATION TO RESURGENCE

‖‖‖

CHAPTER 10 ▶ THE VERY SMALL ISLANDS

1. "Treated Better by Wolves" from *Condition of the Indian Tribes*, Senate Report no. 156. 39th Cong., 2d sess., Washington, D.C.: Government Printing Office, 1867.

2. "We Lost Everything" from *Condition of the Indian Tribes*, Senate Report no. 156. 39th Cong., 2d sess. Washington, D.C.: Government Printing Office, 1867.

3. "The Way Agents Get Rich" from *Life Among the Paiutes: Their Wrongs and Claims* by Sarah Winnemucca Hopkins, edited by Mrs. Horace Mann. Boston and New York: privately printed, 1883.

4. "The Career of Ely Parker" from *The Life of General Ely S. Parker, Last Grand Sachem of the Iroquois and General Grant's Military Secretary*, vol. 23. Buffalo, N.Y.: Publication of the Buffalo Historical Society, 1919.

5. "Annie Makes Her Choice" from *Karnee: A Paiute Narrative* by Lalla Scott. Reno: University of Nevada Press, 1966. Copyright 1966 University of Nevada Press. Used by permission of the publisher.

6. "We Had Everything to Learn" from *The Arapaho Way, A Memoir of an Indian Boyhood* by Althea Bass. New York: Clarkson N. Potter, 1966. Copyright © 1966 by Althea Bass. Reprinted by permission of Clarkson N. Potter, Inc.

CHAPTER 11 ▶ TO LEARN ANOTHER WAY

1. "Responsive and Resistant Students": Part one (Ellis B. Childers) from *School News*, Carlisle Barracks, Pa. vol. 2, no. 11 (April 1882). Part two (Lone Wolf) from "Lone Wolf Returns . . . To That Long Ago Time," as related to Paul Dyck by his adopted son. *Montana, The Magazine of Western History*, vol. 22, no. 1 (January 1972). By permission of the publisher.

2. "He Is Not One of Us" from *Indians of the Americas* by Edwin R. Embree. New York: Houghton Mifflin Co. and The Riverside Press, 1939. Copyright 1939 by Edwin R. Embree. Copyright © renewed 1967 by Kate C. Embree. Reprinted by permission of Houghton Mifflin Co.

3. "What Harm Is in Our Sun-dance?" from *The Old North Trail: Life, Legends and Religion of the Blackfoot Indians* by Walter McLintock. London: Macmillan and Co., Ltd., 1910.

4. "We Will Dance" from *The Indians of British Columbia* by Franz Boas. *Journal of the American Geographical Society of New York*, vol. 28, 1896.

5. "Dr. Fewkes Plays Like a Child" from *Truth of a Hopi* by Edmund Nequatewa. *Bulletin of the Museum of Northern Arizona*, no. 8 (1936), Flagstaff. By permission of the Museum of Northern Arizona.

6. "Judge Wooden Leg Keeps One Wife" from *Wooden Leg: A Warrior Who Fought Custer* by Thomas B. Marquis. Lincoln: University of Nebraska Press, 1962.

CHAPTER 12 ▶ THE FLOOD HAS COME

1. "A House of Our Own" from *The Omaha Tribe* by Francis La Flesche and Alice C. Fletcher. 27th Annual Report, 1905–1906, Bureau of American Ethnology. Washington, D.C.: Smithsonian Institution, 1911.

2. "Luther's Father Stands Alone" from *My People, The Sioux* by Luther Standing Bear. Cambridge: Houghton Mifflin Co. and The Riverside Press, 1928.

3. "Half White and Half Indian" from *Cheyenne Memories* by Margot Liberty and John Stands In Timber. Lincoln: University of Nebraska Press, 1972.

4. "We Want to Tell You Something" from *Big Falling Snow: A Tewa-Hopi Indian's Life and Times and the History and Traditions of his People* by Harold Courlander. New York: Crown Publishers, 1978.

5. "He-na Tom, the Hoodwinker" from *To the American Indian* by Lucy Thompson. Eureka, Calif.: Cummins Print Shop, 1916.

6. "The Dead Did Not Return" from *Speaking of Indians* by Ella Deloria. New York: Friendship Press, 1944. Copyright 1944 by Friendship Press. Used by permission.

CHAPTER 13 ▶ HEARTS ON THE GROUND

1. "Life on the Checkerboard" from *Indians Are People, Too* by Ruth Muskrat Bronson. New York: Friendship Press, 1944.

2. "Big Man's Rules and Laws" from *The Indian Journal*, Eufala, Indian Territory, 27th year, no. 17 (April 24, 1903).

3. "The Outrage of Allotment" from *Conditions in Indian Territory*, Senate Committee Investigation, Senate Report no. 5013. 59th Cong., 2d sess., Pt. 1, November 1906.

4. "Farming and Futility" from "Samples of Pend d'Oreille Oral Literature

and Salish Narratives" by J. Verne Dusenberry, in *Lifeways of the Intermontane and Plains Montana Indians,* edited by Leslie B. Davis. Occasional Papers, no. 1. Bozeman: Museum of the Rockies, 1979. By permission of Museum of the Rockies, Montana State University, Bozeman, Montana.

5. "The Hopi Push of War" from *Me and Mine: The Life Story of Helen Sekaquaptewa* by Helen Sekaquaptewa as told to Louise Udall. Tucson: University of Arizona Press, 1969. By permission of the publisher.

CHAPTER 14 ▶ A TWENTIETH-CENTURY INDIAN VOICE

1. "The Best and the Brightest" from *Report of the Executive Council on the Proceedings of the First Annual Conference of the Society of American Indians,* October 12–17, 1911, Columbus, Ohio. Edited by Arthur C. Parker, Washington, D.C., 1912.

2. "Laughing at Themselves" from "Notes from Adario's Journal" in *The American Indian Magazine,* quarterly journal of the Society of American Indians, spring (January–March) 1916.

3. "From Wassaja to Montezuma" from "Dr. Montezuma, Apache: Warrior in Two Worlds" by Neil M. Clark. *Montana: The Magazine of Western History,* vol. 23, no. 2 (April 1973).

4. "Suddenly a Gate" from *The Fourth World: An Indian Reality* by George Manuel and Michael Posluns. New York: The Free Press, 1974. Copyright © 1974 by George Manuel and Michael Posluns. Reprinted with permission of The Free Press, a division of Macmillan, Inc.

5. "Following the Medicine" from "The Delegation to Washington: A Washo Peyotist Narrative" by Warren L. d'Azevedo. *The Indian Historian,* vol. 6, no. 2 (spring 1973).

6. "Scandal in Oklahoma" from *Oklahoma's Poor Rich Indians: An Orgy of Graft and Exploitation of the Five Civilized Tribes—Legalized Robbery* by Gertrude Bonnin et al. Philadelphia: Office of the Indian Rights Association, 1924.

CHAPTER 15 ▶ INTERLUDE OF HOPE

1. "Hard Times in Sioux Country" from *Lame Deer: Seeker of Visions* by John Fire/Lame Deer and Richard Erdoes. New York: Simon and Schuster, 1972. Copyright © 1972 by John Fire/Lame Deer and Richard Erdoes. Reprinted by permission of Simon & Schuster, Inc.

2. "Neglect Along the Klamath" from "Address of Robert Spott" in *The Commonwealth,* vol. 21, no. 3 (1926).

3. "The Twenties at San Juan" from *Indian Self-Rule*, edited by Kenneth R. Philp. Salt Lake City: Howe Brothers, 1986. By permission of the publisher.

4. "Commissioner Collier Is on Our Side" from *Winter in Taos* by Mabel Dodge Luhan. New York: Harcourt Brace and Co., 1935.

5. "Resisting the Indian New Deal" from *Indian Self-Rule*, edited by Kenneth R. Philp. Salt Lake City: Howe Brothers, 1986. By permission of the publisher.

6. "Debate Over IRA" from *To Be an Indian: An Oral History*, edited by Joseph H. Cash and Herbert T. Hoover. New York: Holt, Rinehart and Winston, 1971. By permission of Herbert T. Hoover.

7. "Reducing Navajo Sheep" from *Navajo Historical Selections*, selected, edited, and translated from the Navajo by Robert W. Young and William Morgan. Department of the Interior. Phoenix: Phoenix Indian School Print Shop, 1954.

CHAPTER 16 ▶ IN AND OUT OF THE MAINSTREAM

1. "Counting Coup in World War Two" from transcript of interview with Joseph Medicine Crow by Peter Nabokov. Billings, Montana, January 1972.

2. "A Code Talker Comes Home" from *The Navajo Code Talkers* by Doris A. Paul. Philadelphia: Dorrance and Co., 1973.

3. "The Menominees Are Terminated" from DRUMS testimony, Hearings on Senate Concurrent Resolution 26, Senate Committee on Interior and Insular Affairs, July 21, 1971.

4. "On Relocation": Part one from *Division Street: America* by Studs Terkel. New York: Pantheon Books, 1967. Copyright © 1967 by Studs Terkel. Reprinted by permission of Pantheon Books, a division of Random House, Inc. Part two from *Cherokee Stories* by Reverend Watt Spade and Willard Walker. Middletown, Conn.: Wesleyan University Laboratory of Anthropology, 1966. By permission of Willard Walker.

5. "Stopping Erosion" from *Navajo Humour* by W. W. Hill, General Series in Anthropology no. 9. Menasha, Wisc.: George Banta Publishing Co., 1943.

CHAPTER 17 ▶ LET'S RAISE SOME HELL

1. "The New Indian Wars" from *Red Power: The American Indians' Fight for Freedom* by Alvin M. Josephy, Jr. New York: American Heritage Press, 1971. By permission of McGraw-Hill, Inc.

2. "Invading Alcatraz" from *Alcatraz, Alcatraz: The Indian Occupation of 1969–71*, a work in progress by Adam Fortunate Eagle. By permission of Heyday Books.

3. "Discovery: The Beeah Tribe" from *ABC—Americans Before Columbus*, April–July 1970.

4. "Birth of AIM" from *Penthouse* interview: Vernon Bellecourt by Richard Ballad. Chicago: *Penthouse Magazine*, July 1973. Reprinted by permission of *Penthouse*. © 1973 Penthouse International, Ltd.

5. "Confrontation or Negotiation" adapted by Gerald Vizenor from *Growing Up in Minnesota: Ten Writers Remember Their Childhoods*, edited by Chester G. Anderson. Minneapolis and St. Paul: University of Minnesota, 1976. By permission of the publisher

CHAPTER 18 ▶ SO LONG AS THIS LAND EXISTS

1. "Going Back" from *ABC—Americans Before Columbus*, August–October 1971.

2. "Hopis and the Love Generation": Part one from *Hopi Voices: Recollections, Traditions and Narratives of the Hopi Indians*, edited by Harold Courlander. Albuquerque: University of New Mexico Press, 1982. Part two from *I Will Die an Indian*, Institute of the American West, Sun Valley Center for the Arts and the Humanities, 1980.

3. "Eskimos and 'The Act' " from *Letters to Howard: An Interpretation of the Alaska Native Land Claims* by Frederick Seagayuk Bigjim and James Ito-Adler. Anchorage: Alaska Methodist University Press, 1974. By permission of Alaska Pacific University Press.

4. "Dark Sky Over Black Mesa" from *Problems of Electrical Power Production in the Southwest*, Senate Hearings of Interior and Insular Affairs Committee, Pt. 5, May 28, 1971.

5. "Indian Children in Crisis" from Robert Coles: review of "Indian Territory" by H. L. Van Brunt in *American Poetry Review* and *New York Review of Books*, March 20, 1975. Reprinted with permission from *The New York Review of Books*. Copyright © 1975 Nyrev, Inc.

CHAPTER 19 ▶ IT'S HARD TO BE INDIAN

1. "What Am I" from DRUMS 1973, Institute of American Indian Arts, Santa Fe, N.M., reprinted in *Wassaja*, San Francisco, July 1973.

2. "Alone and Very Scared" from *Brandon Sun* newspaper, "Dimensions" section, Brandon, Manitoba, Canada, October 6, 1984.

3. "Notes from Indian Country" from *Notes from Indian Country* column by Tim Giago. *Lakota Times*, Rapid City, South Dakota, August 5, 1987. By permission of the publisher.

4. "Before and After Gambling" from *The Rez Road Follies: Canoes, Computers, and Birch Bark Baskets* by Jim Northrup. New York: Kodansha Press, 1997. By permission of the publisher.

5. "Sovereignty Revitalized" from *New Directions in Indian Purpose: Reflections on the American Indian Chicago Conference*. Chicago: Native American Educational Services College Press, January 1988.

6. "Restoring Life to the Dead," excerpted from a life history of Rosemary Cambra by Dr. Lee Davis, currently in manuscript, transcribed from taped interviews conducted in July and August 1990 with Mrs. Cambra and Norma Sanchez.

7. "First and Last Eskimos" from *The First and Last Eskimos* by Robert Coles. Photographs by Robert Harris. Boston: New York Graphic Society, 1978.

8. "Resistance at Oka" from *Canada's Shame: Native Suppression*, a work in progress by Peter Blue Cloud. By permission of the author.

9. "Confronting Columbus Again" by N. Scott Momaday from "View from the Shore: American Indian Perspectives on the Quincentenary," in *Northeast Indian Quarterly*, edited by José Barreiro, vol. 7, no. 3 (fall 1990). By permission of the publisher.

CHAPTER 20 ▶ TOWARDS A NATIVE MILLENNIUM

1. "Thorns in the Side" from *No Battle, No Cry* column by Leslie Logan. *Aboriginal Voices*, Toronto, Canada, March/April 1998. Used by permission of Aboriginal Voices Magazine.

2. "History Repeating itself" from "I Didn't Know I Was Different" by Jenine Dumont in *Writing the Circle: Native Women of Western Canada* compiled and edited by Jeanne Perreault and Sylvia Vance. Norman, Oklahoma: University of Oklahoma Press, 1993. Reprinted by permission of Jeanne Perreault.

3. "Old Names in Charge": Part one from *Mankiller: A Chief and Her People* by Wilma Mankiller and Michael Wallis, New York: St. Martin's Press, 1993. Part two from *Catch the Whisper of the Wind* edited by Cheewa James, Deerfield Beach, Florida: Health Communications, Inc., 1995. By permission of the publishers.

4. "Different Programs" by Bill Bray from *First Person, First Peoples: Native American College Graduates Tell Their Life Stories* edited by Andrew Garrod and Colleen Larimore. Ithaca, New York: Cornell University Press, 1997. Used by permission of Cornell University Press.

5. "Reuniting with Beauty" from "Rose Johnson/Tsosie: Our Testimonies Will Carry Us Through" in *Surviving in Two Worlds: Contemporary Native American Voices* compiled by Lois Crozier-Hogle and Darryl Babe Wilson, edited by Jay Lei-

bold. Austin, Texas: University of Texas Press. Copyright © 1997. Lois Crozier-Hogle, Darryl Babe Wilson, and Jay Leibold. By permission of the University of Texas Press.

6. "Speedboat or Canoe?" from "Unegadihi Speaks" by Watt Scraper. *Red Ink: A Native American Student Publication*, volume 5, number 2, Spring 1997. Reprinted with permission of the publisher.

7. "An Eagle Nation" from *An Eagle Nation* by Carter C. Revard. Tucson, Arizona: University of Arizona Press, 1993. Copyright © 1993 Carter C. Revard. Reprinted by permission of the University of Arizona Press.

8. Part one from *The Zuñis: Self-Portrayals*, by the Zuñi People. Albuquerque: University of New Mexico Press, 1972. Part two from *Myths and Tales of the Chiricahua Apache Indians*, by Morris E. Opler. *Memoirs of the American Folklore Society*, vol. 37, 1942.

ILLUSTRATION CREDITS

Provincial Archives of Alberta   pp. 32, 384

San Francisco Chronicle   p. 185 (by Chris Stewart), 442

Amelia Susman Schultz   p. 8

Smithsonian Institution   pp. 11, 16, 23, 88, 90, 135, 141, 166, 187, 223, 255, 391

Southwest Museum, Los Angeles, California   p. 256

State Historical Society of North Dakota   p. 183

State Historical Society of Wisconsin   p. 386 top

University of Washington Libraries, Special Collections Division (Webster and
    Stevens photo no. 7637)   p. 258

UPI/Bettmann Newsphotos   pp. 309, 355, 374

U.S. Signal Corps, National Archives   pp. 94, 114

Western History Collections, University of Oklahoma Library   pp. 65, 179, 209,
    214, 232

Aaron Yava and Holmgangers Press   pp. 352–53

Yosemite Museum, National Parks Service   p. 298

INDEX

‖‖‖

Page numbers in *italics* refer to illustrations.